A Theory of the Environment and Economic Systems

ADVANCES IN ECOLOGICAL ECONOMICS

General Editor: Robert Costanza, *Director, University of Maryland Institute for Ecological Economics and Professor, Center for Environmental and Estuarine Studies and Zoology Department, USA*

This important series makes a significant contribution to the development of the principles and practices of ecological economics, a field which has expanded dramatically in recent years. The series provides an invaluable forum for the publication of high quality work and shows how ecological economic analysis can make a contribution to understanding and resolving important problems.

The main emphasis of the series is on the development and application of new original ideas in ecological economics. International in its approach, it includes some of the best theoretical and empirical work in the field with contributions to fundamental principles, rigorous evaluations of existing concepts, historical surveys and future visions. It seeks to address some of the most important theoretical questions and gives policy solutions for the ecological problems confronting the global village as we move into the twenty-first century.

Titles in the series include:

Sustainability and Firms
Technological Change and the Changing Regulatory Environment
Sylvie Faucheux, John Gowdy and Isabelle Nicolaï

Valuation and the Environment
Theory, Method and Practice
Edited by Martin O'Connor and Clive Spash

Sustainability in Question
The Search for a Conceptual Framework
Jörg Köhn, John Gowdy, Friedrich Hinterberger and Jan van der Straaten

Capital and Time in Ecological Economics
Neo-Austrian Modelling
Malte Faber, John Proops and Stefan Speck with Frank Jöst

The Economics of Nature and the Nature of Economics
Edited by Cutler J. Cleveland, David I. Stern and Robert Costanza

A Theory of the Environment and Economic Systems
A Unified Framework for Ecological Economic Analysis and Decision-Support
Reinout Heijungs

A Theory of the Environment and Economic Systems

A Unified Framework for Ecological Economic Analysis and Decision-Support

Reinout Heijungs

Centre of Environmental Science
Leiden University
The Netherlands

ADVANCES IN ECOLOGICAL ECONOMICS

Edward Elgar
Cheltenham, UK · Northampton, MA, USA

Published by
Edward Elgar Publishing Limited
Glensanda House
Montpellier Parade
Cheltenham
Glos GL50 1UA
UK

Edward Elgar Publishing, Inc.
136 West Street
Suite 202
Northampton
Massachusetts 01060
USA

A catalogue record for this book
is available from the British Library

Library of Congress Cataloguing in Publication Data

Heijungs, Reinout.
A theory of the environment and economic systems : a unified framework for ecological economic analysis and decision-support / Reinout Heijungs.
p.cm.—(Advances in ecological economics)
Includes bibliographical references and index.
1. Economic development—Environmental aspects. 2. Environmental economics. 3. Decision support systems. I. Title. II. Series.

HD75.6 .H45 2001
333.7—dc21 2001023593

ISBN 1 84064 643 8

Printed and bound in Great Britain by MPG Books Ltd, Bodmin, Cornwall

Contents

Preface x
Conventions, Definitions, and Symbols xii

PART ONE INTRODUCTION

1. The Questions 3
   1.1. Question 1: the attribution problem 3
      1.1.1. Environmental problems: originator versus instigator 3
      1.1.2. Formulation of the attribution problem 4
      1.1.3. Some historical notes on the attribution problem 5
   1.2. Question 2: the position problem 7
      1.2.1. Tools for environmental analysis and decision-support: a small anthology 7
      1.2.2. Formulation of the position problem 9
      1.2.3. Some historical notes on the position problem 10
   1.3. The two-fold answer: unification 11
      1.3.1. Towards a unification of tools 11
      1.3.2. A unified framework 13
      1.3.3. A unified methodology 16
   1.4. The central question 18

2. The Scientific Context 19
   2.1. The epistemological foundation 19
      2.1.1. Failure of the experimental method 19
      2.1.2. Towards an alternative epistemology 22
      2.1.3. Excursus: the epistemology of interpolations 28
      2.1.4. The question of truth 31

2.2. Interdisciplinarity 34
2.2.1. Environmental science, systems analysis, and thermodynamics 34
2.2.2. The role of economics 39
2.2.3. The role of ecology 46
2.2.4. The role of mathematics 47
2.2.5. A theoretical physicist's apology 49

3. Outlook 51
3.1. Economic systems 51
3.2. The environment 51
3.3. The plays 52

PART TWO ECONOMIC SYSTEMS

4. Introduction to Part Two 55
4.1. Some shortcomings of traditional economic theory 55
4.2. Structure of Part Two 58

5. Economic Processes 60
5.1. Representation of an economic process: the production function 60
5.1.1. What is an economic process? 60
5.1.2. Reformulation of the production function: economic and environmental commodities 63
5.1.3. Processes and commodities: a note on terminology 70
5.1.4. The materials and energy balance 72
5.1.5. The labelling of processes and commodities 74
5.2. The assumption of linearity of economic processes 77
5.2.1. The duration of a process 77
5.2.2. Co-transformation of undesired flows 79
5.2.3. The nature of the process data 80
5.2.4. The assumption of fixed technical coefficients 82
5.3. Clusters of economic processes 84
5.3.1. Representation of a process cluster 84
5.3.2. The crossroad: commodity-flow accounting and activity-level analysis 86
5.3.3. System boundaries: which processes to include? 90

5.4. The attribution of environmental interventions to a given external demand 91
5.4.1. The first fundamental equation 91
5.4.2. A simple numerical example 95

6. On Solving the First Fundamental Equation 97
6.1. Does the first fundamental equation necessarily have solutions? 97
6.1.1. The assumption of squareness of the technology matrix 97
6.1.2. Process accounts and commodity accounts 98
6.1.3. Excursus: the relation with economic input–output analysis 104
6.1.4. Excursus: the relation with economic make/use analysis 108
6.1.5. Excursus: the relation with economic equilibrium analysis 113
6.1.6. Are the technology matrix square and the first fundamental equation solvable? 114
6.2. Solution of the first fundamental equation 127
6.2.1. Making a square technology matrix: the allocation procedure 127
6.2.2. The allocation procedure in detail 132

7. Towards Concrete Tools for Environmental Analysis and Decision-Support: Inventory Analysis 136
7.1. General considerations 136
7.2. Derivation of life-cycle assessment 140
7.3. Derivation of substance-flow analysis 150
7.4. The relation with environmental impact assessment 170
7.5. The relation with risk assessment 174

PART THREE THE ENVIRONMENT

8. Introduction to Part Three 179
8.1. From environmental commodities to the environmental problem 179
8.2. Structure of Part Three 181

9. Environmental Processes 183
9.1. Representation of an environmental process 183
9.1.1. What is an environmental process? 183
9.1.2. Analytical description of environmental processes 189
9.1.3. The nature of the process data 196
9.2. Clusters of environmental processes 197
9.2.1. The time-integrated presence or absence of environmental commodities: transient stressors 197
9.2.2. Using the fate matrix to calculate the time-integrated presence or absence 202
9.2.3. The permanent presence or absence of commodities: permanent stressors 204
9.2.4. Using the fate matrix to calculate the permanent presence or absence 209
9.2.5. Combined consideration of the fate of environmental commodities: stressors 211
9.2.6. The second fundamental equation 213
9.2.7. The assumption of linearity of environmental processes and the connection with the epistemological basis 215
9.2.8. Is the fate matrix square? 217

10. Environmental Impacts 219
10.1. Representation of an environmental impact 219
10.1.1. What is an environmental impact? 219
10.1.2. A measure for environmental impacts 225
10.1.3. The third fundamental equation 231
10.1.4. The nature of the impact factors 233

11. The Environmental Problem 238
11.1. Representation of the environmental problem 238
11.1.1. What is the environmental problem? 238
11.1.2. A measure for the environmental problem 240
11.1.3. The fourth fundamental equation 241
11.1.4. The nature of the problem factors 242

12. Towards Concrete Tools for Environmental Analysis and Decision-Support: Impact Analysis 244

12.1. General considerations 244
12.2. Derivation of life-cycle assessment 248
12.3. Derivation of substance-flow analysis 252
12.4. The relation with environmental impact assessment and risk assessment 254

PART FOUR CONCLUSION

13. The Answers 259
13.1. Answer 1: the attribution problem 259
13.1.1. Introduction 259
13.1.2. A product from the cradle to the grave: life-cycle assessment 263
13.1.3. A substance in a region: substance-flow analysis 264
13.1.4. A factory: environmental impact assessment 266
13.1.5. Releases of a chemical: risk assessment 267
13.1.6. Discussion 267
13.2. Answer 2: the position problem 268

14. Further Reflections 272
14.1. The limits of attribution 272
14.1.1. Attribution versus planning analysis 272
14.1.2. Attribution versus scenario analysis 274
14.1.3. Attribution versus improvement analysis 276
14.1.4. Attribution versus origins analysis 278
14.1.5. The meaning of attribution for environmental analysis and decision-support 280
14.2. Final remarks 282
14.2.1. Process and the state of the environment 282
14.2.2. Is there no truth in environmental science? 285
14.2.3. A role within environmental philosophy 287
14.2.4. Post scriptum 288

15. Summary of Findings 290

References 293
Subject Index 314

Preface

This book is the result of research carried out while I was employed by the Centre of Environmental Science (CML) of Leiden University, with the Substances & Products Section. The topic may be described as the unification of a number of tools for environmental analysis and decision-support (notably life-cycle assessment and substance-flow analysis) into one meta-tool. The concrete tools are derived as special cases from that meta-tool. These tools had emerged from practical exercises, had been refined during case studies, and had been adjusted in line with international developments and agreements. What was lacking was a consistent scientific basis, and more specifically, epistemological principles on how to establish knowledge in the field of economy environment interactions.

The idea of deriving life-cycle assessment and substance-flow analysis from one unified principle was made in the Ph.D. thesis of 1993 of Gjalt Huppes, who is now head of the Substances & Products Section. He did not elaborate this idea, however. Two further Ph.D. theses were produced in this section, by Jeroen Guinée in 1995 on the methodology of life-cycle assessment, and by Ester van der Voet in 1996 on the methodology of substance-flow analysis. These three treatises of course have some connections, but do not really build on each other, probably because they were conceived too much in parallel. I decided to work out in detail the idea of deriving analytical tools for environmental decision-support, and was thereby more or less forced to develop once more the methodological principles of life-cycle assessment and substance-flow analysis. This by no means implies that the previous two theses were superfluous; on the contrary, without the existing theories I would never have been able to reinvent them.

So, I reinvented life-cycle assessment and substance-flow analysis, but now using one explicitly formulated set of assumptions. The principles of life-cycle inventory analysis have changed only to a small extent; my recommendations for the design and methodology of substance-flow analysis and life-cycle impact analysis go further. In doing this work, I hope to have contributed to a more scientific foundation of a number of tools that have been and are being applied in practice. This may have some consequences for the validity of previously obtained results; I did not investigate that aspect. But, in some sense more importantly I think, it may also have consequences for the scientific status of these tools. The current situation is that some people believe in a tool and others do not. Other people believe that their specific tool is so "encompassing" or "holistic" that it replaces all other tools. A scientific foundation, a derivation of tools instead of a creation of tools, is necessary to bring believers and non-believers together. A derivation from unified principles, from the meta-tool, makes one realize that every concrete tool takes a "cross-section" out of the actual world, so that none of the tools is sufficiently complete to replace any other tool. Both these aspects are essential in defining the position and potential role of life-cycle assessment, substance-flow analysis, or any other tool for environmental decision-support.

An important remark is that I have often taken one point of view in defining or elaborating a concept or a tool. For instance, I chose the attribution problem as the starting point of this exercise towards a unified approach. The attribution problem poses the question of which environmental problems are to be attributed to which economic activity. There may be good reasons to focus on another question, e.g., what might be called the incremental problem: which environmental problems are created by adding an economic activity to the present situation. With that other question in mind, the analysis and the derivation of tools for environmental decision-support would be different. This is not a matter of one approach being better or worse; it is a small shift of topic with probably large numerical consequences. I hope that the structure of this thesis might be reused to a large extent to deal with such different questions.

The limited private edition of this book that served to obtain my Ph.D. at Leiden University bears the title *Economic Drama and the Environmental Stage. Formal derivation of algorithmic tools for environmental analysis and decision-support from a unified epistemological principle.* It was prepared under the supervision of Professors Helias A. Udo de Haes of Leiden University and Leen Hordijk of Wageningen Agricultural University. Professor Peter Nijkamp of the Free University in Amsterdam acted as the external referee. I owe much to them.

Conventions, Definitions, and Symbols

Boxes indicate throughout summaries of arguments or conclusions. They have been conceived to be as self-containing as possible, so that the impatient reader may skip the main text. Boxes in small print contain important technical summaries.

Quotations have in the main text been put in small print, brackets always indicate modifications, either ellipses or additions, and italics have been deleted in the case of emphasized text and inserted in the case of foreign words or mathematical symbols. Obvious typing errors in quotations have been corrected without notification. Quotations in footnotes have been put within quotation marks.

Mathematical expressions have been set in conformity with normal practice: scalar variables are denoted by italics (e.g., x or X), vectors by lower case bold print (e.g., $\mathbf{x}$), and matrices by upper case bold print (e.g., $\mathbf{X}$). The table summarizes a number of conventions with respect to matrix algebra.

Symbol	Meaning
$\mathbf{0}$	null matrix: $\mathbf{0} = \begin{bmatrix} 0 & 0 & \cdots \\ 0 & 0 & \cdots \\ \cdots & \cdots & \cdots \end{bmatrix}$
δ_{ij}	Kronecker-delta: $\delta_{ij} = \begin{cases} 1 \text{ if } i = j \\ 0 \text{ otherwise} \end{cases}$
$\mathbf{I}$	unit matrix: $\mathbf{I} = \begin{bmatrix} 1 & 0 & \cdots \\ 0 & 1 & \cdots \\ \cdots & \cdots & \cdots \end{bmatrix}$

Symbol	Meaning
$\mathbf{x}$	column vector containing $\mathbf{x} = \begin{pmatrix} x_1 \\ x_2 \\ \dots \\ x_i \\ \dots \end{pmatrix}$
$\mathbf{X}$	matrix containing $\mathbf{X} = \begin{pmatrix} x_{11} & x_{12} & \dots & x_{1j} & \dots \\ x_{21} & x_{22} & \dots & x_{2j} & \dots \\ \dots & \dots & \dots & \dots & \dots \\ x_{i1} & x_{i2} & \dots & x_{ij} & \dots \\ \dots & \dots & \dots & \dots & \dots \end{pmatrix}$
$\mathbf{X}^{-1}$	inverse of a matrix $\mathbf{X}$: $\mathbf{X}^{-1}\cdot\mathbf{X} = \mathbf{I}$
$\mathbf{X}^{\dagger}$	pseudo-inverse of a matrix $\mathbf{X}$: $\lVert \mathbf{X}^{\dagger}\cdot\mathbf{X} - \mathbf{I} \rVert$ = minimal
$\mathbf{X}^{\mathrm{T}}$	transpose of a matrix $\mathbf{X}$: $(x^{\mathrm{T}})_{ij} = x_{ji}$
$\mathbf{x}\cdot\mathbf{y}$, $\mathbf{X}\cdot\mathbf{y}$, $\mathbf{X}\cdot\mathbf{Y}$	symbol to denote multiplication of vectors and matrices with implicit summation: $\mathbf{x}\cdot\mathbf{y} = \sum_i x_i y_i$, $(\mathbf{x}\cdot\mathbf{Y})_j = \sum_i x_i y_{ij}$, $(\mathbf{X}\cdot\mathbf{y})_i = \sum_j X_{ij} y_j$, or $(\mathbf{X}\cdot\mathbf{Y})_{ik} = \sum_j x_{ij} y_{jk}$
$\mathbf{x}\diamond\mathbf{y}$, $\mathbf{X}\diamond\mathbf{y}$	symbol to denote multiplication of vectors and matrices without implicit summation: $(\mathbf{x}\diamond\mathbf{y})_i = x_i y_i$ or $(\mathbf{X}\diamond\mathbf{y})_{ij} = x_{ij} y_j$

Below are a number of frequently recurring terms with their meaning and section of introduction. The terms are often self-referring: it has not been attempted to construct a list of pure definitions, but merely to provide a list for quick reference.

Term	Meaning	Intr'd
activity-level analysis (ALA)	the mode of analysis that gives an answer to the question of flows in satisfying a specified external demand	5.3.2

Term	Meaning	Intr'd
allocation	splitting of an economic process into two or more hypothetical processes in order to increase the number of processes, so that the first fundamental equation may be solved	6.1.6 6.2
attribution problem	the question of which environmental problems are to be attributed to which economic activity	1.1.2
commodity	any "object" that is able to flow from one process to another process, goods (materials, products, services, energy, labour), wastes ("bads" and "disservices"), natural resources, and emissions	5.1.2
commodity-flow accounting	the mode of analysis that gives an answer to the question of flows in relation to a specified time span of economic activity, e.g., one year	5.3.2
damage matrix	the matrix of coefficients that relates environmental processes to economic commodities	9.1.2
economic commodity	commodity that flows from an economic process to an economic process	9.1.1
environmental commodity	commodity that flows from an economic process to an environmental process, from an environmental process to an economic process, or from an environmental process to an environmental process	9.1.1
economic activity	set of economic processes that can be subject to attribution analysis	1.1.1
economic (unit) process	process which converts commodities into commodities and of which the operating time (the active period) can be regulated by human intervention	9.1.1
environmental process	process which converts commodities into commodities and whose operating time (the active period) cannot be regulated	9.1.1
external demand	the quantified set of economic commodities that is supposed to be produced by a certain cluster of economic processes	5.4.1

Term	Meaning	Intr'd
fate matrix	the matrix of coefficients that relate environmental processes to the change that environmental commodities cause for environmental commodities	9.1.2
1st fundamental equation	the relation between the externally demanded economic commodities and the environmental interventions	5.4.1
2nd fundamental equation	the relation between the environmental interventions and the transient and permanent stressors	9.2.6
3rd fundamental equation	the relation between the transient and permanent stressors and the environmental impacts	10.1.3
4th fundamental equation	the relation between the environmental impacts and the one-dimensional environmental problem	11.1.3
goal definition	the analytical phase in which the question to be investigated is formulated, including the economic activity that is the subject of the analysis, and in which a strategy for solution is designed, including the choice of a particular tool	1.3.2
(environmental) impact	the quantified score on each of a number of well-chosen impact categories	10.1.1
impact analysis	the analytical phase in which the environmental problem that is the result of the inputs and outputs that have been identified during the inventory analysis is investigated and evaluated	1.3.2
impact category	member of the set that is accessed during the second step of the impact analysis, and which is assumed to represent a scientifically acknowledged impact type	10.1.1
impact matrix	the matrix of coefficients that map the set of stressors onto the set of impact categories	10.1.3
(environmental) intervention	one element of the set of flows of environmental commodities from an economic process to the environment or *vice versa*; the term is most often applied for a cluster of economic processes	5.3.1

Term	Meaning	Intr'd
intervention matrix	the matrix of coefficients of environmental commodities from an economic process to the environment or *vice versa* for all economic processes	5.4.1
inventory analysis	the analytical phase in which the chosen economic activity is defined in terms of its inputs from and outputs to the environment and from and to other economic processes	1.3.2
operating time	the time period during which an economic process is (analytically) active	5.2.1
permanent stressor	the quantified asymptotical presence or absence of a persistent or non-renewable environmental or economic commodity	9.2.3
position problem	the question concerning the position of a number of the various tools for environmental decision-support	1.2.2
process	locus where commodities are converted into commodities; see economic process and environmental process	1.3.3
(environmental) problem	the one-dimensional measure for the normative perception of "problematicness" of any of the impact categories	11.1.1
(environmental) stressor	the quantified transient or permanent presence or absence of environmental or economic commodities due to the interplay of environmental intervention and environmental processes	9.2.1
technical coefficient	size of a flow of a commodity to or from an economic or environmental process per unit of time	5.2.4
technology matrix	the matrix of coefficients of economic commodities from an economic process to another economic process for all economic processes	5.4.1

Term	Meaning	Intr'd
transient stressor	the quantified time-integrated presence or absence of a persistent or non-renewable environmental or economic commodity	9.2.1

The next table gives a summary of symbol, meaning, and section of introduction of quantities that are used.

Symbol	Meaning	Intr'd
a_{ij}	element indicating the flow of economic commodity i to (when negative) or from (when positive) economic process j	5.4.1
a_i	element indicating the flow of economic commodity i to (when negative) or from (when positive) an economic process	5.1.2
	element indicating the external demand of economic commodity i	5.4.1
$\bar{\mathbf{A}}$	technology matrix containing the technical coefficients $\bar{a}_{ij}$	5.4.1
$\bar{a}_{ij}$	technical coefficient belonging to a_{ij}: $\bar{a}_{ij} = a_{ij}/t_j$	5.4.1
$\mathbf{a}$	vector of inflows and outflows of economic commodities into and out of an economic process	5.1.2
	vector of external demand of economic commodities	5.3.2
$(\mathbf{a})_j$	vector of inflows and outflows of economic commodities into and out of economic process j	5.3.1
$\bar{\mathbf{a}}$	vector of technical coefficients belonging to $\mathbf{a}$: $\bar{\mathbf{a}} = \mathbf{a}/t$	5.2.1
b_{ij}	element indicating the flow of environmental commodity i to (when negative) or from (when positive) process j	5.4.1
b_i	element indicating the flow of environmental commodity i to (when negative) or from (when positive) an economic process	5.1.2
	element indicating the environmental intervention of environmental commodity i	5.4.1

Symbol	Meaning	Intr'd
$\bar{\mathbf{B}}$	intervention matrix containing the technical coefficients $\bar{b}_{ij}$	5.4.1
$\bar{b}_{ij}$	technical coefficient belonging to b_{ij}: $\bar{b}_{ij} = b_{ij}/t_j$	5.4.1
$\mathbf{b}$	vector of inflows and outflows of environmental commodities into and out of an economic process	5.1.2
	vector of environmental interventions of environmental commodities	5.4.1
$(\mathbf{b})_j$	vector of inflows and outflows of environmental commodities into and out of economic process j	5.3.1
$\bar{\mathbf{b}}$	vector of technical coefficients belonging to $\mathbf{b}$: $\bar{\mathbf{b}} = \mathbf{b}/t$	5.2.1
$\mathbf{C}$	fate matrix	9.1.2
c_{ik}	element of the fate matrix indicating the relation between a unit of environmental intervention of environmental commodity k and environmental stressor i	9.1.2
$\mathbf{c}$	vector of time-integrated presences or absences of environmental commodities	9.2.1
c_i	element of $\mathbf{c}$ indicating environmental commodity i	9.2.1
$\check{\mathbf{C}}$	modified fate matrix, in which permanent environmental commodities are removed	9.2.6
$\mathbf{D}$	damage matrix	9.1.2
d_{ik}	element of the fate matrix indicating the relation between a unit of environmental intervention of environmental commodity k and economic stressor i	9.1.2
$\mathbf{d}$	vector of asymptotical presences or absences of environmental or economic commodities	9.2.3
d_i	element of $\mathbf{d}$ indicating environmental or economic commodity i	9.2.3
$\check{\mathbf{D}}$	modified damage matrix, in which permanent environmental commodities are incorporated besides economic commodities	9.2.6
$\mathbf{e}$	vector that contains the contribution to the environmental impact categories of the transient stressors	10.1.3

Symbol	Meaning	Intr'd
$\mathbf{f}$	vector that contains the contribution to the environmental impact categories of the permanent stressors	10.1.3
g	one-dimensional measure of the environmental problem (the problem index)	11.1.2
$\mathbf{g}$	vector that contains problem factors	11.1.3
i, k	index of an economic or environmental commodity	5.2.2
j, l	index of an economic or environmental process	5.3.1
$\mathbf{P}$	matrix of economic and environmental inflows and outflows of a cluster of economic processes: $\mathbf{P} = \begin{pmatrix} \mathbf{A} \\ \mathbf{B} \end{pmatrix}$	5.4.1
$\mathbf{p}$	vector of economic and environmental inflows and outflows of an economic process: $\mathbf{p} = \begin{pmatrix} \mathbf{a} \\ \mathbf{b} \end{pmatrix}$	5.2.2
$\bar{\mathbf{p}}$	vector of technical coefficients belonging to $\mathbf{p}$: $\bar{\mathbf{p}} = \mathbf{p}/t$	5.2.2
$(\mathbf{p})_j$	vector of inflows and outflows of economic and environmental commodities into and out of economic process j: $(\mathbf{p})_j = \begin{pmatrix} (\mathbf{a})_j \\ (\mathbf{b})_j \end{pmatrix}$	5.3.1
p_{ij}	element indicating the flow of economic or environmental commodity i to or from economic process j	5.4.1
p_i	element indicating economic or environmental commodity i of vector $\mathbf{p}$	5.2.2
$\mathbf{q}$	vector of transient and permanent stressors: $\mathbf{q} = \begin{pmatrix} \mathbf{d} \\ \mathbf{c} \end{pmatrix}$	9.2.5
$\mathbf{Q}$	matrix that contains the combination of the fate and damage coefficients: $\mathbf{Q} = \begin{pmatrix} \check{\mathbf{D}} \\ \check{\mathbf{C}} \end{pmatrix}$	9.2.6

Symbol	Meaning	Intr'd
$\mathbf{r}$	vector of environmental impacts: $\mathbf{r} = \begin{pmatrix} \mathbf{f} \\ \mathbf{e} \end{pmatrix}$	10.1.3
$\mathbf{R}$	matrix that contains the impact factors	10.1.3
t	operating time of an economic process	5.2.1
$\mathbf{t}$	vector of operating times of several economic processes	5.4.1
t_j	operating time of economic process j	5.4.1
$\boldsymbol{\tau}$	vector of transmission coefficients	7.3
τ_i	transmission coefficient for commodity i indicating the fraction of commodity i that is to be considered in a substance-flow analysis	7.3
$\boldsymbol{\Theta}$	allocation matrix	6.2.2
θ_{ji}	element of the allocation matrix indicating the fraction of the total input or output of commodity i that is allocated to process j	6.2.2
$\mathbf{x}$	vector of substance flows according to the established approach	7.3
x_i	element of the vector of substance flows according to the established approach, indicating the magnitude of flow number i	7.3
$\boldsymbol{\Xi}'$	matrix that selects the transient stressors from a vector of environmental commodities	9.2.5
$\boldsymbol{\Xi}''$	matrix that selects the permanent stressors from a vector of environmental commodities	9.2.5
$\mathbf{Y}$	matrix of internal substance flows	7.3
y_{ij}	element of the matrix of internal substance flows that represents the amount of the selected substance in commodity i flowing into economic process j (when negative) or from economic process j (when positive)	7.3
$\mathbf{y}$	vector of external substance flows	7.3

Symbol	Meaning	Intr'd
y_i	element of the vector of external substance flows that represents the amount of the selected substance in commodity *i* flowing into the system (when negative) or out of the system (when positive)	7.3

PART ONE

INTRODUCTION

This part introduces the two problems that are the subject of this study. These are:

- The attribution problem: which environmental problems are to be attributed to which economic activities?
- The position problem: what is the relative position of a number of the various tools for environmental decision-support?

Both the attribution problem and the position problem can be resolved by constructing a unified approach for a number of tools for environmental decision-support. This unified approach consists of a general framework and specific methodological steps within that framework. The main focus in this study will be on the methodology.

The unified methodology is based on the notion of economic unit processes, and on the combination of these processes into meaningful clusters of aggregated processes. Here two questions are of interest: which processes are to be clustered, and in what proportion?

The second chapter discusses the scientific position of the work reported here. As the experimental method is not appropriate for answering the attribution problem, a discussion of the epistemological foundation of the work is required. Another section is devoted to a discussion of the interdisciplinary character of the study.

Chapter 1

The Questions

1.1 QUESTION 1: THE ATTRIBUTION PROBLEM

1.1.1 Environmental Problems: Originator versus Instigator

On 3 April 1995, seven members of Greenpeace climbed the 185-metre chimney of an electric power station in Amsterdam and painted the text

S
T
O
P

C
O
2

on the chimney. A national newspaper gave as an argument for this action:

> The environmental group wants to encourage the climate conference in Berlin … to control the release of carbon dioxide.[1]

1 Front page of *De Volkskrant* of 4 April 1995. (Originally in Dutch: '*De milieuorganisatie wil met de actie de klimaatconferentie in Berlijn ... aansporen de uitstoot van kooldioxide*

Why do certain electric power stations emit carbon dioxide? Obviously, these plants do not emit carbon dioxide because the management likes to do so. The plants do so because it is inherently coupled to their method of energy conversion. The answer is therefore that they emit carbon dioxide because they produce electricity by burning fossil fuels.

If this line of reasoning is followed, a next question could be why that plant produces electricity. It does so, not because it likes to produce electricity, but because there is a demand for electricity by industry, by agriculture, by households, etc.

Still one further question is why, say, the aluminium industry exerts a demand for electricity. The obvious answer is that producing aluminium requires power, and that electricity is a good power source in this example.

We might continue posing questions (why do aluminium producers produce aluminium), and we will again obtain an answer (because other industries demand aluminium), an answer which raises new questions (why, say, the automobile industry demands aluminium).

The reason for doing these types of exercises is to examine a question of charge, responsibility, accountability, or, even, blame. True, the electric power station that was the locus of Greenpeace's activity is emitting carbon dioxide; it is the originator. But to what extent is it responsible for it? Who is the instigator? Would it not have been better for Greenpeace to go to an aluminium producer and paint the text "Stop aluminium"? Or even: "Stop electricity"? And to whom should they go with which text?

Obviously, these questions can be asked by any non-governmental organization and can be posed with respect to any economic activity that directly causes or contributes to environmental problems. The question of where to exert pressure can only be answered if we know the answer to a broader, more analytical, question: which environmental problems are to be attributed to which economic activities?

1.1.2 Formulation of the Attribution Problem

The arguments discussed above may lead to a redistribution of "responsibilities":[2] the power station's emission of carbon dioxide is partly attributable

aan banden te leggen.')

2 Responsibility must be understood in a primarily causal sense, without necessarily having any moral connotation (*cf.* Heijungs (1994*a*)).

to the aluminium producer, or to the automobile industry, or perhaps to the consumers that buy or use cars.

In allowing for this type of shifting of responsibilities, there is a danger of nobody actually taking the responsibility. The owners of the electric power station may claim that they emit carbon dioxide for the benefit of the aluminium producers, whereas the aluminium producers may claim that the electricity producers did emit carbon dioxide themselves; after all, they demanded electricity, not carbon dioxide. We see that a proper accounting of responsibilities needs clear rules on deciding which environmental problems to attribute to which economic activities. The design of such rules is a central question in this study. Now we come to the formulation of the attribution problem:

The attribution problem is the question of which environmental problems are to be attributed to which economic activities.

This study gives a procedure for dealing with the attribution problem.[3]

1.1.3 Some Historical Notes on the Attribution Problem

The attribution problem was raised long ago, and a number of answers have been formulated. A quotation from an earlier author gives a clear motivation:[4]

> The Western intellectual tradition has it that one gains knowledge of the universe by focusing attention on some aspects of it. ... It is the purpose of this book to draw attention to the relations between a society's economic activity, as

3 Some readers may wonder why the definition of the attribution problem is not stated in terms of a causal relationship such as: The attribution problem is the question of which environmental problems are caused by which economic activities. The reason will become clear in Section 2.1, where it is argued that there is no unambiguous causal relationship, and that the answer to the attribution problem can never be proven, but rather involves a normative assignment, comparable to the question of which number is to be assigned to 5^{-2} (see in particular Section 2.1.3).

4 Observe the similarity with the terms of Lotka's classic book *Elements of mathematical biology* of 1924, of which Chapter XV bears the title *The stage of the life drama*, the stage being formed by the environmental compartments such as the atmosphere, the aquatic compartment, and the soil.

traditionally defined, and the physical world which provides the stage for a larger drama.[5]

To my knowledge, the term attribution as a procedure to assign environmental problems to economic activities has not often been employed before. In the context of energy analysis Ayres uses the word allocation along with the word attribution:

> It is clear that the total energy consumption of the economy can be allocated among the final goods and services produced, if the energy consumed by each sector is appropriately attributed to those sectors that buy from it, and so on to the last step in the sequence (final consumption).[6]

I introduced the word allocation for it in the following way:

> The complex of economic activities is what I shall call "responsible" … for the complex of environmental problems. In the environmental sciences, one studies this responsibility. One of the key questions here is the following: Which economic activity is responsible for which environmental problem? One can rephrase this as an allocation problem: Which environmental problems are to be allocated to which economic activity?[7]

The term allocation, however, is also used for other purposes, especially with respect to the allocation of scarce resources. The usage of the word in the last quotation was inspired by a very specific meaning, namely the allocation procedure in environmental life-cycle assessment, one tool for environmental analysis and decision-support (see Section 1.2.1).[8] The allocation problem in life-cycle assessment is a sub-problem within the general attribution problem which is the topic of the study of economy environment interactions. The term attribution is preferred in this text for two reasons: it is more neutral than allocation since allocation might suggest some equal distribution, and

5 Victor (1972*a*, p. 17).
6 Ayres (1978, p. 103).
7 Heijungs (1994*a*, p. 8).
8 See, e.g., Huppes & Schneider (1994), where allocation denotes the act of attributing environmental burdens to the various products that are produced by a multi-product process; see also Section 6.2. Unfortunately the meaning of the term allocation has become broadened in the recent discussions in the International Organization for Standardization (ISO), so that one option for allocating is avoiding allocating.

secondly, to reserve the word allocation for the sub-problem encountered in Chapter 6.

Figure 1.1 gives a graphical illustration of the attribution problem.[9] The

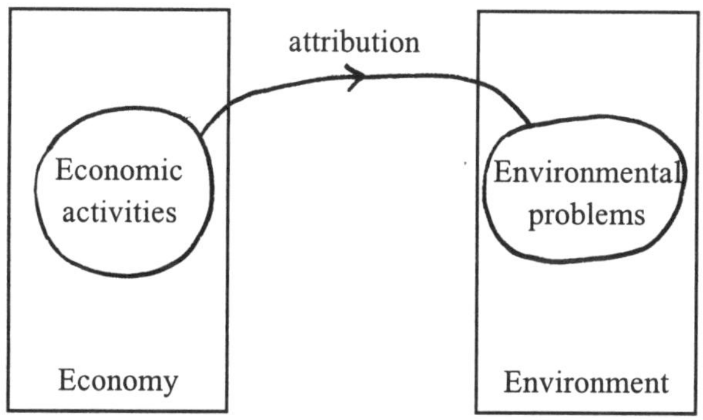

FIGURE 1.1. The attribution problem: which environmental problems are to be attributed to which economic activities?

procedure to isolate economic activities from the total economic system is described in Part Two. The connection with environmental problems is made in Part Three. The attribution problem is finally resolved in Part Four. See Chapter 3 for a more comprehensive overview of the structure of this study.

1.2 QUESTION 2: THE POSITION PROBLEM

1.2.1 Tools for Environmental Analysis and Decision-Support: a Small Anthology

Policy officials dealing with environmental regulation and plant managers dealing with the environmental performance of their facilities face the question of prioritization: some measures for abatement of environmental problems are more relevant than others. Choices are necessary, especially when there is only a limited budget available for environmental investments.

9 Similar figures may be found in Pearce & Turner (1990, p. 30) and in Heijungs (1994*a*, p. 8).

Outside the context of investment decisions, similar questions arise, for instance with respect to preferences among alternatives and balanced policy design. For this purpose, tools for environmental analysis and decision-support tools have been developed.

> Modern industrial society, with its thousands of inter-related products and services, is extremely complex. As a result, business management in this society is also complex and requires a clearly defined management framework to gather and process the information necessary for sound decisions. ... [T]he company must make effective daily decisions using appropriate environmental management tools.[10]

Today's environmental decision-maker has a large number of decision-support tools at hand. Below are just a few examples of terms[11] that may be found in the context of environmental decision-making (*cf.* Beck & Bosshart (1995)):

- clean production (Misra (1996));
- eco-balance (Boustead (1992));
- ecolabelling (Clift (1993));
- ecological balance (Fecker (1992));
- environmental impact assessment (Erickson (1994));
- environmental input–output analysis (Schrøder (1995*a*));
- environmental priority setting (Steen & Ryding (1993));
- industrial ecology (Graedel & Allenby (1995));
- industrial input–output analysis (Duchin (1992));
- industrial metabolism (Ayres & Simonis (1994));
- integrated life-cycle management (Quakernaat & Weenk (1993));
- integrated waste management (White et al. (1995*b*));
- life-cycle assessment (Consoli et al. (1993));
- management of substance chains (Enquete Commission (1994)):
- materials-balance (Kneese et al. (1970));
- materials-process product model (Saxton & Ayres (1975));
- materials-product chains (Kandelaars & Van den Bergh (1996));
- resource and environmental profile analysis (Sauer et al. (1994));

10 White et al. (1995*a*, pp. 171–172).

11 I have restricted the references to those sources that have these terms in their title.

- risk assessment (Van Leeuwen & Hermens (1995));
- substance-flow analysis (Van der Voet (1996));
- sustainable product development (Hansen (1994)).

It is not always clearly defined which of these terms corresponds to a tool, which to a concept, which to an application, etc. (*cf.* De Smet et al. (1997)). Furthermore, some of the terms in the list are synonyms, at least according to some authors. Many of the tools/concepts are ambiguously defined, or are even undefined. Some are developed to quite an extent, and are the exclusive domain of a certain scientific community, probably with their own journal. Some of these terms are no more than powerful metaphors. Some tools/concepts restrict themselves to environmental aspects, while others include more.

1.2.2 Formulation of the Position Problem

Given the large number of tools, concepts, and metaphors, and given the attribution problem, at least three questions can be formulated:

- Which precisely are the tools that are relevant with respect to the attribution problem?
- Which of these tools are appropriate for which types of analysis and decision?
- Is it possible that two equally appropriate tools for a certain type of decision yield conflicting answers?

Remarkably, it is very difficult to answer these questions. It proves to be very difficult to judge the relative merits of the different environmental tools for environmental analysis and decision-support. One may wonder in what sense they do support the process of decision-making: although we try to use the principle of rationality in decision-making, we replace it by some form of revelation: the oracle that is called a tool for decision-support. A highly relevant question is therefore the position problem, which we are now ready to formulate.

The position problem is the question concerning the position of a number of the various tools for environmental decision-support.

As will be shown, the method that is developed in this study to answer the attribution problem allows us to answer this question of relative position as well.

1.2.3 Some Historical Notes on the Position Problem

Beck & Bosshart (1995) devote an entire report to the comparison of a huge number of tools for environmental decision-support. They claim, for instance, that

> it has become difficult to find the right tool for a problem.[12]

Reasons for this include:

- Some of these tools are not described in sufficient detail.
- Some of these tools are defined or described differently by different people.
- Even if the tools are unambiguously defined, the framework and the methodology differ so much between the tools that it is difficult to consider their relative positioning.

Beck & Bosshart phrase it thus:

> a genuine comparison … was for reasons of heterogeneity hardly possible.[13]

Furthermore, they state that

> the conclusions of different tools contradict each other.[14]

This may also be due to an overlap:

> A certain amount of overlap can be identified among the various instruments.[15]

12 Beck & Bosshart (1995, p. 1) (originally in German: '***ausserdem ist es auch schwierig geworden, für ein Problem das richtige Instrument zu finden***').

13 Op. cit. (p. 106) ('*ein wirkliches Miteinander-Vergleichen ... war wegen der heterogenen Materie fast nicht möglich*').

14 Op. cit. (p. 1) ('*widersprechen die Analyseergebnisse verschiedener Instrumente einander*').

15 Anonymous (1995, p. 16).

Another reason may be the enormous number of competing tools:

> Even environmental scientists lose the overview over the existing methods and practitioners have increasing problems to identify the one instrument that is appropriate for the solution of their problems.[16]

On a smaller scale, we may mention Udo de Haes & Huppes (1994), Van der Voet & Heijungs (1994), Tukker & Heijungs (1995), Hofstetter (1996*a*), Anonymous (1996*a*, p. 37 *ff.*), and in particular Anonymous (1995) as instances of comparative research on the position of tools for environmental decision-support. White et al. (1995*a*) discuss the incorporation of some of these tools into a joint framework for decision-support. De Smet et al. (1997) discuss the relationship between the different concepts and tools ("conceptually related programmes") within the context of environmental management.

All these reports follow an object-oriented approach: they define the object of the tool (product, substance, factory), and try to clarify the consequences of this choice of object with respect to scope, usage, and usefulness of the tool. As far as I know, it has never been attempted to follow a "constructive" approach: to make a number of choices on methodology, assumptions, and system boundaries, and describe the object that can be analysed with the resulting tool. This study will employ this latter "bottom-up" approach: first a general set-up will be designed; the connection with concrete tools will be made by making specific choices at some points. It turns out that the tools that are constructed under this rigid derivation differ in a number of respects from the currently existing ones; see Section 13.1.7 for an overview of these differences.

1.3 THE TWO-FOLD ANSWER: UNIFICATION

1.3.1 Towards a Unification of Tools

Above we have seen that there are a large number of tools for environmental analysis and decision-support. All these tools give some form of answer to the attribution problem: of the environmental problems related to a factory, to a

16 Hofstetter (1996*b*, p. 127).

substance, to a product, and so on. We have also seen that the position of many of these tools is unclear. Some are identical or slightly different variants, while others are in fact applications of some other tool, etc.

A harmonization of these tools is highly desirable. Harmonization means that the framework, principles, and/or methods of the tools are adjusted to each other in some way. The most basic level in this respect is a harmonization of terms, so that, for instance, environmental impact has the same meaning within all environmental contexts. A step further in harmonization is that the frameworks – a kind of protocol according to which the tools are defined – are reduced to the same denominator at some level.[17] Probably the highest level of harmonization is that of unification. This means that there is one uniform principle, some meta-tool, from which all concrete tools are derived.[18] In this study, it will be attempted to construct a unified set-up for describing economy environment interactions, and to derive some of the tools for environmental analysis and decision-support from this meta-tool.

The reason for this is twofold (Heijungs (1995*a*)):

- By conforming to one single principle, the relative position of the different tools can be clarified to a much larger extent. As long as the methods are not harmonized, the difference between outcomes will stem from both a difference in object (product, substance, industrial plant, etc.) and a difference in method. If the methods are harmonized, the consequences of the choice of object can be isolated.
- The quality of the tools themselves may be improved by adopting concepts from other tools, whether or not in some modified form.

This study will be concerned with the unification of several tools for environmental analysis and decision-support as an answer to question 2: the

17 Harmonization of terms and frameworks is commonly referred to as standardization. Part of the work of Technical Committee 207 of ISO is devoted to standardization of the terms and framework of environmental management tools.

18 Theoretical physicists are trying to achieve a "grand unification" of the description of the elementary forces of nature into one unified framework (see, e.g., Aitchison & Hey (1982, pp. 287–292)). Unification is regarded as a great step forward in gaining an understanding of nature: the most famous examples are the unification of electricity, magnetism, and light by Maxwell, the unification of electromagnetism and the weak force in quantum chromodynamics, and the unification of the electric, weak, and strong forces in the standard model of Glashow, Salam, and Weinberg.

position problem.

What about question 1: the attribution problem? Many of the different tools for environmental analysis and decision-support listed above give an answer to the attribution problem. For instance: environmental impact assessment gives its own answer to the question of which environmental impacts may be expected by building a certain factory somewhere. Providing a unified set-up of these tools turns out to answer the attribution problem as well.

Thus we can now formulate the answer to the two questions:

> Both the attribution problem and the position problem will be resolved by constructing a unified approach for a number of tools for environmental analysis and decision-support. The construction of such a unified approach, and the derivation of a number of tools for environmental analysis and decision-support (with special attention to life-cycle assessment and substance-flow analysis) is the main topic of this study.

Within the process of unification, we must distinguish two main elements for unification: that of the framework and that of the methodology. The framework can be seen as an overview of the different aspects and procedural steps involved in a certain tool, whereas the methodology is a very specific expression of the operational details within those steps. The two elements will be discussed below.

1.3.2 A Unified Framework

Let me start by quoting the following long excerpt on a comparison of the frameworks of life-cycle assessment (LCA) and risk assessment (RA):

> The structure of the life-cycle assessment technique ... consists of four components:
>
> 1) goal definition and scoping, in which the subject of analysis is defined, the amount of product function produced is fixed in the form of the so-called functional unit, and the scope and some general lines of the study are specified;
> 2) inventory analysis, in which the inputs from the environment (extractions of natural resources, land use, ...) and the outputs to the environment (emissions to air, water and soil, noise, radiation, ...) are compiled for the

entire system;

3) impact assessment, in which these inputs and outputs are interpreted in terms of their contributions (either positive or negative) to a limited number of environmental problems (global warming, acidification, resource depletion, ...);
4) improvement assessment, in which the opportunities for decreasing the product's contribution to these environmental problems are identified and/or prioritized.

The structure of risk assessment follows another procedure ...: exposure assessment, hazard identification, risk characterization, and risk management. There is a strong similarity with the LCA-procedure, nevertheless. Exposure assessment is concerned with emissions as well as with fate, and corresponds thereby to the inventory analysis of LCA and to a part of the impact assessment. Risk characterization deals with toxic parameters; in LCA this takes place in the second part of the impact assessment. Risk characterization combines exposure aspects and hazard aspects; in LCA this is the last part of the impact assessment. Risk management can be seen as an improvement assessment. Goal definition and scoping is implicit. This somewhat concise comparison of the procedures for LCA and RA could be elaborated in more detail to show that design of an encompassing procedural framework is possible. It is tempting to try to cast the several types of environmental analysis into a framework that is similar to the one developed for LCA. In all techniques for environmental decision-support the goal and the scope need to be defined. Probably all of them contain some type of inventory-related stage, in which factual or expected emissions, land use, etc., are compiled. Furthermore, some do proceed with an assessment stage in which impacts are assessed. The improvement assessment is not always part of the decision-support itself, but it is clear that improvement of the environmental performance of plants, products, substance chains, etc., may well be achieved through a prior analysis of the facts.[19]

One may add to this the framework for substance-flow analysis proposed by Van der Voet et al. (1995*a*): definition of the system, quantification of the overview of stocks and flows, and interpretation of the results.[20] This framework assumes an implicit goal definition, since

19 Heijungs (1995*a*, p. 217).

20 That this framework is in development is shown by a recent contribution (Udo de Haes et al. (1997)).

> [a]ll three steps involve a variety of choices and specifications, each of which depends on the specific goal of the study to be conducted.[21]

Furthermore, the second step of the framework might be considered as a quantitative elaboration of the qualitative first step. As the focus of these steps is not really different, it appears more natural to merge these steps into one. Another, still similar, type of structure has been proposed for substance-flow analysis by Tukker et al. (1995, p. 1): inventory analysis, a qualitative classification plus the quantification, and finally a normalization and a valuation. Altogether, these considerations create a framework consisting of three steps: goal definition, definition and quantification of the system, and interpretation of the results.

Built on the arguments presented for risk assessment, life-cycle assessment, and substance-flow analysis, the following framework for solving the attribution problem arises:[22]

- Goal definition: the phase in which the problem to be investigated is formulated, including the economic activity that is the object of the analysis, and in which a strategy for answering the question is designed, including the choice of a particular tool.
- Inventory analysis: the phase in which the chosen economic activity is defined in terms of its inputs from and outputs to the environment and from and to other economic processes, in accordance with the principles of the chosen tool.
- Impact analysis: the phase in which the environmental problems that are the result of these inputs and outputs are investigated and evaluated.

This study concentrates on the inventory analysis of economic activities

21 Van der Voet et al. (1995*a*, p. 91).

22 It may be observed that this framework is very similar to SETAC's framework for life-cycle assessment (see Consoli et al. (1993)), and that there are some deviations to later developments in ISO's TC 207. Even SETAC's terms have not been followed completely here: scoping has been left out, impact assessment has been changed into impact analysis, and improvement assessment has been left out, the reason for these changes being the focus of this study on the attribution problem of environmental problems as they occur or are perceived, not on resolving those problems and not on application in a business context with limited resources and non-environmental arguments.

(Part Two) and the impact analysis into environmental problems (Part Three). Part Four summarizes how the unified approach can be translated into concrete tools for environmental analysis and decision-support; as such it can be seen in connection with a goal definition. See also Figure 3.1.

1.3.3 A Unified Methodology

In order to establish a unified methodology for accounting interactions on the interface of economy and environment, a systematic accounting procedure for economic activities is required. The line of reasoning here is that economic activities (centred around a product, a substance, a firm, a country, etc.) consist of economic unit processes. By making a cluster of the appropriate economic processes in an appropriate proportion, any desired economic activity can be built. For instance, the life cycle of a product is an aggregation of the unit processes that are related to its manufacture, use, disposal, transportation, etc. Similarly, the economic activity of a country is an aggregation of the economic unit processes that take place in that country.

Effectively the unified methodology consists of two notions:

(a) building blocks;
(b) combination rules.

These are described below.

(a) The building blocks are economic (unit) processes.[23] These exist in many varieties, obvious examples being production of steel and passenger transportation by train. Somewhat less obvious examples of economic processes are the consumption of a banana and the incineration of waste. It is difficult to give an exact definition of economic processes, especially at this early point. Gradually, and in particular in Section 5.1.1, a definition will appear which will be further refined in Section 9.1.1. At the moment, it suffices to sketch the general idea: an activity is undertaken by humans to transform commodities (products, materials, services, energy, waste, etc.) into

23 ISO uses the term unit process for the smallest economic activity for which data are collected. This implies that a unit process may be divisible into a number of constituent unit processes, if one is able to collect data on a more detailed level. It indeed implies that what in a particular situation are the unit processes are by definition the smallest building blocks that are used.

(other) commodities. This definition does not contain any notion of want or utility: it is left open whether the desired production of an output commodity is the driving force to operate a process or whether it is the desired elimination of an input commodity (in particular: treatment of waste).

The analytical representation of an economic process is part of the subject of Part Two. For now, it suffices to sketch the general idea in the concise

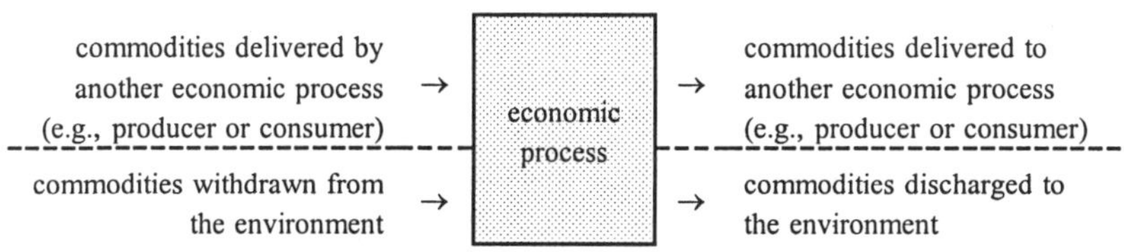

FIGURE 1.2. Structure of an economic (unit) process: commodities are transformed into other commodities.

form of Figure 1.2.[24] Goods, services, waste streams, and raw materials enter the process, which is considered as a black box. Some of these inputs are the output of other economic processes; others are taken directly from the environment. The process has a number of outputs: again products, materials, services, energy, and waste which flow to other economic processes. The other output category are flows to the environment, of which chemicals that are released to air, water, and soil are the most well known.

(b) The second notion of interest is a rule determining how the economic unit processes are to be clustered into systems of economic activity. Here two questions must be discussed: which processes must be clustered and in what proportion.

Huppes (1993) devotes a number of pages to the first question, with an emphasis on the meaningfulness of these clusters:

> One process ... is the most basic unit for the economic object at the society-environment interface. ... If several of these basic processes have been defined, these may be grouped into meaningful aggregates, as the objects of society-environment interface.[25]

24 Similar figures are in Victor (1972*b*, p. 13) and in a somewhat extended form in Huppes (1993, p. 192).

25 Huppes (1993, p. 47).

He distinguishes 13 of these meaningful possibilities: all processes at a certain location, all processes related to a certain product, etc.[26]

He does not discuss the second question: in what proportion should the processes be aggregated. This important question – consider the question of which fraction of an electric power station is to be attributed to an aluminium producer (Section 1.1) – will be discussed in detail in Chapter 5.

1.4 THE CENTRAL QUESTION

Recapitulating the previous sections, the central question of this study can now be formulated.

> This study describes a unified methodology from which a number of tools for environmental analysis and decision-support can be derived. Special attention will be paid to the tools of life-cycle assessment (LCA, related to products) and substance-flow analysis (SFA, related to substances), and some attention to environmental impact assessment (EIA, related to factories and projects) and risk assessment (RA, related to chemicals). Each of these tools gives a particular mode of answer to the attribution problem: which environmental problems are to be attributed to which economic activities. The fact that they are derived from uniform principles enables us to give an answer to the position problem: what is the position of a number of the various tools for environmental decision-support.

The choice of the tools that will be derived in later chapters can be motivated by:

- my desire to concentrate on tools, not on concepts or metaphors, like industrial ecology;
- the fact that these tools are generally considered to be important and different;
- the lack of clarity in the realm of application of these tools.

26 See op. cit. (p. 51). There is a similarity with the much more qualitative-oriented "systems view of waste prevention" in Van Weenen (1990, p. 127 *ff.*).

Chapter 2

The Scientific Context

2.1 THE EPISTEMOLOGICAL FOUNDATION

2.1.1 Failure of the Experimental Method

Any theory which claims to be scientific needs a context of foundation: the knowledge must be derived from certain principles. Statements are therefore only valid if they are based on an epistemological foundation. Consequently, it is necessary to discuss the epistemological basis of the present work.

We can introduce the question of epistemology by analysing the fairly widespread standard for reporting experimental work by the structure: Introduction, Methods, Results, and Discussion. The section on Methods describes in that case – although often quite implicitly – the scientific basis of the work. Anyone can redo the experiment and compare the results with those that are reported.

There are at least two reasons[1] why the experimental approach is not applicable to the work reported here:

(a) One cannot do an experiment in which only one isolated economic activity takes place with the other economic activities "switched off".[2]

1 Oreskes et al. (1994) provide a third reason: the intrinsic "open" nature of the system. This makes all that is argued below all the more true, although from a different argument.

2 This is different from introducing an additional economic activity with all other economic

(b) Even if one could do so, one would not obtain results that would be useful for answering the attribution problem.

Some reflection on these two reasons will not only make the reasons understandable, but will moreover help to formulate an alternative strategy; see Section 2.1.2.

(a) The first point is perfectly explained by Carnap:

> The experimental method has been enormously fruitful. The great progress physics has made in the last two hundred years, especially in the last few decades, would have been impossible without the experimental method. If this is so, one might ask, why is the experimental method not used in all fields of science? In some fields it is not as easy to use as in physics. In astronomy, for example, we cannot give a planet a push in some other direction to see what would happen to it. Astronomical objects are out of reach; we can only observe and describe them. Sometimes astronomers can create conditions in the laboratory similar to those, say, on the surface of the sun or moon and then observe what happens in the laboratory under those conditions. But this is not really an astronomical experiment. It is a physical experiment that has some relevance for astronomical knowledge. Entirely different reasons prevent social scientists from making experiments with large groups of people. Social scientists do make experiments with groups, but usually they are small groups. If we want to learn how people react when they are unable to obtain water, we can take two or three people, give them a diet without liquid, and observe their reactions. But this does not tell us much about how a large community would react if its water supply were cut off. It would be an interesting experiment to stop the water supply to New York, for instance. Would people get frantic or apathetic? Would they try to organize a revolution against the city government? Of course, no social scientist would suggest making such an experiment because he knows that the community would not permit it. People will not allow social scientists to play with their essential needs.[3]

Summarizing: we might do part of the analysis by doing laboratory experiments (as is for instance often done for toxicity tests, which indeed partly give a clue for attributing environmental problems to economic

activities kept constant (*ceteris paribus*). This latter form is – although also not feasible for experimental verification – the relevant question in the case of incremental analysis; see Section 14.1.

3 Carnap (1966, pp. 40–41).

activities), but we cannot do the full experiment because social structures inhibit us from doing so.

(b) The second reason is more fundamental. A self-quotation hopefully clarifies my point here:

> no environmental problems are created by sufficiently narrowly defined economic activities. The environmental assessment constructs a sub-world in which only the isolated economic activities exist. Each sub-world denies the existence of environmental problems.[4]

There are two reasons that an isolated economic activity does not create any environmental problem: the response is highly non-linear (there are for instance many threshold phenomena), and there is a large amount of synergistic and antagonistic factors involved (for instance, the environmental problems associated with emissions of hydrocarbons depend on the presence of nitrogen oxides). These facts mean that it is impossible to incorporate in the development of tools for environmental analysis and decision-support of isolated economic activities a respectable remark like

> There is no scientific basis that a concentration of 5% of a NOEC is any safer than 10%. There is some validity to this claim because how can a non-existing dose-response curve be interpreted? The tacit assumption is that a meaningful dose-response curve exists below the NOEC, *i.e.* there where no response can be measured? Does there?[5]

We are thus led to the conclusion that the attribution problem cannot be studied within empirical science. Because its study is neither a normative science or falls under the humanities, we could, following De Groot (1992, pp. 32–33) infer that it is subject to the rules of formal science: mathematics, logic, etc. Consequently, what is required is the formulation of clear rules to construct sub-worlds (sub-sets of the total economic activity), such that certain consistency rules are met.

> It is the entirety of activities which creates the problems .... This means that it is not correct to predict the impacts in the constructed sub-world by the normal tools that are available in risk assessment or hazard assessment. An interpolation is

4 Heijungs (1998).
5 De Oude (1993, p. 2).

> needed such that every emission, however tiny, contributes a small share to the environmental problems as they occur in the real world. When we require that the sum of the sub-worlds corresponds to the real world, we effectively require that the sum of the parts is equal to the total. This makes that the interpolation techniques must be reductionistic, not holistic.[6]

This implies a possible violation of normal intuitively obtained results, for instance because emissions that remain below toxicological thresholds may nevertheless be taken into consideration for toxic impacts.

Answers to the attribution problem escape experimental verification. Furthermore, they may sometimes defy intuition.

2.1.2 Towards an Alternative Epistemology

In the last quotation above, it was stated that an interpolation is needed. This can be understood by a careful statement of the attribution problem in conjunction with an investigation of the knowledge that is available:

- The question is which environmental problems are to be attributed to a selected economic activity.
- The available knowledge is that the sum of current economic activity creates the sum of current environmental problems.[7]

There is some more knowledge of interest here. Process technology

6 Heijungs (1998).

7 This statement neglects some complications related to a time-lag in the occurrence of environmental problems, as well as environmental problems caused by natural phenomena. One justification for this neglect is that – although there certainly is a time-lag between economic activity and environmental problems and that there is a large variation in the size of this time-lag between different types of environmental impact – the economy environment system can be considered to be in a more or less stationary state: a quasi-stationary state so to speak. A similar assumption is very often made in economic modelling, where equilibrium models are successfully used while growth and innovation to some extent violate the basic assumptions of such models. See also Braat & Van Lierop (1987*b*). As a kind of justification for the neglect of natural causes for environmental problems, we may postulate that the perception of impacts as an environmental problem is only influenced by the deviation from the natural situation, say, before the industrial era.

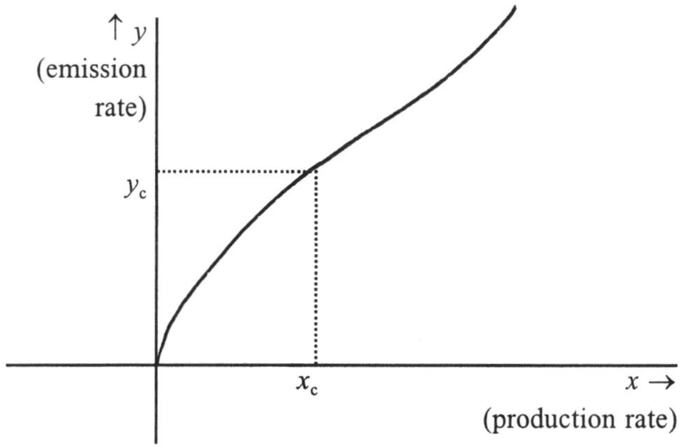

FIGURE 2.1. Relationship between the rate of production of a process and the rate of emission of a chemical.

teaches us how the emission rate (y) of a certain installation may depend on the activity level or production rate (x) of that installation. Typically, a certain pollutant is already emitted when no production takes place (think of a car which emits combustion gases in stationary state). If production increases, the emission rate increases, most often in a non-linear way (see Figure 2.1). Suppose that the current production rate is known to be x_c and the current emission rate is known to be y_c. If one is asked what the emission rate per unit of production rate is, one usually calculates the quantity y_c/x_c. More generally, if one is asked what the emission rate is for an analytical production rate x_a,[8] one calculates

$$y_a = \frac{y_c}{x_c} x_a. \tag{2.1}$$

It is important to observe that this equation totally ignores the available knowledge on the characteristics of the process. Equation (2.1) (which is represented in Figure 2.2) and Figure 2.1 clearly disagree with each other. The only exception to this[9] – the only datum on which there is agreement – is the current situation: the point with the coordinates (x_c, y_c) in Figure 2.1 is the only point of the curve that is satisfied by Equation (2.1).

8 The subscript "a" stands for analytical.

9 Of course there may be more exceptions, like the point (0, 0). In rare cases, like the linear homogeneous case, they even fully agree with each other.

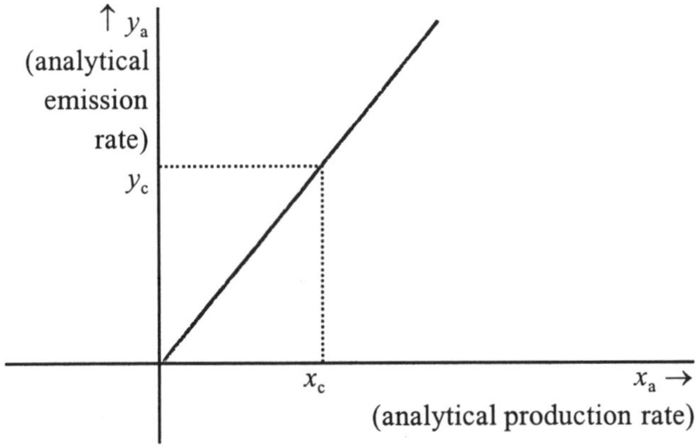

FIGURE 2.2. Relationship between the analytical rate of production and the analytical rate of emission.

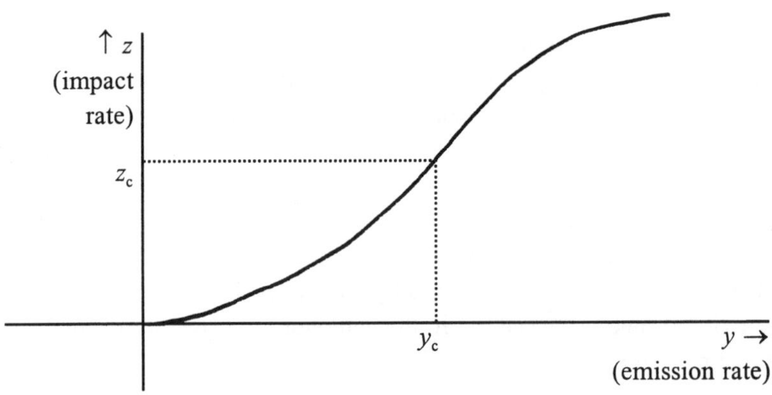

FIGURE 2.3. Relationship between the emission rate of a certain chemical and the resulting environmental impact.

A very similar reasoning can be given for the environmental problems that are generated by the emissions from an installation. Ecotoxicologists have established dose response curves for the relationship between emission rates[10]

10 More precisely, they have established relationships between concentrations and impacts. It will be assumed here that the emission rate of a pollutant and the concentration in the environment are proportional. To facilitate a connection between this paragraph and the previous one, this paragraph will not discuss concentrations but emission rates.

(y) of pollutants and the subsequent environmental impacts (z). This relationship is quite often a mirrored version of the relation between production rate and emission rate (Figure 2.3). In the leftmost part we have a region of no (or negligible) impact. Higher emission rates will produce an impact, but at very high emission rates the slope will level off because all sensitive species are already affected (see also Müller-Wenk (1996)). Denoting the current impact level by z_c, we may write for the environmental impact per unit emission rate z_c/y_c, and for the environmental impact that can be attributed to an analytical emission rate ya

$$z_a = \frac{z_c}{y_c} y_a. \tag{2.2}$$

The same remarks as in the previous paragraph apply: even if we know dose response curves, we apparently discard their use in attributing the environmental impact per unit of current pollution (Figure 2.4).

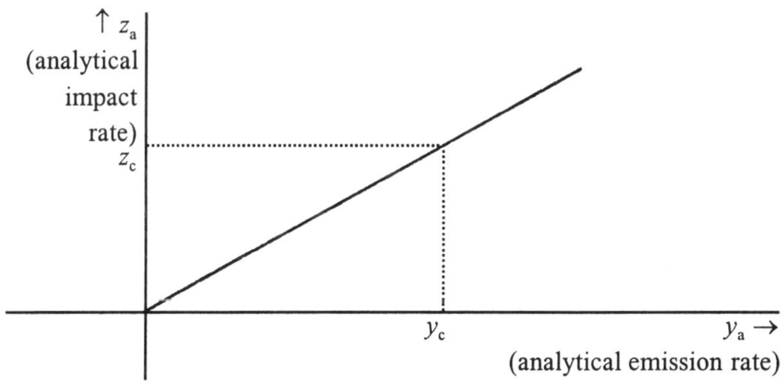

FIGURE 2.4. Relationship between the analytical emission rate and the analytical environmental impact.

There are some good reasons to prefer the use of Equation (2.1) to the use of Figure 2.1 and Equation (2.2) to Figure 2.3, at least for the question of attribution of impacts to activities. A very practical point, of course, is that it is not necessary to know the complete non-linear relationships between production rate and emission rate, between emission rate and environmental impact, etc.; instead it suffices to know the current position on those curves. The second reason is much deeper and deserves additional discussion in this section on the epistemological foundation. The linear attribution principle satisfies three requirements that could have been postulated *a priori*.[11] These are:

- The result of the analysis should be insensitive to the order in which economic activities are analysed.
- The results of the analysis should be insensitive to the amount of economic activity that is analysed.
- The results of a separate analysis of all economic activities should add up to the result of an analysis of the total economic activity.

These points can be illustrated with the analysis of the environmental impacts of a cup and saucer, assuming the non-linear form of the production impact relationship $z = x^2$ and taking $x_{cup} = 3$ and $x_{saucer} = 2$ (in unspecified units). We could state that $z_{cup} = 9$ and that $z_{saucer} = 4$, but also find that $z_{cup\text{-}and\text{-}saucer} = 25$, thereby violating the third principle. If we in contrast state that $z_{saucer} = 16$, because it is an additional contribution to the problem, we would violate the first principle, since an analysis of the saucer prior to the cup would yield $z_{saucer} = 4$ and $z_{cup} = 21$. The second principle is violated with both types of implementations, as we find results of the kind $z_{cup\text{-}and\text{-}saucer} = 25$ and $z_{2\text{-}cups\text{-}and\text{-}saucers} = 100$, which is obviously more than 2 times 25.

There is some trace of realism in these results. For instance, there could be more critical thresholds exceeded when we produce two times as much. In that sense, two products may be more than two times as polluting as one product. But we must keep in mind what the question was: we want to attribute environmental problems to economic activities. If we attribute all current environmental problems to all current activities according to some rule of proportionality, we get results that are more apt for the purpose of analysis.

The order in which burdens are produced becomes immaterial when we do not speak of consequence but of guilt; Steen & Ryding (1993) introduce the example of 11 one-litre cans filling a 10-litre bucket: the last one gives the consequence of one litre spoilt, but all 11 are "guilty"[12] for 1/11th part

11 See Heijungs (1998) for an elaboration of this *a priori* epistemology on the basis of definitions, axioms, and theorems. In that paper, I gave a number of classic examples of axiomatic approaches: Euclid's *Elements*, Spinoza's *Ethics*, and Pāṇini's *Aṣṭādhyāyī*, an ancient Sanskrit grammar. This list may easily be extended with modern achievements, like Debreu (1959) and Fishburn (1988), to name just a few. I furthermore refer to Koopmans' second *Essay* (1959) in favour of axiomatization and Kornai's *Anti-equilibrium* (1971) expressing an opposing view.

12 Again, guilt does not imply a moral idea here; after all, how can a litre be guilty of

of that consequence. Also the marginality of an individual contribution does not mean that it can be neglected:

> No one will die from the emissions of one shaving. But all tiny contributions of all activities together make the environmental problem.[13]

This is exactly the point when the question of holism versus reductionism and between average and marginal contribution comes into the theoretical consideration. Most authors in the field of life-cycle assessment postulate a marginal approach, both for the attribution problem:

> this means that the effects of emissions due to the functional unit are assumed to be additional to normal background concentrations.[14]

and for the allocation procedure:

> we therefore propose that burdens should be allocated between different outputs according to the marginal changes resulting from marginal changes in each output.[15]

Mathematically this means that

$$y_{\mathrm{a}} = \left[\frac{\partial y(x)}{\partial x}\right]_{x=x_{\mathrm{c}}} x_{\mathrm{a}}. \tag{2.3}$$

This form is a linear one, so that the order and the amount of marginal increments is irrelevant. Still, it is not in accordance with the general principles outlined in this study because the previously stated requirement that the sum of the sub-worlds corresponds to the real world is not compatible with this marginal approach.[16] The average attribution rule (Equations (2.1)

something? What is meant here is the aforementioned "responsible for" in the sense that some consequence may be attributed to it.

13 Heijungs & Guinée (1993, p. 4).

14 Heijungs et al. (1992*b*, p. 12). Müller-Wenk (1996) starts from similar principles.

15 Azapagic & Clift (1994, p. 56).

16 It may be argued that, since answers to the attribution problem will be applied, for instance, to rank product alternatives on the basis of the environmental problems that are associated with them and to use this for purchase decisions, the epistemological basis should reflect a marginal principle rather than an average approach. The attribution must in that case be differently formulated: ***Which additional environmental problems will result from a certain***

and (2.2)) is the only one which at the same time satisfies the requirements of order-independency, amount-independency, and 100%-additivity. This does not imply that the marginal approach or any other basic principle is incorrect; see also the next section. Section 14.1 discusses the relevance of a number of alternative epistemological principles in the context of other questions than the attribution problem.

The epistemology of answers to the attribution problem will be based on a fully linear attribution, in order to satisfy the requirements of order-independency, amount-independency, and 100%-additivity. This starting point is different from the idea that is sometimes expressed in some tools for environmental analysis and decision support, where an analysis of marginal changes is central.

The next section argues that the proposed epistemological basis may be regarded as an interpolation and that it thereby escapes validation so that more than one answer to the attribution problem may exist and that this answer may appear counterintuitive. The section is, however, not essential for an understanding of the treatment itself.

2.1.3 Excursus: the Epistemology of Interpolations

In the previous section, it was argued that the attribution problem can be understood as an exercise in interpolation: no economic activities create no environmental problems, all economic activities create all environmental problems, and attribution of environmental problems to part of the economic activities is an interpolation.

In mathematics, the problem of interpolation is an old one. It exists under different names, for instance as analytic continuation. Strikingly, the literature on the foundations of mathematics appears to ignore the epistemological problems that are associated with it.[17] A classic example, the power function

additional economic activity? This question is partly beyond the scope of this study. See, however, Section 14.1 for a number of remarks.

17 That is to say, I was not able to find it. It is missing in books on the philosophy of mathematics like that of Körner (1960), in books on non-empirical epistemology in general like that of Popper (1959), and neither is it discussed in standard books on mathematical analysis.

x^n, will be investigated in this section as an example of how interpolations influence the scientific status of a theory.

An easy and intuitive definition of the power function $y = x^n$ is to multiply n times the number x:

$$y = x^n \equiv \underbrace{x \times x \times \cdots \times x}_{n \text{ times}} . \tag{2.4}$$

This definition clearly restricts the domain of n to the integers 1, 2, 3, ... To be able to assign a value to y if n is fractional, negative, or zero requires an extension to or a modification of the original definition. The accepted approach is to adopt an alternative definition on the basis of a property of the original definition. The property that serves this purpose is the observation that

$$x^{m+n} = x^m \times x^n, \tag{2.5}$$

which is of course only valid for positive integer m and n, as long as the domain of x^n is restricted to positive integers. An interesting situation occurs if one applies this theorem with a positive parameter, say $m = 3$, and an unallowed negative parameter, say $n = -2$, in which case one finds the illegal expression $x^{3-2} = x^3 \times x^{-2}$. Comparison with the neatly defined $x^1 = x^3/x^2$ suggests that it is suitable to identify $x^{-2} = 1/x^2$. More general, one can make the identification

$$x^{-n} = \frac{1}{x^n} \tag{2.6}$$

for all positive integer values of n.

Thus a value of x^{-n} is constructed, not by applying the definition, but by applying a consequence of that definition and extending it to non-defined values of the parameter n. The constructed value of, say, x^{-2}, cannot be verified or validated[18] in the sense that we would multiply -2 x-values with each other according to Equation (2.4). Still, we attach a meaning to these concepts that does not exist under the official definition. I will call the extensions to the original domain interpolations.[19] Defined in this way, the truth of interpolations can by definition not be verified or validated by experiments.

18 See Oreskes et al. (1994) on the difference between verification, validation, and confirmation.

19 These thus include interpolations proper as well as extrapolations.

It is conceivable that someone would assign an alternative value to x^{-2}, i.e. $-x^2$ instead of $1/x^2$. It is important to recognize that this alternative definition does not violate the original definition any more than $1/x^2$ does. True, we would perhaps have to be more careful in applying the rules of addition of powers (Equation (2.5)). The point is that one normally chooses an interpolation such that a maximum of meaning can be assigned with a minimum of violation of original properties. A normative element is therefore involved in choosing a particular mode of interpolation. Others may arrive at another value for x^{-2}, a value that has an equal truth, or rather untruth. In fact, the problem of interpolation or extrapolation beyond what can be experienced could even be considered to be a metaphysical problem:

> There was thus a point at the end of the eighteenth century when philosophers by and large agreed that metaphysics was dead. Kant, who dominated all of Western philosophy for a century, had purportedly shown up this enterprise as inherently and essentially mistaken. It involved after all the extrapolation of our concepts, familiar from daily application in experience, to applications outside the reach of experience – and there cannot be for us even the glimmer of a hope of the possibility of a warrant for such extrapolation. We can spin and weave our words into a rich and colourful tapestry to depict ourselves weaving a likeness of ourselves in the world. But the result must inevitably depict us as hopelessly ignorant of even the conditions under which the woven picture would be true. In science, theorizing can always be harshly brought to a stop, through confrontations arranged within our experience; but purported applications of our concepts outside experience can never be put to the question within experience.[20]

In the above, we spoke of "a minimum of violation of original properties", because interpolations will often challenge common sense to some extent. This does not make them wrong as long as it is clearly stated what has happened and what the assumptions are.[21] Consider for instance x^0: common sense suggests that its value is 0, because a multiplication of 0 x-values does not yield any positive or negative number. The interpolated meaning of x^0, however, is different: $x^{2+0} = x^2 \times x^0$, which implies that $x^0 = 1$ by extension. Again, we see a statement that escapes empirical validation, but now even

20 Van Fraassen (1989, p. 8).

21 One might add to this: and why one chooses a certain option. From an analytical point of view this is of course not compulsory, but it certainly helps in communicating the fruits of research.

worse: it defies intuition. De Groot (1992) says that formal science aims to the construction of formal correctness

> without reference to real-world facts or values.[22]

In this study, I will not go that far. On the contrary, I require that certain real-world facts are part of the theory, but that, where the problem of interpolation comes into play, there can – unfortunately – be no reference to facts. *A priori* values are anyhow outside the present treatment: the answer to the attribution problem is by no means intended to promote recycling or to discourage pesticide use.

The interpolation-like character of an answer to the attribution problem has consequences for the scientific status of that answer: it cannot be validated, alternative contradicting answers may exist and may be equally "true", and the answer may lead to counterintuitive statements.

2.1.4 The Question of Truth

In this study a number of tools for environmental analysis and decision-support will be developed. Quite naturally, the question of their truth will be posed. In particular in life-cycle assessment, the question of truth invokes many discussions. Consider for instance the problem of allocation of multiple processes. One author emphasizes the subjective nature of a choice for any method:

> The example illustrates a case where two reasonable inventories can be established. The first question that arises is then if any of the inventories is objective? In my opinion, the answer is no. Both inventories are "true" and the choice between them is accordingly subjective or maybe political. A second question that arises from the example is: Should the LCA society agree on a standard allocation rule for a similar problem? When discussing this problem, it should be noted that mechanistic rules does not always lead to the right solution. ... When reporting, all options must be mentioned and the choice of allocation model argued. If this is not done, the results should be considered as purely subjective and may compromise the

22 De Groot (1992, p. 12).

> LCA practitioner.[23]

However, another author claims the discussion should be closed:

> Despite this, there remains a small but vociferous group of proponents of this procedure ... [It] cannot be regarded as a serious contender in ecoprofile calculations.[24]

An even stronger statement of this latter desire for absolute clarity is that

> LCA ought to be like mathematics, where people all over the planet can do the same work and get the same answer.[25]

Especially in the area of attributing environmental impacts to isolated economic activities, there is very often the desire to somehow make a link with the real impacts:

> The impacts to be included in LCA/IA should be environmentally relevant and be measurable.[26]

It may be even a motivation to reject papers:

> A scientific paper should, in principle, use the scientific method, *i.e.* there is an hypothesis that can be experimentally tested.[27]

Kornai strongly opposes empirical science and formal science:

> In the logical-mathematical sciences, "truth" is a logical criterion. ... In the real (natural and social) sciences, on the other hand, the only criterion of "truth" is experience, the comparison of assertions with reality.[28]

23 Schmidt (1994, pp. 141–142).
24 Boustead (1994, pp. 3–4).
25 Anonymous (1993, p. 16), quoting J.S. Hirschorn.
26 De Smet et al. (1994, p. 69).
27 Quoted from an anonymous referee report in which the rejection of a paper, which was afterwards rewritten and published as Guinée & Heijungs (1993), is justified.
28 Kornai (1971, p. 8). He admits (loc. cit.) that 'empiricism and observation have played an important part in the development of logical-mathematical sciences'. Furthermore, he states (op. cit. p. 9) that these sciences 'could not build their theories on axiomatical foundations

Popper summarizes the general situation for a science that is not empirical and not purely tautological:

> [Positivists] are constantly trying to prove that metaphysics by its very nature is nothing but nonsensical twaddle – 'sophistry and illusion', as Hume says, which we should 'commit to the flames'. ... The positivist dislikes the idea that there should be meaningful problems outside the field of 'positive' empirical science – problems to be dealt with by a genuine philosophical theory.[29]

In contrast, arguments can also be forwarded concerning the impossibility of a genuine validation of the principles underlying certain tools for environmental analysis and decision-support (*cf.* Oreskes et al. (1994)), and in particular life-cycle assessment. For instance, in the context of the assessment of resource extractions in terms of a depletion score, Guinée & Heijungs (1995) wrote:

> There is no empirically correct method for aggregating extractions of resources to one overall depletion score that can be verified experimentally. In this case, it is necessary to design methods on the basis of logical theoretical reasoning. It is often possible to test methods by detecting logical contradictions, but one cannot truly validate a nonempirical method.[30]

Furthermore, from a paper dealing with the validity of LCA:

> Although it is recognized that no methodology for LCA can thus be "valid" in some empirical sense, we must somehow strive for a methodology that is at least not in contradiction to empirical results, that is internally consistent, and that is to some extent plausible.[31]

In the latter paper, an axiomatic scheme was proposed, which served to prove theorems on the methods for LCA and the nature of the results. Other

which are in contradiction to reality'. With the previous section on interpolations in mind, I think that Kornai is not right in this latter respect. His sharp distinction of real sciences from logical-mathematical sciences, on the other hand, is quite useful, and stresses the hypothetical character of the tools for environmental analysis and decision-support to be developed in this study.

29 Popper (1959, pp. 35–51).

30 Guinée & Heijungs (1995, p. 922).

31 Heijungs (1998).

instances of papers where a set of requirements was used for selection of methods and elements are De Smet et al. (1994) and Heijungs (1995*b*). Another source is Hofstetter (1996*b*):

> The search for "truth" within LCA is an illusion. But we can build models following rules which are derived from axioms. The definition of these axioms asks for "normative" steps.[32]

Here the emphasis is on the intrinsic normative character of life-cycle assessment, which I extend here to tools for environmental analysis and decision-support in general. Subjective choices are necessary in the weighting between different environmental impacts, but normatively decided principles pervade the whole procedure.

> The consequence of the epistemological basis is a possible conflict with intuition and established principles. This is, however, in many cases an inevitable result of an approach that is in accordance with facts, that is internally consistent, and that is to some extent plausible. Full plausibility is thus not always possible.

2.2 INTERDISCIPLINARITY

2.2.1 Environmental Science, Systems Analysis, and Thermodynamics

This study must be seen as an attempt to contribute to the field of environmental science. To be able to appreciate its value, it is necessary to discuss what I understand by environmental science, in particular in relation to some other disciplines: economics, ecology, and mathematics. This section describes some ideas on the content of environmental science. The next sections discuss the role of the other contributing branches of science.

One of the core attributes of environmental science is often claimed to be interdisciplinarity:

32 Hofstetter (1996*b*, p. 130n).

> A key term for environmental science is interdisciplinarity: the integration of contributions from different branches of science.[33]

The title of this study already suggests that two branches of science are involved: economics and environmental science. But there is a contradiction: environmental science is not a science of the environment, but

> ... the interdisciplinary science that is concerned with the relation between society and its environment.[34]

The inconsistency arises from the fact that, whereas economics studies the economy, and social science studies society, environmental science studies more than the environment. One might try to resolve this by using the term ecology for the discipline that studies the environment.[35] In that way, environmental science could claim to encompass social science and ecology. This solution, however, suffers from the fact that what is meant in the current context is much better covered by the term environment than by the term ecology. After all, ecology suggests too strong an emphasis on impacts on biota and their habitat and the like, whereas a much broader meaning is intended here: from impacts related to resource extraction to human toxic releases.

After this clarification of the position of environmental science, it is appropriate to reflect on the position of the environment itself in this type of analytical exercise. A major source of confusion is due to the existence of following terms:

- "the" environment and "its" environment;
- the "natural" environment and the "thermodynamic" environment.

The etymology of the word environment makes one think of surroundings, and the definition

33 Udo de Haes (1991, p. 33) (originally in Dutch: '*Voor de milieukunde is een sleutelbegrip de interdisciplinariteit, ofwel de integratie van bijdragen uit verschillende wetenschappen*').

34 Op. cit. (p. 29) ('*Milieukunde is de interdisciplinaire wetenschap die zich bezighoudt met de relatie tussen de maatschappij en haar milieu*').

35 Some authors do so, see for instance Victor (1972*a*); Pillet & Odum (1987); Idenburg (1993).

> the physical, abiotic and biotic, surroundings of society with which it is in mutual relation[36]

indeed employs that word. It must be stressed, however, that the word surroundings has a relative meaning: the surroundings of a certain something. In environmental science, it is often convenient to distinguish a system (e.g., a factory or a national economy) and an environment:

> a system is considered to consist of a set of related components or elements, each having certain characteristics or attributes with numerical or logical values. ... The set of external systems is called the systems environment. The systems environment generates inputs that are transformed by the system to become outputs. The transformation of inputs is generated by the process operating the system.[37]

The interactions between the system and the environment can be thought of as emissions of pollutants and extractions of resources. It is important to clearly distinguish "the" environment from "its" environment: the latter term corresponds to the relative surroundings-related concept ("a process and its environment"), while the former term has an absolute meaning ("a process and the environment").

Thermodynamics is often argued to be of prime importance in environmental science. There are a number of reasons for this:

- Thermodynamics describes the interactions between a system and its environment (see e.g., Ruth (1993), Amir (1994), Azapagic & Clift (1994)).
- The "first law of thermodynamics"[38] – the law of conservation of mass/energy – implies that energy cannot be created from nothing and that waste cannot be annihilated (see e.g., Kneese et al. (1970), Ruth (1993), Amir (1994)).
- The second law of thermodynamics – that entropy never decreases – postulates certain limits to the performance of the system (see e.g., Kümmel (1989), Ruth (1993), Amir (1994)).

36 Udo de Haes (1991, p. 21) (originally in Dutch: '*de fysieke, niet-levende en levende, omgeving van de maatschappij waarmee deze in een wederkerige relatie staat*').

37 Hettelingh (1989, pp. 5–6).

38 The first law of thermodynamics is one of mere energy conservation.

Despite these superficial similarities, and despite the fact that some thermodynamic concepts can indeed be applied in environmental science, the analogy between the thermodynamic environment and the natural environment fails. The most striking evidence for this is that the existence of environmental problems – which is one of the prime reasons of undertaking environmental analyses at all – is denied by thermodynamics. The thermodynamic environment is assumed to be so huge in comparison to the system that it can exchange heat and matter without limits and without being affected itself. The thermodynamic environment can fulfil its function as a sink and a source without environmental limits. If the exchange between the system and the thermodynamic environment is not optimal, it is due to limits of the system's structure, not of the thermodynamic environment. In short, in thermodynamics there are no environmental problems.

This disqualifies a straightforward application of thermodynamic theory to environmental analysis. It all has to do with the definition of the environment, and with the object of the theory. In thermodynamics, the object is a certain system, and the environment is everything which is not part of the system and therefore not the object. In environmental science the object is the relation between (parts of) society and (parts of) the environment. The object is not a system but an interaction. As the object is not a system, it also does not have an environment (in the thermodynamic sense). This difference of object has remarkable consequences. The natural environment can be limited in its carrying capacity. The performance of the economic system is limited by its own structure, by the structure of the environmental system, and by the nature of the interactions.

This reasoning does not imply a complete rejection of systems analysis and thermodynamics. On the contrary, one of the standard problems in thermodynamics is that of two systems in interaction which are isolated from their shared environment. One of these systems could represent the economic system, the other the environmental system. This amounts to an upgrading of the natural environment from that which is outside the analysis to that which is of equal merit in the analysis. Another very useful concept is the "first law" on which all materials-balances are based. Thirdly, the second law of thermodynamics has been shown to have relevance for environmental science. In general, there is much to admire in the pioneering work of some authors who write on the implications of thermodynamics for economic systems and for environmental repercussions (for instance Georgescu-Roegen (1971) and Ayres (1978)).

Equal merit does not mean a complete analogy in focus and treatment. The systems studied here are the economic system and the environmental system. A healthy environment may be achieved by an absence of production and consumption. A sound economy needs in contrast a healthy environment. There is hence no full similarity. The prime starting point addressed here is the economic system. Sustainable production and consumption must be seen in the context of sustainable environmental quality. The position of the environment is thus ambiguous:

- The environment has system aspects because it is affected by interactions with another system (*in casu* the economic system).
- The environment has environmental aspects because it is an essential condition for a system (*in casu* the economic system).

The system environment duality of the natural environment is a crucial fact for understanding the philosophy of environmental science.

Environmental science, as interpreted in this study, is concerned with more than the natural environment proper. Rather, it is concerned with the interaction between society, and in particular the economic activities therein, and the natural environment.

The scope of this study is thus economic and environmental, hence the branches of science that are involved are economics and ecology in the broader sense, the discipline for which we have no word. Furthermore, the approach that will be followed will to a large extent be based on mathematics.

The next sections describe the role of the three disciplines involved. In particular, it should be emphasized that this study uses only selected aspects from economics, ecology, and mathematics, and can thus not be described as economic, ecologic, or mathematical work. Furthermore, some concepts innate to those disciplines will have a different or very specific meaning in the present work. Awareness of this should prevent the reader from judging the work from a traditional point of view, according to which it will definitely contain serious flaws and deficiencies; see also Section 2.2.5.

2.2.2 The Role of Economics

It is often argued that clean air is a scarce resource, and must therefore be taken into account when doing economic analysis. The field of ecological economics, which has emerged in the last few years, intends to deal with the inclusion of environmental externalities in economic theory.

> Ecological economics is a new transdisciplinary field of study that addresses the relationships between ecosystems and economic systems in the broadest sense.[39]

It turns out that the traditional economic way of thinking may complicate extension of traditional concepts and methods to the study of the causes of environmental problems. Two examples follow. Economists consider resources to be:

> the free gifts of nature, such as land, forests, and minerals; human resources, both mental and physical; and all sorts of manufactured aids to further production, such as tools, machinery, and buildings.[40]

In the context of environmental economics, the distinction between natural resources, human resources and the remaining economic resources must not be neglected, so that it is somewhat strange to list them in one breath.[41] The other example relates to commodities:

> Commodities may be divided into goods and services. Goods are tangible (e.g., cars or shoes), and services are intangible (e.g., haircuts or education). Notice the implication of positive value contained in the terms goods and services.[42]

Although economists apparently see it this way, goods and services need not be associated with positive value. Broken cars, e.g., must be discarded by

39 Costanza et al. (1991, p. 3).
40 Lipsey & Steiner (1978, p. 6).
41 Moreover, environmentalists dislike the habit of speaking of natural resources as being "free gifts". Taking into consideration that the development of energy analysis was stimulated by the publication of *Limits to growth* and the oil crisis, a sentence like 'One can consider the world as a vast store of free energy, available as oil, coal …' (Anonymous (1974, p. 20)) is quite remarkable. The only explanation could be that free energy refers here to Gibbs free energy, but this is unlikely since the rest of the quoted text uses capitalized Free Energy.
42 Lipsey & Steiner (1978, p. 6).

authorized companies who ask for a certain amount of money. This would mean that a broken car, and any waste product in general, would not satisfy the definition of a commodity. We could decide to call positively valued tangibles goods, negatively valued tangible "bads",[43] and together with positively valued services and negatively valued "disservices"[44] call them commodities.[45]

Besides these examples of instances where a critical use of the economic vocabulary is demanded, a deeper conceptual change is required in some places. In Section 1.3.3, for example, we gave less obvious examples of economic processes: the consumption of a banana and the incineration of waste. These examples are less obvious because an economic process is often tacitly equalized with economic production, and production is distinguished from consumption, because it is not "productive". Consider the following sequence of annotated quotations:

> The act of making goods and services is called production and the act of using them to satisfy wants is called consumption.[46]

Here, the distinction between production and consumption is made, such that production seems to produce out of nothing, and consumption seems to consume without producing waste.

> [I]ndustries are productive units which produce nothing but commodities.[47]

This sentence also suggests that industries must be productive, neglecting the fact they are also "consumptive", and underestimating the role of waste

43 Loc. cit., but see also Möller & Rolf (1995, p. 34), who speak of the German *Gut* and *Übel*. Is it a coincidence that English *good*, German *Gut*, Dutch *goed*, and even French *bien* all have that double meaning?

44 If these exist at all. Hooliganism is probably one of those rare examples.

45 In that way we manage to stick to the word commodity. Georgescu-Roegen (1971, p. 218) writes: 'Economics cannot abandon its commodity fetishism any more than physics can renounce its fetishism of elementary particle or chemistry can renounce that of molecule.'. It is, even among economists, not unusual to extend the meaning of commodity to negatively priced or unpriced entities: see for instance Debreu (1959, p. 33): 'The price ... of a commodity may be positive (scarce commodity), null (free commodity), or negative (noxious commodity).'

46 Lipsey & Steiner (1978, p. 6).

47 Anonymous (1968, p. 9).

processing industries.

> The economic activity ... must be divisible into a number of ... producing sectors.[48]

This suggests that consumption is not considered as an economic activity.

> We can define a production process as the process of transformation of commodities and primary inputs into (other) commodities.[49]

This statement is in contradiction with the first two, that production takes place out of nothing; it is unclear what the position of consumption is.

There are at least two problematic aspects at stake:

(a) Is there a difference between production and consumption?
(b) What is the position of waste treatment in the production consumption scheme?

A brief discussion may elucidate the meaning of economic terms in the current context of the attribution problem.

(a) By defining consumption as the act of using certain commodities, it appears to be outruled to use commodities for production. And, *mutatis mutandis*, consumption is defined here as an act which does not produce anything. This problem has been observed a number of times, especially in the context of environmental economics:

> The difference between production and consumption is not as sharp as is often assumed. Particularly in the case of commodities which require energy for their utilization, such as cars, heating equipment, etc., the difference between the production of goods and services and the consumption of goods and services becomes small.[50]

Ayres and Kneese even regard this confusion between production and consumption as a basic reason for environmental neglect:

48 Miller & Blair (1985, p. 7).
49 Konijn (1994, p. 147).
50 Idenburg (1993, p. 13n).

> Almost all of standard economic theory is in reality concerned with services. Material objects are merely the vehicles which carry some of these services, and they are exchanged because of consumer preferences for the services associated with their use or because they can help to add value in the manufacturing process. Yet we persist in referring to the "final consumption" of goods as though material objects such as fuels, materials and finished goods somehow disappear in the void – a practice which was comparatively harmless so long as air and water were almost literally free goods.[51]

To this, they add a footnote:

> We are tempted to suggest that the word consumption be dropped entirely from the economist's vocabulary as being basically deceptive. It is difficult to think of a suitable substitute, however. At least, the word consumption should not be used in connection with goods, but only with regard to services or flows of "utility".[52]

(b) The second problem is that the act of treating or neutralizing waste is outside the general definition of economic production, even if we were to include consumption in production. Even texts which deal with the subject of environmental economics sometimes underestimate the role of waste management as a process:

> the "physical economy" which represents the physical aspects of production, consumption and wastes.[53]

The present text uses the term economic process to include the categories production, consumption, and waste management.

In the last quotation, the term "physical economy" appeared. Much of what is being developed is based on simple physical principles, most notably conservation of matter. The above-mentioned considerations can only be included by making due reference to the physical principles on which they are based. Abandoning the monetary approach to economic analysis and adopting a description in physical terms allows one to introduce unpriced externalities without having to assume shadow prices or other artifacts.[54] Actually, the

51 Ayres & Kneese (1969, p. 284).

52 Op. cit. (p. 284n).

53 Idenburg (1993, p. 13).

54 Pearce & Turner (1990, p. 34) state it like this: 'One thing to note is that all our economy boxes ... were in money terms – that is, if we actually constructed such a table it would

question of whether there is a price or not associated with a certain commodity, whether the price is an ecologically good one, and even, if the price is positive or negative, is unimportant for nearly all analytical exercises that will be undertaken in Part Two.[55]

Similarly, the materials-balance approach rests on the recognition that

> [p]roduction and consumption are intimately involved with real physical materials and energy.[56]

A very important implication of this change of paradigm is that economics – to the extent it is considered in this study – is not a social science:

> Economists are used to thinking of their subject as a social science; so it is, insofar as economics concerns itself with human behavior, as it is expressed in the relationships between buyers and sellers of goods and/or services.[57]

This remark is important because a description of economic activity in physical terms without a declaration of the departure from the viewpoint of social science may lead to the reproach that social science is instrumentalized (Leroy (1995)).[58] Let me emphasize that the work reported here is based on an analysis of observed flows either between economic actors or between economic actors and the environment, without any attempt to explain these observed flows in terms of human behaviour or social utility. Although economics is considered to be a social science, I deprive the economic system in this study from its social components and reduce it to an interplay of processes with transactions of physical flows including services.[59]

show us, for example, the money value of steel as an input to £1 or $1 of automobile output. Although major advances have been made in putting money values on some of the functions of environment ... it must be recognised that [they] will be in physical terms, *i.e.* in tonnes of sulphur oxide, tonnes of coal, etc.'

55 The only exception to this is that it is important to know if the price is positive or negative for the inter-process allocation procedure (Section 6.1).

56 Ayres (1978, p. 4).

57 Op. cit. (p. 5).

58 Consider also Weinberg (1987, p. 14): 'I think a great deal of harm has been done by those from Herbert Spencer on who tried to see the social sciences for example as being based on physics as a model. I think physics is a terrible model for the social sciences. In fact it's probably a terrible model for everything except physics itself.'

59 Of course it remains a science of phenomena that are happening inside society. However, that does not make it a social science, in the sense that it is not oriented towards an explanation

So, the economic system will only be described in terms of observed flows, and no explanatory model for economic behaviour will be assumed or framed. But the same applies to the physical side of the economic system. The flows of commodities to and from economic processes will be described on the basis of observations, but no attempt to explain these phenomena will be undertaken. That is the subject of process technology and related disciplines, where chemical affinity plays a role that could be compared with social utility for the social-scientific side of the economic system. Just as I ignore the social side of social economics, I ignore the physical side of physical economics. This study can therefore be considered to be neither a social-scientific study (gamma-oriented, as the Dutch are used to calling it), nor a natural-scientific[60] study (beta-oriented). It does not explain or predict, which are two hallmarks of these fields of science. It may most appropriately be labelled as a formal science (*cf.* De Groot (1992, p. 12); see also Section 2.1.3), like mathematics and certain branches of philosophy (logic, ontology; see also Section 14.2.3).

Much of the work that will be referred to in Part Two is concerned with economic planning. It is very important to state explicitly that the present work is not about planning but about analysis.

> Economic analysis serves to obtain a clear insight into the structure and the interdependency of a part of the economy. ... Economic planning (or programming) differs from economic analysis, in that it attempts to develop an economic plan (or program) which is derived from certain *a priori* aims, but respects the functioning of the economy.[61]

This confinement of scope has large consequences, especially in relation to the discussion of the epistemological basis. Non-linearities in the relationship between production and emission are important for enviro-economic planning. Not so for the attribution problem; see Section 2.1.2. Similarly, problems arising from the discrete nature of certain economic activities (see Section 5.2.4: one cannot install half a locomotive) are important in planning, but not in attribution. Nothing is being optimized in this study: it is not directed towards a minimization of environmental problems nor to a economically

or prediction of social behaviour.

60 I will throughout use the term "natural science" instead of the ambiguous Anglo-Saxon "science".

61 Paelinck & Nijkamp (*n.d.*, p. 9).

attractive environmental performance. That intriguing subject is left to others (see, e.g., Baumol (1972), Faber et al. (1987) and Bloemhof-Ruwaard (1996)).

A quite large body of economic theory on interindustry economics appears to be useful in answering the questions of this study. Three important restrictions must be kept in mind:

- that the description of economic transactions will be based on observed physical flows, thereby excluding monetary descriptions and any attempt to explain these flows in terms of behaviour;
- that these descriptions also exclude any attempt to explain these flows in terms of physics or chemistry;
- that the aforementioned epistemological principles not only enable but even demand a neglect of the non-linear nature of the actual economic relationships.

It is worthwhile observing that the attribution problem is not characteristic of environmental science. It has been already raised in normal economic science, although no answers to this problem have been discussed:

> Economists, too, should be aware of the difficulty in deciding whether a truck hired by company A from company B and riding on some highway loaded with goods for company C is part of the activity of A, of B, or of C.[62]

A substantial part of this study is therefore devoted to an analysis of selected topics of the analysis of economic activities. One of the surprises is that a formalization of the ideas of life-cycle assessment, a concept on which much methodological development has taken place in the last ten years, is very similar to the economic activity analysis of the early fifties.[63] In fact, the knowledge of economists with respect to the dependency of economic activity and some primary factors of production (e.g., labour) can easily be extended to the environmental factor of production. Put in terms of matrices as a quantification of Figure 1.1:

> Environmental economics is concerned with both matrices .... Moreover it

62 Georgescu-Roegen (1971, p. 212).

63 See the appendix in Heijungs (1996*b*) for a concise overview.

> concentrates on the interactions between the matrices – how the demand for steel affects the demand for water, how changing the size of the economy ("economic growth") affects the functions of the environment, and so on. ... we show how we can use the main body of economic thought to derive important propositions about the linkages between the economy and the environment.[64]

2.2.3 The Role of Ecology

In general, ecology is concerned with organisms in relation to their environment. A much broader meaning is intended throughout this study, however, since it is concerned with so-called environmental problems, a notion which includes much more than a distortion of the relation between organisms and their environment. Rather, it encompasses such diverse aspects as:

- the availability of natural resources for human society;
- the impacts on humans due to the release or presence of toxic substances;
- the impacts on ecosystems due to the release or presence of other contaminants.

As such, the role of ecology in the strict sense will be quite limited.

On the other hand, many of the concepts that play a role in ecology – modelling of the fate of chemicals in the environment, prediction of the impacts of chemicals in relation to the sensitivity of ecosystems – can be used in the modelling of environmental problems, and their attribution to economic activities. A systems approach – such as Odum (1983) describes – could perhaps be envisaged as a foundation for the full structure of environmental processes, impacts, and problems. This has not been attempted, but the starting point proposed by Isard (1968) is one step in that direction.

A number of remarks that have been made concerning the application of economy in this study also apply to the application of ecology, although sometimes a bit differently. In the first place, the linear attribution rules require a neglect of the sophisticated knowledge with respect to cause-effect networks in ecological systems. In the second place, in the same way as economics will be deprived of its aspect as a social science, ecology could be said to be deprived of its aspects as a natural science, in the sense that it will

64 Pearce & Turner (1990, pp. 30–31).

not be attempted to explain or predict ecological phenomena. Only the available knowledge of relationships between, say, dose of a contaminant and impact will be used to develop a formalism for the attribution of environmental impacts to economic activities.

A number of selected elements of ecology will find a place in the theory to be developed, in particular elements dealing with the fate and impacts of chemicals in the environment.

2.2.4 The Role of Mathematics

This study will employ mathematics throughout. This has some disadvantages: some people for whom it might contain relevant information will not read it, others will not fully understand its message, usage of mathematics often suggests highly precise results, etc. This is surely felt to be a problem. The decision to use mathematics nevertheless can be justified by a number of quotations:

> My first point is that the enormous usefulness of mathematics in the natural sciences is something bordering on the mysterious and that there is no rational explanation for it.[65]

Directed to its application in one branch of science:

> The miracle of the appropriateness of the language of mathematics for the formulation of the laws of physics is a wonderful gift which we neither understand nor deserve. We should be grateful for it.[66]

Or in another branch of science:

> Of the chemistry of his day and generation, Kant declared that it was a science but not Science – *eine Wissenschaft, aber nicht Wissenschaft* – for that the criterion of true science lay in its relation to mathematics. This was an old story: for Roger Bacon had called mathematics *porta et clavis scientiarum*, and Leonardo da Vinci

65 Wigner (1960, p. 2).
66 Op. cit. (p. 14).

had said much the same.[67]

Or in yet another branch:

> Though it is perfectly possible to learn economics in a non-mathematical way, one is always then reading a translation rather than the original and that is usually second best. The reason economics is mathematical is not that economists want to seem "scientific", and lust after the intellectual respectability of subjects like physics, but because of its innate nature. It is concerned with quite long chains of reasoning about the interactions among numerical variables in complex systems, and mathematics is the most powerful and effective language we have for doing this.[68]

Or, even stronger, in general:

> This shows that the mathematical language has more to commend it than being the only language which we can speak; it shows that it is, in a very real sense, the correct language.[69]

There are even authors who stress the beauty which unrolls when phenomena are described in mathematical terms:

> I would express my own attitude with more prolixity by saying that such a formula as,
>
> $$\int_0^\infty e^{-3\pi x^2} \frac{\sinh \pi x}{\sinh 3\pi x} dx =$$
>
> $$\frac{1}{e^{2\pi/3}\sqrt{3}} \sum_{n=0}^{\infty} e^{-2n(n+1)\pi} (1+e^{-\pi})^{-2} \times (1+e^{-3\pi})^{-2} \ldots (1+e^{-(2n+1)\pi})^{-2},$$
>
> gives me a thrill which is indistinguishable from the thrill which I feel when I enter the Sagrestia Nuova of Capelle Medicee and see before me the austere beauty of "Day," "Night," "Evening," and "Dawn" which Michelangelo has set over the tombs of Giuliano de' Medici and Lorenzo de' Medici.[70]

67 Thompson (1917, p. 1).
68 McKenna & Rees (1992, p. 1).
69 Wigner (1960, p. 8).
70 Chandrasekhar (1979, p. 61).

However true this may be,[71] mathematics is – in the context of this study – a means, not a purpose:

> Contrary to the belief of many ecologists, systems analysis is not a mathematical technique, nor even a group of mathematical techniques. It is a broad research strategy that certainly involves the use of mathematical techniques and concepts, but in a systematic, scientific approach to the solution of complex problems.[72]

It will be attempted to use mathematics wherever needed, to use words otherwise. A combination of the two will suffice to cover both clear (unambiguous and explicit) formulations as well as comprehensible interpretations.

The linear attribution principles chosen in the preceding section on the epistemological foundation enable a rigid and straightforward mathematical formalization of the theory to be developed. It will be attempted, nonetheless, to exemplify the findings by clear interpretations.

2.2.5 A Theoretical Physicist's Apology

I am a theoretical physicist. I am not an economist, nor an ecologist, nor am I a mathematician. I cannot even claim to be an environmental scientist. Yet, I have tried to combine elements from economics and ecology and I have put them in the language of mathematics. This calls for a word of apology.[73] I

71 Sometimes it is even proclaimed that correct theories necessarily have an aesthetic value, or that an "ugly" theory cannot be correct.

72 Jeffers (1978, p. 1).

73 Compare the British mathematician G.H. Hardy, who wrote towards the end of his life in a humble mood an apology of his work: 'I have never done anything "useful." No discovery of mine has made, or is likely to make, directly or indirectly, for good or ill, the least difference to the amenity of the world. ... Judged by all practical standards, the value of my mathematical life is nil, and outside mathematics it is trivial anyhow' (Hardy (1940, p. 2013)). I will not (yet?) go that far, but I am aware that the value of the present work is, outside a very small circle of people in environmental science, of fairly limited value. Even the relevance for designing environmental policy may be small; see Section 14.1 for a discussion of the limitations due to the focus on the attribution problem. Another parallel that comes up is that of *wasan*, the traditional Japanese mathematics that studied formal problems independent from application in natural science or applied technology: '***Wasanka*** ...

have only a limited knowledge of the disciplines that I bring together. The literature that I studied is a selection, and probably not the best one. The concepts essential to these books sometimes denote different things. I took the liberty to interpret. That is one reason for giving many quotations.[74] Without their knowledge – often the result of monodisciplinary research – I would not have achieved the presented results. Probably it is the destiny of a scientist involved in environmental science – or in any other interdisciplinary field of study – to read, interpret, transform, and integrate books in different branches of science.

considered their neglect of practical problems a sign of sophistication. Scientists, in turn, regarded *wasan* as a useless amusement' (Ravina (1993, p. 223)).

74 The other reason is to emphasize that I – to speak in Newton's words – stood on the shoulders of giants.

Chapter 3

Outlook

3.1 ECONOMIC SYSTEMS

In Part Two, a theoretical model will be developed to attribute environmental flows of natural resources, pollutants, etc. to arbitrarily chosen economic activities. Metaphorically, we may consider this as a kind of jukebox-theatre: select a certain economic "play": a certain product, a certain substance, a certain factory, a certain country, or whatever, play it, and record what is entering and what is leaving the economic actors.

3.2 THE ENVIRONMENT

The inputs entering and outputs leaving the economic actors are delivered, respectively absorbed, by the environment. It is, so to speak, the stage of the theatre which carries the economic actors, and which provides certain services to them. In Part Three, the theoretical model will be extended with an analysis of the consequences of the flows leaving and entering the environment. Some of these flows are more harmful than others, some are more permanent, and some are more essential for sustaining the stage.

It may be observed that the word stage expresses a quite passive function; indeed it is regarded as such in this study.[1] The fact that nature has certain intrinsic qualities, and that an active experience of nature enriches life, is

1 This is also one of the reasons for using the term environmental instead of ecological.

surely recognized, but is not incorporated as such in this study, which concentrates on the functions that the environment fulfils in enabling economic activity.

3.3 THE PLAYS

In Part Four, a number of "plays" will be performed in the "theatre". The part summarizes the derivation of a number of tools for environmental analysis and decision-support as an answer to the attribution problem. These concentrate in particular on products from the cradle to the grave (life-cycle assessment) and on flows of a substance in a region during a time period (substance-flow analysis), but there is also some attention for national economies, factories, and released chemicals.

Figure 3.1 summarizes the general framework and the general structure of this book in relation to the central question of this study.

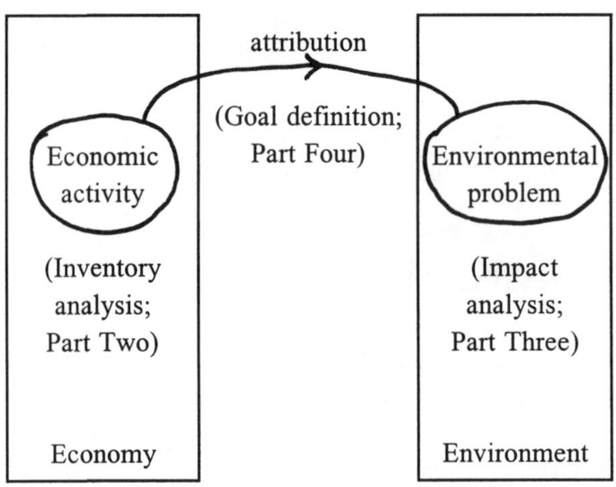

FIGURE 3.1. The attribution problem in relation to the framework developed for it and to the structure of this study.

PART TWO

ECONOMIC SYSTEMS

This part presents a description of a formal method to attribute flows from and to the environment (environmental interventions) to economic activities, which are understood to include economic unit processes and clusters thereof. The method is based on a physical description of economic unit processes along with rules on the clustering of processes, based on a linear combination of these processes in which the operating time of every process plays a crucial role.

Two main families of tools for enviro-economic analysis are developed:

- commodity-flow accounting, in which the operating times of all the processes within a certain region are set to a fixed and equal time period, e.g., one year;
- activity-level analysis, in which the operating times of the processes within the cluster are determined by a specified external demand.

Even if the first mode of analysis is employed, the question will often be turned into one of the second type.

For this reason, and because the second type of analysis is more difficult, a large part of this part is devoted to that form of analysis. The first fundamental equation is derived: an equation which expresses the relationship between the external demand for commodities, the technology matrix that contains the technical coefficients of interactions between economic processes, the intervention matrix of which the elements are technical coefficients of economy environment interactions, and the environmental interventions that can be attributed to the externally imposed demand. The problem of solving the first fundamental equation is discussed, in particular in the typical case of a rectangular technology matrix. Finally, a number of traditional types of analysis are partly derived as special cases from commodity-flow accounting and activity-level analysis: the discussion focuses most notably on life-cycle assessment and substance-flow analysis, but also touches briefly on environmental impact assessment and risk assessment.

Chapter 4

Introduction to Part Two

4.1 SOME SHORTCOMINGS OF TRADITIONAL ECONOMIC THEORY

Nearly all textbooks on economic theory put a strong emphasis on the analysis of economic activity. Welfare is created by economic activities. The value of goods and services, in short, of commodities, is explained by matching supply and demand, the supply being the result of some economic activities (production), and the demand being the result of other economic activities (consumption and production). An understanding of the theory of economic activity is therefore crucial to an understanding of the economy as such.

Traditional textbooks on economics discuss the theory of production: in order to produce a certain amount of output, factors of production are involved on the input side. Classically, these factors of production are mainly capital and labour. The quantitative relationship between the inputs of the various factors of production and the output produced is denoted as the production function:

$$Q = f(K, L), \tag{4.1}$$

where K is the amount of capital, L is the amount of labour, Q is the output produced, and f is a mathematical function which expresses the relationship. All quantities are normally expressed in monetary terms.

This traditional view of the production function is unable to deal with unpriced inputs.[1] Although recognized as an input, natural resources are

1 More extensive discussions can be found in Barbier (1989) and in two recent Dutch theses:

considered as the free gifts of nature; see Section 2.2.2. The natural resource inputs are an example of a class of commodities that is called externalities, although the owner of the land or a mine may ask rent for using the resource. Pigou (1920) was one of the first to discuss the existence and influence of external effects of economic activity. Inclusion of the environment as a source of natural resources and thereby as a factor of production leads to an adaptation of the production function (Daly (1973*a*), Pillet & Odum (1987)):

$$Q = f(K, L, N), \tag{4.2}$$

where N represents the monetarized amount of environment ("natural capital") involved.

This view of economic production is also of limited value. The point is that there are also externalities due to outputs of the economic activity. This becomes even more serious when it is realized that there are often more outputs besides the amount produced Q. Many activities produce a number of outputs: the main product (included in Q), subsidiary products (sometimes included in Q), waste that is to be treated by other economic agents, such as incinerators and waste-water treatment plants (rarely included in Q), and emissions of pollutants to the environment (not included in Q).

To account for undesired outputs (often called "waste", which includes waste residuals for treatment and waste discharges to the environment), a term W is sometimes included in the production function as well (Van den Bergh & Nijkamp (1992))[2]:

$$Q = f(K, L, N, W). \tag{4.3}$$

It should be observed that waste is thus also regarded here as a factor of production. This formulation still suffers from problems in representing outputs beside the main good Q and the waste W: the subsidiary products. Moreover, regarding waste as a factor of production appears to imply that producing more waste increases the productivity of the process; see attempts to reconcile this implication with common understanding (Gross & Veendorp (1990, p. 80), Van den Bergh & Nijkamp (1992, p. 9n)).

One reason for the neglect of waste is that traditional economists consider waste-to-be-processed not as a commodity; see Section 2.2.2. It is chosen here

Heijman (1991) and Noorman (1995).

2 In this way, the production function can be made compatible with the materials-balance principle (see Section 5.1.4), which states that the mass of what enters a process in the long run necessarily equals the mass of what leaves the process. For other formulations, see for instance Smith & Weber (1989) or Gross & Veendorp (1990).

to give a broader meaning to the term commodities, so that this term can be maintained: it includes tangible goods, tangible "bads", intangible services, and intangible "disservices".[3]

A related shortcoming of the traditional view of economics is that it is directed towards production. Consumption is not treated as a standard economic process, because there is no identifiable output Q. One bit of evidence of this is the lack of a "consumption function" of a form similar to Equation (4.1). For similar reasons, waste treatment falls outside this description. In Section 2.2.2, I have given a number of quotations which show that we need to reconceptualize the definition of an economic activity, similar to the redefinition of commodities. Economic activities then include the classical notion of production, consumption, and waste treatment. They must all be seen as transformation of a set of input commodities into a set of output commodities, where again commodity is to be interpreted in the broad sense of goods, services, bads, and disservices.[4]

The main task of the next few chapters will be to develop a consistent physical representation of economic activities, which allows for the description of the flows of all commodities between economic processes and of all flows between economic processes and the environment. The commodities include positively valued products, negatively valued wastes, and – in the present economic tradition – non-valued environmental commodities like natural resources and possible pollutants.

3 One might introduce waste treatment as a service, but that complicates a consistent representation in the sense that the "bad" waste should be left out, to prevent any double counting. When priority is given to the service over the tangible "bad", we are faced with the problem of incomplete mass balance. It is therefore proposed to express every flow of a tangible commodity as a good or a "bad", and to only introduce (dis)services for commodities that are intangible, like electricity, light, and music.

4 Commodities include throughout this study traditional positively valued marketable commodities, like steel, but also negatively valued commodities, like waste-to-be-processed, and non-valued commodities, like surface water and sulphur dioxide emissions.

4.2 STRUCTURE OF PART TWO

The topic of this study requires a full accounting of all inputs and outputs of economic activities. From the discussion above, it is clear that the traditional description of economic activities is not appropriate and must be revised one way or another. This part starts with the formulation of a – for our purposes – improved production function. This by necessity is a physical[5] technical (physico-chemical) representation: we need to know how much of which commodity goes into a process and how much of which commodity leaves that process.[6]

We will see that many standard tools for economic analysis assume that all commodities are expressed in a single unit: a national currency. This enables the addition of quantities that correspond to different commodities: \$8 steel and \$5 electricity make together \$13 commodity. Addition of the corresponding physical quantities is ill defined: we cannot by any means add 8 kg steel and 5 MJ electricity. The establishment of a physical accounting scheme needs a clear and consistent foundation, a topic that requires a new set-up and a critical review of the available methods.

A complex economic activity often involves a series of elementary economic activities. The theory of production will be directed to a comprehensive analytical description of elementary economic activities, or, in short, economic processes. Subsequent rules for the combination of economic processes into clusters that represent complex economic activities follow straightforwardly (Section 5.3).

In Section 5.4 an equation that shows which environmental commodities are involved in the production of an arbitrary external demand is derived. This equation is one of the core equations for this study; it is therefore called the

5 I will use the word "physical" here as an opposition to "monetary". It can denote any quantity in physical, chemical, or technical terms, e.g., kilograms of steel and megajoules of electricity, but also utility-like quantities ("having drunk one cup of coffee") are included in this term.

6 Let it be clear at the outset that the technical representation of an economic process is not necessarily better; the adjective "improved" is only meant to indicate that it is an improved description for the specific problem formulated in the introductory part. Thus, approaches where the monetary description is, at least in part, preserved (e.g., Ayres & Kneese (1969), Victor (1972*a*), Ayres (1978), Perrings (1987), Anderberg et al. (1993), Idenburg (1993)) have an undeniable value of their own. My reason for deviating from their principles is that they are not apt for answering the attribution problem as defined in Section 1.1.2.

first fundamental equation.

Chapter 6 is devoted to solving the first fundamental equation. It turns out that it is very often impossible to find a simple solution to it. The equation involves the inversion of a matrix, which is often not square. Proposals for manipulation of this matrix are discussed.

Finally, in Chapter 7 the arbitrariness of the external demand is reduced to a number of special cases. Here the well-known tools of life-cycle assessment and substance-flow analysis are derived from the principles that were developed in the previous chapters. Some additional remarks are made with respect to environmental impact assessment and risk assessment.

Chapter 5

Economic Processes

5.1 REPRESENTATION OF AN ECONOMIC PROCESS: THE PRODUCTION FUNCTION

5.1.1 What is an Economic Process?

In examining economy environment interactions, it is necessary to reflect on issues such as process, state and change, activity and interaction, stock, flow, and fund. One of the essential concepts of economics is activity. Consumers buy products and services and transform these – after deflection of a non-physical property, utility – into waste; producers make products and deliver services out of other products and services. Non-consuming consumers and non-producing producers, in short, inactive actors, are not interesting for economics; they are effectively supernumerary actors, and in fact don't even exist. Economic activity is change.[1]

But what changes and what is changed? Georgescu-Roegen, in his chapter 'The analytical representation of process and the economics of production', offers a large number of good starting points. First about the meaning of the

1 Some difficulties arise as to what change itself is. A steady-state economy doesn't change with respect to itself, but still requires economic agents. This could be interpreted as that a steady-state economy does change something. This is in contrast with mechanics, where Newton's first law tells us that bodies in uniform motion do not require forces from external agents. In mechanics, in other words, uniform motion is not change – except for change of location – but accelerated motion is.

term process:

> process is a particularly baffling concept, for process is change or is nothing at all. … the intricate issues surrounding the idea of Change have divided philosophers into opposing schools of thought, one holding that there is only Being, the other that there is only Becoming. Science, however, can follow neither of these teachings. Nor can it follow the dialectical synthesis of the two into Hegel's tenet that "Being is Becoming." Science can embrace only the so-called vulgar philosophy according to which there is both Being and Becoming, for by its very nature it must distinguish between object and event.[2]

He proposes the analytical coordinates of a process as

$$\left[\overset{T}{\underset{0}{E_i(t)}};\ \overset{T}{\underset{0}{F_\alpha(t)}},\ \overset{T}{\underset{0}{G_\alpha(t)}}\right], \tag{5.1}$$

where E_i indicates all elements that are only inputs or only outputs of a certain process, F_α indicates all elements that are inputs, and G_α those that are outputs.[3] The subscripts and superscripts 0 and T make explicit that a process has a finite duration, and – analytically – does not exist before $t < 0$ and after $t > T$.[4] The functions $E_i(t)$, $F_\alpha(t)$, and $G_\alpha(t)$ are all non-decreasing by definition.

As he points out, this representation means that any thought of describing what happens inside the process has been given up. A process is represented as a list in which the elements that cross the process's boundary are recorded,

2 Georgescu-Roegen (1971, p. 211).

3 Thus, a process in which corn is used as a seed to grow corn has corn as an input as F_α and as an output as G_α. A material or a certain type of waste is typically denoted by E_i. See below for more examples of the fund categories F_α and G_α.

4 Some remarks concerning the meaning of t and T and their difference must be made. Georgescu-Roegen (1971, p. 135) himself writes: 'there is the confusion between the concepts I have denoted by T and t, a confusion induced by the practice of using the same term, "time," for both. In fact, T represents Time conceived as the stream of consciousness or, if you wish, as a continuous session of "moments," but t represents the measure of an interval (T', T'') by a mechanical clock. … T is an ordinal variable, but t is a cardinal one.' Clearly, the variable t in Equation (5.1) denotes cardinal time, but it is less clear that 0 and T in this equation represent cardinal time as well. In fact, it would be more consistent to replace the symbols 0 and T by T_0 and T_0+T respectively. Even Georgescu-Roegen (op. cit., p. 215) is somewhat loose in jumping to Equation (5.1). For reasons of convenience, of course, the notation $[0, T]$ easily replaces the more meticulous $[T_0, T_0+T]$ in all further discussions.

both with respect to their quality (steel, land) and quantity (in units such as kg and m^2). How the process works is beyond this analysis.

In this representation, those elements that are only inputs or only outputs are described under E_i. A sign convention (positive for an output element, negative for an input element) suffices here.[5] For those elements that are both input and output, a separation is proposed: they fall under F_α when input and under G_α when output. Georgescu-Roegen gives examples of categories for this:

- land, which is used (in the Ricardian sense);
- corn, which is input as a seed and output as a crop;
- hammers which are needed to make new hammers;
- workers, who enter the process rested and leave it tired;
- tools, which are new when input and which are used when output.

It immediately appears that different categories of elements are involved. Some elements enter and leave in the same state and in the same amount, whereas other elements enter and are transformed upon leaving. Georgescu-Roegen extensively discusses the concepts of stock, flow, fund, and service. A stock is an amount at a certain instant of time. Flows are stocks spread out over a time interval. Contrary to what is often thought, flows do not necessarily come out or go into an actual stock, as can be illustrated with the fact that the flow of melted glass that rolls into rolling machines does not accumulate into the stock of melted glass.[6] A further distinction between flows and funds may be useful, flows being consumed and funds being used by a process. Paint is an example of a flow, the ladder of a painter is a fund, because it enters the process and leaves it, although with some scars. In fact, all capital goods are depreciated[7] in using them, and this depreciation requires

5 This sign convention of Georgescu-Roegen (1971) is also followed by, *inter alia*, Koopmans (1951*a*), Georgescu-Roegen (1951), Rosenbluth (1968), Heijungs (1994*b*), and contributors to Schmidt & Schorb (1995). Other authors, e.g., Fava et al. (1991) adopt the opposite convention.

6 It may be worth quoting Pasinetti (1980*a*, p. xiii): 'This opposition between stocks and flows, however, has been the source of many difficulties. Unlike land and labour, "capital" is not something that can be taken as an external element but is something that itself derives from the production process. ... We therefore find ourselves in the presence of something of a hybrid – a stock which is not entirely a stock and which, even in the part that seems to look like a stock, is nevertheless something that by the end of the year has changed from what it was at the beginning.'

7 Georgescu-Roegen (1971, p. 226) speaks of the decumulation as the physical analogue of

an almost fixed amount of time. A machine can be regarded as a fund of services.

Georgescu-Roegen finally ends up with a production function which is in fact a production functional $\mathscr{F}$, *viz.*, a relation from a set of functions to a function:

$$\overset{T}{\underset{0}{Q(t)}} = \mathscr{F}[\overset{T}{\underset{0}{R(t)}}, \overset{T}{\underset{0}{I(t)}}, \overset{T}{\underset{0}{M(t)}}, \overset{T}{\underset{0}{W(t)}}; \overset{T}{\underset{0}{L(t)}}, \overset{T}{\underset{0}{K(t)}}, \overset{T}{\underset{0}{H(t)}}], \tag{5.2}$$

where R are natural resource inputs, I are material inputs from other processes, M are maintenance requirements, Q are product outputs, and W are waste outputs. Furthermore, L is Ricardian land, K is capital proper, and H is labour power. The first five categories are flows, the last three are funds.

> A central element in the description and representation of economic processes is the production function, a function that summarizes the relationships between the output of a process and the different inputs. An important element which is often neglected in production functions is the operating time of the process.

5.1.2 Reformulation of the Production Function: Economic and Environmental Commodities

The above representation is very general, and it is intended to be so. Still, it is designed within the context of fairly traditional economics, not of ecological economics. A number of alterations are required to safeguard clarity in the environmental context. These concern:

(a) What is comprised by waste?
(b) Can materials be an output?
(c) Are there waste inputs?
(d) Are there product inputs and maintenance outputs?

(a) The category waste output (W) is of a mixed nature. We must distinguish economic flows from environmental flows. This means that we must properly define the category waste flows, thereby distinguishing between

depreciation of a capital good.

waste from one process that is processed (incinerated, dumped, recycled, cleaned, etc.) by another process, and waste from one process that is released into the natural environment (as gaseous, aqueous or solid emission). The first type of waste might be called economic waste or inter-process waste, whereas the second type might be called environmental waste or extra-process[8] waste. I will simply use the term waste for waste that is processed somewhere, and the term emission for waste that is released into the environment.

(b) The category *I* describes material inputs from other processes. This means that there must be processes which have those materials as an output. These could be understood under the term product outputs (category *Q*). It appears to be strange, or at least confusing, however, to employ different terms for the same commodity, depending on one's point of view. Something which is called a good for the producer must not be called a material by the recipient. As the difference in meaning between the words product and material is too vague to allow for a discrimination, and a distinction in the present context is not needed, the word goods could be proposed as an encompassing term.

(c) What applies to goods also applies to "bads": waste generated by a process is by definition treated in another process. This implies that waste can also be input to a process.

(d) Obviously, what holds for a material also holds for a product: any good, be it a material or a product, can be exchanged between processes. There is a complicated relation with decumulation of capital goods, however. A machine that enters a production facility needs maintenance in the form of service and spare parts. The service is clearly a fund, not a flow. The machine itself may be replaced gradually in twenty years' time, without an actual retired machine coming out of the process. Only the parts that were replaced came out of the process during a number of years, maybe even labelled as waste. Accumulated over time, however, a retired machine did come out, although not recognizable as such. Then, how fundamental is the distinction between flows and funds? Georgescu-Roegen goes into the difference between use and consumption, between durable and non-durable, and arrives at a criterion of identity of an associated output element, although he admits that this

8 Extra-process means here that the waste is not flowing to another economic process. It still flows to a process, namely to an environmental process, like degradation or transport.

> classification is, of course, dialectical because we find no tool in the positivist paraphernalia for recognizing sameness.[9]

In the end, he goes into the units of measurement of flows and funds:

> The amount of a flow is expressed in units appropriate to substances (in the broad sense) – say pounds, quarts, feet, etc. The rate of flow, on the other hand, has a mixed dimensionality, (substance)/(time). The situation is entirely reversed in the case of services. The amount of service has a mixed dimensionality in which time enters as a factor, (substance)×(time). If a plant uses one hundred workers during a working day (eight hours), the total of the services employed is eight hundred man × hours. If by analogy with the rate of flow we would like to determine the rate of service for the same situation, by simple algebra the answer is that this rate is one hundred men, period.[10]

Although the appearance of time in an expression like mass/time or mass × time often has a profound meaning, it cannot be regarded as a simple test for flow-ness or fund-ness. An amount of electricity can be expressed in kWh (kilowatt × hours) or in MJ (megajoule), simply because the unit of joule "hides" a time aspect. Some professionals charge costs per hour (e.g., a painter) whereas others charge per unit of service (e.g., a barber). This means that a process could require 5 man hours of painting and others 3 units of haircutting. The questions of sameness, dimensions, etc. make the distinction between funds and flows not less true, but reduce its importance somewhat to a non-fundamental topic.

Ultimately, the production function turns out to be a hybrid construction, which reflects the ambiguous meaning of the word production, a meaning which comprises both physical production and economic value generation. A waste incinerator is an illustrative example of a process which does not properly fit into the normal framework of a production function: it needs goods (fuel) and bads (waste streams) as inputs, and it produces goods (heat or electricity) and bads (fly ash) as outputs, and has furthermore fund requirements (capital, labour) and environmental flow characteristics (natural resources, emissions). The economic production of this type of process can not easily be cast into a form $Q(t)$.[11]

9 Op. cit. (p. 225).
10 Op. cit. (pp. 227–228).
11 Unless one is only interested in generation of economic value, of course.

For this reason, it is necessary to give equal treatment to non-productive aspects of a process, and to effectively abandon the idea of a production function.[12] Georgescu-Roegen gives, before turning to the production function(al) $\mathcal{F}$ in Equation (5.2), a general representation of a process:

$$[\overset{T}{\underset{0}{R(t)}},\ \overset{T}{\underset{0}{I(t)}},\ \overset{T}{\underset{0}{M(t)}},\ \overset{T}{\underset{0}{Q(t)}},\ \overset{T}{\underset{0}{W(t)}};\ \overset{T}{\underset{0}{L(t)}},\ \overset{T}{\underset{0}{K(t)}},\ \overset{T}{\underset{0}{H(t)}}]. \tag{5.3}$$

With the above considerations in mind, it seems inevitable to refrain from selecting one of these parameters to be placed in front of this expression, like Q in Equation (5.2). This can be made more explicit by exploiting the form

$$0 = \mathcal{F}[\overset{T}{\underset{0}{R(t)}},\ \overset{T}{\underset{0}{I(t)}},\ \overset{T}{\underset{0}{M(t)}},\ \overset{T}{\underset{0}{Q(t)}},\ \overset{T}{\underset{0}{W(t)}};\ \overset{T}{\underset{0}{L(t)}},\ \overset{T}{\underset{0}{K(t)}},\ \overset{T}{\underset{0}{H(t)}}]. \tag{5.4}$$

Summarizing the adaptations proposed for the purpose of describing processes within the context of economy environment interactions, the analytical representation of a process assumes the following form:

$$0 = \mathcal{F}[\overset{T}{\underset{0}{G(t)}},\ \overset{T}{\underset{0}{W(t)}};\ \overset{T}{\underset{0}{R(t)}},\ \overset{T}{\underset{0}{E(t)}}], \tag{5.5}$$

where the following categories have been discerned:

(a) economic[13] commodities: goods (G), wastes (W);
(b) environmental[14] commodities: natural resources (R), emissions (E).

12 Von Neumann (1945/1946) implicitly disregards the traditional production function. He states (p. 2): 'In each process P_i ($i = 1, \ldots, m$) quantities a_{ij} (expressed in some units) are used up, and quantities b_{ij} are produced, of the respective goods G_j ($j = 1, \ldots, n$). The process can be symbolised in the following way: P_i: $\sum_{j=1}^{n} a_{ij}G_j \rightarrow \sum_{j=1}^{n} b_{ij}G_j$.' Observe that the process P_i is thereby treated as a mathematical function (analogous to f: $x \rightarrow y$) which maps a collection of inputs onto a collection of outputs, *viz.*, the (production) process is the (production) function.

13 The word economic here only denotes the fact that the commodities flow from economic process to economic process. There is no principal relation with monetary criteria. The fact that (flows of) environmental commodities may be charged by the government does not make them economic commodities. For similar reasons, a release to the sewage system is an economic commodity flow because the flow is towards a sewage treatment plant, even if there is no price per litre effluent.

14 Victor (1972*a*) distinguishes the same categories, calling the latter ecologic commodities. He is however not clear about the position of inter-process waste: '[M]aterial inputs, on their first introduction into the economy, will be called ecologic commodities. However, once the material is being processed for further use or is satisfying the demand of a final consumer,

Here, funds and flows have together been called commodities, because it is the nature of what is flowing that defines the name: sometimes it is a lamp, sometimes it is energy, sometimes it is light.

(a) Goods comprise materials, products, services, energy, etc. They also comprise labour: labour is a flow (or a service) flowing from a man, woman, or animal, to a process. Men, women, and animals in their turn can be described as economic "facilities" which require inputs (food, shelter) in order to produce outputs (labour).[15] Wastes basically comprise goods with a negative value, although this will most often be discarded materials and products. It is often convenient to group goods and wastes into one group, which will be called economic commodities and will be denoted by A. Thus, A comprises G and W in Equation (5.5). And, in this context, economic commodities comprise goods, services, bads, and disservices.[16]

(b) Examples of natural resources are mineral ores and fossil fuels, animals and plants, wind and sunlight, but also land surface, atmospheric oxygen, etc. Emissions comprise chemical pollutants in solid, aqueous or gaseous form, but also radiation, sound and other potential environmental stressors.[17] Environmental flows therefore also comprise funds, such as land

it will be referred to as an economic commodity. Only when it is discarded by an economic agent, that is a producer or a consumer, and so leaves the economy, does it become once again, an ecologic commodity. ... Factories, machines and consumer goods are all economic commodities. Waste products discharged into the air, into water courses or onto land are all ecologic commodities' (op. cit., p. 54). In neglecting inter-process waste as an economic commodity, he effectively denies the existence of an anti-pollution industry (see Leontief (1970)). Although I agree with Victor's statement (p. 49) that 'Leontief spends no time at all in defining' anti-pollution, and that a monetary interpretation of it is cumbersome, I think that a physical accounting scheme would save the materials-balance principle, and that a proper modelling of transactions between industries demands the postulate of waste as an economic commodity. The point is that as long as the waste does not cross the economy environment border, it is no environmental commodity, and can therefore never create environmental problems. Victor's criticism is mainly caused by Leontief's inappropriate use of the word "pollution" in the term "anti-pollution industry". This industry does not eliminate pollutants as Leontief put it (p. 266) but prevents a certain economic commodity (waste-to-be-processed) from becoming an environmental commodity (emission).

15 Newman (1962, p. 59) describes the situation as that 'workers are produced like any other commodity, requiring definite inputs of wheat and wine, etc. in order to produce the given amount of labor time'.

16 We thus deviate from the normal economic meaning of the term commodity; see Section 2.2.2.

17 And, of course, non-stressor outputs. In fact, a full accounting of physical flows requires the inclusion of all types of flow, those that flow to and from other economic processes, and

and sound.[18] Furthermore, natural resources are normally inputs to a process, and emissions are outputs, but some exceptions occur. CO_2, normally being an output, is an input for the process forestry. This leaves room for regarding it either as a resource input, or as a "negative emission". Soil sanitation is a process which clearly has pollutants as an inflow. Dumping cadmium in an old cadmium mine could be seen as a "negative resource extraction". For may practical purposes, however, it will be sufficient to have one category of environmental flows, resources flowing to a process and emissions flowing out of it. It will therefore be convenient to merge R and E into one category, environmental commodities. These will be denoted by B. This B thus comprises flows of natural resources as well as flows of pollutants.

The combination of goods G and wastes W into economic flows A of commodities which flow from process to process, and the combination of natural resources R and emissions E into environmental flows B which flow from process to the environment and *vice versa* gives a very concise production functional:

$$0 = \mathscr{F}[\overset{T}{\underset{0}{A(t)}}, \overset{T}{\underset{0}{B(t)}}]. \tag{5.6}$$

Obviously, all elements A and all elements B may consist of several items. To emphasize this, they will be written as vectors instead of scalars. At the same time, we will adopt the convention of using lower case symbols to denote vectors, in order to reserve capital letters for matrices; see the list of conventions on page xii. Thus a and A are scalar quantities, $\mathbf{a}$ is a vector, and $\mathbf{A}$ is a matrix. We thus rewrite the production functional of an economic process as

$$0 = \mathscr{F}[\overset{T}{\underset{0}{\mathbf{a}(t)}}, \overset{T}{\underset{0}{\mathbf{b}(t)}}]. \tag{5.7}$$

those that flow to and from the environment. Not all environmental flows are necessarily of environmental interest. For instance, the input of oxygen in combustion processes is often neglected in environmental analyses, as is the emission of vapour by those processes. They should, in principle, be recorded, however, if only for reasons of a materials and energy balance (Section 5.1.4).

18 Sound which is perceived as noise or annoyance may disturb humans, animals, and ecosystems. Production of sound has a fund characteristic, because it is the combination of noise level (in dB) and duration (in hours) that determines what will happen. Sound is therefore an example of an output fund. Again, it can in the current context be treated as analogous to flows, provided that the dimensions of all flows are taken care of.

The elements of the vectors **a** and **b** will in general be of different dimensions, e.g., kg, MJ, piece, etc. The vector **b** that represents the flows of commodities entering and leaving the environment is called the vector of environmental interventions of the unit process. A graphical illustration of an economic process, as a more detailed form of Figure 1.2, is given in Figure 5.1.

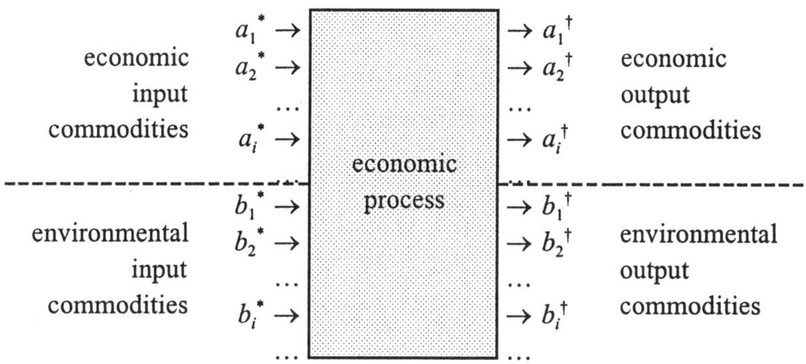

* Only when negative, else zero or absent.
† Only when positive, else zero or absent.

FIGURE 5.1. An economic process: economic commodities and environmental commodities are flowing in and out.

A consistent representation of environmental consequences of economic activities requires a consistent representation of economic processes. For this, a completely physical representation is adopted, in which all inputs entering and outputs leaving an economic process are denoted by elements of a vector. A distinction can be made between flows of economic commodities to and from other economic processes, and flows of so-called environmental commodities to and from the environment. These latter flows are called the environmental interventions of the economic unit process. Inputs are represented by negative numbers, outputs by positive numbers. The adopted form differs very much from the usual form for a number of reasons:

- the fact that a process in general generates more than one output (be it positively or negatively priced, or zero-priced) is taken into account;
- negatively priced inputs can easily be included as an input;
- from a physical standpoint none of the commodities takes a special position, in that it is put on the other side of the equality sign;
- the duration of a process is made explicit.

The definition of economic commodities as those commodities that flow between two economic processes implies that they are the input of at least one process as well as the output of at least one process.

5.1.3 Processes and Commodities: a Note on Terminology

In the discussion above, the terms process and commodity have been employed. A process was defined as an entity that could be characterized by three aspects: the input commodities, the output commodities, and the duration. The commodities could be divided into economic and environmental commodities, the economic commodities into goods, services, bads, and disservices.

It should be noted that many other terms occur in literature: ecologic commodities (Isard (1968), Victor (1972*a*)), the flow-fund concept (Georgescu-Roegen (1971)), the deposit-fund-flow distinction (Finnveden (1996*a*)), etc. With respect to processes, a number of related terms exist (see Anonymous

(1968, p. 9), Konijn (1994, p. 146*ff.*)): industries, activities, establishments. These all relate to some sort of (cluster of) processes. In the present text, these terms are sometimes used in conjunction,[19] but as a general rule, the word process is reserved to denote the most elementary level of transformation or activity.

Another remark concerns the adjectives economic and environmental. Process is normally used to indicate certain economic activities. There are environmental processes as well; evaporation and degradation are only two examples. These will be addressed in Part Three. For now, it will normally suffice to speak of a process, with occasional specification of its nature: economic or environmental.

Although we have discussed extensively the difference between economic and environmental commodities, between goods and bads, between waste and emission, and between flows and funds, it should be kept in mind that the most important conclusion is that a full accounting of inputs and outputs of a process is most crucial. The neglect of waste and emission as a "byproduct" of economic processes (*cf.* the traditional production function of Equation (4.1)) is symptomatic of the fact that classical economic theory overlooks the environment as an essential collective good. Although the traditional production function is under the influence of ecological considerations sometimes extended to incorporate the environment as a factor of production, the homogeneity of the output remains a problem in dealing with waste management systems, let alone pollution. The only consistent answer to the challenge of describing environmental consequences of economic production is a full accounting of inputs and outputs, regardless of their name, nature, role, or price:

> This discussion should make clear the point that often a classification of commodities involves somewhat arbitrary decisions. ... But while arbitrary elements do enter any classification system, for the purposes of our conceptual framework it makes no difference how we classify commodities, provided there is full accounting of all inputs and outputs of all commodities relevant for the problem being examined.[20]

19 The reason for this is that it is sometimes necessary in referring to other authors.
20 Isard (1968, p. 93).

Occasionally, some terms that are employed in this study differ from the terms that can be found in other literature. Most probably, the term "process" will give the largest problems: possible synonyms are activity, sector, industry, and establishment; moreover the adjective "economic" in "economic process" will often be omitted.

5.1.4 The Materials and Energy Balance

A well-known fact that goes back to Lavoisier is the law of conservation of mass: matter cannot be created nor can it be destroyed. In fact, this phenomenon may partly be held responsible for the existence of environmental pollution:

> Nature does not permit the destruction of matter except by annihilation with antimatter, and the means of disposal of unwanted residuals ... is by discharge to the environment, principally watercourses and the atmosphere.[21]

A somewhat more recent (going back to Mayer) but equally fundamental law is the first law of thermodynamics, which states that energy cannot be created nor can it be destroyed. Apparent violations of these laws may be reconciled by Einstein's equation which expresses the equivalency of matter and energy: not matter, not energy, but matter-energy is conserved.[22] Another refinement of the balancing principle is that, under exclusion of nuclear reactions, there is a conservation of matter on the level of the individual atoms: there is hydrogen balance, a helium balance, a lithium balance, and so forth.[23]

If a process is to be described by its incoming and outgoing flows, mass

21 Ayres & Kneese (1969, p. 283).

22 Observe that this will lead to a reformulation of the materials-balance principle. A simple calculation reveals that the "mass loss" of a large electric power plant is about 1 kg per year, of which about one-third is electric mass, and two-thirds is heat mass (March (1996)). This amount is much less than the emission of CO_2, comparable with the emission of benzo(a)pyrene, and much more (a factor of 1000) than the emission of dioxines (Frischknecht et al. (1993)).

23 Even more precise is to state that there are balances for all isotopes of all elements (^1H, ^2H, ^3H, ^3He, ^4He, ^6He, etc.), as well as for energy. And even this statement is not exactly true, as the mass of Na and the mass of Cl combine in a lower mass of NaCl, the excess of mass being released in the form of available energy.

and energy figures must balance. The amount of, say, copper going into a process must leave it if we assume a steady-state situation. If the process is not in a steady state, accumulation of stocks may occur. By a careful accounting of stock changes, we can still maintain the mass- and energy-balance principle. It is however one of the essentials of economic theory that a state of (near) equilibrium applies, at least in the long run. In that case, total input necessarily equals total output (Ayres (1993)). In theory, stock changes can easily be incorporated in the formalism: the increase of the copper stock of the process is the amount of copper entering the process (through input commodities, i.e., negatively valued elements of **a** and **b**) minus the amount of copper leaving it (through output commodities, i.e., positively valued elements of **a** and **b**). Thus, the stock change from $t = 0$ to $t = T$ can be calculated. It should be noted, however, that the premise of representing a process in terms of the flows that cross the process boundaries implies that the stock that is present inside the process cannot be calculated. Another remark here is the fact that accumulation can only be deduced by comparing figures relating to input flows and output flows, but not in a direct way: the accumulated flow cannot be observed from outside the process. See also Section 7.3 for a couple of additional remarks in the context of substance-flow analysis.

It is for many reasons very unfortunate that the materials and energy flows that are recorded do not balance:

> in some cases, process data used in LCAs actually violate the laws of physics. Yet the data are commonly used such a way that their inconsistency – physical impossibility – is effectively obscured.[24]

The result is unreliable data, unreliable results, and mistrust from industry or society. The issue of data quality must at least be raised (see Fava et al. (1994), Weidema (1994), Lee et al. (1995), Lindfors et al. (1995*e*)). Moreover, one can often easily use the materials- and energy-balancing principle to fill data gaps or to adapt apparently wrong figures; see Ayres (1994*a*, p. 213 *ff.*) for a discussion.

On the other hand, it must be acknowledged that the power of the materials- and energy-balance principle is limited in practice:

24 Ayres (1994*a*, p. 208).

> To quantify all these entries is extremely demanding. This is the main problem with the material balance principle. Moreover, not every item in the material balance is relevant from an environmental point of view.[25]

It therefore seems advisable to use these principles when feasible.

By constructing material balances for the different elements as well as an energy balance, an idea of the reliability of the process data can be obtained. Moreover, these balancing principles can be used to fill data gaps or to adapt apparently wrong figures. The possibility to apply this principle is, however, limited in practice.

5.1.5 The Labelling of Processes and Commodities

All processes and all commodities may be given a number of attributes to characterize their nature: a name, a label to represent geographical characteristics, a label to represent temporal characteristics, etc. In the next sections, a matrix representation of processes and flows of commodities will be constructed. Matrix representations do not require any information with respect to names and representativeness labels. For matrix operations it suffices to denote processes and commodities by a unique set of coordinates ("process 216" and "economic commodity 97"). The connection between the matrix operations and an interpretation requires, however, a translation between coordinates in an abstract space ("97, 216") and a meaningful description ("polyethylene bag, packing potatoes"). Although this translation is not the topic of this study, some words must be devoted to it in order to point the way to application in practice, and to provide solutions for a number of difficulties that will be met.

In principle, process names may be defined at any level of aggregation: from individual facilities ("steel production by means of equipment *x* at factory *y* on day *z*") to world averages over a decade ("steel production by means of average world technology during the 1980s"). Construction of average data may proceed in two ways: either by compiling these data by hand or from statistical sources, or by constructing a mixing process which

25 Idenburg (1993, p. 27).

has definite amounts of steel from different specified factories as an input, and which has average steel as an output. From this, it will be clear that commodity names must be assigned depending on process names. A process that is called "average French steel production" produces, of course, "average French steel".[26] Furthermore, it may be allowed or even necessary to introduce a spatial and/or temporal differentiation at this place. This is quite usual, see, e.g., Ginsburgh & Waelbroeck:

> We will be assuming that there is a finite number *r* of commodities differentiated by time and place, as well as by type. A ton of wheat today in New York is not a ton of wheat available in New York six months from now, or in Rotterdam today.[27]

For the environmental commodities one further attribute must be mentioned: the environmental compartment in which it is present. From a descriptive point of view, phenol in air, mercury in air, and mercury in water can be considered as three distinct environmental commodities. Of course, phenol in air and mercury in air are more different than mercury in air and mercury in water. They are so – from a chemical perspective. In the analysis of processes in the environment (Section 9.1) this chemical perspective will be ignored. There are environmental processes, like evaporation, that convert a chemical in one compartment into the same chemical in another compartment, and there are environmental processes, like degradation, that convert one chemical in a compartment into another chemical in the same compartment. They will be represented within the same analytical terms. A fine differentiation of environmental compartments ("phenol in the Everglades") is of course required when a very rigid connection with environmental impacts is desired. The highly aggregated nature of what will follow (see the closing remarks of Section 5.4.1) poses, however, practical and fundamental

26 The labelling of commodities has been discussed in the context of regional input–output analysis. See, e.g., Paelinck & Nijkamp (*n.d.*, p. 254): 'In the most general way, a certain flow *x* (for instance, goods or services) can be provided with a seven-fold index: $({}^{k}_{i,j}x^{k'}_{i',j'})_t$, which represents a flow of commodity *j*, produced in a certain production process *i* at location *k*, to production process *i'* at location *k'*, which uses commodity *j* as an intermediate product for commodity *j'*, while the index *t* stands for the time period concerned.' This clearly shows that the number of attributes that may be assigned to a certain flow is quite large.

27 Ginsburgh & Waelbroeck (1981, p. 3).

limitations on the possibilities of such rigid connections. The attribution of environmental impacts (see Chapter 10) is therefore proposed to be limited to generic impact information.

In going to a form of analysis that is feasible in practice, transportation processes produce some complications. In a very strict description, we would have a process "transportation of steel from Northern France to Italy" which has the commodities "steel in Northern France" and "fuel" as an input and the commodity "steel in Italy" as an output along with a number of environmental commodities. As there are for instance also processes that are called "transportation of eggs from Northern France to Italy" and "transportation of steel from Eastern France to Italy", the number of processes and the number of commodities will be extremely large. Practical calculations will then be hindered by formidable memory requirements. Therefore, in practice less pure but more workable options may be conceived and applied.

One further aspect needs to be discussed here, as it will have consequences for the types of analysis that will be derived later (see also Section 5.3.3). These are the attributes of space and time that may be given to each process. Regardless of the exact name of the commodities and processes, a process may be given a label to indicate the place where it is operative and the time during which it is (or was, or will be) operative. Other attributes may be given to each commodity as well: function, form, value, etc, but these attributes will not be important for the further discussion in this study.

> Giving names to processes and commodities is from a theoretical point of view not of particular interest, although it is absolutely required for an easy understanding in practice. Furthermore, some labels may be attached to the processes; two of these – those for the place where and the time when a process is operative – will be used in later sections.

5.2 THE ASSUMPTION OF LINEARITY OF ECONOMIC PROCESSES

5.2.1 The Duration of a Process

In the previous section, a general production functional was defined. No specific form of $\mathscr{F}$ was assumed. Following several authors in different contexts (Von Neumann (1945/1946), Koopmans (1951*a*), Georgescu-Roegen (1951, 1971), Gale (1960), Saxton & Ayres (1975), Heijungs (1994*b*)), it may be convenient for certain forms of economic analysis to make the assumption of linearity;[28] see however Section 5.2.4. The most explicit statement of the assumptions is by Koopmans:

> The first of these [assumptions] is divisibility: we assume that each activity is capable of continuous proportional expansion or reduction. ... The second assumption is additivity: we assume that any number of activities can be carried out simultaneously without modification in the technical ratios by which they are defined. ... The two assumptions can be fused in the statement that we postulate the existence of a finite set of basic activities, ... such that any possible state of production can be represented by a linear combination of basic activities.[29]

Assuming this linearity, the production function can be written as being proportional with time. This gives that

$$\mathbf{a}(t) = \bar{\mathbf{a}}t; \ \mathbf{b}(t) = \bar{\mathbf{b}}t; \ (0 \leq t \leq T), \tag{5.8}$$

where $\bar{\mathbf{a}}$ and $\bar{\mathbf{b}}$ are technical coefficients and t is the time[30] at which the

28 Von Neumann (1945/1946, p. 2) makes the assumptions implicitly: 'In the actual economy, these processes P_i, $i = 1, \ldots, m$, will be used with certain intensities x_i, $i = 1, \ldots, m$. That means that for the total production the quantities ... must be multiplied by x_i. We write symbolically: $E = \sum_{i=1}^{m} x_i P_i$. $x_i = 0$ means that process P_i is not used.'

29 Koopmans (1951*a*, p. 36).

30 Most authors do not use the interpretation in terms of a time. Von Neumann (1945/1946) speaks about intensities, Chenery & Clark (1959) and Saxton & Ayres (1975) about activity levels. In Heijungs (1994*b*), I called it the quantitative occurrence of the process. The only instance where the interpretation of a time is made that I am aware of is Georgescu-Roegen (1971, p. 238 *ff.*); see also Heijungs (1998). A set of these parameters, one for each process

process's accumulated flows are being measured.[31] Recall that inputs are denoted with negative elements of a and b, while outputs are positive, in accordance with other authors (Koopmans (1951*a*), Rosenbluth (1968), Heijungs (1994*b*)). Observe furthermore the units involved: elements of $\mathbf{a}$ and $\mathbf{b}$ are in general expressed as amounts, e.g., in kg and MJ, while the technical coefficients, elements of $\bar{\mathbf{a}}$ and $\bar{\mathbf{b}}$ are expressed as rates of flows, e.g., in kg/hr and MJ/hr.

As an example assume a process which creates one commodity "*a*"[32] along with an environmental flow "*b*". A certain amount of production can be achieved by simply "turning the process on" for a certain amount of time. The time (t)[33] needed to produce an accumulated amount a of commodity "*a*" is simply given by

$$t = \frac{a}{\bar{a}}. \tag{5.9}$$

Even if the total active time period (the operating time) of the process is T, a time period t is needed for the production of an amount a. We could say that a fraction t/T of the process's total output $a(T)$ is attributed to the production of an amount a. The linearity of economic production means that 31 seconds of electricity generation is equivalent to a fraction of one-millionth of one year's production of that electricity generator.[34]

in a certain economic system, is sometimes called a program (Chenery & Clark (1959, p. 85)); hence the term linear programming for one of the techniques to determine the program.

31 The relationship $\mathscr{F}[\mathbf{a}(t)_0^T, \mathbf{b}(t)_0^T] = \begin{pmatrix} \mathbf{a}(t) - \bar{\mathbf{a}}t \\ \mathbf{b}(t) - \bar{\mathbf{b}}t \end{pmatrix}$ makes the formal connection between Equations (5.7) and (5.8).

32 The symbol a denotes the amount of the commodity of the type "*a*". a is thus a quantity of the quality "*a*".

33 Again, one might discuss if t or T is the relevant symbol here. The time at stake is not a historic-chronological stream of consciousness, but an interval that can in principle be measured with a clock; this makes t the preferred symbol. On the other hand, recognition of the fact that T in Equation (5.8) is a time interval as well, and that it defines the duration of the process, would make one prefer the symbol T. For practical reasons, the symbol t will be used in this text.

34 This statement deserves some additional discussion as to the exact meaning of t: is it clock time or is it some form of "effective time"? For instance, most plants run in one week time something like 40 hours of production, which is definitely less than the 168 clock hours in one week. The meaning of the technical coefficients is such that they are based on clock time. This means that changes in production volume due to holidays, strikes, seasonal effects, etc. are included as an average in the technical coefficients. A normal time span during

> Fully in line with the previously stated axiom of linear calculus (Section 2.1.2), the operating time that is to be attributed to a process for a certain level of production is calculated using assumptions on the continuous nature of economic processes.

5.2.2 Co-transformation of Undesired Flows

It is an unfortunate fact of life that, while producing a certain amount of product or material, all kinds of "undesired flows" are also "turned on" during this time interval, so that

$$b = \bar{b}t. \tag{5.10}$$

In other words, eliminating the process's operating time t from the expression, the environmental flow b associated with producing an amount a is given by[35]

$$b = \bar{b} \cdot \bar{a}^{-1} \cdot a. \tag{5.11}$$

In general there will be more than one environmental commodity involved; hence the vector notation $\mathbf{b} = \bar{\mathbf{b}}t$ instead of $b = \bar{b}t$. A similar remark applies to the economic commodities. The productivity **a** of processes in general and their associated environmental flows **b** can thus be described by the process vector **p**, which assumes the form

$$\mathbf{p} = \begin{bmatrix} \mathbf{a} \\ \mathbf{b} \end{bmatrix} = \bar{\mathbf{p}}t = \begin{bmatrix} \bar{\mathbf{a}} \\ \bar{\mathbf{b}} \end{bmatrix} t, \tag{5.12}$$

where **p** is the accumulated flow produced by turning on the process characterized by the specific parameters $\bar{\mathbf{p}}$ for a time interval t. The vector **p** is embedded in a commodity space (Koopmans (1957, p. 7); Debreu (1959, p.32)).

In writing **a** instead of a, we thus emphasized the fact that more than one economic commodity is involved. Apart from the flow for which we "turned

which a reasonable estimate of these technical coefficients can be obtained is the calendar year. This is also the time span that is normally used in statistical declarations. Notice that a (quasi) steady-state situation is assumed here (*cf.* Section 5.2.3).

35 The peculiar form employed here can be explained by comparison with the more general form of Equation (5.29).

on" the process, other commodities will flow as well: co-products and by-products, but also "undesired" economic commodities, such as the input of electricity and the output of waste-to-be-processed.

For similar reasons we wrote **b** instead of b. The elements b_i of the vector **b** will be referred to as the environmental interventions.

One last notational remark for future reference: elements of the **a** and **b** vectors may be indexed by a subscript i to denote different economic or environmental commodities:

$$\mathbf{a} = \begin{pmatrix} a_1 \\ a_2 \\ \ldots \\ a_i \\ \ldots \end{pmatrix} \text{ and } \mathbf{b} = \begin{pmatrix} b_1 \\ b_2 \\ \ldots \\ b_i \\ \ldots \end{pmatrix}, \tag{5.13}$$

with similar expressions for the vectors of technical coefficients.

> The observation that the operating time of a process causes not only economic commodities to flow, but also environmental commodities to flow, means that a predefined economic production determines the environmental interventions according to the process's technical coefficients.

5.2.3 The Nature of the Process Data

The previous discussion assumes that data on the flows of commodities into and from economic processes can be represented by simple technical coefficients $\bar{\mathbf{a}}$ and $\bar{\mathbf{b}}$. Assuming for the moment that this is so,[36] the problem arises of how to find these data.

One obvious way is to measure the inflows and outflows of all commodities that enter and leave a process within a certain time span, e.g., one year, and to construct the technical coefficients by dividing the observed flows (a_i, b_i) by this time span (t):

36 See however Section 5.2.4.

$$\bar{a}_i = \frac{a_i}{t}, \ \bar{b}_i = \frac{b_i}{t}, \ \forall i. \tag{5.14}$$

In this measurement procedure it is assumed that the time span is long enough to average out fluctuations related to daily, weekly, or yearly variations, but small enough to guarantee that the process is in a quasi-steady state.

An alternative is to construct the data by means of models (see, e.g., Schuler (1995)). This is of course required when an estimation of future processes is to be made, but it can also be done for those processes for which measurements are absent, hard to make, incomplete, or unreliable.[37]

Another aspect which is relevant in the context of the nature of the process data is the level of aggregation. One may for reasons of convenience deliberately aggregate several unit processes of the same type to represent a typical technology or a typical branch. For instance, one could add the flows of the different electric power stations in a certain country in one process, "average electricity production". The operating time that is required to produce a certain amount of electricity is in that situation smaller than the operating time when only one of the constituting processes was used. The process data represent in that case not a concrete production facility, but a virtual one.

We see that in many cases the basic data will not be data in the true sense of the word, but will be the result of certain manipulations to find, to correct, to complement, or to adjust data according to certain aims.

The technical coefficients $\bar{a}_i$ and $\bar{b}_i$ can be obtained by:

- measuring flows a_i and b_i during a certain time span t and calculating the average rate of flow;
- predicting the rates of flow by process-technological models;
- correcting and completing measured rates of flow on the basis of models, materials and energy balances;
- constructing typical rates of flow by aggregation of processes of the same type, e.g., to construct data for a certain technology of processing.

37 See the discussion of the materials and energy balance in Section 5.1.4.

As the focus of this study is theoretical, the practical – perhaps even insurmountable! – difficulties of finding workable data are not discussed.[38] It should be stressed that the existence of a theoretical structure often stimulates the collection of data in practice. In that sense, an impractical theory may become feasible in due time.

5.2.4 The Assumption of Fixed Technical Coefficients

In the description above, a proportionality of inputs and outputs with time was assumed. This was translated into the concept of technical coefficients $\bar{a}_1$, $\bar{a}_2$, …, $\bar{b}_1$, $\bar{b}_2$, …, such that

$$a_i = \bar{a}_i t;\ b_i = \bar{b}_i t;\ (0 \leq t \leq T);\ \forall i. \tag{5.15}$$

Within the context of economic input–output analysis (see also Section 6.1.3), the validity of these technical coefficients is often discussed. Fixed technical coefficients imply constant returns to scale and can thereby be represented by a linear homogeneous unconstrained production function (Miller & Blair (1985, p. 11 *ff.*)). It seems obvious to make this assumption:

> it is almost tempting to argue that production functions will necessarily exhibit constant returns to scale. The view is that if, in some sense, all inputs are, say, tripled, what is there to prevent all outputs from being tripled?[39]

Fixed technical coefficients, however, imply more: it is necessary to postulate a strict non-substitutability of production factors. If one of them is reduced by a factor of two, production will drop by a factor of two, and a factor of two of all other factors of production is idle.[40] This is in contradiction with the most common forms of production functions (see Equation (4.1)), of which

38 See Hemming (1995) for an overview of databases that could be useful. A problematic aspect of most (or all?) databases that are described in that report is that the process inputs and outputs are not stated as flows per time unit, but per standard unit of commodity, e.g., per 1000 kg steel. This one missing data element means that all these databases can only be used for studies of the activity-level analysis type, not for studies of the commodity-flow accounting type (see Section 5.3.2). This restricts their use to life-cycle assessment, excluding susbtance-flow analysis, environmental impact assessment, and risk assessment.

39 Baumol (1972, p. 281).

40 A more elaborate treatment of production functions within the context of input–output analysis is to be found in Miller & Blair (1985, p. 11 *ff.*).

the Cobb–Douglas form[41] is the most well known. There are good reasons to reject simple forms of substitution:

> To conceive of capital as a near-perfect substitute for resources, as is frequently done under the influence of Cobb-Douglas type production functions, is to believe that one can make the same house with twice as many saws, but half the lumber.[42]

The background of this problem lies mainly in the switch to physical coordinates instead of monetary ones:

> Underlying the basic concept of a production function – and absolutely essential to it, is the notion of substitutability. ... Economists have given less attention, however, to the physical constraints on the possibility of free substitution between fundamentally different factors. ... As an example of complementarity or synergy, take the relationship between tractors and gasoline in agriculture. They are linked together: Neither is of any use without the other. Hence there is absolutely no possibility of substitution between them. ... One is led, in short, to conclude that neoclassical production functions are basically inappropriate for the materials-processing sectors of the economy. More specifically, they effectively violate thermodynamic principles, by implicitly permitting labor or capital to "create" (or "destroy") material or energy inputs.[43]

Nevertheless, the premise of fixed technical coefficients

> is certainly never absolutely true, even in those cases where chemistry and engineering dictate fixed proportions between some ingredient and output.[44]

Furthermore, the substitution theorem (Samuelson (1951)) states that for a certain class of processes, fixed technical coefficients represent the most efficient way of production. For probably related reasons, Gale (1960) distinguishes "linear models of exchange" (p. 260 *ff.*) from "linear models of

41 The Cobb–Douglas production function is in its bare form $Q = K^{\alpha}L^{\beta}$, where α and β are coefficients.

42 Daly (1995, p. 154). One solution here is to define unsubstitutable categories (like actors and resources) which contain substitutable subcategories (like labour and capital within actors and different materials within resources); see Van den Bergh & Nijkamp (1994).

43 Ayres (1978, p. 39–40).

44 Baumol (1972, p. 505).

production" (p. 294 *ff.*).

It must be recalled (see Section 2.1.2) that the particular objective of this study is not a classical operations analysis for planning purposes. It is a theoretical analysis for descriptive purposes: it seeks to answer which environmental problems are to be attributed to a certain economic activity. Therefore, the validity of the assumptions of fixed technical coefficients, the limited availability of some inputs, or the indivisibility of some inputs[45] can be ignored, simply because we are constructing a virtual sub-world, deduced from the full world. This means that the discussion about the validity of the assumptions of activity analysis are pointless within the present treatment. The purpose is to distribute observed facts according to some set of consistent rules among restricted parts of the world. It is perfectly legitimate to state that one plastic bag requires 10^{-10} electricity generator, although fractional plants do not exist. See also Section 14.1 for a discussion of seemingly similar questions that necessarily employ non-linear rules.

> Although the assumption of fixed technical coefficients is not completely justified for the purposes of planning, the particular question of this study and the epistemological basis of its answers inevitably lead to this linear attribution rule.

5.3 CLUSTERS OF ECONOMIC PROCESSES

5.3.1 Representation of a Process Cluster

Having described the analytical representation of one single economic process, the next stage is to analyse the representation and the analytical properties of clusters[46] of processes. Two or more processes can be merged by drawing a boundary around those two, and treating the combination as one single

45 Quoting Baumol (1972, p. 281): 'We cannot install half a blast furnace or half a locomotive'. Furthermore, Koopmans (1957, pp. 150–154) makes an interesting connection between the failure of the hypotheses of fixed technical coefficients and the existence of indivisible commodities.

46 Alternatively called process chains (Ayres (1993, p. 18)), aggregates (Huppes (1993, p. 47)), and systems (Baccini & Bader (1996, p. 54)).

process, a "meta-process". Clustering, of course, is straightforward. As processes themselves are described as a black box, without knowledge of what happens inside, one cannot tell whether some particular analytical coordinates belong to a unit process or to a meta-process.

Whilst making clusters is easy, the question of which types of clustering make sense is much more difficult. One can of course make a cluster of two or three arbitrary processes, but why should one? In practice, it turns out that some types of clustering are of particular interest.

Before discussing the clusters in detail, it is necessary to adjust the notation so as to allow for indicating different processes. An additional subscript j will suffice: a_{ij} represents the flow of economic commodity i to or from process j, whereas b_{ij} represents that of environmental commodity i to or from process j. Recall that negative values of a_{ij} and b_{ij} denote flows to process j (inputs), while flows from process j (outputs) are indicated by positive values.

The analytical description of a cluster of processes is easy, as it is itself a process. The only problem is to keep track properly of the different elements within the categories **a** and **b**. Clustering two processes amounts to

$$\begin{aligned}(\mathbf{p})_{1+2} &= \begin{pmatrix}(\mathbf{a})_{1+2}\\(\mathbf{b})_{1+2}\end{pmatrix} = \\ (\mathbf{p})_1+(\mathbf{p})_2 &= \begin{pmatrix}(\mathbf{a})_1\\(\mathbf{b})_1\end{pmatrix}+\begin{pmatrix}(\mathbf{a})_2\\(\mathbf{b})_2\end{pmatrix} = \begin{pmatrix}(\mathbf{a})_1+(\mathbf{a})_2\\(\mathbf{b})_1+(\mathbf{b})_2\end{pmatrix},\end{aligned} \tag{5.16}$$

where $(\mathbf{p})_{1+2}$ refers to the cluster of the processes that are characterized by $(\mathbf{p})_1$ and $(\mathbf{p})_2$ respectively.[47] Extension of this equation to more than two clusters is straightforward.

Equation (5.16) is a crucial step forward in answering the attribution problem. It states that a certain economic activity, namely the cluster that consists of a number of economic processes, produces a certain external economic flow (which may be consumed or exported) along with a certain external environmental flow. In that sense, we may say that the environmental flows **b** are to be attributed to the economic flows **a**. The environmental flows will be referred to as the environmental interventions that can be attributed to

47 The fact that the process representation of a composition of two processes is denoted by the same symbols as the representation of its constituent processes emphasizes that there is no fundamental difference between one process or an aggregate of several processes.

the cluster of economic processes and hence to the external flow of economic commodities.

In making such a cluster of processes two questions arise:

- Which processes will be clustered?
- What is the operating time of every process within the cluster?

Before entering into the question of the boundaries of a cluster, the aspect of operating time will be discussed.

> The analytical representation of a unit process also allows an analytical representation of clusters of several economic processes. Two main questions are which processes should be included for the analysis of meaningful clusters, and how the operating times of the processes within the cluster should be chosen.

5.3.2 The Crossroad: Commodity-Flow Accounting and Activity-Level Analysis

A fundamental question about the role of time arises as soon as the specific parameters that build $\overline{\mathbf{p}}$ are used. The description of the cluster assumes the form

$$(\mathbf{p})_{1+2} = (\overline{\mathbf{p}})_1 t_1 + (\overline{\mathbf{p}})_2 t_2 = \begin{pmatrix} \overline{\mathbf{a}}_1 \\ \overline{\mathbf{b}}_1 \end{pmatrix} t_1 + \begin{pmatrix} \overline{\mathbf{a}}_2 \\ \overline{\mathbf{b}}_2 \end{pmatrix} t_2, \tag{5.17}$$

a form which allows for a different choice of t_1 and t_2. A crossroad of main categories of analysis occurs here:

(a) the operating time of the processes can be explicitly externally imposed, e.g., by choosing a certain time span for all processes;

(b) the operating time of the processes can be implicitly imposed by stating boundary conditions in the form of a certain external demand.

(a) The first possibility corresponds to types of analysis in which a certain period, usually one year, is chosen as the overall operating time of the processes. Substance-flow analysis is an example of this type of analysis, in

which a well-defined set of processes is taken into account for the full operating time, most often one year.

(b) The second possibility corresponds to types of analysis in which a certain externally delivered function determines the operating time of every individual process. Life-cycle assessment is an example here: a societal function, say 20 years of painted wall, requires fixed amounts of associated processes, e.g., 2 seconds of paint production and 10 hours of painting.[48]

The crossroad which follows from the two principles for choosing the operating times of the processes within a cluster of processes naturally yields two categories of analysis.

(a) The first will be referred to as commodity-flow accounting (CFA). As a definition we could use the following: Commodity-flow accounting is a method of systematically quantifying the mutual relationships among the various sectors of a complex economic system and the relationships of this system with the environment.[49]

(b) The second will be referred to as activity-level analysis (ALA). For activity analysis the following definition is proposed: Activity-level analysis is an analysis in which the quantities of each of several activities contributing directly to objectives (or "final demand") are specified; from this it is desired to determine the magnitudes of each of the supporting activities, as well as their total requirement for commodities from outside the system.[50]

As an example of both categories of analysis, consider the cluster of two

48 Observe that funds and flows in Georgescu-Roegen's sense are treated here in an identical manner. If a flow of 12 kg steel is needed, it could be argued that, say, 20 seconds of a certain steel production process is required, even if the steel is needed in small amounts over many years. On the other hand, if 80 MJ electricity is required, one can translate this mathematically into, say, 15 seconds of a certain electricity generation process, although practical considerations can mean that in reality a continuous electricity demand of, say, one-millionth electricity generation process takes place. Even this point can in principle be solved by installing a condenser which stores energy. The point is that there is a difference between flows and funds, but that this difference need not appear in all types of theoretical exercises, that the difference is dialectical, and that it is even technology-dependent. The time-interpretation is elaborated more completely in Heijungs (1998).

49 Modified from Leontief (1986, p. 2339): 'Input–output analysis is a method of systematically quantifying the mutual relationships among the various sectors of a complex economic system.'

50 Modified from Wood & Dantzig (1951, p. 16): 'the quantities of each of several activities contributing directly to objectives (or 'final demand') are specified …; from this it is desired to determine the magnitudes of each of the supporting activities, their total requirement for commodities from outside the system'.

simplified processes: fuel production and electricity generation. There are two economic commodities: fuel and electricity, and two environmental commodities: SO_2 and waste heat. These commodities can be seen as objects in an abstract space which is spanned by a unit vectors such as (1, 0, 0, 0) and (0, 1, 0, 0). The meanings of the coordinates are

$$\begin{pmatrix} 1\text{ l fuel} \\ 1\text{ MJ electricity} \\ 1\text{ g } SO_2 \\ 1\text{ MJ waste heat} \end{pmatrix} \text{ or } \begin{pmatrix} 1\text{ l fuel/hr} \\ 1\text{ MJ electricity/hr} \\ 1\text{ g } SO_2\text{/hr} \\ 1\text{ MJ waste heat/hr} \end{pmatrix}, \tag{5.18}$$

depending on whether $\mathbf{p}$ or $\bar{\mathbf{p}}$ respectively is indicated.[51] Process 1 represents production of fuel; process 2 production of electricity. They have as hypothetical coordinates in this space:

$$(\bar{\mathbf{p}})_1 = \begin{pmatrix} 3 \\ -3 \\ 0 \\ 2 \end{pmatrix} \text{ and } (\bar{\mathbf{p}})_2 = \begin{pmatrix} -1 \\ 10 \\ 5 \\ 2 \end{pmatrix}. \tag{5.19}$$

So, for example, process 1 uses 3 MJ electricity/hr to produce 3 l fuel/hr and 2 MJ waste heat/hr.[52]

(a) The CFA category of analysis corresponds to taking a fixed operating time for both processes, say, $t_1 = t_2 = 500$ hr. This gives:

$$\mathbf{p} = \begin{pmatrix} 3 \\ -3 \\ 0 \\ 2 \end{pmatrix} \times 500 + \begin{pmatrix} -1 \\ 10 \\ 5 \\ 2 \end{pmatrix} \times 500 = \begin{pmatrix} 1000 \\ 3500 \\ 2500 \\ 2000 \end{pmatrix} \tag{5.20}$$

which amounts to a net[53] economic production of 1000 l fuel and 3500 MJ

51 It is remarkable that the possible flow-aspect of the commodity space is almost always overlooked. The only author of whom I know that he recognizes it is Koopmans (1957, p. 7): 'Depending on the application, these amounts may be interpreted as rates of flow per unit of time, maintained at a constant level for an indefinite period; or each number ... may be regarded as a quantity made available during just one specified period out of a number of successive periods.'

52 It will be clear that these numerical examples are completely fictitious. They merely illustrate the procedure instead of representing phenomena happening in the real world.

53 It can be observed that the gross economic production is higher: 1500 l fuel and 5000 MJ

electricity, and net environmental outflows of 2500 g SO_2 and 2000 MJ waste heat.

(b) The ALA category of analysis corresponds to imposing a fixed outflow of commodities, say 250 l fuel and 200 MJ electricity. This results in a commodity-balance equation[54] for the economic commodities:

$$\mathbf{a} = \begin{pmatrix} 250 \\ 200 \end{pmatrix} = \begin{pmatrix} 3 \\ -3 \end{pmatrix} \times t_1 + \begin{pmatrix} -1 \\ 10 \end{pmatrix} \times t_2 \tag{5.21}$$

which can be solved and therefore determines two operating times: $t_1 = 100$ hr and $t_2 = 50$ hr. The environmental part of the balance can be completed as

$$\mathbf{b} = \begin{pmatrix} 0 \\ 2 \end{pmatrix} \times 100 + \begin{pmatrix} 5 \\ 2 \end{pmatrix} \times 50 = \begin{pmatrix} 250 \\ 300 \end{pmatrix}. \tag{5.22}$$

An external demand of 250 l fuel and 200 MJ electricity thus requires 100 hr of fuel production and 50 hr of electricity production and produces an environmental outflow of 250 g SO_2 and 300 MJ waste heat.[55]

A major crossroad of types of analysis is related to a different type of question:

- commodity-flow accounting is the mode of analysis that gives an answer to the question of interprocess flows, net flows, and gross flows in relation to a specified time span of economic activity, e.g. one year;
- activity-level analysis is the mode of analysis that gives an answer to the question of interprocess flows, net flows, and gross flows in satisfying a specified external demand.

electricity, but that these amounts are not available for external demand. Furthermore, one can easily read off the interprocess flows, e.g., 1500 MJ electricity from electricity production to fuel production. In economic input–output analysis as well as in economic activity analysis, obtaining gross and interprocess figures is often the aim of the analysis.

54 Observe that we thus distinguish the materials and energy balance within a process and the commodity balance between processes within a cluster. The materials and energy balance is a physical fact, although the observed data will often show a surplus or a deficit; see Section 5.1.4. The commodity balance is of an entirely different nature: it is imposed by the analyst. It also does not require that the materials and energy balance is satisfied.

55 Again, gross values of the different flows can be calculated as well, as can the interprocess flows.

5.3.3 System Boundaries: Which Processes to Include?

In discussing the time aspect of clusters of processes, the question of cluster boundaries was postponed in order to discuss first the crossroad which creates the two types of analysis. Obviously, any choice with respect to the processes to be included can be made.[56] Some choices, however, are easier to interpret than other choices. Of special interest is the choice for all processes within a certain region. This can be an administrative region: a facility, a company, a country, or a supra-national body, such as the OECD. It can also be an ecological region: the Rhine basin, the arctic, etc. Besides regions, some other possibilities could make sense: processes of a certain industrial kind (e.g., all refineries), processes dealing with particular substances (e.g., mercury), processes involved in the life cycle of a certain product (e.g., window frames), etc.; see Huppes (1993, p. 51) for a range of possibilities. These are related to categories of activities and to categories of substances. Some of these choices can also be combined, e.g., in a study of European paint industry with respect to only organic solvents. For the moment, however, the selection of processes in the analytical cluster will mostly be based on geographical considerations: a region's economic activities. Furthermore the time during which the process was, is, or will be active may be of interest. If all processes in 1990 are included, those processes that were active in earlier years and those that were or will be active in later years must be excluded. There is consequently a need for an appropriate labelling system of processes; see also Section 5.1.5. The consequences of the choices themselves will be elaborated in Chapter 7.

> The question of how to aggregate economic processes into a cluster can be answered by addressing two main questions: which processes and how much of every process. The first question consists of three smaller questions: on the region, on the type of process, and on the substances involved. The second question must be answered by either giving the operating time of all processes, or by stating an external flow and requiring that the cluster produce this flow.

56 Saxton & Ayres (1975, p. 195) write in a similar context that 'the set of materials and processes included in the system is relatively arbitrary. In other words, the "system" may be the whole economy or a small subset of it – say, a region, an industry, a single firm, or even an individual plant.' See also Huppes (1993, pp. 47–52).

5.4 THE ATTRIBUTION OF ENVIRONMENTAL INTERVENTIONS TO A GIVEN EXTERNAL DEMAND

5.4.1 The First Fundamental Equation

If a study of the activity-level analysis type is performed, the operating time of the processes is not stated, but has to be calculated. If a study of the commodity-flow accounting type is performed, things are different: the operating times are imposed. However, when a change in external demand or in technology is assumed,[57] the problem is likely to turn into a problem of the activity-level analysis type: a certain external flow is imposed and the problem is to calculate the operating time of every process such that the external demand is satisfied. The associated environmental flows are calculated in a next step. Thus, for both types of analysis the problem of finding operating times often occurs. Moreover, as the calculation procedure of activity-level analysis is more involved than that of input–output analysis, it will be given more attention throughout the rest of this section.

Let the external demand[58] of economic commodity i be given as a_i. The flows of economic commodities of process j is also given; the technical coefficients are denoted by $\bar{a}_{ij}$. The set of equations to be solved is the following:

$$\begin{aligned} \bar{a}_{11}t_1 + \bar{a}_{12}t_2 + \cdots + \bar{a}_{1j}t_j + \cdots &= a_1 \\ \bar{a}_{21}t_1 + \bar{a}_{22}t_2 + \cdots + \bar{a}_{2j}t_j + \cdots &= a_2 \\ \cdots &= \cdots \\ \bar{a}_{i1}t_1 + \bar{a}_{i2}t_2 + \cdots + \bar{a}_{ij}t_j + \cdots &= a_i \\ \cdots &= \cdots \end{aligned} \tag{5.23}$$

or in matrix notation as

57 Strictly speaking, studying the influence of a change in external demand or technology is outside the scope of attribution analysis.

58 This external demand comprises the consumers' demand, the demand due to export, but may also consist of a negative term to represent import.

$$\begin{pmatrix} \bar{a}_{11} & \bar{a}_{12} & \cdots & \bar{a}_{1j} & \cdots \\ \bar{a}_{21} & \bar{a}_{22} & \cdots & \bar{a}_{2j} & \cdots \\ \cdots & \cdots & \cdots & \cdots & \cdots \\ \bar{a}_{i1} & \bar{a}_{i2} & \cdots & \bar{a}_{ij} & \cdots \\ \cdots & \cdots & \cdots & \cdots & \cdots \end{pmatrix} \cdot \begin{pmatrix} t_1 \\ t_2 \\ \cdots \\ t_j \\ \cdots \end{pmatrix} = \begin{pmatrix} a_1 \\ a_2 \\ \cdots \\ a_i \\ \cdots \end{pmatrix}, \tag{5.24}$$

or even more concisely as

$$\bar{\mathbf{A}} \cdot \mathbf{t} = \mathbf{a}. \tag{5.25}$$

The matrix $\bar{\mathbf{A}}$ is usually called the technology matrix (Koopmans (1951*a*, p. 37), Chenery & Clark (1959, p. 84)).

This equation can be solved[59] for **t** by inverting the technology matrix $\bar{\mathbf{A}}$ and postmultiplying it with the vector of external demand **a**:

$$\mathbf{t} = \bar{\mathbf{A}}^{-1} \cdot \mathbf{a}. \tag{5.26}$$

The environmental part of the processes transforms according to the values in **t**:

$$\begin{pmatrix} b_1 \\ b_2 \\ \cdots \\ b_k \\ \cdots \end{pmatrix} = \begin{pmatrix} \bar{b}_{11} & \bar{b}_{12} & \cdots & \bar{b}_{1j} & \cdots \\ \bar{b}_{21} & \bar{b}_{22} & \cdots & \bar{b}_{2j} & \cdots \\ \cdots & \cdots & \cdots & \cdots & \cdots \\ \bar{b}_{k1} & \bar{b}_{k2} & \cdots & \bar{b}_{kj} & \cdots \\ \cdots & \cdots & \cdots & \cdots & \cdots \end{pmatrix} \cdot \begin{pmatrix} t_1 \\ t_2 \\ \cdots \\ t_j \\ \cdots \end{pmatrix}, \tag{5.27}$$

or compactly

$$\mathbf{b} = \bar{\mathbf{B}} \cdot \mathbf{t}. \tag{5.28}$$

The matrix $\bar{\mathbf{B}}$ will be called the intervention matrix, since its coefficients represent interventions of the different economic processes in the environment: inputs (mainly extractions of resources) and outputs (mainly emissions of chemicals). Substituting the calculated value for **t** gives

$$\mathbf{b} = \bar{\mathbf{B}} \cdot \bar{\mathbf{A}}^{-1} \cdot \mathbf{a}. \tag{5.29}$$

This is a very fundamental equation: it expresses the relation between a

59 The problem that a solution does not always exist is postponed until Section 6.1.

certain level of consumption and the associated environmental flows, i.e., extractions of natural resources and emissions of pollutants. Because of its importance in this study it is regarded as a fundamental equation, and it will be referred to as the first fundamental equation.[60] It expresses that there are three places which enable abatement of environmental degradation:

- one corresponding to the structure of the economic process environmental commodity interactions (the intervention matrix $\bar{\mathbf{B}}$);
- one corresponding to the structure of the economic process economic commodity interactions (the technology matrix $\bar{\mathbf{A}}^{-1}$);
- one corresponding to the external demand (the consumers' external demand vector **a**).

Attempts to reduce environmental problems may accordingly be classified into:

- measures which affect the structure of the economic process-environment commodity interactions (e.g., emission reduction);
- measures which affect the structure of the economic process-economic commodity interactions (e.g., energy saving);
- measures which affect the external demand (e.g., ecotax).

Although the equation, when rewritten in words

$$\begin{aligned}&\textbf{environmental intervention} = \\ &\textbf{intervention matrix}\cdot\textbf{technology matrix}^{-1}\cdot\textbf{external demand}\end{aligned} \tag{5.30}$$

suggests some resemblance with the "master equation" (see Graedel & Allenby (1995, p. 5)):

$$\begin{aligned}&\text{Environmental impact} = \\ &\text{population}\times\frac{\text{GDP}}{\text{person}}\times\frac{\text{environmental impact}}{\text{unit per capita GDP}}\end{aligned} \tag{5.31}$$

it will be clear that the latter is much more tautological, as the term "environmental impact" enters the equation on both sides of equality sign. The

60 It should be observed that there are alternative forms to express the same idea. See, for instance, Möller & Rolf (1995) and Will (1996, p. 16 *ff.*) for a number of elaborations. See also Heijungs (1994*b*). Futhermore, the form that is derived by Kneese et al. (1970, p. 77) will be discussed in Section 6.1.3.

former equation expresses environmental impact in terms of the structure of the economy.[61]

Lastly, observe that the vector **p** which summarizes the aggregated processes into the external flows can be written as

$$\mathbf{p} = \begin{bmatrix} \mathbf{a} \\ \mathbf{b} \end{bmatrix} = \begin{bmatrix} \mathbf{a} \\ \bar{\mathbf{B}}\cdot\bar{\mathbf{A}}^{-1}\cdot\mathbf{a} \end{bmatrix}, \tag{5.32}$$

an expression which clearly demonstrates the fact that **p** is an aggregation over several processes, but which nevertheless makes clear that the environmental interventions **b** are determined by the structure of the economy, expressed by the technology matrix $\bar{\mathbf{A}}$ and by the intervention matrix $\bar{\mathbf{B}}$. An important consequence of this aggregation is that information with respect to the distribution in time of the environmental flows is lost. Although the

TABLE 5.1. The commodity-process representation of clusters of economic processes, including the vector of external flows.

economic or environmental commodity	economic process					external flow
	1	2	...	j	...	
"a_1"*	a_{11}	a_{12}	...	a_{1j}	...	a_1
"a_2"	a_{21}	a_{22}	...	a_{2j}	...	a_2
...	...	...	...	...	...	...
"a_i"	a_{i1}	a_{i2}	...	a_{ij}	...	a_i
...	...	...	...	...	...	...
"b_1"	b_{11}	b_{12}	...	b_{1j}	...	b_1
"b_2"	b_{21}	b_{22}	...	b_{2j}	...	b_2
...	...	...	...	...	...	...
"b_k"	b_{k1}	b_{k2}	...	b_{kj}	...	b_k
...	...	...	...	...	...	...

* See footnote 32 of this chapter for an explanation of the quotation marks.

61 In Moll (1993, p. 26) a related form is presented. Here environmental effects are equal to the product of population size, consumption per capita, and intensity. Although not further defined, it appears that this intensity is again a tautological environmental impact per unit of consumption.

elements of **b** are constructed from contributions from different processes at different times and in different places, the value itself represents some "overall emission" or "overall extraction". This has consequences for the possibilities of assigning environmental problems to these overall environmental flows; see Part Three. Furthermore, the aggregation of the columns that build the technology matrix and the intervention matrix can be illustrated in the form of Table 5.1. It may also be abbreviated as

$$\begin{pmatrix}\mathbf{P} & \mathbf{p}\end{pmatrix} = \begin{pmatrix}\mathbf{A} & \mathbf{a} \\ \mathbf{B} & \mathbf{b}\end{pmatrix} = \begin{pmatrix}\bar{\mathbf{P}}\cdot\mathbf{t} & \mathbf{p}\end{pmatrix} = \begin{pmatrix}\bar{\mathbf{A}}\cdot\mathbf{t} & \mathbf{a} \\ \bar{\mathbf{B}}\cdot\mathbf{t} & \mathbf{b}\end{pmatrix}, \tag{5.33}$$

where an aggregation over the columns of the matrices yields the vectors:

$$\sum_j (\mathbf{P})_j = \mathbf{p},\ \sum_j (\mathbf{A})_j = \mathbf{a}, \text{ and } \sum_j (\mathbf{B})_j = \mathbf{b}. \tag{5.34}$$

> The environmental consequences of a certain external demand can be found by application of the first fundamental equation. This equation is as follows:
>
> $$\mathbf{b} = \bar{\mathbf{B}}\cdot\bar{\mathbf{A}}^{-1}\cdot\mathbf{a}$$
>
> where **a** is the external demand vector of economic commodities, $\bar{\mathbf{A}}$ is the technology matrix of which the coefficients represent the interprocess rates of flow, $\bar{\mathbf{B}}$ is the intervention matrix of which the coefficients represent the rates of flow of the interventions of the processes in the environment, and **b** is the total amount of environmental interventions that can be attributed to the external demand vector **a**.

5.4.2 A Simple Numerical Example

To illustrate the use of the formalism, the previous example with two processes and two commodities will be elaborated; see Equation (5.19) for a description of the problem. The technology matrix is

$$\bar{\mathbf{A}} = \begin{pmatrix}3 & -1 \\ -3 & 10\end{pmatrix}, \tag{5.35}$$

the intervention matrix is

$$\bar{\mathbf{B}} = \begin{pmatrix} 0 & 5 \\ 2 & 2 \end{pmatrix}, \tag{5.36}$$

and the consumers' external demand is

$$\mathbf{a} = \begin{pmatrix} 1000 \\ 3500 \end{pmatrix}. \tag{5.37}$$

The inverse of the technology matrix is

$$\bar{\mathbf{A}}^{-1} = \begin{pmatrix} 0.37 & 0.037 \\ 0.11 & 0.11 \end{pmatrix}. \tag{5.38}$$

From this, we can compute two intermediate results:

$$\bar{\mathbf{B}} \cdot \bar{\mathbf{A}}^{-1} = \begin{pmatrix} 0.56 & 0.56 \\ 0.96 & 0.11 \end{pmatrix} \text{ and } \bar{\mathbf{A}}^{-1} \cdot \mathbf{a} = \begin{pmatrix} 500 \\ 500 \end{pmatrix}, \tag{5.39}$$

as well as the environmental flow:

$$\mathbf{b} = \begin{pmatrix} 2500 \\ 2000 \end{pmatrix}. \tag{5.40}$$

It is this latter vector of 2500 g SO_2 and 2000 MJ waste heat that can be attributed to the external demand vector of 1000 l fuel and 3500 MJ electricity.

The same procedure can be applied to clusters of many economic processes in which many economic and environmental commodities are involved. Two problems may arise:

- as the computation becomes more involved, more sophisticated numerical methods than a plain matrix inversion may be required (see Frischknecht & Kolm (1995) for some proposals);
- as the computation is centred around the inverse of the technology matrix, the equation fails to give an answer if this matrix is not invertible, either because it is not square or because it is singular.

The next chapter is devoted to this second problem. The first problem is not discussed further.

Chapter 6

On Solving the First Fundamental Equation

6.1 DOES THE FIRST FUNDAMENTAL EQUATION NECESSARILY HAVE SOLUTIONS?

6.1.1 The Assumption of Squareness of the Technology Matrix

The first fundamental equation $\mathbf{b} = \bar{\mathbf{B}} \cdot \bar{\mathbf{A}}^{-1} \cdot \mathbf{a}$ presupposes that $\bar{\mathbf{A}}$ is invertible or, in other words, that the economic commodity balance $\bar{\mathbf{A}} \cdot \mathbf{t} = \mathbf{a}$ can be solved uniquely. This poses severe restrictions to the formalism. The first of these is that the number of equations and the number of unknowns be equal, or in other words, that the matrix $\bar{\mathbf{A}}$ must be square. The second one is that the equations be independent from each other, or in other words, that the determinant of the matrix $\det(\bar{\mathbf{A}})$ be different from 0 and that the matrix is hence non-singular.

Notice that the requirement of squareness does not necessarily mean that each process produces one single type of commodity, and that each commodity is produced by one single process. In fact, there is no reason to associate certain processes with certain commodities: the expression "the process of electricity generation" is in fact a misnomer when this processes coproduces marketable steam. The situation is even more compelling for "the process of chlorine production", which produces chlorine as well as caustic soda, the revenues being approximately equivalent. Nevertheless, within the framework of economic input–output analysis and derivations thereof, there is a constant tendency to impose a (near) one-to-one correspondence between a process (or sector, or industry, or establishment) and a commodity. Before turning to the relation with input–output analysis (Section 6.1.3), some aspects of the discussion on industry accounts versus commodity accounts are presented (Section 6.1.2).

Another relevant source of information is the economic make/use analysis, which nowadays often forms the basis of input–output tables. Make/use analysis is quite similar in its principles to the formalism which was sketched above. The derivation of input–output tables, and other manipulations with the make/use matrices, also requires a discussion of how to deal with rectangular matrices (Section 6.1.4). A third type of important models is the equilibrium models (Section 6.1.5).

From these discussions, a number of proposals for solving the first fundamental equation in the case of a non-square technology matrix are given, along with a discussion of the appropriateness of these solutions in the present context.

> Application of the first fundamental equation requires that the technology matrix be invertible. The problem of whether a solution always exists, or whether some pseudo-solution can be found, is discussed in connection with two traditional forms of economic analysis: input–output analysis and activity analysis.

The next discussion is to a very large extent based on the technology matrix $\bar{\mathbf{A}}$. It will not come as a surprise that the environmental aspect is absent in this discussion: it is only introduced in the intervention matrix $\bar{\mathbf{B}}$. Neither will it be surprising that many of the references are from outside the environmental circle, and are sometimes even much older than the environmental literature.

6.1.2 Process Accounts and Commodity Accounts

Input–output analysis (alternatively indicated as interprocess[1] analysis) has

1 In input–output analysis, the emphasis is not so much on elementary economic processes, but

TABLE 6.1. A very simple physical input–output table.

	into				
from	process 1	process 2	households	total	unit & nature
process 1	0	500	1000	1500	l fuel
process 2	1500	0	3500	5000	MJ electricity

been set up (Leontief (1936)) as a process-to-process approach: economic transactions are registered as process–process interactions. Although the system has been developed mainly for transactions in monetary units, the approach works for physical flows as well (see, e.g., Leontief (1986)).[2] An example of an input–output table is given in Table 6.1.[3]

The first input–output study (Leontief (1941)) had to be restricted to a rather coarse classification of processes into only nine industry categories, such as "agriculture and foods" and "minerals industry". One important reason for this was the virtual absence of computational devices:

> The total number of multiplications involved in the practical solution of our problem exceeds 450,000. This task alone would mean a two-year job, at 120 multiplications per hour. Fortunately, the recent invention of the Simultaneous Calculator by Professor Wilbur of the Massachusetts Institute of Technology has made it possible to perform all the necessary computations in a small fraction of the time they otherwise would have required. This apparatus solves nearly automatically a system of nine simultaneous linear equations.[4]

on highly aggregated clusters thereof, usually called sectors or industries. The principles of analysis, however are identical, so that the present text will use the term process instead of sector or industry.

2 Some additional remarks on this point will be made later; see for instance Section 6.1.4, where it is argued that certain mathematical operations are only meaningful for financial accounting schemes.

3 This input–output table represents an open model, since the external demand is exogenously determined. A closed model contains the households (consumers) as one of the processes, absorbing a number of consumer products as input commodities, and providing labour as an output commodity. In an open model, labour is most often described as a primary input instead of an interindustry (or: interprocess) flow. Furthermore, input–output tables often have additional rows and/or columns to denote imports and exports. In the section on regional substance-flow analysis (Section 7.3), this point will be treated in more detail.

4 Leontief (1941, p. 74).

The coarseness of the classification implies that very heterogeneous commodities are lumped together. This observation gives a guideline for the principle of classification: the classification of industries should be such that each firm is assigned to an industry on the basis of the goods or services it produces (Konijn (1994, p. 48)).

Even if it is accounted for that some processes produce more than one function, the general tendency is to keep a correspondence between a process and a commodity in mind. The terms "coproduct" and "primary sector" are striking reminiscences of this phenomenon, as is the following quotation:

> Most of the commodity outputs will be produced by the primary sectors, but not all. Sectors may also produce each others' commodities as so called secondary products. ... Secondary output is smaller than primary output. This stylized fact is represented by the assumption that primary output dominates secondary output, for every commodity.[5]

It is only seldom that a full independence of processes and commodities is expressed:

> It is true that an industry and its primary product will have the same name .... However, in an abstract sense, we shall regard any industry as potentially capable of producing any commodity; and among those commodities which it does in fact produce, we shall treat the industry's primary product in essentially the same way as any of its secondary products[6]

and

> In principle, however, there is no reason why the number and definition of commodities should have a one-to-one relationship with the definition and classification of industrial sectors.[7]

One observation is that the distinction between process (activity, sector,

5 Ten Raa (1995, p. 88). It must be kept in mind that many of these texts relate to analyses in monetary terms. In physical terms, it is not possible to say which of two outputs dominates, since the choice of the physical unit is arbitrary. An airline company for example produces two commodities: passenger transport and cargo transport. It can well be that the first dominates in volume terms, whereas the latter dominates in mass terms.

6 Edmonston (1952, p. 560).

7 Chenery & Clark (1959, p. 160).

industry, establishment; see also Section 5.1.3) and commodity is very often either overlooked or treated without care.[8] Nearly all input–output tables contain, like the example table above, rows that indicate process outputs, but that bear commodity names. This has to do with an assumption that is only seldomly explicitly stated:

> Each commodity (or group of commodities) is supplied by a single industry or sector of production. Corollaries of this assumption are (*a*) that only one method is used for producing each group of commodities; and (*b*) that each sector has only a single primary output.[9]

This means that input–output analysis by itself is essentially incompatible with the fact that almost every process deals with several output commodities:

> Multiple production can be a disturbing factor in input–output modelling and analysis.[10]

Or, stronger, that

> ... it is sufficient to point out that it is the practical and theoretical problems due to the lack of correspondence between commodities and industries that render commodity-by-industry analysis preferable to inter-industry analysis.[11]

Especially when the coordinates of a process contain negatively valued economic outputs (waste-to-be-processed) and environmental outputs (emissions), the one-to-one correspondence of processes and commodities fails.[12] This was exactly the reason for the rejection of the traditional concept

8 Recall that Leontief (1936, p. 69) spoke about the category "agriculture and foods", the former being a sector, the latter being a commodity.

9 Chenery & Clark (1959, pp. 33–34).

10 Konijn (1994, p. 60).

11 Rosenbluth (1968, p. 256).

12 It should be observed that there are environmental extensions to economic input–output analysis, where allowance is paid to the fact that each process produces besides "its" commodity one or more pollutants by means of emission coefficients per sector per pollutant. See Victor (1972*a*, p. 25 *ff.*) and Miller & Blair (1985, p. 236 *ff.*) for an overview, and Cumberland (1966) and Daly (1968) for two early examples. Energy analysts have also pretty promptly observed the theoretical complications that are associated with input–output analysis; see in particular Boustead & Hancock (1979, p. 94 *ff.*).

of the production function in Section 4.1.

Interestingly, Ghosh (1958) proposed an alternative input–output approach, one in which each process transforms one commodity into several outputs.[13] This model has been criticized severely (see e.g., Oosterhaven (1988)). The point I would like to make is that the traditional input–output model is probably almost equally artificial in its assumptions as the alternative of Ghosh. Ghosh has tried to escape one problematic assumption but at the expense of the introduction of another very similar one.

Input–output analysis has been described so far as a process-by-process account: the numbers represent transactions between processes. It must be mentioned that to solve the problems raised above, commodity-by-commodity accounts have been constructed:

> If a firm produces more than one product, to which industry should this firm then be assigned? This problem leads to the distinction between functional and institutional input–output tables.[14]

The process-by-process tables are the institutional tables referred to, because they represent transactions between institutions: how much of process *j*'s output is needed as input for process *l*. This makes the flows observable, which is a great advantage in their compilation by statistical agencies. Commodity-by-commodity tables, or functional tables, contain numbers which represent how much of commodity *i* is used to produce commodity *k*, regardless of the process that produces this commodity. Functional tables are therefore models: the flows cannot be observed but must be constructed, and there are problems in finding the proper modelling procedure.

A much more radical solution is the introduction of the commodity-by-industry tables:

> A more realistic classification scheme that accounts for industrial production by commodity type rather than industry category eliminates this somewhat clumsy and biased accounting of secondary production.[15]

13 Ayres (1978, p. 100) also discusses output coefficients along with the more familiar input coefficients, and concludes that the two approaches are incompatible. Schrøder (1995*a*, p. 20) chooses to use output coefficients.

14 Konijn (1994, p. 49).

15 Miller & Blair (1985, p. 155).

However, some claim that an eventual conversion to input–output tables should be made:

> However, the input–output method presented numerous difficulties ..., especially concerning the registration of secondary products .... Therefore, a new system was constructed ... frequently denoted as the "make/use framework". ... So, now we have a splendid statistical system which describes in detail the input and outputs of industries. But, with this new system we cannot perform input–output analysis in the way we used to, without (re-)constructing an input–output table from the system of make and use matrices.[16]

Others, on the other hand, hold that input–output analysis (in the quotation called inter-industry analysis) should be abolished:

> One might have thought that with the development of linear programming and activity analysis, and the demonstration that the inter-industry analysis can be regarded as a special case of these more flexible models, inter-industry analysis would be abandoned, or at least substantially modified. Yet nothing of the sort has taken place. ... This paper presents a plea for the abolition of inter-industry analysis and its replacement by what we shall call, for lack of a better name, commodity-by-industry analysis. We shall try to demonstrate that there is nothing inter-industry analysis can do that cannot be done equally well by commodity-by-industry analysis, and a good many things that the latter can do better.[17]

The overall conclusion is that the use of commodity-by-process[18] accounts – which in the normal economic context were already described as superior – are indispensable when extending the framework to negatively valued economic commodities and to environmental commodities. Nearly every process produces more outputs than the one which constitutes the *raison d'être* of the process: it generates inter-process waste (waste-to-be-treated by another process) and it generates emissions.[19]

16 Konijn (1994, pp. 6–7).
17 Rosenbluth (1968, p. 255).
18 That is to say, the above cited commodity-by-industry tables.
19 One could even say – with Sraffa (1960) – that every process generates capital goods as well.

One of the basic assumptions of input–output analysis – that every process produces exactly one homogeneous output – is not compatible with the fact that many processes produce products, co-products, by-products, undesirable wastes, and undesirable emissions. Since it is essential for an attribution of environmental problems to economic activities to keep track of all commodities that enter and leave a process, input–output analysis is not a good tool for this purpose.

Notwithstanding the further choice for commodity-by-process accounts, the following section will briefly discuss the position of input–output analysis with respect to our present approach.[20] The section is not essential for an understanding of the principles of the approach to the attribution problem and may be skipped, along with Section 6.1.4 and 6.1.5.

6.1.3 Excursus: the Relation with Economic Input–Output Analysis

Suppose that indeed all processes produce one unique homogeneous valuable output commodity. In that case, an input–output table as shown in Table 6.2 can be drawn up.[21]

The parameter z_{jl} represents the amount of process j's commodity[22] that is used up by process l. Evidently, all parameters z_{jj} represent self-inputs, a phenomenon which will most probably occur if a coarse classification of industries is used, as is the case for, e.g., the process "agriculture", where agricultural products (e.g., wheat) are used to produce agricultural products (e.g., meat).[23] The total output[24] of process j (denoted by d_j) is given by the

20 The above-stated neglect of input–output analysis is of course based on theoretical arguments. It can be useful as a surrogate for the theory proposed in this study if there is insufficient data to do (parts) of the analysis. See *inter alia* Woo et al. (1977), Van Engelenburg et al. (1994), Ayres (1994*b*), Dohnomae et al. (1994), Lave et al. (1995) and Wilting (1996) for a discussion of the (partial) replacement of a process-analytical approach by an input–output-analytical approach. See Chapman (1974) for a comparison of results obtained with these methods.

21 Most input–output tables contain more rows and columns, containing data on labour, capital, imports and exports, investments, and so on. The part that is contained in the matrix **Z** is the matrix of interindustry flows.

22 I have tried to speak consistently of "process j's commodity" instead of "commodity j", to explicate that it is not a commodity-by-process table but a process-by-process table.

23 Georgescu-Roegen (1971, p. 256 *ff.*) argues that consistency requires that the diagonal elements be zero. See also my remarks in Section 6.1.4.

24 Observe that it makes sense to define the total output as an aggregation over the jth row,

TABLE 6.2. General structure of the interprocess part and the external demand part of an input–output table.

	into						
from	process 1	process 2	...	process l	...	households	total
process 1	z_{11}	z_{12}	...	z_{1l}	...	z_1	d_1
process 2	z_{21}	z_{22}	...	z_{2l}	...	z_2	d_2
...	...	...	...	...	...	...	...
process j	z_{j1}	z_{j2}	...	z_{jl}	...	z_j	d_j
...	...	...	...	...	...	...	...

sum of all sectors' inputs of process j's commodity $\left(\sum_l z_{jl}\right)$ plus the external demand of process j's commodity (z_j), so that

$$d_j = z_j + \sum_l z_{jl}. \tag{6.1}$$

It is customary to define technical coefficients $\bar{z}_{jl}$ as process l's input of process j's commodity per unit output of process l:

$$\bar{z}_{jl} = \frac{z_{jl}}{d_l}. \tag{6.2}$$

A further postulate is that the technical coefficients are independent of the consumers' external demand and hence of the production volume of the processes. This postulate explains the fact that these coefficients $\bar{z}_{jl}$ are named "technical" (see also Section 5.2.4): it is assumed that they are only affected by a change of technology. The equation for the total output can now be rewritten as

whereas the total input, an aggregation over the lth column has no meaning in a physical input–output table. This fact is acknowledeged ("... in practice most input–output tables are constructed in value terms [...]. The last row shows the combined value of all outputs absorbed by each of the three sectors. Such column totals could not have been shown in [a physical input–output table] since the physical quantities of different inputs absorbed by each sector cannot be meaningfully added." (Leontief (1986, p. 2340)), but since input–output theory is founded on monetary tables, some of the equations somewhere require the existence of these column totals.

$$d_j = z_j + \sum_l \bar{z}_{jl} d_l. \tag{6.3}$$

By rearrangement[25] this leads to

$$(\mathbf{I} - \bar{\mathbf{Z}}) \cdot \mathbf{d} = \mathbf{z}, \tag{6.4}$$

where **I** is the unit matrix of the appropriate dimension. This equation can be solved for **d** as

$$\mathbf{d} = (\mathbf{I} - \bar{\mathbf{Z}})^{-1} \cdot \mathbf{z}. \tag{6.5}$$

The expression $(\mathbf{I} - \bar{\mathbf{Z}})^{-1}$ is generally known as the Leontief inverse.[26]

We can observe the similarity between the expression $\mathbf{z} = (\mathbf{I} - \bar{\mathbf{Z}}) \cdot \mathbf{d}$ and the previous $\mathbf{a} = \bar{\mathbf{A}} \cdot \mathbf{t}$. The vector **d** contains the total output of each process, whereas the vector **t** contains the duration or activity level of each process, a somewhat related quantity. The vector **a** contains the consumers' external demand for the different commodities, whereas the vector **z** contains their external demand for the different processes' outputs.[27] If, under the assumptions of one-to-one correspondence of processes and commodities, **a** and **z** coincide, a relationship between the matrix of technical coefficients $\bar{\mathbf{Z}}$ and the technology matrix $\bar{\mathbf{A}}$ can be established, provided that the ordering of the commodities (the rows of $\bar{\mathbf{A}}$) corresponds to the unique outputs of the processes (the rows of $\bar{\mathbf{A}}$, as well as the rows and the columns of $\bar{\mathbf{Z}}$).[28] It reads

$$\bar{\mathbf{A}} \cdot \mathbf{t} = (\mathbf{I} - \bar{\mathbf{Z}}) \cdot \mathbf{d}. \tag{6.6}$$

We may expand on this a little more to illustrate some of the conceptual

25 Evidently, $z_j = \sum_l -\bar{z}_{jl} d_l + d_j$, which can be rewritten as $z_j = \sum_l (-\bar{z}_{jl} d_l + \delta_{jl} d_l)$ where δ is the Kronecker-delta.

26 It is most appropriate here to refer to the analog of the first fundamental equation in Kneese et al. (1970). Combination of their equations (3) and (4b) on page 77 gives, in our notation: $\mathbf{b} = \bar{\mathbf{B}} \cdot (\mathbf{I} - \bar{\mathbf{Z}})^{-1} \cdot \mathbf{z}$, an equation that is very close to our first fundamental equation, but that has the disadvantage of being based upon an input–output structure instead of a process-by-commodity structure.

27 The difference is so subtle that I have chosen to magnify it by using different symbols for the external demand for commodities (*d*) and the external demand for industries' outputs (*a*). Even Rosenbluth (1968), although textually distinguishing the meaning of the two, uses the same symbol.

28 This is a problematic restriction; see below for a discussion.

problems of physical input–output tables of the process-by-process type. Suppose that there are m commodities and n processes. Clearly, $(\mathbf{I}-\bar{\mathbf{Z}})\cdot\mathbf{d}$ is $(n \times n) \times (n \times 1)$, and therefore $(n \times 1)$. $\bar{\mathbf{A}}\cdot\mathbf{t}$ is $(m \times n) \times (n \times 1)$, and therefore $(m \times 1)$. In other words, the dimensions of the expressions on the left-hand side and the right-hand side do not necessarily match. Even when they do match, the occurrence of joint production poses problems in attributing commodities to processes.

We will not be concerned too much with input–output tables, and even less with input–output tables of the commodity-by-commodity type. Nevertheless it is useful to introduce the latter at this point, in order to refer to them where appropriate. The input of the ith commodity in producing the kth commodity will be indicated by a coefficient z_{ik}.[29] The associated technical relationship is expressed by

$$\bar{z}_{ik} = \frac{z_{ik}}{d_k}, \tag{6.7}$$

where $d_k \left(= z_k + \sum_i z_{ik}\right)$ is the total production of the kth commodity.[30]

> By going in some detail into the mathematics of physical input–output analysis, the inadequacy of it becomes apparent: the semantic confusion between a process and "its commodity", the interpretational difficulties of the self-inputs, the problematic relationship between the external demand of commodities and the external demand of process outputs, etc.

29 We will keep things simple by not introducing separate symbols for commodity-by-commodity tables and process-by-process tables. Here, it suffices that the indices are different: z_{ik} denotes an element of a commodity-by-commodity table, while z_{jl} denotes an element of a process-by-process table.

30 A badly defined quantity is introduced here: $\sum_i z_{ik}$ has in a physical accounting scheme a mixed dimension: MJ + kg + pieces + … In monetary analyses, this problem is absent (or perhaps hidden).

6.1.4 Excursus: the Relation with Economic Make/Use Analysis

A concept closely related to the input–output structure, as well as to the technology matrix approach, is the framework of make tables and use tables (see, e.g., Miller & Blair (1985), Konijn (1994), Ten Raa (1995)).[31]

The use table is a table which lists for each process the amount of every commodity that is used. Reserving the columns for the processes and the rows for the commodities, the use table assumes the form of a matrix **U**, in which u_{ij} denotes the use of commodity i by process j.

Similarly, the make table lists the commodity output of every process. Normally, columns are reserved for the commodities instead of processes, while rows represent processes.[32] To avoid any confusion here, we will make use of the transposed make matrix $\mathbf{V}^{\mathrm{T}}$ instead of the normal make matrix **V**. Thus, v^{T}_{ij} denotes the make of commodity i by process j (and is therefore equal to v_{ji}).

Once more, the assumption of constancy of technical coefficients can be made. That is, it is assumed that the activity structure of each process is linear, such that

31 Other authors (e.g., Ayres (1978), Manara (1980)) introduce these concepts without calling them make matrix and use matrix. Victor (1972*a*, p. 56) defines an accounting scheme with 17 matrices and vectors, one of which (his **A**) might be called a use matrix, and another (his **D**) might be called a make matrix. Van Rijckeghem's (1967) transaction matrix (lower case x) is a use matrix; his output matrix (upper case X) a make matrix, while his technology matrix (lower case a) is a commodity-by-commodity matrix. Observe furthermore that Georgescu-Roegen's definition of a unit process in terms of $((a_i; b_i))$ in which an "economic transformation is the possibility of obtaining $(b_1, b_2, \ldots, b_n)$ from $(a_1, a_2, \ldots, a_n)$" (Georgescu-Roegen (1951, p. 99)) corresponds to a use vector and a make vector, a number of which make up the use matrix and the make matrix.

32 According to Konijn (1994, p. 72), the reason for this lies in the mixed accounting scheme, which contain commodities as well as industries to denote columns and rows. In the present notation (*cf.* Gigantes (1970)):

	industries	commodities	external demand	total
industries	—	$\mathbf{V}^{\mathrm{T}}$	—	—
commodities	**U**	—	**a**	**d**
total	—	$\mathbf{d}^{\mathrm{T}}$	—	—

Recall that there are no industry totals in a physical accounting scheme. Victor (1972*a*, p. 56), Ayres (1978, pp. 96–97), and Pearce & Turner (1990, p. 34) use a similar accounting scheme, with extensions to environmental commodities.

$$u_{ij} = \bar{u}_{ij} t_j \tag{6.8}$$

represents the technological input structure. For the technological output structure, different procedures exist (Miller & Blair (1985), Konijn (1994), Ten Raa (1995)):

- the commodity-based technology assumption: each commodity is produced in its own specific way, irrespective of the process by which it is produced;
- the process-based technology assumption:[33] each process has its own specific way of production, irrespective of its output commodity mix.

Furthermore, some other proposals haven been made, see Ten Raa et al. (1984) for a critique.

It is assumed here that the processes are elementary or pure, i.e., they are not an aggregate of several processes. Hence, we must assume that there are no subsidiary outputs, and that all outputs are strictly proportional, i.e., we must follow the process-based technology assumption. This amounts to[34]

$$v^{\mathrm{T}}_{ij} = \bar{v}^{\mathrm{T}}_{ij} t_j. \tag{6.9}$$

It is clear that the technology matrix $\bar{\mathbf{A}}$ can be easily derived from the use matrix and the make matrix in the case of the process-based technology assumption. Process j uses an amount $\bar{u}_{ij}$ of commodity i and makes an amount $\bar{v}^{\mathrm{T}}_{ij}$ of that commodity; in other words a net production of $-\bar{u}_{ij} + \bar{v}^{\mathrm{T}}_{ij}$ (a quantity that may well be negative) results. This is exactly what the corresponding coefficient of the technology matrix $\bar{a}_{ij}$ should represent. We thus find that

$$\bar{\mathbf{A}} = \bar{\mathbf{V}}^{\mathrm{T}} - \bar{\mathbf{U}}. \tag{6.10}$$

A consequence of the choice for the process-based technology assumption is

33 Also called industry-based technology assumption.

34 As noted before, most writers do not make an interpretation in terms of operating times t_j of the processes. It is, however, difficult to conceive of an overall process characteristic to be used for constructing technical coefficients if there is more than one output and if the accounting units are not monetary. For instance, Victor (1972*a*, p. 72) proposes the same equation as the one written down here, but in the form to $v^{\mathrm{T}}_{ij} = \bar{v}^{\mathrm{T}}_{ij} \times \sum_i v^{\mathrm{T}}_{ij}$, where $\sum_i v^{\mathrm{T}}_{ij}$ denotes the total output of process j. In a physical accounting scheme with more than output, this quantity could bear the nonsensical unit of 5 apples + 3 pears.

that

$$\begin{aligned} a_{ij} &= v^{\mathrm{T}}_{ij} - u_{ij} \\ &= \bar{v}^{\mathrm{T}}_{ij} t_j - \bar{u}_{ij} t_j \\ &= \bar{a}_{ij} t_j \end{aligned} \tag{6.11}$$

in accordance with the basic premise of Section 5.2.1.

Clearly, the make matrix and use matrix can be used to calculate the technology matrix. The converse is, however, not true. The technology matrix cannot be used to compile the make matrix and the use matrix, because it provides only information about net outputs, and lacks information about output flows that are partly used as an input flow. It can be questioned whether this is a problem: internal flows are from a phenomenological point of view uninteresting as long as we define a process by its resulting flows, without any attempt to describe what is inside (see also Section 6.1.3).

As a side remark, the relation between the make/use framework and the input–output framework is summarized, a topic that is dealt with extensively by Konijn (1994), as well as by Miller & Blair (1985) and Ten Raa (1995). We will restrict this to the derivation[35] of the commodity-by-commodity table under the commodity-based technology assumption, as this is the only method that does not violate the basic principles of input–output analysis (Konijn (1994, p. 122)). The coefficient $\bar{z}_{ik}$ represents the input of the ith commodity for producing one unit of commodity k. Process j produces an amount $\bar{v}^{\mathrm{T}}_{kj}$ of this latter commodity. Multiplying these and aggregating over all commodities k gives the amount of commodity i needed by process j, a quantity which is by definition equal to $\bar{u}_{ij}$. We thus find

$$\bar{u}_{ij} = \sum_k \bar{z}_{ik} \bar{v}^{\mathrm{T}}_{kj} \tag{6.12}$$

or in matrix notation

$$\bar{\mathbf{U}} = \bar{\mathbf{Z}} \cdot \bar{\mathbf{V}}^{\mathrm{T}}, \tag{6.13}$$

which enables one to calculate the input–output matrix as

$$\bar{\mathbf{Z}} = \bar{\mathbf{U}} \cdot (\bar{\mathbf{V}}^{\mathrm{T}})^{-1} \tag{6.14}$$

It is immediately clear that this poses strict requirements to the make matrix $\bar{\mathbf{V}}^{\mathrm{T}}$: in order to be invertible it should be square (see Konijn (1994, p. 116 *ff.*)). We are back to the problem introduced in Section 5.4.1. The next

35 The derivation was first presented by Van Rijckeghem (1967).

section is devoted to the question of whether this is the case, and, if not, how to proceed.

It may finally be interesting to observe that the commodity-based technology assumption leads to an answer to the first fundamental equation, even if the technology matrix is (or rather, the make and use matrices are) not square. The validity of the procedure for solution can, however, be seriously doubted. Although mathematically correct, the procedure lacks a consistent interpretation because badly defined sums of different commodities are involved.

The procedure (see, e.g., Ayres (1978, p. 102); Konijn (1994, p. 116)) makes use of the following sums:[36] the sum of all produced amounts of commodity i:

$$x_i = \sum_j v^{\mathrm{T}}_{ij}, \qquad [4.15]\ (6.15)$$

and the sum of all commodities that are produced by process j:

$$y_j = \sum_i v^{\mathrm{T}}_{ij}. \qquad [4.16]\ (6.16)$$

It is this latter quantity y_j which lacks meaning in a physical accounting scheme. For the first of these sums, a balance equation holds per commodity:

$$x_i = \sum_j u_{ij} + a_i. \qquad [4.17]\ (6.17)$$

For the second one, a similar balance equation could be proposed (Ayres's [4.18]), but it is not needed in the further derivation here.

The technical input coefficients are in principle the familiar input coefficients of the use table ($u_{ij} = \bar{u}_{ij} t_j$), but an alternative definition is to be used here:[37]

$$u_{ij} = \bar{u}'_{ij} y_j. \qquad [4.19]\ (6.18)$$

For the technical output coefficients, the commodity-based technology assumption is followed; this means that not the previous $v^{\mathrm{T}}_{ij} = \bar{v}^{\mathrm{T}}_{ij} t_j$ is used, nor even $v^{\mathrm{T}}_{ij} = \bar{v}'^{\mathrm{T}}_{ij} y_j$, but that the technical coefficients are defined in terms

36 Here I chose to elaborate Ayres's derivation; since his notation is different from mine and also internally not unambiguous (the same symbols denote sometimes commodities and sometimes processes), I have added in brackets the numbers of his equations in order to facilitate a comparative analysis.

37 I have used a primed symbol to distinguish this technical coefficient from the one that was used before.

of the market share of commodity i[38]:

$$v^{\mathrm{T}}_{ij} = \bar{v}''^{\mathrm{T}}_{ij} x_{i}. \qquad [4.20]\ (6.19)$$

The definition of y_j and the equation of the technical output coefficients $\bar{v}''^{\mathrm{T}}_{ij}$ lead to

$$y_j = \sum_i \bar{v}''^{\mathrm{T}}_{ij} x_i, \qquad [4.21]\ (6.20)$$

whereas the definition of x_i and equation of the technical input coefficients $\bar{u}'_{ij}$ give

$$x_i = \sum_j \bar{u}'_{ij} y_j + a_i. \qquad [4.22]\ (6.21)$$

These two equations give, when substituted into each other,

$$x_i = \sum_j \bar{u}'_{ij} \sum_l \bar{v}''^{\mathrm{T}}_{lj} x_l + a_i \qquad [4.23]\ (6.22)$$

or in matrix form

$$\mathbf{x} = \bar{\mathbf{U}}' \cdot \bar{\mathbf{V}}'' \cdot \mathbf{x} + \mathbf{a} \qquad [4.23a]\ (6.23)$$

and

$$y_j = \sum_i \bar{v}''^{\mathrm{T}}_{ij} \sum_k \bar{u}'_{ik} y_k + \sum_i \bar{v}''^{\mathrm{T}}_{ij} a_i \qquad (6.24)$$

or in matrix form

$$\mathbf{y} = \bar{\mathbf{V}}'' \cdot \bar{\mathbf{U}}' \cdot \mathbf{y} + \bar{\mathbf{V}}'' \cdot \mathbf{a}. \qquad (6.25)$$

These equations can finally be solved to give the desired expressions for x_i and y_j:

$$\mathbf{x} = (\mathbf{I} - \bar{\mathbf{U}}' \cdot \bar{\mathbf{V}}'')^{-1} \cdot \mathbf{a} \qquad [4.24]\ (6.26)$$

and

$$\mathbf{y} = (\mathbf{I} - \bar{\mathbf{V}}'' \cdot \bar{\mathbf{U}}')^{-1} \cdot \bar{\mathbf{V}}'' \cdot \mathbf{a}, \qquad [4.25]\ (6.27)$$

where **I** is the unit matrix of the appropriate dimension.[39] As the formulation in which we are interested is not one for x_i or y_j but one for the operating times t_j, we may rewrite the last equation as

$$t_j = \frac{\bar{u}'_{ij}}{\bar{u}_{ij}} y_j = \frac{\bar{u}'_{ij}}{\bar{u}_{ij}} \left((\mathbf{I} - \bar{\mathbf{V}}'' \cdot \bar{\mathbf{U}}')^{-1} \cdot \bar{\mathbf{V}}'' \cdot \mathbf{a} \right)_j, \qquad (6.28)$$

38 Here a double primed symbol had to be used, unfortunately.

39 Observe that the last two equations use the non-transposed matrix $\bar{\mathbf{V}}''$ instead of $\bar{\mathbf{V}}''^{\mathrm{T}}$.

where any i can be chosen to find the ratio $\frac{\overline{u'}_{ij}}{\overline{u}_{ij}}$.

One might wonder if this last equation for t_j may be employed with the implicit or explicit neglect that a badly defined quantity (y_j) was used to derive it. One could argue that, as long as the result does not contain these problematic terms, its use is legitimate.[40] On the other hand, one should be aware of the conceptual difficulties involved in using a theorem of which the proof contains a badly defined variable. For this latter reason, I have chosen here not to follow the apparently easy way of making the commodity-based technology assumption to circumvent the problem of inverting non-square matrices. Perhaps unfortunately, we must face the fact that the commodity-based technology assumption is in conflict with the assumption that the inflows and the outflows of a process depend proportionally on the operating time of the process; see Equation (5.8).

The theory of make/use analysis does not offer a better starting point than the analysis in terms of the technology matrix does. On the contrary: the procedure is more complicated and not entirely unambiguous.

The availability of data and the fact that the technology matrix can be derived from the use and make matrices means that this type of analysis can be useful for practical reasons. There is one further definite theoretical advantage in studying the relation between the technology matrix, the input–output matrix, and the make/use matrices: the problem of rectangularity has been discussed extensively. The following section gives an overview of the different solutions to the problem of rectangularity.

6.1.5 Excursus: the Relation with Economic Equilibrium Analysis

Equilibrium analysis in fact comprises a set of diverse types of economic models which have in common that they study the simultaneous maximization of some objective function (usually profit). The fact that this is done for each sector (or process) at the same time guarantees that the programming of

40 A comparison could be made with the use of complex numbers to do calculations in the field of electric phenomena. Regardless of the interpretational aspects of imaginary currents, one may apply the results if they contain only real numbers.

economic activities is consistent. Equilibrium models have two essential parts: a set of interindustry relationships, and a pricing system along with an objective function.

This study is about attribution analysis, and thus about a consistent attribution of environmental problems as they occur, without entering into the question of equilibrium or disequilibrium and without the question of profit maximization. As such, equilibrium analysis has little to offer to the problem of attribution, except for the theory of interindustry transactions. And for this, it appears (*cf.* Von Neumann (1945/1946), Debreu (1959), Ginsburgh & Waelbroeck (1981), Parmenter (1982), Bergman (1990)) that either input–output modelling or – to a much greater extent – activity analysis or make/use analysis is used. In that sense, the development of equilibrium analysis is of great interest for the theoretical analysis of this study, but not so much for the equilibrium aspect.

The theory of equilibrium analysis is especially useful in the present study for the ideas that are developed in relation to input–output analysis, activity analysis, and make/use analysis.

6.1.6 Are the Technology Matrix Square and the First Fundamental Equation Solvable?

Is the technology matrix (or, equivalently, the make matrix and the use matrix) square or is it rectangular? As said above, we can give it any desired size by aggregating processes and aggregating commodities. Apart from these manipulations, opinions on this differ to a large extent. Some say that the matrix is square:

> We shall now suppose two of the commodities to be jointly produced by a single industry (or rather by a single process, as it will be more appropriate to call it in the present context). … In these circumstances there will be room for a second, parallel process which will produce the two commodities by a different method and, as we shall suppose at first, in different proportions. Such a process will not only be possible – it will be necessary if the number of processes is to be brought to equality with the number of commodities so that the prices may be determined. We shall therefore go a step further and assume that in such cases a second

> process or industry does in fact exist.[41]

Among those that say it is not, some say that there are more commodities than processes:

> If we include joint products in our input–output accounts, then there will be more commodities than industries ....[42]

Others hold that the converse is true:

> [The technology matrix] includes the Leontief ... matrix as a special case in which the number of activities is equal to the number of commodities. When there is some choice of activity, however, the number of activities *n* will be larger than the number of commodities *m*, and the matrix will no longer be square.[43]

All these statements are based on theoretical reflections. "Empirical" evidence[44] suggests that there are more commodities than processes:

> ... the Dutch make and use matrices of 1987 comprise about 800 commodities and 250 industries.[45]

It is generally felt that at one stage or another a square matrix must be constructed, and that it is possible to do so:

> A ... practical difficulty is that there are normally more commodities than industries, so the industry-commodity input and output matrices are not square, whereas an industry-industry input–output matrix (by definition) must be square; that is, it must have the same number of rows and columns. This involves disaggregation of industries to the commodity level and reaggregation of commodities to the industry level.[46]

It is tempting to establish a general theory which works for all three cases

41 Sraffa (1960, p. 43).
42 Miller & Blair (1985, pp. 166–167).
43 Chenery & Clark (1959, p. 84).
44 The quotation marks should remind one that this empirical evidence can be traced back to human origin: the tables are constructed, and are not just found in nature.
45 Konijn (1994, p. 116).
46 Ayres (1978, p. 98).

(more commodities than processes, more processes than commodities, or an equal number of them), related to the theory exposed by Ten Raa (1995, p. 95 *ff.*). In order to keep the following discussion simple, we will assume for the time being that there are more commodities than processes. It should be possible to use the same ideas that are being developed in the case of more processes than commodities.[47] Application in the case of an equal number of processes and commodities is easy in any case.

For now, consider an extension of the previous example: there are two processes and three commodities, steam being a by-product of process 2; the processes are described in Table 6.3.

TABLE 6.3. Example of a cluster of processes with a rectangular technology matrix.

commodity	process 1	process 2
l fuel/hr	3	−1
MJ electricity/hr	−3	10
kg steam/hr	−1	2

The technology matrix is now rectangular:

$$\bar{\mathbf{A}} = \begin{pmatrix} 3 & -1 \\ -3 & 10 \\ -1 & 2 \end{pmatrix}. \tag{6.29}$$

Suppose furthermore that the external demand is as before, without any consumer demand for steam:

47 It is questionable to what extent this situation exists. This can only occur when one commodity is produced by more than one process. One might suggest that electricity is an example of such a commodity: it may be produced by several types of installations: coal plants, nuclear facilities, hydro plants, etc. If all these processes were taken in consideration, there would be many more processes than commodities. It is not unreasonable, however, to distinguish several types of electricity by their origin, and to introduce another process "electricity mixing", which has coal electricity, nuclear electricity, hydroelectricity, etc. as input in a certain proportion, and which has the homogeneous commodity "electricity on the grid" as an output; see also Section 5.1.5.

$$\mathbf{a} = \begin{bmatrix} 1000 \\ 3500 \\ 0 \end{bmatrix}. \tag{6.30}$$

Clearly, the matrix $\bar{\mathbf{A}}$ cannot be inverted, and the operating times of the two processes $\mathbf{t}$ can not be determined.

Let us first review the types of solutions that have been formulated in different contexts. These are:

(a) reducing the number of commodities by aggregating commodities;
(b) expanding the number of processes by splitting processes;
(c) treating secondary products as primary products of another sector;
(d) treating the external demand as a minimum, and allowing for a surplus;
(e) using pseudo-inverses to calculate an approximate solution to the external demand;

These solutions will be considered in more detail below.[48]

(a) The first way of solving the problem of rectangularity is to merge commodities, so as to merge rows:

> We shall assume that the number *m* of commodities exceeds the number *n* of industries. ... If a model is desired in which total final demand can be specified and is to be produced precisely, the commodity classification must be aggregated so that there will be exactly *n* commodities. The system will then have exactly *n* equations to determine the *n* industry operating levels ....[49]

For example, suppose that we choose to aggregate the commodities electricity and steam into the commodity energy, that energy is measured in MJ, and that 1 MJ electricity is equivalent to 1 MJ energy while 1 kg steam is equivalent to 2 MJ energy. A modified table will result (Table 6.4). We thus arrive at a square invertible technology matrix. The operating times of the processes is found to be

48 Another, perhaps more systematic, categorization of such options is introduced by Heijungs & Frischknecht (1998).

49 Rosenbluth (1968, pp. 257–260). A similar description is in Konijn (1994, p. 117).

TABLE 6.4. Modified square technology matrix obtained by aggregation of commodities.

commodity	process 1	process 2
l fuel/hr	3	−1
MJ energy/hr	−5	14

$$\mathbf{t} = \begin{pmatrix} 3 & -1 \\ -5 & 14 \end{pmatrix}^{-1} \cdot \begin{pmatrix} 1000 \\ 3500 \end{pmatrix} = \begin{pmatrix} 473 \\ 419 \end{pmatrix}. \quad (6.31)$$

It will be clear that this is not a very elegant solution: things that are different are lumped together and treated as being similar for computational reasons:

> The need to aggregate the commodities is an important drawback of the commodity technology model.[50]

After all, if process 1 is run during 473 hr and process during 419 hr, we end up with

$$\mathbf{a} = \begin{pmatrix} 1000 \\ 2770 \\ 365 \end{pmatrix} \quad (6.32)$$

so with 365 kg steam instead of 730 MJ electricity. So we have an economic system which produces commodities in other quantities than desired by consumers, simply because we could not otherwise calculate what to produce.

(b) The second solution is to split a multiple process into a number of virtual single processes:

> Reallocation (sometimes referred to as redefinition) of secondary production … requires that a firm allocate its inputs between the production of primary and secondary products; in effect, it is necessary to break the firm into two independent sub-firms – one a producer of the primary product and the other a producer

50 Konijn (1994, p. 117).

of the secondary product.[51]

For example, we would split process 2 into a process (2a) that produces electricity without steam and a process (2b) that produces steam without electricity; the input of fuel must be distributed among these two processes

TABLE 6.5. Modified square technology matrix obtained by splitting processes.

commodity	process 1	process 2a	process 2b
l fuel/hr	3	-0.7	-0.3
MJ electricity/hr	-3	10	0
kg steam/hr	-1	0	2

according to some rule; see Table 6.5. The new technology matrix is again square and invertible. The operating times of the processes are

$$\mathbf{t} = \begin{pmatrix} 3 & -0.7 & -0.3 \\ -3 & 10 & 0 \\ -1 & 0 & 2 \end{pmatrix}^{-1} \cdot \begin{pmatrix} 1000 \\ 3500 \\ 0 \end{pmatrix} = \begin{pmatrix} 472 \\ 491 \\ 236 \end{pmatrix}. \qquad (6.33)$$

This solution has the disadvantage of the difficulty in finding factors to split processes: a fairly weak statement of this difficulty is that

> [m]ost firms do not record data in a form that permits this accounting easily ....[52]

In the example, 70% of the steel consumption of the original process was allocated[53] to electricity and 30% to steam, but any distribution is arguable and debatable. Interestingly, this is exactly the way most practitioners of energy analysis and of environmental life-cycle assessment solve the problem

51 Miller & Blair (1985, p. 154).

52 Loc. cit.

53 In this study, we will use the term allocation for the procedure of splitting a process into two or more processes in order to expand the number of columns of the technology matrix to make it square. In economic literature, the terms reallocation and redefinition are sometimes employed; in the literature of life-cycle assessment the term allocation is dominant but other terms (partitioning, attribution) occur as well.

of multiple production (see Anonymous (1974, pp. 57–59) for energy analysis and Consoli et al. (1993, pp. 20–21) for life-cycle assessment); debate focuses there on the operationalization of this procedure (*cf.* Huppes & Schneider (1994), Boustead (1994)). The allocation procedure is – implicitly – aimed at the construction of a square technology matrix (see Heijungs (1994*b*, p. 74), Schmidt (1995, p. 100)). Another serious consequence is that the operating times of process 2a and process 2b are different. As the processes are one in reality, we cannot turn on one half of the process for a longer time than the other half of the process. For analytical purposes – giving an answer to the attribution problem – we may be satisfied with this description, but for macroeconomic scenario calculations we must be aware of somehow reconciling process 2a and process 2b.

(c) The third solution assumes that there exists a process that produces steam without producing electricity. This process (number 3) is – as it were – subtracted from the original multiple process:

> ... each secondary product is transferred from the industry actually producing it to the industry producing it as a primary product.[54]

This procedure is in economic literature referred to as redefinition, although it must be repeated that procedure *(b)* is also sometimes referred to by this term. In the literature of life-cycle assessment the terms substitution method and avoided impacts are used in connection with this procedure. Suppose that there is a process which makes 1 kg steam/hr out of 0.5 MJ electricity/hr. This generates a new table: see Table 6.6. Again, the new technology matrix

TABLE 6.6. Modified square technology matrix obtained by subtracting an "avoided" process.

commodity	process 1	process 2	process 3
l fuel/hr	3	−1	0
MJ electricity/hr	−3	10	−0.5
kg steam/hr	−1	2	1

is square and invertible. The operating times are

54 Konijn (1994, p. 96).

$$\mathbf{t} = \begin{pmatrix} 3 & -1 & 0 \\ 3 & 10 & -0.5 \\ -1 & 2 & 1 \end{pmatrix}^{-1} \cdot \begin{pmatrix} 1000 \\ 3500 \\ 0 \end{pmatrix} = \begin{pmatrix} 492 \\ 475 \\ -458 \end{pmatrix}. \tag{6.34}$$

A problematic aspect of this solution is the negative operating time of the third process:

> ... when faced with a set of nonnegative final demands ... it would be meaningless in an economy to find that one or more of the necessary gross outputs ... were negative.[55]

At a micro level, this can be interpreted as avoided, comparable with the delivery of electricity to the grid by waste incinerators, thereby avoiding combustion of fossil fuels. This method is sometimes employed in the context of life-cycle assessment, especially for recycling processes (see, e.g., Tillman et al. (1994) and Huppes & Schneider (1994)). Again, we must be careful not to extend negative operating times to the macro scale.[56] In fact, the existence of negative production levels has been one of the problems in using and interpreting input–output analysis.[57] A very serious disadvantage is of course that the non-existence of avoided activities makes the choice of what is actually being avoided quite cumbersome. If there are two modes of steam production, which one is avoided in this example?

> The commodity technology assumption seems to be most applicable to cases of subsidiary production ..., since in those cases the technology of primary and secondary product are independent. However, the commodity assumption does not exclude cases where two or more commodities are produced in the same way. ... Only if one of both commodities is produced elsewhere as well but in a different way, the commodity assumption is not valid.[58]

Still more intricate is the point that there is not always an alternative process which produces one single commodity, e.g., there is no process which produces petrol without co-producing heavy oil.

55 Miller & Blair (1985, p. 36).

56 Alternatively, an interpretation in terms of a change of economic activity could be allowed for; see, e.g., Miller & Blair (1985, p. 36n).

57 Hawkins & Simon (1949) were the first to discuss conditions for non-negativity.

58 Konijn (1994, p. 98).

The most serious argument against this method refers back to the requirement of 100%-additivity. If we subtract a steam production process when considering pure electricity, and an electricity production process when considering pure steam, it is unlikely that the sum of these two systems yields the original multiple process. Reserving primed quantities for the subtracted process, we have

$$\begin{aligned}\mathbf{p}_{\text{electricity}} &= \mathbf{p}_{\text{multiple}} - \mathbf{p}'_{\text{steam}} \\ \mathbf{p}_{\text{steam}} &= \mathbf{p}_{\text{multiple}} - \mathbf{p}'_{\text{electricity}}\end{aligned} \tag{6.35}$$

and thus

$$\mathbf{p}_{\text{electricity}} + \mathbf{p}_{\text{steam}} = 2\mathbf{p}_{\text{multiple}} - \mathbf{p}'_{\text{steam}} - \mathbf{p}'_{\text{electricity}} \neq \mathbf{p}_{\text{multiple}}. \tag{6.36}$$

This is in contradiction with the basic postulate of 100%-additivity, which requires the ≠ to be replaced by an equality sign.

(d) The fourth solution allows for an approximate solution of the external demand, in the sense that a surplus of commodities is produced.

> If we permit surpluses, we then have an infinite variety of ways in which any given bill of goods can be produced and we must choose a way which will in some significant sense minimize the surpluses. For this we require some economizing principle, and once this is introduced we have a standard linear programming problem that can be solved by the standard methods.[59]

For example, this could amount to stating the problem in terms of an objective function

$$\text{minimize} \sum_j \pi_j t_j \tag{6.37}$$

where π_j is the price of running process j during one hour, and in terms of constraints like

$$\begin{pmatrix} 3 & -1 \\ 3 & 10 \\ -1 & 2 \end{pmatrix} \cdot \begin{pmatrix} t_1 \\ t_2 \end{pmatrix} \geq \begin{pmatrix} 1000 \\ 3500 \\ 0 \end{pmatrix} \tag{6.38}$$

$$t_1,\ t_2 \geq 0.$$

In the present context, financial optimization appears a bit strange, as the task

59 Rosenbluth (1968, p. 261).

is to find an answer to the attribution problem. An alternative formulation could be merely to require that the external demand is met

$$\begin{pmatrix} 3 & -1 \\ 3 & 10 \\ -1 & 2 \end{pmatrix} \cdot \begin{pmatrix} t_1 \\ t_2 \end{pmatrix} \geq \begin{pmatrix} 1000 \\ 3500 \\ 0 \end{pmatrix}, \tag{6.39}$$

by putting the operating times to

$$\mathbf{t} = \begin{pmatrix} 500 \\ 500 \end{pmatrix} \tag{6.40}$$

and henceforth producing a surplus of 500 kg steam. In the literature of life-cycle assessment, this method is sometimes encountered in connection with the method referred to as system expansion (see Tillman et al. (1994)).

An obvious disadvantage is of course the existence of a surplus. The task was to attribute environmental problems to selected economic activities. It turned out to be impossible to fulfil this task, and what we have done is in some sense a close approximation to the original task.

(e) The last solution discussed here makes use of the concept of pseudo-inverses.[60] The pseudo-inverse of $\bar{\mathbf{A}}$ is

$$\bar{\mathbf{A}}^{\dagger} = \begin{pmatrix} 0.36 & 0.045 & -0.045 \\ 0.11 & 0.11 & 0.0039 \end{pmatrix}. \tag{6.41}$$

This leads to operating times given by

$$\mathbf{t} = \begin{pmatrix} 523 \\ 498 \end{pmatrix}. \tag{6.42}$$

This amount of activity produces an output of

60 Any matrix $\mathbf{A}$ of dimension $(m \times n)$ with $m \geq n$ can be subject to singular value decomposition, i.e., it can be decomposed into a column-orthogonal matrix $\mathbf{U}$ of dimension $(m \times n)$, a diagonal matrix $\mathbf{D}$ of dimension $(n \times n)$, and an orthogonal matrix $\mathbf{V}^{\mathrm{T}}$ of dimension $(n \times n)$: $\mathbf{A} = \mathbf{U}\cdot\mathbf{D}\cdot\mathbf{V}^{\mathrm{T}}$. The system of m equations in n unknowns $\mathbf{A}\cdot\mathbf{x} = \mathbf{y}$ can now be "solved" through $\mathbf{x} = \mathbf{V}\cdot\mathbf{D}\cdot\mathbf{U}^{\mathrm{T}}\cdot\mathbf{y}$. The word "solved" means here that the solution for $\mathbf{x}$ is not an exact solution of the equation, but represents the closest solution in the sense that $\|\mathbf{A}\cdot\mathbf{x}-\mathbf{y}\|$ is minimized. The term $\mathbf{V}\cdot\mathbf{D}^{-1}\cdot\mathbf{U}^{\mathrm{T}}$ is known as the pseudo-inverse of $\mathbf{A}$ and may be represented as $\mathbf{A}^{\dagger}$. See, e.g., Press et al. (1989, p. 61 *ff.*), Golub & Van Loan (1989, p. 243), or Stewart & Sun (1990, p. 101 *ff.*) for details.

$$\mathbf{a} = \begin{pmatrix} 1070 \\ 3412 \\ 473 \end{pmatrix}. \tag{6.43}$$

A definite disadvantage of this approach is that the external demand is not satisfied for any of the commodities. For some there is a surplus, for others there is a shortage. This procedure gives a solution that satisfies as closely as possible the external demand.[61] In some cases, the approximation may be a precise solution; see Section 6.2.1 for a discussion of this special case.

> It appears that the technology matrix is in practice often not square. There are at least five methods for finding a solution to the first fundamental equation in this case. All these solutions lead to different results (see Table 6.7) and all have a number of disadvantages (see Table 6.8).

Above, we discussed the first fundamental equation along with the fact that it is very often not possible to solve it because the technology matrix is not square. Five proposals to generate a solution in any case were discussed, all of them having some disadvantages (Table 6.8).

Considering the central question of this study – which environmental problems are to be attributed to which economic activity? – a choice for *(a)*, *(d)* or *(e)* is not very satisfying: in that case there would be an answer, but it would be an answer to another question.

The problem of using method *(b)* is purely methodological: main lines of thought are here a socio-economic allocation (e.g., Huppes (1993)) and a physico-chemical allocation (e.g., Boustead (1994)).

61 To be more precise: the output is a least squares approximation to the external demand. It can be doubted whether this distance can be given any meaningful interpretation: the analysis is in physical, not monetary, terms, which means that we are minimizing a quantity with the unit $\sqrt{(\text{l fuel})^2 + (\text{MJ electricity})^2 + (\text{kg steam})^2}$, a completely nonsensical entity! It is, however, not only the interpretation that is the problem: the approach is sensitive for the choice of units. If fuels are measured in m^3 instead of in l, another result is found: $\mathbf{t} = \begin{pmatrix} 1700 \\ 875 \end{pmatrix}$ and $\mathbf{a} = \begin{pmatrix} 4400 \\ 3500 \\ 0.023 \end{pmatrix}$. It is therefore a form of solution that is sensitive for a choice of units, something which is generally considered as a criterion for inappropriateness.

TABLE 6.7. The degree to which the external demand is satisfied in the case of a non-square technology matrix.

method	l fuel	MJ electricity	kg steam
reducing the number of commodities by aggregating commodities (*a*; Page 117)	1000	2770	365
expanding the number of processes by splitting processes (*b*; Page 119)	1000	3500	0
treating secondary products as primary products of another sector (*c*; Page 120)	1000	3500	0
treating the final demand as a minimum, and allowing for a surplus (*d*; Page 122)	1000	3500	500
using pseudo-inverses to calculate an approximate solution to the final demand (*e*; Page 123)	1070*	3412*	473*
desired external demand	1000	3500	0

* Based on the units l fuel, MJ electricity, and kg steam. Other units yield a different result.

The problem of using method *(c)*, finally, is two-fold. First we have the violation of the epistemological rule of 100%-additivity. Furthermore, this option implies choices with respect to technological state and historical developments. It must be decided which process is actually being avoided or substituted. It is impossible to give an answer to this question: one can observe which processes are there, but one cannot figure out which processes are not there because they have been replaced by other processes. Moreover, there are many commodities which are only produced in a joint production process: the process of cow breeding produces milk, meat, skins, calves, manure, and some more commodities. If we are only interested in milk, we would need information on the processes of meat production, skin production, calf production, etc., in order to subtract them from the multiple-output process of cow breeding. These processes actually do not exist without each other: there is only one joint process of cow breeding. Similar remarks apply to chlorine/sodium production: although there are processes which produce sodium from Na_2CO_3 without making chlorine (see Kleijn et al. (1994)), it seems a bit strange to say that this process is nowadays avoided because sodium is normally coproduced along with chlorine. For these reasons, the

TABLE 6.8. Disadvantages of the methods for solving the first fundamental equation for a non-square technology matrix.

method	disadvantage
reducing the number of commodities by aggregating commodities (*a*; Page 117)	deviations from external demand
expanding the number of processes by splitting processes (*b*; Page 119)	unclear how to split
treating secondary products as primary products of another sector (*c*; Page 120)	unclear which process is avoided
treating the external demand as a minimum, and allowing for a surplus (*d*; Page 122)	deviations from external demand
using pseudo-inverses to calculate an approximate solution to the external demand (*e*; Page 123)	deviations from external demand

method of redefinition appears less pure a solution than method *(b)*.[62]

> The method for finding a solution to the first fundamental equation that is on theoretical grounds superior is the allocation procedure, in which processes are split to expand the number of processes so that the technology matrix becomes square.

How this allocation is performed in practice is discussed in the next section.

62 In a slightly different context – a discussion of drawbacks of the commodity-based technology assumption – the same arguments can be found. This is so because the commodity-based technology assumption is inspired by the belief that each commodity is produced in one unique way, a belief which is obviously unjustified: "There are numerous examples of commodities that are produced in more than one way, for example many petrochemical products. Also, secondary products are often produced in a different way than when they are produced as primary products." (Konijn (1994, p. 144)).

6.2 SOLUTION OF THE FIRST FUNDAMENTAL EQUATION

6.2.1 Making a Square Technology Matrix: the Allocation Procedure

Having chosen the allocation method (*b*), we face three questions:

- When is allocation required?
- Which processes are to be allocated in those cases?
- How do we allocate those processes?

Allocation is meant to expand the number of columns of the technology matrix, so that it becomes square and – hopefully – invertible. Strictly speaking, allocation is only required when the technology matrix is rectangular instead of square. This implies that allocation would only take place after completion of the technology matrix, so after data on the inputs and outputs of economic commodities into and out of every process involved have been compiled. A problem which then arises is: which process or processes should be split? A very obvious answer appears to be to apply the procedure to those processes that produce more than one economic output commodity:

> ... it is necessary to break the firm into two independent subfirms – one a producer of the primary product and the other a producer of the secondary product.[63]

This answer is, at least in the present context of environmental extensions to the economic analysis, wrong for two reasons:

- if waste-to-be-processed is also an economic output commodity, allocation appears to be superfluous (or even wrong);
- if waste-to-be-processed is an economic input commodity, allocation appears to be necessary in many cases.

The notion of economic value seems to be important here.

An economic process is a transformation of commodities into commod-

63 Miller & Blair (1985, p. 154).

ities. But an economic process is more than that: nearly all flows of economic commodities are associated with monetary value. An economic process is therefore also a transformation of value into value. Some of the commodities are goods and materials, others are bads and disservices. The criterion for categorizing a commodity as a good or a bad is the value that is assigned to it: goods and services have a positive value, while bads and disservices have a negative value.

The relative value is not an attribute of a certain commodity, but the position it assumes for a certain economic process. Goods and services that are the input of a process are costs for that process; this makes them have a negative relative value for that process. In contrast, bads and disservices that are the input of a process are benefits for that process, which gives them a positive relative value. On the output side, the situation is reversed: goods and services are benefits, and have a positive relative value; "bads" and "disservices" are costs, and have a negative relative value. In conclusion: the list of economic commodities that flow to and from a process can be split into four groups:

- input goods and services;
- input bads and disservices;
- output goods and services;
- output bads and disservices.

It can now be stated that input bads and disservices and output goods and services are the commodity flows that are the *raison d'être* of the process, and that the other types of commodity flows (input goods and services, output bads and disservices, as well as all environmental flows) must be allocated to the former two categories of commodity flows (Figure 6.1; see for instance Heijungs et al., (1992*b*), p. 22 *ff.*; Huppes (1993), p. 192 *ff.*; Huppes & Schneider (1994)).

From this observation, three elementary types of allocation may be distinguished:

- more than one output good or service (coproduction, multi-output process);
- more than one input bad or disservice (combined waste handling, multi-input process);

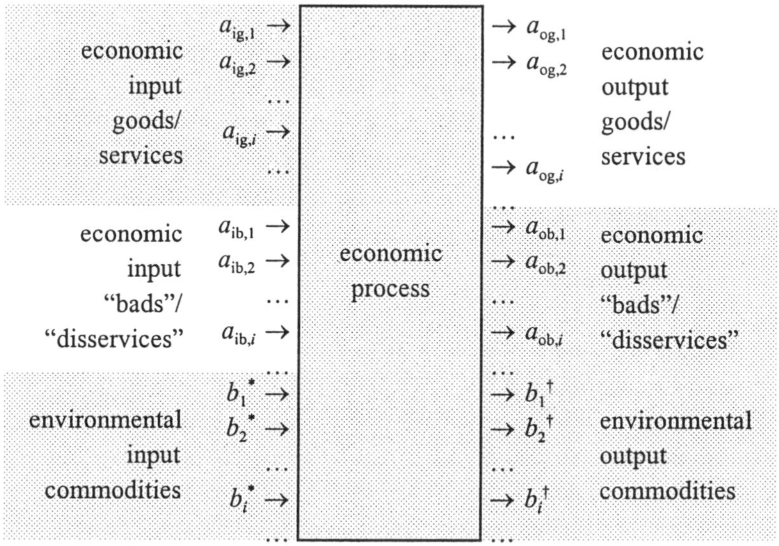

* Only when negative, else zero or absent.
† Only when positive, else zero or absent.

FIGURE 6.1. The allocation procedure: undesired flows (shaded) are to be allocated to desired flows.

- one input bad or disservice and one output good or service (recycling,[64] input–output process).

It appears that allocation must be performed on the level of the individual process. This means that it can be performed prior to the construction of the technology matrix and independently of the process cluster in which it is included. So we can strive for a certain degree of universality of the allocation procedure. We can even consider allocated processes to be more elementary than the joint process that has been observed.[65] This could induce one to

64 Recycling is also sometimes understood to convert a good into a more valuable good, e.g., positively priced scrap into basic iron. According to the strict definition given above, this situation should, however, be considered as ordinary production. In the case that a consumer deflects a positively valued service ("utility") from a product and afterwards discards a positively valued used product, we speak of coproduction (Huppes (1993, p. 214n) and Huppes (1994, p. 84n)).

65 In fact, sometimes it is a statistical procedure which means that a small cluster of processes is observed instead of its constituent parts.

compile a database of allocated processes instead of observed processes.[66] It must, however, not be forgotten that the allocation procedure is a highly speculative procedure, on which a lot of discussion is going on (see, e.g., Huppes & Schneider (1994)). This means that it is from a scientific point of view recommendable to collect the observed or predicted process data, and to perform an allocation on the processes therein when needed.

Every economic process that has more than one output good/service or input bad/disservice must in principle be allocated. It is preferable to accomplish this before processes are put into a cluster, but only after a proper recording of the observed or predicted process data.

A last not unimportant remark is that it is not always necessary to apply an allocation procedure to multiple processes. If we have a process that produces iron layers from bare iron, and a process that produces iron circles and miscellaneous iron out of iron layers, it is normal industrial practice to feed back the miscellaneous iron to the production process of iron layers. Suppose that economic commodity 1 is iron layers, economic commodity 2 is iron circles, and economic commodity 3 is miscellaneous iron; bare iron is for simplicity left out. Process 1 is production of iron layers, process 2 is production of iron plates. The technology matrix and the external demand are supposed to be given by

$$\bar{\mathbf{A}} = \begin{pmatrix} 10 & -10 \\ 0 & 8 \\ -2 & 2 \end{pmatrix} \text{ and } \mathbf{a} = \begin{pmatrix} 0 \\ 16 \\ 0 \end{pmatrix}. \qquad (6.44)$$

It is immediately clear that the operating times of the two processes are simply 2 and 2 (hr). The formalism described unfortunately has more difficulties in proving this obvious fact. The formalism expects a square technology matrix because the rectangular one cannot be inverted. There are two possibilities: miscellaneous iron has a positive value whence process 2 is multiple because it produces two valuable outputs, or it has a negative value whence process 1 is multiple because it processes waste and produces a valuable good. Both options will be briefly considered.

66 Actually, almost all databases of economic processes that include figures on environmental flows consist of allocated data.

Using the allocation procedure for process 2 gives a square technology matrix:

$$\bar{\mathbf{A}} = \begin{pmatrix} 10 & -10\theta & -10(1-\theta) \\ 0 & 8 & 0 \\ -2 & 0 & 2 \end{pmatrix}, \tag{6.45}$$

which can be inverted to yield for almost every choice of the allocation parameter θ the operating times

$$\mathbf{t} = \begin{pmatrix} \frac{1}{10\theta} & \frac{1}{8} & \frac{1-\theta}{2\theta} \\ 0 & \frac{1}{8} & 0 \\ \frac{1}{10\theta} & \frac{1}{\theta} & \frac{1}{2\theta} \end{pmatrix} \cdot \begin{pmatrix} 0 \\ 16 \\ 0 \end{pmatrix} = \begin{pmatrix} 2 \\ 2 \\ 2 \end{pmatrix}. \tag{6.46}$$

The other options would apply the allocation procedure to process 1 and start with the square technology matrix

$$\bar{\mathbf{A}} = \begin{pmatrix} 10 & 0 & -10 \\ 0\theta & 0(1-\theta) & 8 \\ 0 & -2 & 2 \end{pmatrix}, \tag{6.47}$$

which also yields the operating times

$$\mathbf{t} = \begin{pmatrix} 2 \\ 2 \\ 2 \end{pmatrix} \tag{6.48}$$

as a final result.

We see here a remarkable result: on the one hand the operating times are independent of the allocation parameters; on the other hand the operating times of the "virtual" processes that make a real process are equal. This means that discussions on the exact choice of the allocation parameter is in these cases pointless: any choice produces the same results.

We could also achieve this result without going into an allocation procedure and calculating the pseudo-inverse of the rectangular technology matrix; see also option *(e)* of Section 6.1.5. We easily find

$$\mathbf{t} = \bar{\mathbf{A}}^{\dagger} \cdot \mathbf{a} = \begin{pmatrix} 0.096 & 0.125 & -0.019 \\ 0 & 0.125 & 0 \end{pmatrix} \cdot \begin{pmatrix} 0 \\ 16 \\ 0 \end{pmatrix} = \begin{pmatrix} 2 \\ 2 \end{pmatrix}. \tag{6.49}$$

This is in this exceptional case an exact solution; this can be observed by calculating the distance between external demand the approximated supply:

$$\| \mathbf{a} - \bar{\mathbf{A}} \cdot (\bar{\mathbf{A}}^{\dagger} \cdot \mathbf{a}) \| \tag{6.50}$$

which is in this case exactly 0.

The physical interpretation of this example is that of closed-loop recycling: all miscellaneous iron is returned to the producing facility; the amount that is needed in addition is supplied from the outside. It is a quite generally acknowledged[67] fact that closed-loop recycling can do without an allocation procedure.

> It is advisable to determine if the first fundamental equation can be solved exactly in the case of a rectangular technology matrix by means of pseudo-inversion. If this is not the case, one must go back to the elementary processes and apply an allocation procedure to all multiple processes.

6.2.2 The Allocation Procedure in Detail

Technically, allocation is the converse of clustering. In clustering, however, information on the individual processes inside is being lost. This means that "declustering" requires the incorporation of new information. This is exactly the problematic aspect of allocation, and it is one of the major sources of disagreement in the field of life-cycle assessment; see Section 2.1.4 for a number of quotations which illustrate the unresolved nature of the problem.

Suppose that a certain process is represented by the coordinates

67 Actually, it is quite often heard but not so often written down. Most textbooks discuss in a chapter on allocation the three main types – coproduction, combined waste handling, and open-loop recycling – without discussing closed-loop recycling. For instance, in Lindfors et al. (1995*d*, p. 6), it is stated that allocation of open-loop recycling may be avoided by treating it as closed-loop recycling. Despite the truth of this statement, the method to actually find a solution has to my knowledge not been discussed before, and certainly not in terms of a pseudo-inverse (see Heijungs & Frischknecht (1998)).

$$\mathbf{p} = \begin{bmatrix} \mathbf{a} \\ \mathbf{b} \end{bmatrix} = \begin{bmatrix} a_{\mathrm{og},1} \\ a_{\mathrm{og},2} \\ a_{\mathrm{ib},1} \\ a_{\mathrm{ib},2} \\ a_{\mathrm{ig},1} \\ a_{\mathrm{ig},2} \\ a_{\mathrm{ob},1} \\ a_{\mathrm{ob},2} \\ b_1 \\ b_2 \end{bmatrix}, \tag{6.51}$$

where $a_{\mathrm{og},1}$ is the first output good or service, $a_{\mathrm{og},2}$ is the second output good or service, $a_{\mathrm{ib},1}$ is the first input bad or disservice, etc. The allocation procedure amounts to:

$$\begin{bmatrix} a_{\mathrm{og},1} \\ a_{\mathrm{og},2} \\ a_{\mathrm{ib},1} \\ a_{\mathrm{ib},2} \\ a_{\mathrm{ig},1} \\ a_{\mathrm{ig},2} \\ a_{\mathrm{ob},1} \\ a_{\mathrm{ob},2} \\ b_1 \\ b_2 \end{bmatrix} \rightarrow \begin{bmatrix} a_{\mathrm{og},1} & 0 & 0 & 0 \\ 0 & a_{\mathrm{og},2} & 0 & 0 \\ 0 & 0 & a_{\mathrm{ib},1} & 0 \\ 0 & 0 & 0 & a_{\mathrm{ib},2} \\ \theta_{15}a_{\mathrm{ig},1} & \theta_{25}a_{\mathrm{ig},1} & \theta_{35}a_{\mathrm{ig},1} & \theta_{45}a_{\mathrm{ig},1} \\ \theta_{16}a_{\mathrm{ig},2} & \theta_{26}a_{\mathrm{ig},2} & \theta_{36}a_{\mathrm{ig},2} & \theta_{46}a_{\mathrm{ig},2} \\ \theta_{17}a_{\mathrm{ob},1} & \theta_{27}a_{\mathrm{ob},1} & \theta_{37}a_{\mathrm{ob},1} & \theta_{47}a_{\mathrm{ob},2} \\ \theta_{18}a_{\mathrm{ob},2} & \theta_{28}a_{\mathrm{ob},2} & \theta_{38}a_{\mathrm{ob},2} & \theta_{48}a_{\mathrm{ob},2} \\ \theta_{19}b_1 & \theta_{29}b_1 & \theta_{39}b_1 & \theta_{49}b_1 \\ \theta_{1\,10}b_2 & \theta_{2\,10}b_2 & \theta_{3\,10}b_2 & \theta_{4\,10}b_2 \end{bmatrix}. \tag{6.52}$$

This may be summarized as

$$\mathbf{p} \rightarrow \boldsymbol{\Theta} \cdot \mathbf{p}, \tag{6.53}$$

where $\boldsymbol{\Theta}$ is the matrix of allocation factors. It is subject to a number of restrictions described below.

In the first place, the principle of "declustering" implies that a "reclustering" of allocated processes retrieves the original process. In formula:

$$\forall i: \sum_j \theta_{ji} p_i = p_i, \tag{6.54}$$

which means that the sum of the allocation factors that belong to the same commodity must be equal to one:

$$\forall i: \sum_j \theta_{ji} = 1. \tag{6.55}$$

A second requirement is that the allocated processes are fully allocated, that is, they will not again give rise to non-square technology matrices. This can be translated into the requirement that every allocated process has exactly one output of good or service or exactly one input of bad or disservice. In the example above, we see the consequence of this as a diagonal structure for the first 16 elements of the allocation matrix $\boldsymbol{\Theta}$: $\begin{pmatrix} 1 & 0 & 0 & 0 \\ 0 & 1 & 0 & 0 \\ 0 & 0 & 1 & 0 \\ 0 & 0 & 0 & 1 \end{pmatrix}$. In general, however, the order of the economic commodities will be such that this diagonal is not easily detectable.

These are the only two formal requirements.[68] All further proposals for the exact values of the allocation factors are speculative. In the literature of life-cycle assessment, some further requirement are sometimes proposed:

- All allocation factors, except those for the output goods/services and the input bads/disservices, must be the same for the different commodities within one process. This means in the example above $\theta_{15} = \theta_{16} = \ldots, \theta_{25} = \theta_{26} = \ldots$, etc.[69]
- All allocation factors must have a value between zero and one: $0 \leq \theta_{ji} \leq 1$.
- The allocation factors must be based on the ratio of the mass (or any other physical parameter) or on the ratio of the economic value (or

68 Among the requirements found in literature that I reject is the one that each of the allocated processes should not violate the laws of physics (Boustead (1994, p. 2)). Any allocation method will yield from cow breeding a number of process that violate the laws of physics. If it didn't, the allocated process could have been found in reality.

69 This is a requirement that is very often implicitly made.

any other economic parameter) of the output goods/services and/or the input bads/disservices. This would, for instance for θ_{15}, mean that

$$\theta_{15} = \frac{a_{og,1}}{a_{ib,1} + a_{ib,2} + a_{og,1} + a_{og,2}} .$$ [70]

None of these rules can be proven with the same rigour as is applied to the other manipulations of process data and technology matrix.[71] It is an unfortunate fact that the indeterminateness of the allocation procedure is a barrier to a straightforward application of the formalism put forward in this study (*cf.* Ten Raa (1988)).

There is as yet no universal rule for performing the allocation procedure. There are some requirements which follow from the epistemological principles of the attribution problem (especially 100%-additivity), and in addition some other requirements are sometimes proposed. These are, however, not universally acknowledged and are from a scientific point of view speculative, because they are beyond the realm of the epistemological basis of this study.

70 Here the largest difference in opinion can be found, with obvious consequences for the numbers that will be obtained. Boustead (1994, p. 19) writes: "The choice of partitioning method is clearly important since it can significantly affect the final result. However, it is equally clear that there is no single, overwhelming scientific reason for choosing any specific procedure. As a result, the choice is almost arbitrary."

71 The same argument applies to energy analysis. For instance, Chapman (1974, p. 93) states that "... there is no 'correct' solution."

Chapter 7

Towards Concrete Tools for Environmental Analysis and Decision-Support: Inventory Analysis

7.1 GENERAL CONSIDERATIONS

In Section 5.3, two main types of analysis were defined:

- commodity-flow accounting, in which the operating time of every process is externally imposed, in order to calculate the flows between economic processes and between the environment and the various economic processes within a certain region;
- activity-level analysis, in which the operating time of every process is determined by an externally imposed external demand, again in order to calculate the flows between economic processes and between the environment and the various economic processes within a certain region.

The next sections, 5.4, 6.1, and 6.2, concentrated on the ALA type of calculation: the first fundamental equation and the problems encountered in solving it. The discussion assumed the form of a calculation problem: given an economic structure in the form of a technology matrix $\bar{\mathbf{A}}$ and the intervention matrix $\bar{\mathbf{B}}$, we can for any external demand vector $\mathbf{a}$ compute the vector of environmental interventions $\mathbf{b}$. We have not yet faced the question of selecting an appropriate external demand for a meaningful ALA. Neither did we discuss the meaning of the CFA type of analysis. This chapter is devoted to the question of making a meaningful and feasible analysis.

Starting from ALA, we first observe that we may naturally specify any desired external demand of commodities in the vector **a**. This may thus be an arbitrarily composed basket of commodities. However, for the purpose of analysis, it is often required to concentrate on one unit of one particular commodity (see also Section 1.1.3):

> The accounting models ... are all essentially designed to help find answers to one class of question, which is always of the form How much material/energy/pollutant "*X*" is used or generated directly/indirectly in or by process/commodity/product/sector or final demand category "*Y*"?[1]

A strongly related concept is the Leontief multiplier (Miller & Blair (1985, p. 100 *ff.*)), of which the output multiplier is the most interesting here:

> An output multiplier for sector *j* is defined as the total value of production in all sectors of the economy that is necessary in order to satisfy a dollar's worth of final demand for sector *j*'s output.[2]

So, a special form of the external demand will be introduced: there is only one economic commodity for which there is a non-zero external demand. Consequently, the vector **a** consists of a large array of zeroes, with only one non-zero element. The type of analysis obtained with this restriction is commonly referred to as environmental life-cycle assessment of products.[3] See Section 7.2 for a full discussion.

The other main type of analysis is the CFA. Here we may choose a certain period, usually one year, and calculate all flows of economic and environmental commodities through the economic system and to and from the environment. However, also here we may wish to concentrate on a particular commodity or set of commodities, typically a substance or a substance group:

> An appropriately chosen combination of possibly few substances allows an

1 Ayres (1978, p. 95).
2 Miller & Blair (1985, p. 102).
3 It should be emphasized at this early stage that not all exercises in literature indicated by the term life-cycle assessment comply with the interpretation given here.

efficient and qualified characterization of the metabolism.[4]

Here the main approach is to calculate all flows, but to present only the flows of the selected commodity or commodities. This will typically be a substance or a group of substances, hence the name substance-flow analysis for this mode of analysis.[5] Instead of a substance, the indicator commodity may also be a material, a product, or energy. Material-flow analysis and energy analysis are some of the terms that are used for those types of analysis. Here, they are all understood to be covered by the term substance-flow analysis. Section 7.3 is devoted to an extensive description.

The situation can be summarized as follows; see Figure 7.1. From one

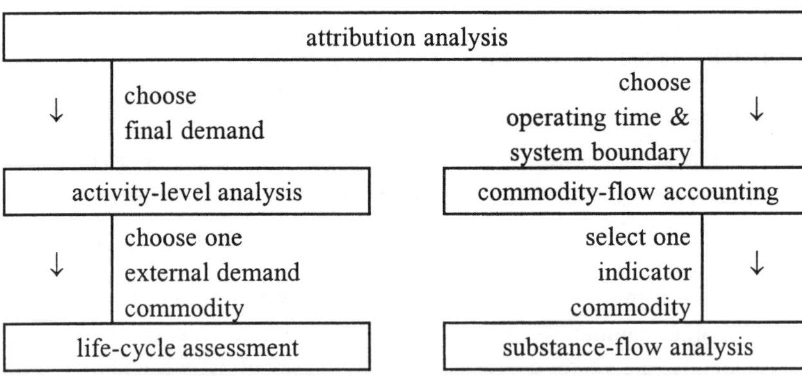

FIGURE 7.1. The crossroad of types of analysis yields two branches, from which two major analytical tools can be derived.

analytical principle in approaching the attribution problem – the clustering of economic processes by means of a linear combination involving operating times – two main modes of analysis are derived: activity-level analysis and commodity-flow accounting. A further concretization towards existing tools for environmental analysis and decision-support is provided by concentrating

4 Baccini & Bader (1996, p. 49) (originally in German: "*Eine geschickt gewählte Kombination möglichst weniger Indikatorstoffe erlaubt eine effiziente und treffende Charakterisierung des Stoffwechsels.*").

5 Again, not all types of analysis that may be encountered under this name are covered by the description to be given below.

ALA on one commodity and by presenting CFA on the basis of one substance. The former analysis corresponds to life-cycle assessment, the latter to substance-flow analysis.

From activity-level analysis, one can derive the tool of life-cycle assessment by making the restriction that the external demand vector contains only one non-zero element. In similar vein, one can derive from commodity-flow accounting the tool of substance-flow analysis by presenting only those fractions of the commodity flows that are associated with a particular substance (or material or product or energy).

Besides these two concrete tools, other possible elaborations can be envisioned; see also Sections 7.4 and 7.5. We will briefly touch on environmental impact assessment and risk assessment.

The derivation of life-cycle assessment and substance-flow analysis is illustrated by a simple example with hypothetical data. It is customary to represent the processes and their interactions in a flow chart, sometimes called a process tree (Figure 7.2). The process data for the four processes in the process tree are given in Table 7.1.[6]

We can easily identify the technology matrix as

$$\bar{\mathbf{A}} = \begin{pmatrix} 0 & 0 & 0 & 1 \\ 0 & 0 & 10 & -0.001 \\ -1 & 0 & 0 & 0.001 \\ 0 & 1000 & -100 & -0.1 \end{pmatrix} \tag{7.1}$$

and the intervention matrix as

$$\bar{\mathbf{B}} = \begin{pmatrix} 2 & 0 & 5 & 0 \\ 0 & 5000 & 0 & 0 \\ 0 & -3000 & -40 & 0 \end{pmatrix}. \tag{7.2}$$

These matrices will be used in the examples on life-cycle assessment and substance-flow analysis below.

6 This format was presented first in Heijungs et al. (1992*a*) and Heijungs (1994*b*); for elaborations see *inter alia* several contributors to Schmidt & Schorb (1995).

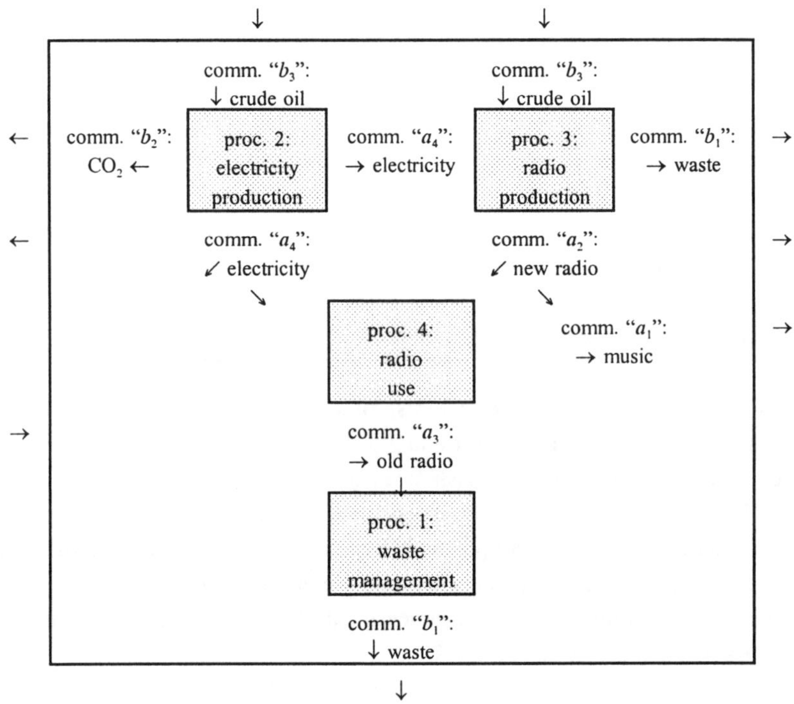

FIGURE 7.2. A simple process cluster; processes are indicated by boxes; the commodity flows are drawn as arrows.

7.2 DERIVATION OF LIFE-CYCLE ASSESSMENT

In the literature,[7] environmental life-cycle assessment (LCA) is defined as an

> ... objective process to evaluate the environmental burdens associated with a product, process, or activity by identifying and quantifying energy and material usage and environmental releases .... The assessment includes the entire life cycle of the product, process, or activity, encompassing extracting and processing raw materials; manufacturing, transportation, and distribution; use/re-use/mainten-

7 Some standard references to the methodology of life-cycle assessment as understood within the present context are: Fava et al. (1991), Anonymous (1992), Heijungs et al. (1992*a*; *b*), Consoli et al. (1993), Guinée (1995), Lindfors et al. (1995*a*, 1995*b*, 1995*c*), and Curran (1996).

TABLE 7.1. Hypothetical data for four economic processes, used to illustrate the derivation of several tools.

	process			
commodity	1: waste management	2: electricity production	3: radio production	4: radio use
"a_1": hr(/hr)* music	0	0	0	1
"a_2": (/hr)* new radio	0	0	10	-0.001
"a_3": (/hr)* old radio	-1	0	0	0.001
"a_4": MJ(/hr)* electricity	0	1000	-100	-0.1
"b_1": kg(/hr)* waste	2	0	5	0
"b_2": kg(/hr)* CO_2	0	5000	0	0
"b_3": kg(/hr)* crude oil	0	-3000	-40	0

* The unit "/hr" in parenthesis must be added for the technical coefficients of the processes, not for the external flow (see also Section 5.3.2).

ance; recycling; and final disposal.[8]

Life-cycle assessment is, among other things, intended to compare the environmental consequences of products that fulfil equivalent functions, thereby taking into account the upstream and downstream activities, such as production of the product and the waste handling of the scrap from the production processes as well. The introduction of the concept of a life cycle means that a small economic system is created that is self-supporting: no imports from or exports to other economic systems take place. There is an interaction with the environment though, and knowing it is exactly the aim of the LCA.[9]

From the discussion above, we can regard life-cycle assessment as a form of activity-level analysis in which the external demand is restricted to one economic commodity output. There are no other flows of economic commodities into or out of the cluster. There are, however, flows of environ-

8 Fava et al. (1991, p. 1).

9 More precisely, the interaction in terms of flows is studied in a life-cycle inventory analysis, whereas the environmental problems associated with it is studied in life-cycle impact assessment (or analysis); see Part Three for a discussion of environmental impacts connected to environmental flows.

mental commodities into and out of the cluster. The calculation of these environmental flows – the environmental interventions – is the aim of the analysis; a secondary aim is often to gain insight into the magnitudes and types of the flows of economic commodities between economic processes. The first aim can be formulated as finding

$$\mathbf{b} = \bar{\mathbf{B}} \cdot \bar{\mathbf{A}}^{-1} \cdot \begin{pmatrix} 0 \\ 0 \\ \dots \\ a_i \\ 0 \\ \dots \end{pmatrix} . \tag{7.3}$$

The second aim cannot be formulated in such a strict way, because a formulation depends on the exact aim; see, however, Heijungs et al. (1992*b*, p. 116 *ff.*) for some examples. Very often it is desired to leave out one of the summations implied by Equation (7.3), in order to be able to study the contributions of the individual processes to the total environmental flow. That is, one studies the matrix

$$\begin{pmatrix} \mathbf{P} & \mathbf{p} \end{pmatrix} = \begin{pmatrix} \mathbf{A} & \mathbf{a} \\ \mathbf{B} & \mathbf{b} \end{pmatrix} \tag{7.4}$$

where

$$\mathbf{A} = \bar{\mathbf{A}} \diamond \bar{\mathbf{A}}^{-1} \cdot \mathbf{a} \text{ and } \mathbf{B} = \bar{\mathbf{B}} \diamond \bar{\mathbf{A}}^{-1} \cdot \mathbf{a} \tag{7.5}$$

where the symbol $\diamond$ is defined as shorthand for the product of two vectors $(\mathbf{a} \diamond \mathbf{b})_i = a_i b_i$, of a vector and a matrix $(\mathbf{a} \diamond \mathbf{B})_{ij} = a_i b_{ij}$, or of a matrix and a vector $(\mathbf{A} \diamond \mathbf{b})_{ij} = a_{ij} b_j$.

In LCA, the subject of the analysis is an amount of function that is fulfilled by a product system, which is understood as the cluster of economic processes which are involved in producing a certain externally delivered service. The specification is referred to as the functional unit. A typical functional unit could be "listening for 5 hours to the radio". Observe that the concept of a life cycle implies that no material products are left after the life cycle has been completed: the small part of the radio that has been depreciated must be treated in a waste management facility. The external demand vector **a** consists therefore of one single economic commodity: 5 hours of radio-listening. The other economic commodities are internal flows only:

among them are radios and electricity, but also commodities that are more indirectly involved: steel, oil products, trucks, and much more. If we apply the rules strictly, every conceivable commodity is involved somewhere. This in turn implies that every conceivable process is involved somewhere. The qualitative flow chart of processes, the process tree, is thus in a theoretical sense the same for every product system (*cf.* Hofstetter (1996*b*)). The amount involved, however, is for most of these commodities extremely small, e.g., the amount of pencils involved in producing 1 MJ electricity is negligible. There is therefore in practice a distinct process tree for every product system.[10]

In the following example on radio listening we have included only a small number of processes and commodities; we have for instance excluded all broadcasting activities. The external demand is

$$\mathbf{a} = \begin{pmatrix} 5 \\ 0 \\ 0 \\ 0 \end{pmatrix}, \tag{7.6}$$

which corresponds to a functional unit of 5 hours of listening to a radio.

The first fundamental equation (see Section 5.4.1) $\mathbf{b} = \bar{\mathbf{B}} \cdot \bar{\mathbf{A}}^{-1} \cdot \mathbf{a}$ gives an easy answer to the question of determining the environmental interventions:

$$\mathbf{b} = \begin{pmatrix} 0.125 \\ 2.75 \\ -1.67 \end{pmatrix} \tag{7.7}$$

or in other words, 0.125 kg of dumped waste,[11] 2.75 kg of emitted CO_2, and 1.67 kg of extracted crude oil.[12]

10 With the compilation of extensive databases (*cf.* Frischknecht et al. (1993)) and dedicated software, we are on the way to involving every process and every commodity in every product system.

11 This is not waste-to-be-processed, as it is considered to flow directly to the environment. The old radio can be regarded as waste-to-be-processed instead.

12 The equation $\mathbf{t} = \bar{\mathbf{A}}^{-1} \cdot \mathbf{a}$ yields the operating times of the processes: $\mathbf{t} = \begin{pmatrix} 0.005 \\ 0.00055 \\ 0.0005 \\ 5 \end{pmatrix}$, so

The inventory analysis is the part of life-cycle assessment that is concerned with the calculation of flows of environmental commodities due to the life cycle of a certain product. It can be derived from activity analysis by choosing one unit of economic commodity as a external demand; this corresponds to the functional unit. In addition to the environmental flows, one may reveal the flows between the different economic processes as well.

The example above was relatively straightforward because it did not involve a rectangular technology matrix: no allocation was needed. We may complicate the example by assuming that the electric power plant (process 2) coproduces along with electricity valuable steam as well. Assuming the process vector to be

$$\mathbf{(p)}_2 = \begin{pmatrix} 0 \\ 0 \\ 0 \\ 1000 \\ 500 \\ 0 \\ 5000 \\ -3000 \end{pmatrix}, \tag{7.8}$$

where the fifth row is the inserted "kg(/hr) steam", the new technology matrix is no longer square, and therefore not invertible:

$$\bar{\mathbf{A}} = \begin{pmatrix} 0 & 0 & 0 & 1 \\ 0 & 0 & 10 & -0.001 \\ -1 & 0 & 0 & 0.001 \\ 0 & 1000 & -100 & -0.1 \\ 0 & 500 & 0 & 0 \end{pmatrix}. \tag{7.9}$$

An allocation procedure must be applied to the multiple process of electricity/steam production:

0.005 hr of waste management, 0.00055 hr of electricity production, 0.0005 of radio production, and 5 hours of radio use. This supplies an easy interpretation of the meaning of the intermediate calculations of LCA (see also Heijungs (1998)).

$$(\mathbf{p})_2 = (\mathbf{p})_{2a} + (\mathbf{p})_{2b} = \begin{bmatrix} 0 \\ 0 \\ 0 \\ 1000 \\ 0 \\ 0 \\ \theta_{17} \times 5000 \\ \theta_{18} \times -3000 \end{bmatrix} + \begin{bmatrix} 0 \\ 0 \\ 0 \\ 0 \\ 500 \\ 0 \\ \theta_{27} \times 5000 \\ \theta_{28} \times -3000 \end{bmatrix}, \tag{7.10}$$

where θ_{17}, θ_{27}, θ_{18}, and θ_{28} are allocation factors such that $\theta_{17} + \theta_{27} = 1$ and $\theta_{18} + \theta_{28} = 1$. Any further choice for these allocation factors θ is speculative (see Section 6.2.2); nevertheless for this example we must take some value: $\theta_{17} = \theta_{18} = 0.8$ and $\theta_{27} = \theta_{28} = 0.2$.

The allocated technology matrix is now square and invertible:

$$\bar{\mathbf{A}} = \begin{bmatrix} 0 & 0 & 0 & 0 & 1 \\ 0 & 0 & 0 & 10 & -0.001 \\ -1 & 0 & 0 & 0 & 0.001 \\ 0 & 1000 & 0 & -100 & -0.1 \\ 0 & 0 & 500 & 0 & 0 \end{bmatrix}, \tag{7.11}$$

whereupon the further procedure is identical to the one previously described. Applying the new intervention matrix

$$\bar{\mathbf{B}} = \begin{bmatrix} 2 & 0 & 0 & 5 & 0 \\ 0 & 4000 & 1000 & 0 & 0 \\ 0 & -2400 & -600 & -40 & 0 \end{bmatrix}, \tag{7.12}$$

we find the environmental interventions that are to be attributed to 5 hours of radio listening:

$$\mathbf{b} = \begin{bmatrix} 0.012 \\ 2.20 \\ -1.34 \end{bmatrix}, \tag{7.13}$$

which of course is different from that before. In fact, the environmental flows have decreased, a fact which can be understood by the observation that the gain in environmental loadings has been transferred[13] to the coproduced allocated amount of 500 kg/hr steam.

> An essential element of the inventory analysis of LCA in solving the first fundamental equation is the allocation procedure, in which multiple processes are split into several effectively independent processes.

In the definition of LCA, we defined a vector of external demand of the form $\mathbf{a} = \begin{bmatrix} 0 \\ 0 \\ \cdots \\ a_i \\ 0 \\ \cdots \end{bmatrix}$: all flows of economic commodities except one – the commodity that delivers the functional unit – are zero by definition. This implies a very ambitious task: every economic commodity that is somewhere involved in producing the functional unit must be traced back to flows of environmental commodities. This means, for instance, that the very small depreciation of the electricity plant that produces the electricity for listening to the radio must be seen as an economic input of a very small fraction of an electricity generator which consequently must be compensated by an economic process "production of an electricity generator". Even if we could manage to include this process, we would next be confronted with the depreciation of machinery, trucks, etc. In practice, therefore, many flows, especially of capital goods and of materials of which only a very small amount is needed, are neglected.[14] This can be done in three ways:

(a) The very small number which denotes the depreciation of the capital good is explicitly put to zero.
(b) A new economic process is added which makes a capital good out of nothing.

13 Of course the operating time of process 2b is 0 here.
14 A term which is sometimes used for these flows is *pro memoria*. Here they will be called truncated flows.

(c) The technology matrix and the external demand vector are split into a "solvable" and an "unsolvable" part.

We will briefly discuss these three possibilities.

(a) This solution is not recommendable, since it hides the fact that this figure is not equal to zero, and it does not allow for an easy reincorporation once data for the production of capital goods are known.

(b) This solution has the practical disadvantage that the technology matrix becomes larger, which might put severe requirements on computer capacity with regard to matrix inversion. Another disadvantage is that a process is included of which nothing is known and which moreover violates material and energy balances.

(c) This option is the preferred solution. It is demonstrated below. Suppose that in the original radio example data on the depreciation of the electricity generator are known: 10^{-12} electricity plant/hr. Suppose in addition that the process of producing an electricity plant is not known. These two assumptions give a new technology matrix

$$\bar{\mathbf{A}} = \begin{pmatrix} 0 & 0 & 0 & 1 \\ 0 & 0 & 10 & -0.001 \\ -1 & 0 & 0 & 0.001 \\ 0 & 1000 & -100 & -0.1 \\ 0 & -10^{-12} & 0 & 0 \end{pmatrix}, \tag{7.14}$$

where a fifth row with the meaning "(/hr) new electricity plant" has been added.[15] The proposed solution is to create a new technology matrix $\bar{\mathbf{A}}'$ that contains the first four rows, and a matrix $\bar{\mathbf{A}}''$ that contains the fifth row, and do a similar thing for the external demand vector:

$$\bar{\mathbf{A}} = \begin{pmatrix} \bar{\mathbf{A}}' \\ \bar{\mathbf{A}}'' \end{pmatrix} \text{ and } \mathbf{a} = \begin{pmatrix} \mathbf{a}' \\ \mathbf{a}'' \end{pmatrix}. \tag{7.15}$$

The modified first fundamental equation is now:

15 For simplicity, no sixth row "old electricity generator" has been added, although it is assumed that the process "electricity plant dismantling" is not known.

$$\begin{bmatrix} \mathbf{a}'' \\ \mathbf{b} \end{bmatrix} = \begin{bmatrix} \bar{\mathbf{A}}'' \\ \bar{\mathbf{B}} \end{bmatrix} \cdot \bar{\mathbf{A}}'^{-1} \cdot \mathbf{a}'. \tag{7.16}$$

This form strongly suggests that truncated flows of economic commodities are to be treated in a way which is identical to the way flows of environmental commodities are treated. A redefined intervention matrix can make this suggestion even stronger: the definition

$$\bar{\mathbf{B}}' = \begin{bmatrix} \bar{\mathbf{A}}'' \\ \bar{\mathbf{B}} \end{bmatrix} \text{ and } \mathbf{b}' = \begin{bmatrix} \mathbf{a}'' \\ \mathbf{b} \end{bmatrix} \tag{7.17}$$

leads to a modified first fundamental equation which is after all not so modified:

$$\mathbf{b}' = \bar{\mathbf{B}}' \cdot \bar{\mathbf{A}}'^{-1} \cdot \mathbf{a}'. \tag{7.18}$$

Here, we have in fact categorized truncated flows of economic commodities as environmental commodities. Continuing the example, we find

$$\bar{\mathbf{A}}' = \begin{bmatrix} 0 & 0 & 0 & 1 \\ 0 & 0 & 10 & -0.001 \\ -1 & 0 & 0 & 0.001 \\ 0 & 1000 & -100 & -0.1 \end{bmatrix} \tag{7.19}$$

for the modified technology matrix and

$$\bar{\mathbf{B}}' = \begin{bmatrix} 0 & -10^{-12} & 0 & 0 \\ 2 & 0 & 5 & 0 \\ 0 & 5000 & 0 & 0 \\ 0 & -3000 & -40 & 0 \end{bmatrix} \tag{7.20}$$

for the modified intervention matrix. The modified external demand vector is

$$\mathbf{a}' = \begin{bmatrix} 5 \\ 0 \\ 0 \\ 0 \end{bmatrix}; \tag{7.21}$$

the last row's zero has been replaced to the still unknown vector of environmental interventions $\mathbf{b}'$. We may now apply the modified first fundamental equation to find

$$\mathbf{b}' = \begin{pmatrix} -0.55 \cdot 10^{-16} \\ 0.12 \\ 2.75 \\ -1.67 \end{pmatrix}; \tag{7.22}$$

an expression which shows the flows of environmental commodities along with the flows of truncated economic commodities.[16]

If, for reasons of data unavailability, certain flows of economic commodities cannot be balanced by processes producing that good or service or by processes annihilating that bad or disservice, the commodity can be categorized as a pseudo-environmental commodity. This means that the truncated amounts are calculated for presentation along with the flows of environmental commodities instead of being balanced.

The discussion above was inspired by the practical problem of lacking data on the production of every good or service or the annihilation of every "bad" or "disservice". Sometimes reasons are given to deliberately exclude certain processes from the economic system, e.g., because the aim is to concentrate on those processes that take place in a certain region. In that case, there will be many economic commodities that are not produced or annihilated within the system, but are instead imported from outside the system or exported to the outside. Concepts like the ecological footprint or the ecological rucksack[17] rely on these ideas. The approach to be followed in these cases would be identical to the approach for truncated flows. In fact, we might consider these imported and exported flows as truncated as well. There is a problem of categorization, however, in the sense that one may doubt if this question can be answered by a life-cycle assessment, or if the tool of substance-flow analysis (see the next section) is more appropriate. See also Van der Voet & Heijungs (1994) for a number of attribution-related questions that are

16 By incorporating the truncated economic flows into the set of environmental flows, we are close to replacing "the environment" by "its environment"; see Section 2.2.1.

17 The ecological footprint is the "area of productive land required to maintain a population's consumption level", while the ecological rucksack is the "volume of material throughput required to maintain a consumption level" (taken from a text that has by now already disappeared from http://www.oneworld.org/overviews/cities/girardet_urbanage.html).

somewhere between the question of pure LCA and pure SFA. Another issue to be addressed in these large-scale questions is of course the appropriateness of the assumption of linearity; see Section 14.1 for a number of remarks.

One last aspect that is worth mentioning is related to the popular wording "cradle-to-grave"analysis to indicate that LCA looks in two directions beyond the use phase and encompasses production and waste treatment as well. We also often see the term "cradle-to-gate" analysis which then means that the waste treatment phase, and also often the use phase, have not been studied. The object of the analysis is in that case not a function, but a material or a product, like 1 kg PVC. We may incorporate these two modes of LCA into the current scheme by observing that a "cradle-to-grave" analysis has a function as the functional unit: a service which represents a non-tangible commodity, and that a "cradle-to-gate" analysis has a product or material as the functional unit: a good which represents a positively valued tangible commodity. We can then easily identify one missing class of analysis, that may be called a "gate-to-grave" analysis, which has a waste material as functional unit: a bad which represents a negatively valued tangible commodity. Thus an LCA of waste treatment is not a "cradle-to-grave" analysis but a "gate-to-grave" analysis.[18]

7.3 DERIVATION OF SUBSTANCE-FLOW ANALYSIS

In the literature,[19] substance-flow analysis (SFA) is defined as

> ... a method for the description and modelling of the flows and stocks of one substance or a group of substances in the economy and environment of a region.[20]

One essential ingredient here is that the flow of one substance or one group of substances is followed in its course through the economy,[21] with special

18 Another way of saying the same thing is put forward by White et al. (1995*b*, p. 42): "the 'cradle' of waste, in households at least, is usually the dustbin.".

19 Some major sources for the methodology of substance-flow analysis (or a similar type of analysis with a different name) are: Van der Voet et al. (1995*a*; 1995*b*) and Van der Voet (1996), Schrøder (1995*a*; 1995*b*), and Baccini & Bader (1996).

20 Van der Voet et al. (1995*a*, p. 91).

21 The substance's flow through the environment will be dealt with in Part Three.

attention to the flows that cross the boundary between economy and environment (i.e., those processes in which the substance passes from an economic commodity into an environmental commodity or *vice versa*).

The set-up of the formalism presented above as commodity-flow accounting can be fully applied. That is to say, in principle a full regional economy is modelled. However, in the presentation of the results, it is not the environmental flows **b** that are interesting, but all flows in so far as they contain the substance or substance group under study. We may envisage modelling the full system and cover it with a "coloured" transparency, such that only the flows of interest are visible to the observer. Suppose that we have chosen to observe the flows of cadmium, and that commodity 1 is pure cadmium, commodity 2 is batteries, and commodity 3 is electricity. The SFA is now obtained by applying a "cadmium filter" that fully displays the flows of commodity 1, that partly displays the flows of commodity 2, and does not display the flows of commodity 3. In other words, we design a vector of transmission coefficients that represents the cadmium content of every commodity flow. Denoting the transmission coefficient of commodity i by τ_i, a transmission vector

$$\boldsymbol{\tau} = \begin{pmatrix} \tau_1 \\ \tau_2 \\ \cdots \\ \tau_i \\ \cdots \end{pmatrix} \tag{7.23}$$

is constructed. In the example of cadmium one might have $\tau_1 = 1$ kg Cd per kg Cd, $\tau_2 = 0.01$ kg Cd per battery, and $\tau_3 = 0$ kg Cd per MJ electricity.

The actual flow of commodity i to or from process j is p_{ij}, which amounts to a_{ij} for an economic commodity and b_{ij} for an environmental commodity.[22] Multiplication of τ_i with this flow gives the flow of the selected substance or substance group[23] to or from process j, a quantity that will be denoted by y_i:

22 As always, negative elements denote flows into the process; positive elements flows out of it.

23 There are two options in the case of a substance group, e.g., heavy metals. The first is that τ_1 indicates the amount of heavy metal per unit of commodity 1, regardless of the nature of the heavy metal. The second is that there are several transmission vectors, $(\boldsymbol{\tau})_1$ for, say, lead, $(\boldsymbol{\tau})_2$ for, say, mercury, etc., with consequently several substance-flow matrices and vectors

$$y_{ij} = \tau_i p_{ij}. \tag{7.24}$$

The matrix of interprocess substance flows **Y** is consequently given by[24]

$$\mathbf{Y} = \boldsymbol{\tau} \diamond \mathbf{P}. \tag{7.25}$$

The substance flows related to the external flows are then given by

$$\mathbf{y} = \boldsymbol{\tau} \diamond \mathbf{p}. \tag{7.26}$$

To illustrate the procedure according to the present formalism, we take up the example of the previous section. Consider the simple cluster of economic processes of four processes[25] with ten non-zero flows; see Figure 7.2 and Table 7.1. Suppose that we have chosen an operating time of 1000 hr. Then we find as an overview of all flows in the matrix of commodity flows **P**:

$$\mathbf{P} = \bar{\mathbf{P}}t = \begin{pmatrix} \bar{\mathbf{A}} \\ \bar{\mathbf{B}} \end{pmatrix} t = \begin{pmatrix} 0 & 0 & 0 & 1000 \\ 0 & 0 & 10000 & -1 \\ -1000 & 0 & 0 & 1 \\ 0 & 1000000 & -100000 & -100 \\ 2000 & 0 & 5000 & 0 \\ 0 & 5000000 & 0 & 0 \\ 0 & -3000000 & -4000 & 0 \end{pmatrix}, \tag{7.27}$$

from which the external flows can be found by aggregation over all columns:

$(\mathbf{Y})_1$, $(\mathbf{Y})_2$, … and $(\mathbf{y})_1$, $(\mathbf{y})_2$, … Furthermore, the procedure described here is not necessarily restricted to substances in the strict sense (Cd, PVC, etc.) or substance groups (heavy metals, chlorinated compounds, etc.), but might also be applied to energy, materials (like concrete), products (like semiconductors), etc. See also Moll (1993, p. 66 *ff.*) and Van der Voet (1996, pp. 4–5) for a discussion on this. We may thus also regard energy analysis (see, e.g., Anonymous (1974), Boustead & Hancock (1979), Nieuwlaar (1988)) as a special case of substance-flow analysis. The end of this section discusses more completely the position of materials and energy in SFA.

24 See the beginning of the previous section for an explanation of the symbol ◇.

25 Processes are referred to as nodes in Van der Voet et al. (1995*a*), as systems in Schrøder (1995*a*), and as balance volumes (German: *Bilanzvolumina*) in Baccini & Bader (1996).

$$\mathbf{p} = \begin{pmatrix} \mathbf{a} \\ \mathbf{b} \end{pmatrix} = \begin{pmatrix} 1000 \\ 9999 \\ -999 \\ 899900 \\ 7000 \\ 5000000 \\ -3040000 \end{pmatrix}. \qquad (7.28)$$

Next the filtering of the substance of interest takes place. Suppose that carbon has been chosen as substance, and that the transmission coefficients are given by

$$\tau = \begin{pmatrix} 0 \\ 1.455 \\ 1.455 \\ 0 \\ 0.727 \\ 0.273 \\ 0.455 \end{pmatrix}, \qquad (7.29)$$

which means that 1 hr music contains 0 kg carbon, 1 new radio contains 1.455 kg carbon, etc. Application of this filter to the matrix **P** gives the flows of carbon between the processes and between the processes and the environment within 1000 hr of economic activity:

$$\mathbf{Y} = \tau \diamond \mathbf{P} = \begin{pmatrix} 0 & 0 & 0 & 0 \\ 0 & 0 & 14545 & -1.455 \\ -1455 & 0 & 0 & 1.455 \\ 0 & 0 & 0 & 0 \\ 1455 & 0 & 3636 & 0 \\ 0 & 1363636 & 0 & 0 \\ 0 & -1363636 & -18182 & 0 \end{pmatrix}, \qquad (7.30)$$

and an external flow of

$$\mathbf{y} = \tau \diamond \mathbf{p} = \begin{bmatrix} 0 \\ 14544 \\ -1453 \\ 0 \\ 5091 \\ 1363636 \\ -1381818 \end{bmatrix}. \qquad (7.31)$$

It may be observed that it makes sense to calculate column totals of the matrix **Y** and the vector **y**: all these column totals are zero. This must be the so for reasons of the materials-balance principle; see Section 5.1.4.

The interpretation of the vector of external substance flows **y** is as follows: 1000 hour of economic activity in the region that contains the economic processes 1 to 4 may be held responsible for a number of inflows of carbon from outside (y_3 = −1453 kg C in old radios and y_7 = −1381818 kg C in crude oil) and for a number of outflows to the outside (y_2 = 14544 kg C in new radios, y_5 = 5091 kg C in waste and y_6 = 1363636 kg C in CO_2). For the economic commodities (y_1 to y_4) the inflows from and the outflows to the outside may be understood as imports from and exports to other regions. For the environmental commodities (y_5 to y_7) the inflows from and the outflows to the outside may be interpreted as extractions of natural resources and emissions of chemicals, the environmental interventions.

The inventory analysis is the part of substance-flow analysis that is concerned with the calculation of flows of economic and environmental commodities in a certain time period. The flows of the substance of interest can easily be obtained by a filtering procedure.

In accordance with Van der Voet et al. (1995*a*) the analysis of the effectiveness of measures is one important application of substance-flow analysis. This means that either certain changes in process characteristics are postulated, or that some external flows are changed with consequences for the operations within the system. An example of the first type is a reduction of the material needed to produce a radio, i.e., a change of $\bar{p}_{73}$. Another example is the establishment of a backflow of old radios for recycling into new ones, i.e., a change of $\bar{p}_{34}$ and $\bar{p}_{33}$. Examples of measures of the second type are a reduction of the import of old radios (i.e., a change of p_3) and a reduction of the use of radios (i.e., a change of p_1). All these parameters can in principle be changed, and their effects can be studied. For instance, if $\bar{p}_{73}$ is reduced one will find that flows of new and old radios will contain less carbon, as will the flow of waste from process 1. If there is a backflow of old radios, process 1 will be less operative. It may be that it will close for some hours per week, thus reducing all coefficients of process 1 by the same factor of, say, 0.9, with subsequent consequences for the waste flows. A similar thing happens when the import of old radios is reduced: the process of waste management will become less operative. A reduction of radio use (say, turning off the radio for 8 hours per day) will reduce all technical coefficients of process 4 by 1/3, which will in consequence affect the operative periods of all other processes.

Consider in more detail the externally imposed reduction of imports of old radios from 999 to a mere 700, the other external flows of economic commodities remaining the same (*ceteris paribus*). This leads to an equation of the following type:

$$\mathbf{p} = \begin{pmatrix} 0 & 0 & 0 & 1 \\ 0 & 0 & 10 & -0.001 \\ -1 & 0 & 0 & 0.001 \\ 0 & 1000 & -100 & -0.1 \\ 2 & 0 & 5 & 0 \\ 0 & 5000 & 0 & 0 \\ 0 & -3000 & -40 & 0 \end{pmatrix} \cdot \begin{pmatrix} t_1 \\ t_2 \\ t_3 \\ t_4 \end{pmatrix} = \begin{pmatrix} 1000 \\ 9999 \\ -700 \\ 899900 \\ ? \\ ? \\ ? \end{pmatrix}. \qquad (7.32)$$

This equation very much resembles the first fundamental equation which was developed for the life-cycle analysis approach, not for the substance-flow analysis approach. Nonetheless, we see the first fundamental equation making its appearance here. The economic part (the submatrix consisting of rows and columns 1 to 4) can be solved and is found to yield

$$\mathbf{t} = \begin{pmatrix} 701 \\ 1000 \\ 1000 \\ 1000 \end{pmatrix}. \qquad (7.33)$$

The interpretation is that process 1, waste management, will become less operative: it will close down for 0.701 of the time, thereby effectively yielding reformulated process coordinates:

$$(\mathbf{p})_1 = \begin{bmatrix} 0 \\ 0 \\ -0.701 \\ 0 \\ 0 \\ 1.402 \\ 0 \\ 0 \end{bmatrix}. \tag{7.34}$$

The modified performance of the waste management process may be inserted in the matrix of technical coefficients:

$$\overline{\mathbf{P}} = \begin{bmatrix} 0 & 0 & 0 & 1 \\ 0 & 0 & 10 & -0.001 \\ -0.701 & 0 & 0 & 0.001 \\ 0 & 1000 & -100 & -0.1 \\ 1.402 & 0 & 5 & 0 \\ 0 & 5000 & 0 & 0 \\ 0 & -3000 & -40 & 0 \end{bmatrix}, \tag{7.35}$$

and this matrix may be multiplied by the scalar $t = 1000$ hr to produce the vector of external flows

$$\mathbf{p} = \begin{bmatrix} 1000 \\ 9999 \\ -700 \\ 899900 \\ 6402 \\ 5000000 \\ -3040000 \end{bmatrix}. \tag{7.36}$$

Finally, the flows of the substance of interest can again be calculated by applying the transmission vector τ:

$$\mathbf{Y} = \begin{pmatrix} 0 & 0 & 0 & 0 \\ 0 & 0 & 14545 & -1.455 \\ -1020 & 0 & 0 & 1.455 \\ 0 & 0 & 0 & 0 \\ 1020 & 0 & 3636 & 0 \\ 0 & 1363636 & 0 & 0 \\ 0 & -1363636 & -18182 & 0 \end{pmatrix} \tag{7.37}$$

and

$$\mathbf{y} = \begin{pmatrix} 0 \\ 14544 \\ -1018 \\ 0 \\ 4656 \\ 1363636 \\ -1381818 \end{pmatrix}. \tag{7.38}$$

Comparison with Equations (7.30) and (7.31) reveals the difference with the situation before a reduction of the imports of old radios.

> When the influence of certain scenarios or abatement measures are calculated with the substance-flow analysis, the problem is converted into an analysis of the activity analysis type: a certain external demand is imposed and the new effective operating times of all processes are established, from which the environmental interventions and other interprocess flows can be calculated.

A last point of interest at this stage is the role of flows that accumulate into a stock. Suppose that the analytical representation of process 1 is given by

$$(\bar{\mathbf{p}})_1 = \begin{bmatrix} 0 \\ 0 \\ -1 \\ 0 \\ 1.5 \\ 0 \\ 0 \end{bmatrix}, \tag{7.39}$$

so there is not 2 kg/hr of waste leaving the process but only 1.5. Application of τ (Equation (7.29)) gives for the associated vector of carbon flows in 1000 hr

$$(\mathbf{y})_1 = \tau \Diamond (\bar{\mathbf{p}})_1 t = \begin{bmatrix} 0 \\ 0 \\ -1455 \\ 0 \\ 1090 \\ 0 \\ 0 \end{bmatrix}, \tag{7.40}$$

which implies that the carbon balance of the process shows a surplus of 365 kg in 1000 hr. Assuming that there is no inaccuracy or incompleteness in the observed flows (see Section 5.1.4), that the transmission vector τ represents the real carbon content, and that there has been no nuclear conversion process of carbon, there is only one possibility: there is a stock of carbon, for example in the form of old radios or of stored waste, and this stock has increased during the operating time of 1000 hr. Although there are possibilities to represent stocks and flows within the same formalism (see, e.g., Georgescu-Roegen (1971), Van der Voet et al. (1995*b*), and Baccini & Bader (1996)), it must be doubted whether it makes sense to do so. An argument for this is the previously discussed assumption that a process is to be described by the elements that cross its boundary (Section 5.1.1). Explicit quantification of accumulations of stocks is at variance with this point of view.[26] Nonetheless,

26 In this respect, the position of stocks in the substance-flow diagram (Van der Voet (1995*a*, p. 93)) is also somewhat peculiar: whereas accumulation in a stock "occurs in products that

accumulation of stocks is an important phenomenon, which could even fit within the situation of a steady state.[27] The quantity

$$(\Delta y)_j = \sum_i y_{ij} \tag{7.41}$$

can therefore be interpreted as the accumulation (or decumulation when negative) of the stock in process j during the operating time of the process.

> Knowledge of stocks is in disagreement with the previously stated principle that a process is defined by the flows that cross its boundary. The only thing that can be observed with respect to stocks are changes thereof (*viz.* accumulation or decumulation). Only a very careful book-keeping can account for unaccounted flows, which apparently have gone to or have come from a stock.

Next we will compare the procedure for substance-flow analysis outlined above with the established procedures for SFA. These would handle the example above in a quite different way. The several carbon-containing flows are labelled x_1 to x_9 according to the scheme of Figure 7.3. Flows x_3 to x_6 are flows of economic commodities, flows x_1 and x_2 are environmental inflows, and flows x_7 to x_9 are environmental outflows. We can easily establish the correspondence between the elements of $\mathbf{x}$ and $\mathbf{y}$. For instance, x_1 corresponds to the inflow of the 7th commodity to the 2nd process: $x_1 = -y_{72}$, and x_4 corresponds to the exported surplus of new radios and is therefore given by the total amount of new radios produced (y_{23}) minus the amount of new radios that is used up by the region ($-y_{24}$). The full correspondence is given by

are produced but not discarded in the same year" (op. cit., p. 94), and the production and consumption are regarded as economic processes (op. cit., p. 95), the substance-flow diagram draws the flow of substance that is accumulated into a stock as leaving the economic processes.

27 This situation is sometimes referred to as a quasi-steady state (*cf.* Baccini & Bader (1996)): all flows are time-independent, but the stocks (which are not represented in the analysis) may be changing at a constant rate.

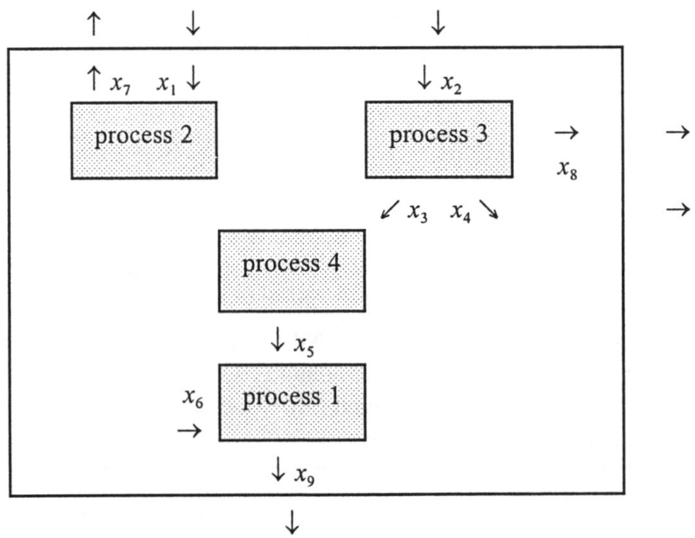

FIGURE 7.3. Process tree for the established SFA methodology for the same example as in Figure 7.2.

$$
\begin{aligned}
x_1 &= -y_{72}\\
x_2 &= -y_{73}\\
x_3 &= -y_{24}\\
x_4 &= y_{23}+y_{24}\\
x_5 &= y_{34}\\
x_6 &= -y_{31}-y_{34}\\
x_7 &= y_{62}\\
x_8 &= y_{53}\\
x_9 &= y_{51}
\end{aligned}
\qquad (7.42)
$$

We first consider the simple example of only three processes, leaving out process 2 as well as the flows x_1 and x_7. A set of equations is constructed using a combination of physico-chemical relationships, the observed flows in the base year, and educated guesswork. Three types of equations occur:

- balance equations based on conservation laws, one for each process (here: $x_5 + x_6 = x_9$, $x_2 = x_3 + x_4 + x_8$, and $x_3 = x_5$);
- formulae based on assumed causal relationships with fixed technical

coefficients[28] determined by observations from the base year[29] (here for instance $x_8 = \alpha(x_3 + x_4)$ and $x_4 = \beta x_3$, with $\alpha = 0.25$ and $\beta = 9996$);
- fixed parameters usually relating to external demand or initial supply (here for instance $x_3 = 1.455$ and $x_6 = 1453$).

Combination of these seven equations gives a matrix equation that can be solved for x_2 to x_6, x_8 and x_9:

$$\begin{pmatrix} 0 & 0 & 0 & 1 & 1 & 0 & -1 \\ 1 & -1 & -1 & 0 & 0 & -1 & 0 \\ 0 & 1 & 0 & -1 & 0 & 0 & 0 \\ 0 & 0.25 & 0.25 & 0 & 0 & -1 & 0 \\ 0 & -9996 & 1 & 0 & 0 & 0 & 0 \\ 0 & 1 & 0 & 0 & 0 & 0 & 0 \\ 0 & 0 & 0 & 0 & 1 & 0 & 0 \end{pmatrix} \cdot \begin{pmatrix} x_2 \\ x_3 \\ x_4 \\ x_5 \\ x_6 \\ x_8 \\ x_9 \end{pmatrix} = \begin{pmatrix} 0 \\ 0 \\ 0 \\ 0 \\ 0 \\ 1.455 \\ 1453 \end{pmatrix}. \tag{7.43}$$

The solution of this equation is found by inversion:

28 Schrøder (1995*a*) speaks in this context of performance variables (PVs), while Baccini & Bader (1996) speak of transfer coefficients (German: *Transferkoeffizienten*).

29 For these observations, we take from Equations (7.30) and (7.31): $x_1 = 1363636$, $x_2 = 18182$, $x_3 = 1.455$, $x_4 = 14544$, $x_5 = 1.455$, $x_6 = 1453$, $x_7 = 1363636$, $x_8 = 3636$, and $x_9 = 1455$.

$$\begin{bmatrix} x_2 \\ x_3 \\ x_4 \\ x_5 \\ x_6 \\ x_8 \\ x_9 \end{bmatrix} = \begin{bmatrix} 0 & 1 & 0 & -1 & 1.25 & 12496 & 0 \\ 0 & 0 & 0 & 0 & 0 & 1 & 0 \\ 0 & 0 & 0 & 0 & 1 & 9996 & 0 \\ 0 & 0 & -1 & 0 & 0 & 1 & 0 \\ 0 & 0 & 0 & 0 & 0 & 0 & 1 \\ 0 & 0 & 0 & -1 & 0.25 & 2499 & 0 \\ -1 & 0 & -1 & 0 & 0 & 1 & 1 \end{bmatrix} \cdot \begin{bmatrix} 0 \\ 0 \\ 0 \\ 0 \\ 0 \\ 1.455 \\ 1453 \end{bmatrix} = \begin{bmatrix} 18182 \\ 1.455 \\ 14544 \\ 1.455 \\ 1453 \\ 3636 \\ 1454 \end{bmatrix}. \tag{7.44}$$

It appears that this traditional way of modelling substance flows leads to the same results. That is to say, for the situation in the base year, there is no difference in result between the proposed and the established procedure for SFA.

That may not come as a surprise: after all, the determination of the coefficients that build the matrix in Equation (7.43) was based on observations from the base year. This exercise thus only proves that no errors were made in constructing the equations and coefficients. The real test is the prediction of the effectiveness of abatement measures. We will repeat here the example of reducing the import of old radios for waste management. In the original example, the amount was reduced from 999 to 700. Now, we must specify the carbon flows, not the radio flows. Each radio was assumed to have a carbon content of 1.455 kg C per old radio. Therefore we must change the fixed parameter $x_6 = 1453$ (= 1.455 × 999) into $x_6 = 1019$ (= 1.455 × 700). This gives instead of Equation (7.44):

$$\begin{pmatrix} x_2 \\ x_3 \\ x_4 \\ x_5 \\ x_6 \\ x_8 \\ x_9 \end{pmatrix} = \begin{pmatrix} 18182 \\ 1.455 \\ 14544 \\ 1.455 \\ 1018 \\ 3636 \\ 1019 \end{pmatrix}, \qquad (7.45)$$

again in full accordance with Equation (7.37), where the flows of carbon were predicted with the first fundamental equation.

Once more, it appears that the traditional way of doing SFA yields the same results as the one that is proposed in this study, although their appearance is quite different. Two questions can now be raised:

- Is the agreement between established and proposed method indeed more universal than can be seen by one or two examples?
- Is there, either from a theoretical or from a practical perspective, a preference for one of the approaches?

To begin with the second question, we can observe that those who developed the established approach encounter a number of problems. It is necessary to construct a number of equations, and to determine values of coefficients. This means that the procedure is quite demanding with respect to time and effort, and that errors may be easily introduced:

> Setting up of a system of equations in a consistent way is the most difficult step for this type of modelling.[30]

One specific problem is that the first class of equations rests on the materials-balance principle. This principle is undeniably valid, but is sometimes difficult to apply, especially when some harmless or otherwise

30 Van der Voet et al. (1995*c*, p. 136). (Originally in Dutch: "*Het opzetten van het stelsel vergelijkingen op een consistente wijze is voor deze modelvorm de methodisch moeilijkste stap*".)

uninteresting substance flows (such as H_2O, N_2, and O_2) were not recorded. Nevertheless the established system

> ... requires each node to have one balancing item.[31]

In other words, one of the flows to and from each process is given the status of balancing item, so that any shortage or surplus of mass is compensated by adjusting the measured value of that flow.

Another problematic issue is that another class of equations is based on presumed causal relationships. It may be difficult to decide what exactly are the causal relationships involved. Moreover, the number of equations that must be specified is fixed for a particular situation. Two instances of evidence are:

> The total number of valves (PVs) necessary and sufficient to control all flows and funds in the system ... is therefore four.[32]

and

> A complete determination of the system requires another $N_{tot}-N = 6$ equations.[33]

This fact could induce one to produce the required number of equations without a careful consideration of the possibility thereof.

The last point raised here is that it is difficult properly to include disconnected processes, such as the process of electricity production in the analysis of carbon substance flows above. This appears to be a very serious point, which has to my knowledge not been discussed before and is therefore discussed in more detail below (see also Heijungs (1997*a*)).

In the case of inclusion of process 2 in the previous simplified example, we could of course observe the flow x_1, the carbon flow due to the flow of crude oil to the electricity plant. We could easily add two equations to the system: the balance equation $x_1 = x_7$ and the fixed parameter $x_1 = 1363636$. This would produce the correct result for the base year, and it would also

31 Van der Voet et al. (1995*a*, p. 138).
32 Schrøder (1995*a*, p. 19).
33 Baccini & Bader (1996, p. 102). (Originally in German: "*Volle Bestimmtheit des Systems verlangt also noch $N_{tot}-N = 6$ unabhängige Gleichungen.*")

produce the correct result if the parameter that fixes x_6 were changed if the last coefficient of the right-hand side of the last equation were changed from 1453 into 1019. The correct results would in that case be predicted – by accident! If for example the process data had included the fact that waste management of old radios consumes electricity, we would have seen a difference in the results. The proposed method would have recognized that the consumption of crude oil and the release of CO_2 by the electricity plant would have decreased because of the reduced activity level of the waste treatment plant. The established methods would have difficulties in seeing that, as the connection of process 2 to process 1 is not via carbon, but via electricity. It could resolve that problem by not fixing x_1, but by establishing a formula for it. As a causal relationship we would postulate that $x_1 = \gamma(x_3 + x_4) + \delta x_3 + \varepsilon(x_5 + x_6)$, on the grounds that the use of crude oil (to which x_1 is related) for electricity generation depends in a multilinear way on the amount of radios produced (to which $x_3 + x_4$ is related), on the amount of radios used (to which x_3 is related), and on the amount of old radios treated (to which $x_5 + x_6$ is related). It is, however, impossible to derive a concrete value for the parameters γ, δ, and ε on the basis of the flows x_3, x_4, x_5, x_6, and x_7 alone. For this we would have to go into the full process characteristics:[34] the information that is present in the vectors of technical coefficients $\overline{\mathbf{p}}$. Thus we see that the apparently time-gaining step of the established procedure for SFA in not collecting information on the flows that are not the topic of the study creates a weak point in the further analysis of consequences of abatement measures. The information of causal relationships otherwise than via the substance under consideration itself is simply necessary to establish the relations between the flows of that substance in a cluster of processes. True, the compilation of data on every conceivable commodity going into and leaving a process is time-consuming, and might seem superfluous if the interest is in one substance only. But it is essential, since the causalities run via all commodities. The

34 Somewhat related to this is the issue of allocation of multiple processes in the case of a rectangular technology matrix. Suppose once more that process 2, production of electricity, is replaced by a process that coproduces steam. If we want to attribute carbon flows to a changed demand for electricity, an allocation of the input of crude oil and the output of CO_2 of the multiple process to the non-existing single process of electricity production is required. This manipulation is straightforward in the proposed approach. One way to include it in the established approaches is to incorporate the allocation factors (see Section 6.2.2) in the coefficients γ, δ, and ε that represent the causal relationships between input of crude oil and output of CO_2 on the one hand and need for electricity on the other hand.

appealing aspect of the proposed approach to SFA is that it is able to establish relations between weakly coupled processes, and that it moreover does so in an extremely simple way. Balancing items need not be introduced (they may be introduced, but not necessarily) and formulae need not be established, because all formulae are automatically implied in the first fundamental equation.[35] A further advantage is that it is possible to use a common database of technical coefficients of economic processes that can be used for life-cycle assessments, as well as for substance-flow analyses of every possible substance or substance group.

In conclusion, it is argued here to follow the proposed approach for the following reasons:

- there is a unified approach for life-cycle assessment and for substance-flow analysis;
- it is possible to use a common database of economic processes for these tools;
- the apparently difficult procedure of establishing physico-chemical relationships and of finding the associated coefficients can be completely avoided;
- although an incomplete mass balance should still stimulate additional data collection (Ayres (1994*a*)), a complete balance is no longer a necessary requirement.

Of course, there are also advantages of the established approach over the proposed one. In the first place, working with coefficients that can be established on the basis of sophisticated reflection instead of using automatically calculated technical coefficients leads to a greater flexibility. In particular, it opens the way to dynamic modelling (see Van der Voet et al. (1995*b*, pp. 142–143), and in particular Baccini & Bader (1996, p. 221 *ff.*)) and to non-linear modelling (see op. cit. (p. 100 *ff.*)). It is argued here that these extensions (of which the added value in practice has not yet really been investigated) might be interesting for scenario studies on the future of environmental problems and on the effectiveness of abatement measures, but that they are not of interest in the context of the attribution problem. The

35 It is perhaps useful to emphasize that there is nothing new or magic about automatic formula generation: the concept of fixed technical coefficients that is introduced in going from an input–output table to an input–output analysis is more than 50 years old.

epistemology of attribution (Section 2.1) requires linearity and implies a steady state.

> A number of problematic aspects of the established approach to substance-flow analysis (the fact that a balancing item must always be introduced, the difficulties involved in establishing causal relations, and how to include apparently disconnected processes, or even multiple processes) are absent in the approach that is proposed in this study. This is an argument in favour of the proposed method for SFA over the established approaches.

A more formal treatment of the question of correspondence between the traditional and the proposed approach to SFA closes the theoretical part of this section. Assume that we have a system that consists of one process with n flows. Then the proposed method would describe this as follows:

$$\begin{aligned} x_1 &= \bar{x}_1 t \\ x_2 &= \bar{x}_2 t \\ \dots &= \dots \\ x_n &= \bar{x}_n t \end{aligned} . \quad (7.46)$$

Given n values of the technical coefficients $\bar{x}_1$, $\bar{x}_2$, ..., $\bar{x}_n$, this system of equations is undetermined unless we specify either t or one of the flows x_1, x_2, ..., x_n. Suppose that we specify $x_1 = y$. Then it follows that

$$\begin{aligned} x_1 &= y \\ x_2 &= \bar{x}_2 \frac{y}{\bar{x}_1} \\ \dots &= \dots \\ x_n &= \bar{x}_n \frac{y}{\bar{x}_1} \end{aligned} . \quad (7.47)$$

We thus find

$$x_i = \frac{\bar{x}_i}{\bar{x}_1} y \quad (7.48)$$

for each of the n flows.

The traditional approach would proceed quite differently. Three categories of equations would be made:

- a balance equation $a_1x_1 + a_2x_2 + \ldots + a_nx_n = 0$, with the coefficients $a_1, a_2, \ldots, a_n = \pm 1$;
- one fixed parameter, as above $x_1 = y$;
- a number of $n-2$ remaining formulae of the form $b_{k1}x_1 + b_{k2}x_2 + \ldots + b_{kn}x_n = 0$, where the coefficients b express assumed causal relationships.

These three classes of equations can be combined into one system of equations:

$$\begin{aligned} a_1x_1+a_2x_2+\cdots+a_nx_n &= 0 \\ x_1 &= y \\ b_{11}x_1+b_{12}x_2+\cdots+b_{1n}x_n &= 0 \\ b_{21}x_1+b_{22}x_2+\cdots+b_{2n}x_n &= 0 \\ \cdots &= 0 \\ b_{n-2,1}x_1+b_{n-2,2}x_2+\cdots+b_{n-2,n}x_n &= 0 \end{aligned} \tag{7.49}$$

or in matrix form:

$$\begin{pmatrix} a_1 & a_2 & \cdots & a_n \\ 1 & 0 & \cdots & 0 \\ b_{11} & b_{12} & \cdots & b_{1n} \\ b_{21} & b_{22} & \cdots & b_{2n} \\ \cdots & \cdots & \cdots & \cdots \\ b_{n-2,1} & b_{n-2,2} & \cdots & b_{n-2,n} \end{pmatrix} \cdot \begin{pmatrix} x_1 \\ x_2 \\ \cdots \\ x_n \end{pmatrix} = \begin{pmatrix} 0 \\ y \\ 0 \\ 0 \\ \cdots \\ 0 \end{pmatrix} \tag{7.50}$$

Abbreviating the square matrix as **Z**, we thus find

$$\mathbf{Z} \cdot \mathbf{x} = \begin{pmatrix} 0 \\ y \\ 0 \\ 0 \\ \cdots \\ 0 \end{pmatrix}, \tag{7.51}$$

from which the flows **x** can be found as

$$x_i = (\mathbf{Z}^{-1})_{i2}y \tag{7.52}$$

for each of the n flows.

Comparison of Equations (7.48) and (7.52) shows that, at least for this simple one-process system, the traditional and the proposed procedure are in full agreement with each other. It also shows that the equivalence holds for each choice of the coefficients b that express the causal relationships and that somehow enter the matrix **Z**. Hence, the proposed description is always equivalent to the traditional one, but rests on the measurement of technical coefficients as flow rates, circumventing the apparently painstaking causal modelling.

The situation for more than one process is not really different. The main feature that enters the analysis is that there should be exactly one externally imposed flow (like x_1 above). Hence, for situations where more than one flow is externally determined (see, e.g., Van der Voet (1995*b*, p. 139)) there is no correspondence with the proposed procedure. In fact, a system of connected processes on the basis of purely technical coefficients (like the proposed one) is incompatible with the external determination of more than one flow (as is done in the traditional approach).

> It can be proven that the traditional approach to SFA, which includes modelling equations to account for assumed causal relationships, is under some conditions fully equivalent to the proposed approach, in which the relationships are expressed in an implicit way, as is done for input–output analysis. These conditions refer to a complete proportionality of all input and output flows of each process in the system.

We return finally to the question of choosing a material, a product or energy instead of a substance as the indicator commodity. There is no theoretical problem in defining the transmission vector τ in such a way that it represents the flow of a material (like steel), a product (like light bulbs) or energy in the chosen region in the chosen time period. Moll (1993, p. 67 *ff.*) discusses "energy life cycle assessment", "material life cycle assessment", and "product life cycle assessment", but these classes do not represent exactly the same as is meant in the present context, and belong more to the previous section on life-cycle assessment than to the present one. Closer in that respect are texts like Brunner & Baccini (1992) and Bringezu (1993) for materials-flow analysis (MFA). Energy analysis, in the sense of Chapman (1974) and Boustead & Hancock (1979), most often concentrates on the energy requirements and/or performance of a product, and can therefore be seen as a somewhat limited LCA, or at least some tool of the ALA type. Energy analysis of the CFA type studies the metabolism of energy of a region, and therefore comes much closer to what Odum (1983) describes, albeit for ecosystems. This section shows that there is no principal reason why there could not be a variant to energy analysis that is concerned with the energy metabolism of a region. Choosing a product as indicator commodity (product-flow analysis) must for similar reasons be distinguished from analysing the life cycle of a product. Again, this section demonstrates its existence.

Despite these possibilities for choosing a substance, a material, a product or energy, all these tools go back to exactly the same type of formalism: the one that is described in this section as substance-flow analysis.

7.4 THE RELATION WITH ENVIRONMENTAL IMPACT ASSESSMENT

Environmental impact assessment (EIA) is a procedure

> ... whereby an assessment is made of the environmental impact which may be expected to result from the activity alternatives.[36]

or, alternatively stated, it

> ... is the process of identifying and evaluating the consequences of human actions on the environment ...[37]

The first definition clearly restricts the scope of the EIA to an activity. This is in contrast to the two approaches discussed in the preceding sections, which both displayed aspects of chain analysis.[38] The second definition is less clear

36 Anonymous (1981, p. 108).

37 Erickson (1994, p. 3).

38 The ALA type of analysis by definition includes exactly those processes that are connected with a certain function that can be externally demanded; this set of connected processes is often referred to as a chain, hence the terms chain analysis and chain management. Strictly speaking, the situation is not that clear for the CFA type of analysis. Here all processes that take place in a certain region in a certain time period are included, even if they are not

with respect to this, but later introduces the term "project" to be the focus of the EIA. An EIA is usually aimed at assessing the environmental impacts of a factory, a road, a recreational zone, and so on. This means that the analysis usually involves two types of activities:

(a) regular activities, such as operation and maintenance of the facility;
(b) singular activities, such as construction and dismantling of the facility.

As the facility is located somewhere, the impacts under consideration are normally restricted to impacts confined to the area. For instance, if the topic is a highway, aspects like noise, odour, landscape degradation and risks are included as far as they relate to the construction of the road and to the use of the road by traffic. Other aspects, such as depletion of fossil fuels or landscape degradation caused somewhere else by removing sand, etc. are typically excluded. Sometimes acidification caused by fuel combustion is excluded as well.

(a) Let us first concentrate on the regular operation of a certain factory. Typically, a factory includes a number of installations, all of which can be described by the process representation of the previous sections. That is, a factory consists of a number of unit processes $(\mathbf{p})_1$, $(\mathbf{p})_2$, ... Some of the commodities produced by one of these processes may be the input of the other processes, e.g., the factory may generate its own electricity. Other economic commodities are imported from or exported to other factories or consumers.

As an example, consider a factory which produces polyethylene (PE), and which consists of two processes: production of PE and production of electricity. The – hypothetical – data are given in Table 7.2. The process data are specified in unit coordinates like kg/hr, which implies that the factory produces 100 kg PE/hr, 20 kg waste/hr, etc. It effectively acts as a metaprocess with coordinates

connected with each other. Via interindustry transactions, most industries will usually be somehow connected, but there is no fundamental reason for this to be the case. Nevertheless, SFA and MFA are often said to analyse chains, and to be tools for chain analysis.

TABLE 7.2. Example data of a factory which consists of a PE production process and an electricity generation process.

commodity	process 1: PE production	process 2: electricity production
kg polyethylene/hr	100	0
MJ electricity/hr	-10	10
kg waste/hr	20	0
kg oil/hr	90	-20
kg SO_2/hr	20	10

$$\bar{\mathbf{p}}_r = \begin{pmatrix} 100 \\ 0 \\ 20 \\ -110 \\ 30 \end{pmatrix}, \qquad (7.53)$$

where the subscript "r" indicates the fact that the regular activities are denoted. When the factory is "turned on" for two hours, the figures double to 200 kg PE, etc. In general:

$$\mathbf{p}_r = \bar{\mathbf{p}}_r t = \begin{pmatrix} 100 \\ 0 \\ 20 \\ -110 \\ 30 \end{pmatrix} t, \qquad (7.54)$$

where t is the operating time during which the factory is active.

Notice that we have so far had no need to distinguish between economic and environmental commodities. This distinction must be made when an inventory of environmental extractions and releases is to be made. Then, we could say that 100 kg PE/hr and 20 kg waste/hr are delivered to other economic agents, that 110 kg oil/hr is supplied by other economic agents, and that 30 kg SO_2/hr is released to the environment. In a subsequent stage of EIA, the resulting impact from the 30 kg SO_2/hr could be investigated.

The economic commodities are left for what they are. Although 100 kg PE/hr could produce horrible impacts, depending on the application and the further processing, and the elimination of 20 kg waste/hr and the production of 110 kg oil/hr certainly has a number of environmental impacts, these are not considered as a part of the factory's operation. As such, they are by definition outside EIA. Taking them into account would amount to expanding the horizon of the EIA to production and consumption chains, a topic that is reserved for LCA.

(b) Thus far, only the regular activities, mainly operating the factory, have been investigated. To account for the singular activities, like the construction of the factory, the share of the constructing processes that were required for installing the factory needs to be calculated. One could easily imagine a computation which yields a $\mathbf{p}_s$ for the singular activities. Computation of the total exchange of commodities would then simply yield

$$\begin{aligned}\mathbf{p} &= \mathbf{p}_r + \mathbf{p}_s \\ &= \bar{\mathbf{p}}_r t + \mathbf{p}_s\end{aligned} \qquad (7.55)$$

However, the notion of capital depreciation over the long term blurs the distinction between regular and singular activities.[39] The transactions table (Table 7.2) can be made more consistent by introducing another row for the commodity "factory", and another column for the process "factory construc-

TABLE 7.3. Modified data of the PE plant, including construction to replenish depreciated capital equipment.

commodity	process 1: PE prod.	process 2: electricity prod.	process 3: factory constr.
kg/hr polyethylene	100	0	0
MJ/hr electricity	-10	10.005	-0.005
factory/hr	-0.001	0	0.001
kg/hr waste	20	0	0.02
kg/hr oil	90	-20	-0.01
kg/hr SO_2	20	10	0.001

tion". A proper accounting would now yield something like Table 7.3. This modification enables one to employ the form

39 Once again, the distinction between flows of materials and funds of services proves to be dialectical (Georgescu-Roegen (1971, p. 225)).

$$\mathbf{p} = \bar{\mathbf{p}}t \tag{7.56}$$

where

$$\bar{\mathbf{p}} = \begin{bmatrix} 100 \\ 0 \\ 0 \\ 20.02 \\ -110.01 \\ 30.001 \end{bmatrix} \tag{7.57}$$

to include both regular and singular activities.

With the procedure described above, we have turned the problem of environmental impact assessment into the problem of commodity-flow accounting for a very restricted region: the small area where a certain factory is located or the area where a road is situated.

The inventory analysis part of environmental impact assessment of an activity may assume the same form as that of commodity-flow accounting with a very restricted region as system boundary.

7.5 THE RELATION WITH RISK ASSESSMENT

Risk assessment (RA), or environmental risk assessment (ERA), is sometimes defined as a

> ... systematic process for describing and quantifying the risks associated with hazardous substances, processes, action, or events.[40]

More often, however, its domain is restricted to the risks due to chemical substances:

> ... the identification and quantification of the risk resulting from a specific use or occurrence of a chemical compound including the determination of dose-response

40 Covello & Merkhofer (1993, p. 3).

> relationships and the identification of target populations.[41]

As is already clear from the term "target population", it most often concentrates on the risks due to toxic impacts.

Risk assessment was already briefly outlined in a quotation in Section 1.3.2. Of particular interest in this part on attributing environmental interventions (i.e. emissions) to economic activities is the step of exposure assessment:

> The component ... that estimates the emissions, pathways and rates of movement of a chemical in the environment, and its transformation or degradation ...[42]

This component is thus of a very mixed nature: for the time being our sole interest is in the emissions. Sometimes this part of the risk assessment is split off and called release assessment:

> Release assessment involves quantifying the extent to which a risk source releases or otherwise introduces risk agents into the human environment.[43]

In that case the exposure assessment concentrates on the processes that take place in the environment. Here this division into release assessment and exposure assessment will be followed as it fits better the structure of this study.

The release assessment aims at predicting the emission rate of the chemical of interest in the region under consideration. Therefore, the procedure for substance-flow analysis (Section 7.3) can again be applied to find the data required.

The inventory analysis of risk assessment aims at a prediction of the emission of a selected substance by the economic activity of a certain region during a fixed time period, e.g., one year. The method that has been developed for substance-flow analysis suffices to derive these data.

41 Tas & Van Leeuwen (1995, p. 357).
42 Op. cit. (p. 347).
43 Covello & Merkhofer (1993, p. 35).

PART THREE

THE ENVIRONMENT

This part extends the discussion on environmental interventions that was the offspring of the previous part on environmental problems. Three stages of analysis are distinguished:

- the inclusion of environmental processes, such as degradation, transport, formation, and growth, leading to the time-integrated presence or absence of degradable and renewable environmental commodities and the permanent presence or absence of persistent and non-renewable commodities that is to be attributed to an economic activity;
- the connection of the presence or absence of environmental commodities (the so-called stressors) to impacts on the environment;
- the connection of these impacts to environmental problems, that is, the degree of "undesiredness" of the environmental impacts as perceived by society.

The analysis of fate leads to a distinction being made between transient stressors and permanent stressors. These may be attributed to an inventory table by means of the second fundamental equation. This equation involves clusters of environmental processes and the integration over an infinite time for transient stressors and the asymptotical amount for permanent stressors.

The analysis of the attribution of environmental impacts according to the epistemological principles from the introductory part introduces the concept of impact factors. These factors indicate the contribution of a unit amount of stressor to an impact category. The procedure for obtaining the impact factors is beyond the epistemological scope of this study. The formal relationship between stressors and impacts is expressed by the third fundamental equation.

A similar story holds for the attribution of the environmental problem to environmental impacts. Here it is the fourth fundamental equation that links impacts to the problem, as perceived by an individual or by a group of individuals. The problems factors which are needed for the interpretation and aggregation into the one-dimensional problem measure are once more beyond the epistemological scope of this work.

Chapter 8

Introduction to Part Three

8.1 FROM ENVIRONMENTAL COMMODITIES TO THE ENVIRONMENTAL PROBLEM

In Part Two, it was argued that a description of the environmental problems that are associated with sets of economic activities requires a full accounting of physical flows between processes, and between a process and the environment. The part was to a large extent devoted to the first fundamental equation: given a certain external demand, what are the environmental interventions – the inflows from and outflows to the environment of environmental commodities? It must be realized, however, that an answer to the main question of this study (which environmental problems are to be attributed to which economic activities) is far from complete with that answer. The only thing we now know about is interventions: flows of natural resources from the environment and flows of chemical substances into the environment.

An analysis of the resulting environmental problem is the topic of this part. When dealing with this subject, a first question of course is what exactly is understood by the term environmental problem. If we look at different sources on environmental problems, we are confronted with a number of not fully unambiguous definitions and a large heterogeneous array of examples: disappearance of birds or forests, household waste, depletion of the ozone layer, decrease in reproductivity of mammals, destruction of historic buildings by acid precipitation, and increase of the world population are all sometimes considered as environmental problems. In general, we can state that environmental problems are only recognized as such when they are perceived as a problem by society. Thus there is an intrinsic value-bound aspect in the definition of an environmental problem. Likewise, statements with respect to the importance of the various environmental problems necessarily involve subjective judgements.

This subjective nature does not imply that an exact treatment of environmental problems is impossible. On the contrary: the subjective judgements involved must be fitted one way or another in the general structure that has been constructed to answer the attribution problem. There are various formal methods that enable this task, for example multicriteria analysis or decision theory in general. And, secondly, subjective judgements with respect to environmental problems can be related to scientifically established relationships between pollutants and impacts and between resources and depletion-related phenomena. It will be attempted to analyse the environmental problems that are the result of interactions between economy and environment in terms of natural scientific knowledge with respect to transport, degradation, and formation of substances in the environment, natural scientific knowledge with respect to environmental impacts due to the presence of pollutants and due to the absence of natural resources, and social scientific knowledge with respect to the way society perceives environmental impacts as an environmental problem.

The analysis can therefore be split into three parts.

- A first stage in this analysis is the representation of environmental processes, such as degradation and transport of chemicals and formation or growth of natural resources.
- A second stage is a description of the impacts that are caused by the (temporary or permanent) presence of pollutants in air, water, or soil, and by the (temporary or permanent) reduction of the amounts of available natural resources. Examples of these impacts could be acidification, global warming, and resource depletion.
- A final stage is an assessment of the overall importance of these (temporary or permanent) impacts. This is the most subjective stage of the analysis, as it involves opinions on the relative importance of different impact categories.

The final synthesis is then a mere combination of the different elements that have been discussed.

> The analysis that was presented in the previous part produced an inventory table that contains a list of environmental interventions: inflows and outflows of environmental commodities that are attributed to a certain economic activity. This part discusses the next stage of the analysis: the interpretation of the environmental interventions with respect to fate, the resulting environmental impacts, and the societal opinion with respect to the degree to which these impacts are perceived as a problem.

8.2 STRUCTURE OF PART THREE

From the above considerations, the structure of this part is fairly simple.

Section 9.1 discusses the environmental process in a way which resembles the discussion of economic processes in Section 5.1 and 5.2. Of course there will be some emphasis on the difference between economic and environmental processes, as well as on the consequences for the further analysis. The next section (9.2) discusses – as in Part Two – the representation of clusters of processes, but now of course processes of the environmental type. These two sections together discuss the aspect that is commonly referred to as the fate of pollutants; however, in a context that is broader than pollutants but that includes natural resources as well. The discussion ends with the second fundamental equation, an equation which expresses the relation between environmental interventions (*viz.* extractions and emissions of environmental commodities) and environmental stressors, which are defined as the time-integrated presence or absence of degradable or renewable environmental commodities or the permanent presence or absence of persistent or non-renewable environmental commodities or economic commodities.

Chapter 10 is devoted to the representation of the environmental impacts that are the result of the (temporary or permanent) presence or absence of certain commodities. An attribution rule – the third fundamental equation – is derived to convert environmental stressors into environmental impacts, and is illustrated on a default list of impact categories.

Chapter 11 enables the final transition to the environmental problem, which is conceived as the societal importance that is attached to the various environmental impacts to which man and his environment are exposed. The attribution rule that is derived is called the fourth fundamental equation, and allows us to map the environmental impacts that are attributed to an economic activity to a single number that is regarded as a measure of the environmental problem.

The impact analysis of the selection of tools for environmental decision-support is derived in Chapter 12. This derivation is much shorter than the one for the inventory analysis in Part Two. On the other hand, there are more substantial deviations from the existing approaches for life-cycle assessment, substance-flow analysis, etc.

Chapter 9

Environmental Processes

9.1 REPRESENTATION OF AN ENVIRONMENTAL PROCESS

9.1.1 What is an Environmental Process?

The previous part included many statements on economic processes and on commodities, both of an economic and of an environmental nature. It seems natural to extend the discussion to include environmental processes, and this extension should appear to be straightforward. It was probably Isard who was the first to suggest such a procedure:

> … the ecologic system is considered as a very large set of interdependent activities, involving as inputs and outputs many commodities, only a few of which correspond to those of the economic system.[1]

Characteristics of the economic processes which were used to develop a theoretical set-up of economy environment interactions were their flexibility of operating times, their linearity with respect to this operating time, and the existence of technical coefficients.

There is an important similarity between economic and environmental processes. Both of them can be regarded as phenomenological evidences of

1 Isard (1968, p. 86).

transformations of commodities into commodities. We have seen that the economist's traditional view of economic processes dealing with economic commodities is too narrow. Every economic system requires the cooperation of environmental sources and environmental sinks. Economic commodities can only be converted into other economic commodities by means of cotransformation of natural resources into emissions. Or, using the entropic principle:

> ... the economic process consists of a continuous transformation of low entropy into high entropy, that is, into irrevocable waste or, with a topical term, into pollution.[2]

The representation of an economic process was cast into the form $\mathbf{p} = \begin{pmatrix} \mathbf{a} \\ \mathbf{b} \end{pmatrix}$, where **a** represents flows of economic commodities and **b** flows of environmental commodities.

At the same time, environmental processes convert environmental commodities into environmental commodities, some of which are the input or the output of economic processes.

> Not only do [environmental processes] feed upon each other, that is provide each other with inputs, but also to the exogenous economic system they furnish final outputs or deliveries (in the sense of exports to the economic system). In turn these ecologic activities are dependent on the economic system (that is currently require or receive from it) various commodities (in the sense of imports) to be used as inputs.[3]

What Isard aims at is the environmental commodity cod, a fish that is an input for the economic process of sport fishing. He extends the traditional economic thinking of production to define the environmental processes that together constitute the food chain that is involved in the environmental process of cod production. For instance (see Table 9.1), to produce 1 kg of cod, 8.333 kg of carnivorous invertebrates are required, along with 1.167 kg of small fish and 1.167 kg of herring. 1 kg of carnivorous invertebrates are produced by means of 10 kg of herbivorous invertebrates, of which 1 kg in its turn requires 10 kg of detritus. He ends up with the environmental process

2 Georgescu-Roegen (1971, p. 281).
3 Isard (1968, p. 86).

TABLE 9.1. Analogue for the technology matrix, after Isard (1968, p. 91). The columns represent environmental processes.

environmental commodity	environmental process: plankton prod.	all marine plant prod.	detritus prod.	herbivorous invertebrates prod.	herring prod.	small fish prod.	carnivorous invertebrates prod.	cod prod.
plankton (kg)	1	0	0	0	−10	0	0	0
all marine plants (kg)	0	1	−1	0	0	0	0	0
detritus (kg)	0	0	1	−10	0	0	0	0
herbivorous invertebrates (kg)	0	0	0	1	0	−10	−10	0
herring (kg)	0	0	0	0	0	0	0	−1.167
small fish (kg)	0	0	0	0	1	1	0	−1.167
carnivorous invertebrates (kg)	0	0	0	0	0	0	1	−8.333
cod (kg)	0	0	0	0	0	0	0	1

of plankton production. Altogether, economy and environment are modelled as each other's complement (see Figure 9.1).[4]

Similar work has more recently been reported by others:

> The set of production activities comprehends both economic production activities and natural production activities of all living organisms as components of the food web (bioactivities). With regard to the transformation of matter and energy there is no principal difference between economic and natural production activities[5]

Observe that only the correspondence between economic and environmental processes is highlighted, not their difference.

A more drastic modification is the introduction of non-productive processes.[6] In the previous part, it was shown that an extension of the

4 A similar structural analogy between the economic and the environmental subsystem is suggested by the substance-flow diagram (Van der Voet (1995*a*, p. 93)).

5 Strassert (1993, p. 514).

6 Recall that a non-productive process is understood to mean a process that does not produce a "beautiful" commodity, such as an amount of iron or a car in the case of economic processes, or a tree or a fish in the case of environmental processes.

		economic processes	environmental processes
		agricul-ture, textile industry, refineries ...	cod growth, herring growth, plankton growth ...
economic commodities	wheat cloth oil ...	technology matrix	—
environmental commodities	cod herring plankton ...	intervention matrix	see Table 9.1

FIGURE 9.1. Isard's linkage of economic and environmental processes (adapted from Isard (1968, p. 87)).

traditional concept of commodities to include bads and disservices besides the traditional goods and services enabled the inclusion of non-productive economic processes like waste treatment (which is not waste annihilation, but conversion of waste into other commodities). The associated non-productive environmental processes are processes which convert pollutants into other commodities. Examples are transport, e.g., from air to water, and degradation of pollutants into other chemicals. These are processes that involve only environmental commodities. There are a number of suchlike environmental processes that involve economic commodities as well. Examples are the processes of erosion and of acidification, affecting economic commodities like crops and buildings.[7]

The criterion of categorizing a process as being economic or environmental is therefore not the set of commodities that is involved. It is the ability to regulate the operating time that makes a process an economic process. The operating time of the economic processes was a central concept in the previous part. It was possible to "turn on" a process for definite duration, at least in theory, such as in the case where 0.0005 hr of radio production was

7 These aspects are sometimes considered to represent environmental impacts. In this part, "events" which convert a set of input commodities into a set of output commodities are treated as environmental processes, and "events" which affect the state of certain entities (e.g., the temperature on earth) are treated as environmental impacts; see Chapter 10 for a discussion of environmental impacts.

needed to satisfy an external demand of 5 hr of music. In principle, it is indeed possible to run the process for that specific duration.

For environmental processes, the situation is entirely[8] different. Human beings possess no power over them. These processes run on their own as they obey natural laws instead of economic laws. A nuclear reactor, turned on for only one second, may produce environmental commodities that are subject to environmental decay processes that take millions of years to complete. Similarly, we cannot give orders to the cod to consume carnivorous invertebrates for a specific time. They just eat, be it sufficient or not to satisfy the consumers' demand for cod.

Although Isard's suggestion to treat environmental processes like economic processes makes sense, it must be adapted for reasons of the fundamental difference between the two categories of processes. In fact, Isard fails to define the formal difference between economic processes and environmental processes, and between economic commodities and environmental commodities.[9] On the basis of the discussion above, the following definitions emerge:

- Economic processes are processes which convert commodities into commodities and of which the operating time (the active period) can

8 Of course there will always be dialectical in-betweens. A fire converts a house into ash and smoke; the duration of the fire cannot be fully controlled, but the fire-brigade can to some extent do so. It seems rather odd to categorize a fire under economic processes, but it can be doubted whether environmental process is a more proper categorization. Another problem is posed by chemical reactions which take place in a chemical factory. Stopping is often impossible. Many biological or chemical processes that are categorized as economic suffer from this problem: can one turn on a composting process for a short while? Still another difficult point is that many economic processes are turned off by cutting the supply of one of the inputs, e.g., by switching off electricity. The environmental process of, say, degradation obviously stops if the supply of the chemical-to-be-degraded is stopped. Is there a real difference? These issues will be left as philosophical questions to be clarified outside the present discussion. Actually, the categorization of processes into owned and unowned processes (Rescher (1996)) is a philosophical development which might have implications for a better definition.

9 He admits this omission, adding a comment on its deliberate character: "... while a classification of processes as economic and ecologic may facilitate our comprehension of a problem, basically such classification is not essential for analysis, provided all processes relevant for a problem are identified and accurately described in an empirical manner." (Isard (1968, pp. 93–94)). Other authors either stick to giving examples of processes of the two kinds (e.g. Van der Voet et al. (1995*a*, p. 95)), or hold that the separation is somehow imposed by the method instead of the other way around (Fischer-Kowalski et al. (1994)).

be regulated by human intervention.

- Environmental processes are processes which convert commodities into commodities and of which the operating time (the active period) cannot be regulated.
- Economic commodities are commodities that flow from an economic to an economic process.
- Environmental commodities are commodities that flow from an economic process to an environmental process, from an environmental process to an economic process, or from an environmental process to an environmental process.[10]

We end by stating a number of complications in the extension of the conceptual representation of economic processes to environmental processes:

- environmental processes run autonomously, and we cannot turn them on for a limited time period;[11]
- environmental processes proceed non-linearly in the course of time;
- the course of environmental processes depends on aspects such as background concentrations.[12]

These arguments mean that the description of environmental processes must be cast in a form that differs from the treatment of economic processes. The general format remains exactly the same, however; see Figure 9.1 which

10 Commodities that flow from an economic process to an economic process via an environmental process are according to this definition environmental commodities. Two instances of such commodities are dioxins that are emitted by an incineration process and that somewhere enter the food-processing industries, and PCBs that are emitted by a factory and that are the input of soil sanitation activities.

11 Connected to this is the fact that environmental processes are not confined to a limited space. In the case of economic processes, we could speak of "this particular steel producer" or "this particular waste incinerator", and henceforth calculate the operating time required to produce a certain demand. For environmental processes the situation is quite different. We can never speak of "this particular algae producer" or "this particular phenol degrader", as environmental processes have no boundaries except for the environmental compartment itself.

12 A comparison with the situation for economic processes may illustrate this point: the characteristic behaviour of a steel factory does not much depend on the amount of produced steel or the stock of iron that is present in the warehouses. Only a shortage of the iron stocks has a clear influence. For some economic processes, such a dependency is more visible: the performance of public transport systems stagnates if too many people use them.

illustrated the concept of an economic process and which could have been exactly duplicated here, the only difference being a replacement of "economic process" by "environmental process".

> Although environmental processes, like fish production and substance degradation, have many aspects in common with economic processes, the role of the operating time is quite different. This aspect serves here as the defining property of an environmental process.

Having defined the nature of an environmental process, we proceed to describe it analytically.

9.1.2 Analytical Description of Environmental Processes

If the set-up of Isard (1968) were to be followed, degradation and transport phenomena of chemicals would be described as in Table 9.2.[13] This,

TABLE 9.2. Representation of degradation and transport of chemicals similar to Table 9.1.

	environmental process	
environmental commodity	degradation	transport
1 (kg substance x in compartment y)	−1	−1
2 (kg substance x' in compartment y)	1	0
3 (kg substance x in compartment y')	0	1

however, can hardly be described as an analytical representation: it is merely a tautology. It is well known that parameters like the degradation rate and the mobility of chemicals are important characteristics for environmental considerations. These are absent in the above description: it is a representation in which the fate of chemicals is not represented in an appropriate way. A representation similar to that of economic processes with the inclusion of the

13 Observe that the rows of this table represent three different commodities, two of which are different in a chemical sense and two of which are different with respect to their position. See also Section 5.1.5 for a discussion on this topic.

empirical conversion rates[14] does not improve the situation.

The fate of chemicals can be modelled by fairly simple laws which follow from elementary chemistry and ecology (see, *inter alia*, Mackay (1991), Hemond & Fechner (1994), Cowan et al. (1995)). Here we will briefly discuss the analytical representations of:

(a) degradation, as an example of a chemical process;
(b) transport, as an example of a physical process.

(a) Degradation means that a certain substance gradually disappears by chemical reactions or biological transformations. Chemists and toxicologist often employ first-order kinetics to describe these reactions (Schrap et al. (1994)). Denoting the amount of chemical 1 which is present at time t by $b_1(t)$, a degradation law is postulated in which the rate of decay $\frac{\mathrm{d}b_1(t)}{\mathrm{d}t}$ is proportional to the amount present $b_1(t)$:

$$\frac{\mathrm{d}b_1(t)}{\mathrm{d}t} = -\kappa b_1(t), \tag{9.1}$$

where κ is the degradation constant (or: decay constant). This differential equation can be solved to yield an explicit expression for $b_1(t)$:

$$b_1(t) = b_1(0)e^{-\kappa t}. \tag{9.2}$$

The conservation laws (see also Section 5.1.4) tell us that decay of a substance implies the creation of another substance, the reaction product, so that the amount of another chemical, say chemical 2 of which the amount present at time t is given by $b_2(t)$, increases according to $\frac{\mathrm{d}b_2}{\mathrm{d}t} = -\frac{\mathrm{d}b_1}{\mathrm{d}t}$. This means that we have

$$\frac{\mathrm{d}b_2(t)}{\mathrm{d}t} = \kappa b_1(t), \tag{9.3}$$

so that

14 The degradation process would look like $\begin{pmatrix} -400 \text{ kg/hr substance } x \text{ in compartment } y \\ 400 \text{ kg/hr substance } x' \text{ in compartment } y \\ 0 \text{ kg/hr substance } x \text{ in compartment } y' \end{pmatrix}$.

$$b_2(t) = b_2(0) + b_1(0)(1 - e^{-\kappa t}), \tag{9.4}$$

neglecting stoichiometric details.[15]

(b) The second example of an environmental process is transport, e.g., diffusion from one environmental compartment to the other. The assumption that is often made here is that the rate of transport is proportional to the weighted difference in concentrations in the two interacting compartments. If the amount[16] in the other compartment is denoted by $b_3(t)$, the kinetics is described by

$$\frac{\mathrm{d}b_1(t)}{\mathrm{d}t} = \lambda b_3(t) - \mu b_1(t), \tag{9.5}$$

the parameters λ and μ being measures of the mobility or diffusivity and also implying some partition coefficient.[17] The solution of this differential equation is

$$b_1(t) = b_1(0)e^{-\mu t} + \lambda e^{-\mu t}\int_0^t e^{\mu t'} b_3(t')\mathrm{d}t', \tag{9.6}$$

an equation which clearly exhibits a dependency on the evolution of $b_3(t)$.

The above two examples demonstrate two of the points exposed in Section 9.1.1:[18]

- environmental processes proceed non-linearly in the course of time;
- the course of environmental processes depends on aspects such as

15 Of course, this is a very simplistic representation of the process of formation of an environmental commodity. Especially for self-reproductive commodities (*in casu* biotic resources), the growth of the reserve also depends on the size of the population; see, e.g., Plourde (1970) who proposes $\frac{\mathrm{d}b_2(t)}{\mathrm{d}t} = \alpha b_2(t) - \beta(b_2(t))^2$. Neglecting the quadratic term, this form can actually be incorporated into the present framework.

16 For reasons of convenience, the laws are stated in terms of amounts and not in terms of concentrations. A careful introduction of volumes in the equations would complicate the notation without providing more insight.

17 In equilibrium we have $\frac{\mathrm{d}b_1(t)}{\mathrm{d}t} = 0$ and hence $\frac{b_3(\infty)}{b_1(\infty)} = \frac{\mu}{\lambda}$. This latter quantity is often denoted the partition coefficient K_{31} related to compartment 3 and 1 (Van den Berg et al. (1995, p. 38)).

18 The other point (environmental processes run autonomously, and we cannot turn them on for a limited time period) was used as the definition of an environmental process in Section 9.1.1.

background concentrations.

This makes it clear that in the present context it is senseless as well as impossible to model environmental processes as activities which convert commodities into commodities according to certain technical coefficients, in a way similar to the specification of degradation and intermedia transport processes in Table 9.2. We definitely need another representation. This representation necessarily involves an analysis of a complex of interdependent environmental processes. In other words, we must direct our attention to the analysis of clusters of environmental processes instead of the individual environmental process. For instance, if we consider the cluster that encompasses the processes of degradation and diffusion, we must take into consideration the combined effects on the commodities (*cf.* Van de Meent (1993)):

$$\frac{\mathrm{d}b_1(t)}{\mathrm{d}t} = \left(\frac{\mathrm{d}b_1(t)}{\mathrm{d}t}\right)_{\text{degradation}} + \left(\frac{\mathrm{d}b_1(t)}{\mathrm{d}t}\right)_{\text{diffusion}}. \tag{9.7}$$

Substitution of Equations (9.1) and (9.5) gives the full cluster description for environmental commodity 1:

$$\frac{\mathrm{d}b_1(t)}{\mathrm{d}t} = -\kappa b_1(t) + \lambda b_3(t) - \mu b_1(t). \tag{9.8}$$

A more complete discussion of representing clusters of environmental processes is presented below.

The facts that environmental processes proceed non-linearly in the course of time and that they are dependent on aspects such as background concentration, along with the fact that the operating time cannot be controlled, mean that an alternative analytical description of environmental processes must be developed to answer the attribution problem. This new set-up must be based on the notion of essentially interwoven clusters of environmental processes.

Before turning to the representation and properties of clusters of environmental processes, some more should be said on the representation of individual environmental processes within the representation of clusters thereof. The discussion above was based on some specific examples of environmental processes. For the purpose of the general treatment it is necessary to generalize the concepts somewhat. As we had in the example above the equations

$$\begin{aligned}\frac{\mathrm{d}b_1(t)}{\mathrm{d}t} &= -\kappa b_1(t)+\lambda b_3(t)-\mu b_1(t)\\ \frac{\mathrm{d}b_2(t)}{\mathrm{d}t} &= \kappa b_1(t) \qquad , \\ \frac{\mathrm{d}b_3(t)}{\mathrm{d}t} &= \lambda b_1(t)-\mu b_3(t)\end{aligned} \tag{9.9}$$

a multilinear relationship between amount and rate of change can be postulated on the grounds of the form of the degradation and transport processes. This leads to a generalization into

$$\forall\ i\!:\ \frac{\mathrm{d}b_i(t)}{\mathrm{d}t} = \sum_k c_{ik} b_k(t) \tag{9.10}$$

or in matrix notation

$$\frac{\mathrm{d}\mathbf{b}(t)}{\mathrm{d}t} = \mathbf{C}\cdot\mathbf{b}(t). \tag{9.11}$$

Here, the coefficients c_{ik} represent the net effects of all degradation and transport processes. In the example $\mathbf{C}$ is given by

$$\mathbf{C} = \begin{pmatrix} -\kappa-\mu & 0 & \lambda \\ \kappa & 0 & 0 \\ \lambda & 0 & -\mu \end{pmatrix}. \tag{9.12}$$

The matrix $\mathbf{C}$ will be called the fate matrix, and is in some sense the environmental analogue of the technology matrix $\bar{\mathbf{A}}$. Apart from the ontological difference of the technology matrix representing economic processes and the fate matrix representing environmental processes, there is a more sophisticated difference. The columns of the technology matrix represent individual processes; the coefficients denote the inputs and the outputs of commodities per unit of time into and from a process. As such, the columns of the technology matrix indicate which input commodities can be converted into which output commodities and at what rate.[19] In contrast, the columns of the fate matrix do not represent individual processes. The elements in a certain column represent what happens with a particular environmental

19 Often, terms like "cooking recipes" (Leontief (1970, p. 263)) are used to indicate this idea.

commodity: does it stay where it is (like commodity 2), is it being degraded (like commodity 1) or will it be transported (like commodity 1 and 3)? They do so not for one environmental process but for the aggregate of them. Furthermore, they do not give any indication of an actual time rate. These coefficients only tell us that there are fixed coefficients of fate, in the sense that, say, one mass unit of SO_2 can produce 0.03 mass units of H^+. The question of what is the rate of H^+ production is outside this analysis. To emphasize the fact that the fate matrix is not a matrix of technical coefficients like the technology matrix $\bar{\mathbf{A}}$ and the intervention matrix $\bar{\mathbf{B}}$, and that it is therefore not derived from a matrix of observable flows (**A** and **B** respectively), the bar is omitted and the matrix is given the plain symbol **C**. See Section 9.2.7 for a discussion of the nature of the process data that are placed in the fate matrix.

We saw above that economic processes involve flows of economic and environmental commodities. We also argued that environmental processes also involve flows of both types of commodities. The fate matrix **C** expresses only the influence of environmental processes on environmental commodities. It is in that sense comparable to the technology matrix $\bar{\mathbf{A}}$ that expresses the influence of economic processes on economic commodities. The counterpart of the technology matrix is the intervention matrix $\bar{\mathbf{B}}$: the matrix that expresses how economic processes affect environmental commodities. We are now in a position to define the still lacking counterpart of the fate matrix **C**: the matrix that expresses how economic commodities are affected by environmental processes. The idea is that the amount of economic commodity 1 ($a_1(t)$) is affected by the presence of environmental commodity 1 ($b_1(t)$). For instance, building materials disappear gradually due to the presence of certain corrosive pollutants. A typical relationship could be

$$\frac{\mathrm{d}a_1(t)}{\mathrm{d}t} = -\nu b_1(t), \tag{9.13}$$

where ν is a coefficient that depends on corrosive properties. The general relationship here can be postulated as

$$\forall\ i: \ \frac{\mathrm{d}a_i(t)}{\mathrm{d}t} = \sum_k d_{ik} b_k(t) \tag{9.14}$$

or compactly as

$$\frac{\mathrm{d}\mathbf{a}(t)}{\mathrm{d}t} = \mathbf{D}\cdot\mathbf{b}(t), \tag{9.15}$$

where **D** is the matrix of coefficients that relate environmental processes to the damage that environmental commodities cause for economic commodities.[20] This matrix **D** will therefore be called the damage matrix. In the example we have

$$\mathbf{D} = \begin{pmatrix} -\nu & 0 & 0 \end{pmatrix}. \tag{9.16}$$

Now, finally, we are able to supply Table 9.1 with the analytical description that we have developed so far: the left upper part contains the technology matrix $\bar{\mathbf{A}}$, the left lower part the intervention matrix $\bar{\mathbf{B}}$, the right lower part the fate matrix **C**, and the right upper part the damage matrix **D**; see Figure 9.2.

	individual economic processes	cluster of environmental processes
economic commodities	technology matrix: $\bar{\mathbf{A}}$	damage matrix: **D**
environmental commodities	intervention matrix: $\bar{\mathbf{B}}$	fate matrix: **C**

FIGURE 9.2. Completed version of Figure 9.1 with the four matrices.

20 This damage must be understood as a purely physical damage: the amount of building material, harvest, or cultural heritage that is lost, without (yet) any relation to the economic value or societal importance of this damage. Another relevant remark here is that the damage not only relates to the disappearance of goods or the appearance of bads (like sludge from canals that has to be removed), but might also relate to the appearance of goods (e.g., increased crop growth due to an increased concentration of CO_2) or to the disappearance of bads (e.g., the corrosion of deposited waste). The word "damage" is in fact too negative to cover these positive influences as well, but is used here for lack of an alternative.

The characteristics of environmental processes can be cast in two matrices: the fate matrix that expresses the inputs and outputs of environmental commodities of the environmental processes, and the damage matrix that expresses the inputs and outputs of economic commodities of these environmental processes. The fate matrix **C** relates the rate of change of the amounts of environmental commodities to the amounts themselves:

$$\frac{d\mathbf{b}(t)}{dt} = \mathbf{C} \cdot \mathbf{b}(t).$$

The damage matrix **D** relates the rate of change of the amounts of economic commodities to the amounts of environmental commodities:

$$\frac{d\mathbf{a}(t)}{dt} = \mathbf{D} \cdot \mathbf{b}(t).$$

9.1.3 The Nature of the Process Data

The data with respect to the environmental processes differ from those of the economic processes (Section 5.1.3). It does not suffice here to measure the inputs and outputs of a process during some time period. Instead, we must construct the fate matrix by means of differential equations that represent models for environmental processes.

In general, the matrix will contain quite some chemical-specific parameters (such as the octanol water partition coefficient, the solubility, the vapour pressure, etc.) as well as a number of environment-specific parameters (the areas of the compartment (such as air, water, and soil), the temperature, the wind speed, etc.); see, e.g., Mackay (1991) and Van de Meent et al. (1993). There is a rich and steadily developing literature with respect to the modelling of the fate of chemicals. Despite competing principles (for instance, fugacity (Mackay (1991)) versus concentration (Van de Meent et al. (1991))), and competing equations for modelling certain environmental processes, there appears to be quite some convergence as to the results (Cowan et al. (1995)).

The fate matrix will also contain coefficients that are related to other environmental commodities than chemicals, especially to the "fate" of natural resources. Most important parameters here are the rate of formation (or: growth) and the rate of consumption of other environmental commodities. The damage matrix contains information on the transformation of economic commodities (conversion of buildings into ruins, increased growth of crops) due to the presence of environmental commodities. At this time, not much is known about the resource aspects of the fate matrix and about the damage matrix. Also, the formation of reaction products (or: decay products) by degradation of chemicals is an area that is not usually covered by multimedia models. The present structure, however, enables an easy incorporation once coefficients are known. More complex forms of the formation of reaction products, such as the increase of heavy-metal mobility due to acidification of the soil, could in theory be inserted as well.

> The fate matrix and the damage matrix contain coefficients that must be found by modelling environmental processes. The best-developed aspects that can be used to construct a fate matrix are the transport and degradation of chemicals, that are modelled by multimedia models. The aspects of decay products, resource growth, and transformation of economic commodities still need further attention.

9.2 CLUSTERS OF ENVIRONMENTAL PROCESSES

9.2.1 The Time-Integrated Presence or Absence of Environmental Commodities: Transient Stressors

If we operate a nuclear reactor for, say, one second, we must take the environmental consequences for more than one second into account. On the other hand, after millions of years, the impacts have ceased to exist. So, we must not look at the impacts that occur after an infinite time. Neither must we look at the impacts after, say, 100 years. We must look at what happens in the period between the introduction of a radioactive substance into the environment and the time of disappearance, which is usually infinity. To be more precise, what must be taken into account is the time-integrated environmental impacts from $t = 0$ to $t = \infty$.[21]

21 One may consider discounting future problems. In that case, there is no simple time-integration here, but a modified form with a parameter indicating the rate of time preference. This discounting is not applied here, as it introduces value-bound elements into the analysis of facts that is discussed in this chapter. Should one consider discounting future problems

The same argument applies to impacts of hazardous chemicals. The environmental impacts of the release of a pollutant during a short time period must be accounted for during the total period that the pollutant or its decay products can be found in some compartment of the environment.[22] Moreover, it is the cumulated impacts which must be accounted for, and an infinite time period is the only guarantee of a full accounting of cumulated impacts.

If a chemical is released at $t = 0$ in an amount b_1,[23] we now postulate that a measure of the environmental exposure[24] to that chemical is given by the time-integrated amount of the pollutant present in some compartment:

$$c_1 = \int_0^\infty b_1(t)\mathrm{d}t. \tag{9.17}$$

Observe that this quantity c_1 is not a concentration; neither is it a mass: its unit is kg·hr, and the quantity will be called the time-integrated presence of the chemical.

The function $b_1(t)$ can be of a complicated nature. For instance, if we study the amount of a pollutant that can be found in an aquatic environment when an atmospheric emission of that pollutant has taken place, we will see no aquatic amounts at $t = 0$, then a gradual rise because of intermedia transport, and a final exponential tail. The proposed measure of environmental

in Chapter 11, one is forced to redo parts of the analysis that is undertaken in Section 9.2. See also Section 9.2.3 for a brief discussion in a related context.

22 Some authors distinguish besides the economy (or technosphere) and the environment (or ecosphere), the substrate (or lithosphere) in which pollutants are considered to be immobilized without being able to induce adverse impacts. The term lithosphere is sometimes considered to be too narrow, because *inter alia* the upper atmosphere, the deeper groundwater and the sediments are included in this term as well. This study uses the term environment to include also the substrate. The fact that no organisms are living there does not give a principal reason to exclude these parts of the world from the environment. In Chapter 10, we will see that the impact factors are zero in these regions, so that they indeed do not contribute to what is perceived as an environmental problem. For practical reasons, however, one may define some parts of the environment as being outside the analytical environment.

23 We use the symbol $b_i(t)$ to indicate the time-dependent amount of a certain environmental commodity that is present somewhere. The environmental intervention is denoted by a plain b_i. Thus, in the absence of a background level of the chemical due to non-anthropogenic or previous anthropogenic releases, $b_i(0) = b_i$.

24 We speak with caution here of a measure of the exposure, and not of a measure of the impact, as the intrinsic capacity to cause harm (e.g., the toxicity or the radiative forcing) is not (yet – see Chapter 10) taken into account.

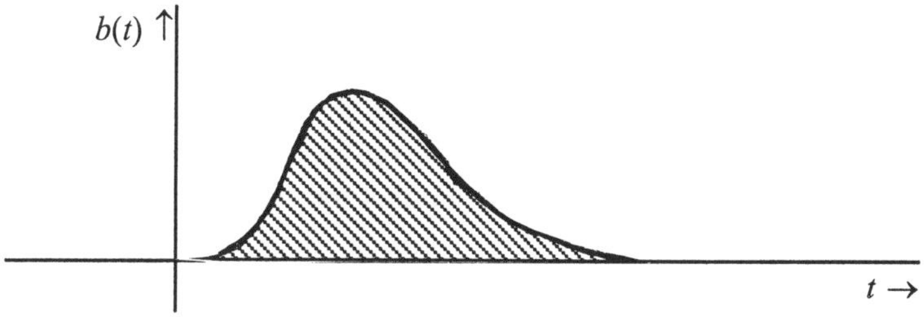

FIGURE 9.3. A measure of environmental exposure.

exposure to the chemical is graphically illustrated in Figure 9.3.

An example may illustrate this. If a chemical decays[25] according to

$$\frac{db_1(t)}{dt} = -\kappa b_1(t), \tag{9.18}$$

then the measure of the environmental exposure c_1 to commodity 1 turns out to be

$$c_1 = \frac{b_1}{\kappa}. \tag{9.19}$$

For a more general situation we may extend the definition of the time-integrated presence of a certain chemical in a certain compartment as:

$$\mathbf{c} = \int_0^\infty \mathbf{b}(t)\mathrm{d}t, \tag{9.20}$$

where the elements c_i and b_i of the vectors **c** and **b** denote time-integrated presences and amounts related to environmental commodity *i*. Another extension applies to the situation where there is already a certain steady-state background[26] b_{bg} of the chemical and where $b(0)$ is therefore given by $b(0) = b_{bg} + b$:

$$\mathbf{c} = \int_0^\infty (\mathbf{b}(t) - \mathbf{b}_{bg})\mathrm{d}t, \tag{9.21}$$

25 The situation for persistent substances is discussed in Section 9.2.3.

26 A later discussion on the relation between background levels and the coefficients of the differential equations will reveal some further properties; see Sections 9.2.2 and 9.2.7.

which is illustrated for one compartment in Figure 9.4.[27] It should be observed that usage of the term "presence" is in fact inspired by the situation without a background concentration (Figure 9.3). In including background concentrations (Figure 9.4), the word receives a more abstract meaning, because there is already a certain amount present. What is meant by "presence" is therefore the surplus to the background.

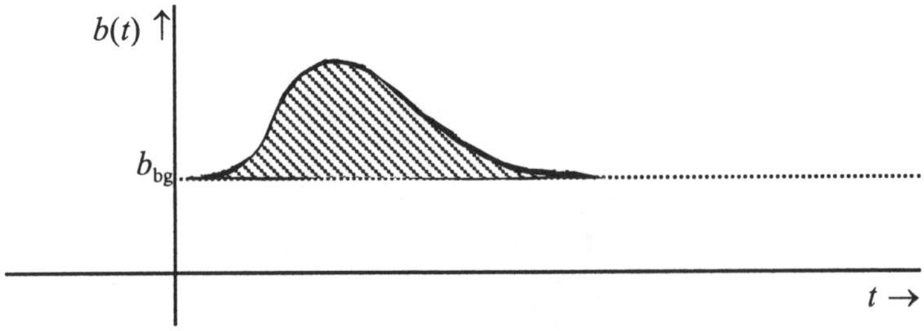

FIGURE 9.4. Interpretation of the measure of environmental exposure in the case of a background level.

Looking back to Isard's scheme of cod production, does it fit into the analytical description proposed above? It does. If we realize that the environmental process of degradation of substance x corresponds to a conversion of substance x into substance x', it is a small further step to give this process an alternative name: formation of substance x'. The two terms "degradation" and "formation" are in fact members of the same family of conversion processes. Transport can be seen as another member: substance x in compartment y is converted into substance x in compartment y'.[28] It can therefore be concluded that all environmental processes can be regarded as phenomenological evidences[29] of conversion processes of commodities into commodities: either by degradation, by formation, or by transport.

27 A steady-state background concentration will be the result of a continuous environmental intervention flow ϕ. This means that the homogeneous differential equation (9.11) changes into $\frac{d\mathbf{b}(t)}{dt} = \mathbf{C}\cdot\mathbf{b}(t) + \phi$. It is easily shown that $\mathbf{b}_{bg} = \mathbf{b}(\infty) = -\mathbf{C}^{-1}\cdot\phi$.

28 Here, again, we see that the same chemical in two different compartments can be regarded as two different commodities; see Section 5.1.5.

29 I write phenomenological because the environmental processes are – like the economic processes in Section 5.1 – considered as a black box here.

A consequence of this analogy is that, whereas output-related impacts should be measured by the time-integrated presence of environmental commodities, input-related impacts should be measured by the time-integrated

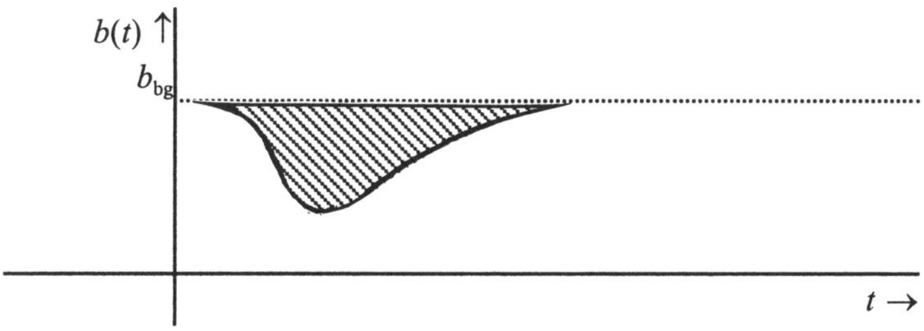

FIGURE 9.5. Time-integrated absence for environmental inputs like natural resources.

absence[30] of environmental commodities (Figure 9.5).[31] The procedure is fully equivalent in a mathematical sense: the fate matrix contains coefficients that relate to presence and coefficients that relate to absence of environmental commodities.[32] The resulting number c can represent either a presence or an absence: a positive value indicates a time-integrated presence and a negative value indicates a time-integrated absence.

The time-integrated presence or absence of environmental commodities is a concept that plays an important role in this chapter. We introduce the term

30 It should be emphasized that the word absence denotes here a reduced presence, as is illustrated in Figure 9.5. It therefore does not mean that an environmental commodity is "not there", but merely that the amount that is "there" is reduced by a certain amount.

31 Like the restriction of Figure 9.4 to degradable substances, Figure 9.5 is only valid for renewable resources. The approach to be followed for non-renewable resources is discussed in Section 9.2.3 together with that of persistent substances.

32 Use of the word fate is of course inspired by the discussion on pollutants. Its use is extended here to cover, e.g., growth of extracted resources as well. This can be justified on two grounds: the regeneration of a resource determines the fate of the reserve, and the fact that formation and degradation are considered to be identical means that regeneration of resources implies the disappearance (and thereby the fate) of other environmental commodities.

environmental stressors (Wegener Sleeswijk & Heijungs (1996))[33] (or briefly: stressors) to indicate in general the result of the calculations of the fate of the environmental commodities that are introduced by environmental interventions. The time-integrated presence of degradable commodities and the time-integrated absence of renewable commodities will then be referred to as transient stressors, to indicate their transient nature. In Section 9.2.3 we will introduce in contrast permanent stressors to account for the permanent presence or absence of persistent and non-renewable commodities.

The time-integrated presence or absence of an environmental commodity is used for including environmental processes in the attribution of environmental problems to economic activities. In principle it involves constructing and solving a set of differential equations that are based on chemical, physical, and biological processes in the environment: degradation, formation, transport, growth, etc. The result of these calculations is referred to as the set of transient stressors. The time-integrated presence or absence of environmental commodities is defined as the vector **c**:

$$\mathbf{c} = \int_0^\infty (\mathbf{b}(t) - \mathbf{b}_{\text{bg}})\mathrm{d}t,$$

where the vector $\mathbf{b}(t)$ contains the amounts of environmental commodities at time t, and $\mathbf{b}_0$ is the amount that was present before the economic activity was begun at $t = 0$.

9.2.2 Using the Fate Matrix to Calculate the Time-Integrated Presence or Absence

The problem of working with the time-integrated presence or absence **c** is that it is a very elaborate and time-consuming procedure to calculate it:

33 This term is inspired by Fava et al. (1993, p. 11): "Stressors are conditions that may lead to human health or ecological health impairment or to resource depletion", although its meaning in the present context is different from the one introduced there. Although the term may appear to suggest that stress indeed is exerted, the meaning here is devoid of an impact connotation. Stressors are in principle defined independently from impacts.

- first we must draw up a system of differential equations for $\frac{d\mathbf{b}(t)}{dt}$;
- next we have to solve this system and express $\mathbf{b}(t)$;
- finally we have to integrate this over t.

It is therefore tempting to investigate the existence of short-cuts for this procedure. One such short-cut is provided by a theorem due to Heijungs (1995*a*, p. 219). If a system of differential equations is given by

$$\frac{d\mathbf{b}(t)}{dt} = \mathbf{C}\cdot\mathbf{b}(t) + \boldsymbol{\phi}, \tag{9.22}$$

then the steady-state solution is given by

$$\mathbf{b}_{bg} = -\mathbf{C}^{-1}\cdot\boldsymbol{\phi}. \tag{9.23}$$

Furthermore, the time-integrated presence or absence defined by

$$\mathbf{c} = \int_0^\infty (\mathbf{b}(t) - \mathbf{b}_{bg})dt \tag{9.24}$$

due to a release $\mathbf{b}$ at time $t = 0$ is found by

$$\mathbf{c} = -\mathbf{C}^{-1}\cdot\mathbf{b}. \tag{9.25}$$

In other words, we may apply the equation

$$\mathbf{c} = -\mathbf{C}^{-1}\cdot\mathbf{b} \tag{9.26}$$

instead of the complicated three-step procedure described above. It is no longer necessary to solve the system of differential equations and to integrate over an infinite time. It suffices to construct the system of differential equations, and to invert the matrix of coefficients. That is, it suffices to establish the fate matrix $\mathbf{C}$ and to invert it. Indeed, as $-(-\kappa)^{-1} = \frac{1}{\kappa}$, we see how easy it is to derive Equation (9.19) with this theorem.

An alternative interpretation for the table of degradation and intermedia transport processes can now be conceived: the columns of the matrix $\mathbf{C}$ do not denote environmental processes (conversions of commodities into commodities), but denote lists of fate coefficients. An element of the matrix $-\mathbf{C}^{-1}$, say $(-\mathbf{C}^{-1})_{ik}$, denotes a measure of the time-integrated exposure to commodity i due to a unit emission (or extraction) of commodity k.[34]

34 Recall the meaning of commodity in this context: phenol and mercury are two different commodities, but mercury in air and mercury in water are different commodities as well (see

The negative inverse of the fate matrix is therefore a very important quantity, as it allows one easily to calculate the time-integrated presence or absence of environmental commodities that are connected to an environmental intervention **b**. The elements of **b** represent inputs (negative) and outputs (positive), and are found by means of the first fundamental equation $\mathbf{b} = \bar{\mathbf{B}} \cdot \bar{\mathbf{A}}^{-1} \cdot \mathbf{a}$ that was derived in Section 5.4.1. The time-integrated presence and absence of environmental commodities, the transient stressors **c**, can thus directly be found from the identity

$$\mathbf{c} = -\mathbf{C}^{-1} \cdot \bar{\mathbf{B}} \cdot \bar{\mathbf{A}}^{-1} \cdot \mathbf{a}, \tag{9.27}$$

where $\bar{\mathbf{A}}$ is the technology matrix, $\bar{\mathbf{B}}$ is the intervention matrix, **C** is the fate matrix, and **a** is the external demand for a certain amount of economic commodities.

> The time-integrated presence or absence of degradable or renewable environmental commodities can easily be found by using the fate matrix. The short-cut is to postmultiply the negative inverse of the fate matrix with the vector of environmental interventions:
>
> $$\mathbf{c} = -\mathbf{C}^{-1} \cdot \mathbf{b}.$$

9.2.3 The Permanent Presence or Absence of Commodities: Permanent Stressors

The procedure developed so far is only applicable to emissions of degradable substances and extractions of renewable resources. The example in the previous section already poses difficulties: the fate matrix **C** of Equation (9.12) cannot be inverted because it has a zero determinant. The reason for this is that the second column of **C** contains only zeroes, which reflects that none of the differential equations contains a dependency on $b_2(t)$. If, for instance, differential equation for commodity 2 contained a term via which

Section 5.1.5). The fate matrix **C** shows how environmental commodities that were released in some form lead to a time-integrated exposure in all types of forms. Many entries of **C** will be zero, as it is well known that an emission of phenol to water will not lead to a mercury-related exposure.

matter disappeared, e.g., $\frac{db_2(t)}{dt} = \kappa b_1(t) - \mu b_2(t)$, the fate matrix would have been invertible. In the present situation the time-integrated exposure to commodity 2 increases with the integration time and therefore is infinitely high in the case of an infinite integration time. A similar situation occurs for non-renewable natural resources: the time-integrated absence is infinite if no regeneration term is included. The same problem also exists for economic commodities that are affected by the presence or absence of environmental commodities: the corrosion of building materials is in principle permanent.

There are several ways to solve this problem:

(a) allow for infinitely high scores;
(b) always introduce a degradation or regeneration mechanism;
(c) use a finite integration time;
(d) introduce time discounting;
(e) review the definition of the measure of exposure.

The relevance and implications of each of them will be explored below.

(a) Allowing for infinitely high scores at first seems to be the best choice: emission of infinitely persistent chemicals and extraction of infinitely non-renewable resources is considered to be more serious than the emission of any degradable substance or the extraction of any renewable resource. This, however, creates some problems. Apart from the computational difficulties involved in finding an expression for the exposure **c**, there is the problem that we still want to discriminate between 1 kg and 2 kg of a persistent chemical, and similarly between 1 kg and 2 kg of a non-renewable resource. By stating that all of them lead to an infinite score, we would not be able to see the distinction of amounts, let alone of intrinsic differences in hazard and abundance respectively. An emission of one gram of a noble gas would in that case be equally – infinitely – bad as an emission of 10 kg of a heavy metal.[35]

(b) The introduction of a degradation mechanism conforms to the belief that ultimately all pollutants will be destroyed.[36] It is questionable whether

35 One may try to resolve this by going into Cantor's theory of transfinite numbers, where a comparison of different kinds of inifinity is possible.

36 It could be argued that the introduction of a degradation mechanism in the deep sediment is justified by the fact that the substance has become immobilized, and that impacts are no

this is true, and whether it makes sense to postulate so. In the first place some pollutants are really very persistent, and a crude estimation of a degradation time, say 10^{12} hr, may well be outside reality by quite a few orders of magnitude. In the second place, the law of conservation of matter implies that by degradation of a substance another substance is created.[37]

(c) Instead of an infinite integration time, we could reduce the integration time to some finite value, say, t_{int} and define the time-integrated exposure as $\mathbf{c} = \int_0^{t_{\text{int}}} (\mathbf{b}(t) - \mathbf{b}_{\text{bg}})\mathrm{d}t$. Here again, we are faced with a quite arbitrary decision with large consequences: what is t_{int}? In some contexts, a few hundred years is used (e.g., for climate change impacts; see Shine et al. (1990, p. 58)), but it could also be argued that the estimated future time span of existence of life on earth should be the parameter of concern.

(d) Time discounting means that impacts in the future are considered to be less important than impacts now. One formal way to achieve this is to introduce a discounting term e^{-rt} in the definition of the time-integrated presence or absence: $\mathbf{c} = \int_0^{\infty} (\mathbf{b}(t) - \mathbf{b}_{\text{bg}})e^{-rt}\mathrm{d}t$, where r is the rate of discounting. Time discounting means that the time-integrated exposure converges to a finite value, even when $b(t)$ does not vanish. Apart from the technical advantage of being able to deal with persistent pollutants and the theoretical disadvantage of introducing another quite arbitrary parameter r, there are a number of ethical problems associated with discounting (see, e.g., Pearce & Turner (1990, p. 217 *ff.*)).

(e) The last solution discussed here is to define another measure of environmental exposure for those pollutants that would otherwise lead to infinite measures. One measure for this could be the (asymptotical) amount of permanently present or absent commodity. This measure may be argued from the consideration that the increased accumulated stock of a certain pollutant is that quantity that is to be attributed to the economic activities that contribute to that increase. The commodities that do not lead to infinitely high

longer likely to occur. This latter fact may in itself be true. It is however not an argument that the chemical has degraded. Although immobile and not exerting impacts, it is still there. This case should therefore be considered in a pure fate analysis (this chapter) and only be dropped in an impact analysis (Chapter 10).

37 Excluding the conversion of matter into available energy through Einstein's equation.

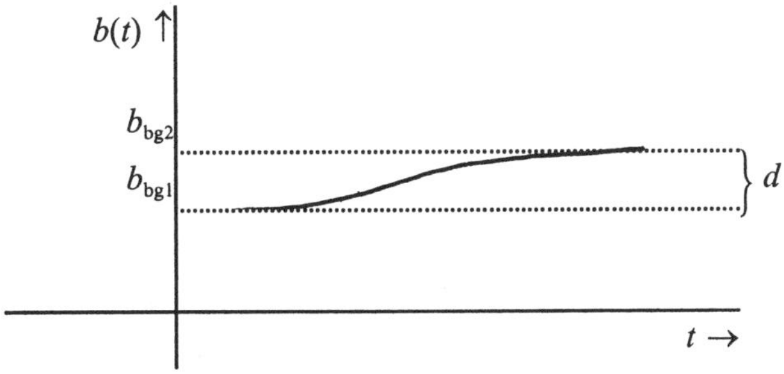

FIGURE 9.6. The asymptotical increase d of background concentration due to the release of a persistent chemical.

scores can then be treated in the usual way: $\mathbf{c} = \int_0^\infty (\mathbf{b}'(t) - \mathbf{b}_{bg}')\,dt$ where $\mathbf{b}'(t)$ represents those elements of the original vector $\mathbf{b}(t)$ that correspond to degradable chemicals and renewable resources. The persistent chemicals and non-renewable resources are then put in a separate vector $\mathbf{b}''(t)$, and the measure of environmental exposure to those environmental commodities is defined as $\mathbf{d} = \lim_{t\to\infty} (\mathbf{b}''(t) - \mathbf{b}_{bg}'')$. This option is sketched in Figure 9.6 and illustrated with an example below.

The example fate matrix of Equation (9.12) could not be inverted because there was no steady-state solution for $b_2(t)$. Therefore we split the vector $\mathbf{b}(t)$ into two vectors: one vector $\mathbf{b}'(t)$ containing $b_1(t)$ and $b_3(t)$ and the other vector $\mathbf{b}''(t)$ containing $b_2(t)$:

$$\mathbf{b}(t) = \begin{bmatrix} \mathbf{b}''(t) \\ \mathbf{b}'(t) \end{bmatrix} \tag{9.28}$$

If we reduce the fate matrix by excluding the second row and the second column, we end up with a set of differential equations for the remaining environmental commodities which have been put into the vector $\mathbf{b}'(t)$:

$$\frac{d\mathbf{b}'(t)}{dt} = \mathbf{C}' \cdot \mathbf{b}'(t) = \begin{bmatrix} -\kappa-\mu & \lambda \\ \lambda & -\mu \end{bmatrix} \cdot \mathbf{b}'(t). \tag{9.29}$$

The reduced fate matrix $\mathbf{C}'$ can easily be inverted and multiplied by the reduced vector of environmental interventions (see Equation (9.26)):[38]

$$\mathbf{c} = -\mathbf{C}'^{-1}\cdot\mathbf{b}' = \frac{1}{-\lambda^2+\kappa\mu+\mu^2}\begin{bmatrix} -\mu & -\lambda \\ -\lambda & -\kappa-\mu \end{bmatrix}\cdot\mathbf{b}'. \tag{9.30}$$

For the differential equation that was left out and for the economic commodities that are the input or output of environmental processes, another procedure may be followed. The entries of $\mathbf{b}(t)$ that were left out in defining $\mathbf{b}'(t)$, *viz.* $\mathbf{b}''(t)$, can be merged into the vector of economic commodities $\mathbf{a}(t)$ such that the vector $\mathbf{a}'(t)$ that is defined by

$$\mathbf{a}'(t) = \begin{bmatrix} \mathbf{a}(t) \\ \mathbf{b}''(t) \end{bmatrix} \tag{9.31}$$

can be constructed. For this vector, the system of differential equations

$$\frac{\mathrm{d}\mathbf{a}'(t)}{\mathrm{d}t} = \mathbf{D}'\cdot\mathbf{b}(t), \tag{9.32}$$

where $\mathbf{D}'$ is the modified[39] damage matrix, holds. For the example (*cf.* Equation (9.16)), this matrix is given by

$$\mathbf{D}' = \begin{bmatrix} -\nu & 0 \\ \kappa & 0 \end{bmatrix}. \tag{9.33}$$

Solving the differential equations for $\mathbf{a}'(t)$ enables one to define the amount of commodities that is in the end permanently present or absent as[40]

$$\mathbf{d} = \lim_{t\to\infty}(\mathbf{a}'(t)-\mathbf{a}_{\mathrm{bg}}'). \tag{9.34}$$

The increased or decreased permanent amounts of environmental or economic commodities are referred to as permanent stressors. Together with the transient stressors that represent the time-integrated amounts, they constitute the class of (environmental) stressors. Note that transient stressors

38 The procedure to transfer environmental commodities to the vector of economic commodities could be considered as the mirror version of how to account for truncated economic commodities; see Section 7.2.

39 It is reduced with respect to the number of columns and expanded with respect to the number of rows.

40 The inclusion of $\mathbf{a}_{\mathrm{bg}}'$ ensures that only the difference is attributed to the economic activity. This quantity **d** expresses the permanent amount of economic or environmental commodity that is present or absent that can be attributed to an environmental intervention **b**.

are calculated with a fate model that includes degradation (or growth) and intermedia transport, while the fate calculation of permanent stressors involves only transport. Of course, the decision which stressor is permanent and which is transient may be difficult in some cases. How persistent are persistent chemicals? Are fossil fuels renewable or not?[41] The answers to these questions determine to which category a certain commodity and thereby its associated stressor belongs.

> The asymptotical increase or decrease of the permanent amount of environmental commodities is defined as a measure for the exposure to persistent chemicals and non-renewable resources. This measure is also applicable to the appearance or disappearance of economic commodities. These commodities are jointly referred to as permanent stressors. The expression again involves the construction of a set of differential equations which need to be solved. It does not involve integration over time, however. Persistent chemicals and non-renewable resources cannot be treated with the time-integrated measure. Splitting them off from $\mathbf{b}(t)$ and putting them together with $\mathbf{a}(t)$ in $\mathbf{a}'(t)$, the expression for the permanent stressors $\mathbf{d}$ is
>
> $$\mathbf{d} = \lim_{t\to\infty}(\mathbf{a}'(t) - \mathbf{a}_{\mathrm{bg}}').$$
>
> The degradable chemicals and renewable resources can then be put in the vector $\mathbf{b}'(t)$ and the expression for the transient stressors formulated to
>
> $$\mathbf{c} = \int_0^\infty (\mathbf{b}'(t) - \mathbf{b}_{\mathrm{bg}}')\mathrm{d}t.$$

9.2.4 Using the Fate Matrix to Calculate the Permanent Presence or Absence

In Section 9.2.2, a time-saving trick was introduced to calculate directly the time-integrated presence and absence of transient commodities. A very similar

41 There is even a connection to almost metaphysical questions, like the stability of matter (it has, for instance, been claimed that the proton could have a half-life of some 10^{31} years) and the existence of the earth (do we need to take extremely long decay times into consideration, if astrophysicists tell us that the earth will have ceased to exist long before?).

short-cut can be applied for the permanent presence and absence of permanent commodities.

Observing that the solution of the differential equation for $\mathbf{a}'(t)$ is given by

$$\mathbf{a}'(t) = \mathbf{a}_{\mathrm{bg}}' + \mathbf{D}' \cdot \int_0^t \mathbf{b}'(t')\mathrm{d}t', \tag{9.35}$$

it is easily found that

$$\mathbf{d} = \mathbf{D}' \cdot \int_0^\infty \mathbf{b}'(t)\mathrm{d}t. \tag{9.36}$$

The theorem (Heijungs (1995*a*)) that enabled the short-cut that was described in the context of the fate matrix (Section 9.2.2) can also be applied to the damage matrix. By absence of an offset **f**, we find that

$$\mathbf{d} = \mathbf{D}' \cdot -\mathbf{C}'^{-1} \cdot \mathbf{b}'. \tag{9.37}$$

We are now still missing one term, corresponding to the possibility of directly emitting persistent pollutants or directly extracting non-renewable resources, represented by the term $\mathbf{b}''$. This term can of course simply be added to the amount of persistent pollutant that is created by environmental processes or the amount of non-renewable resources that vanishes due to environmental processes. That is, we have to replace the last equation by

$$\mathbf{d} = \mathbf{D}' \cdot -\mathbf{C}'^{-1} \cdot \mathbf{b}' + \mathbf{b}''. \tag{9.38}$$

Calculation of the permanent presence or absence of persistent or non-renewable environmental commodities and of economic commodities can, as in Section 9.2.2, be facilitated by using the fate matrix. The procedure is then

$$\mathbf{d} = \mathbf{D}' \cdot -\mathbf{C}'^{-1} \cdot \mathbf{b}' + \mathbf{b}'',$$

where $\mathbf{D}'$ and $\mathbf{C}'$ represent the modified damage matrix and the reduced fate matrix, and $\mathbf{b}''$ represent the direct interventions of persistent and non-renewable environmental commodities. The modified form for the transient stressors then becomes

$$\mathbf{c} = -\mathbf{C}'^{-1} \cdot \mathbf{b}'.$$

9.2.5 Combined Consideration of the Fate of Environmental Commodities: Stressors

Similar to the vector **p** that was introduced in Section 5.2.2 to summarize the flows of economic and environmental commodities via $\mathbf{p} = \begin{pmatrix} \mathbf{a} \\ \mathbf{b} \end{pmatrix}$, a vector of stressors **q** may be introduced that summarizes the time-integrated presence or absence of transient commodities (Sections 9.2.1 and 3.3.2) and the permanent presence or absence of permanent commodities (Sections 9.2.3 and 9.2.4). That is, we define **q** as

$$\mathbf{q} = \begin{pmatrix} \mathbf{d} \\ \mathbf{c} \end{pmatrix}. \tag{9.39}$$

Observe that the permanent amount **d** has a dimension that is different from that of the time-integrated amount **c**: if an element of **b** is expressed in kg, for instance of a hazardous substance, the corresponding element of **c** is expressed in kg·hr and the corresponding one of **d** is expressed in kg.

Once more, as in Section 5.4.1, we may rewrite the vector **q** as

$$\mathbf{q} = \begin{pmatrix} \mathbf{d} \\ \mathbf{c} \end{pmatrix} = \begin{pmatrix} \mathbf{D}' \cdot -\mathbf{C}'^{-1} \cdot \mathbf{b}' + \begin{pmatrix} \mathbf{0} \\ \mathbf{b}'' \end{pmatrix} \\ -\mathbf{C}'^{-1} \cdot \mathbf{b}' \end{pmatrix}, \tag{9.40}$$

where **0** denotes the null vector of the dimension of **a**, such that $\begin{pmatrix} \mathbf{0} \\ \mathbf{b}'' \end{pmatrix}$ has the same dimension as $\mathbf{a}'$. This equation for **q** clearly shows the linear dependency on the elements of **b**. It also explains the fact that **q** is the result of the aggregation of several environmental processes.

Finally, it is important to establish a formal procedure to deduce $\mathbf{b}'$ and $\mathbf{b}''$ from **b**, etc. In the example we simply had

$$\mathbf{b}'(t) = \begin{pmatrix} 1 & 0 & 0 \\ 0 & 0 & 1 \end{pmatrix} \cdot \begin{pmatrix} b_1(t) \\ b_2(t) \\ b_3(t) \end{pmatrix} \text{ and } \mathbf{b}''(t) = \begin{pmatrix} 0 & 1 & 0 \end{pmatrix} \cdot \begin{pmatrix} b_1(t) \\ b_2(t) \\ b_3(t) \end{pmatrix}. \tag{9.41}$$

From this the general forms

$$\begin{bmatrix} \mathbf{b}''(t) \\ \mathbf{b}'(t) \end{bmatrix} = \begin{bmatrix} \Xi'' \\ \Xi' \end{bmatrix} \cdot \mathbf{b}(t) \tag{9.42}$$

can be deduced, where Ξ' and Ξ'' are the matrices that select elements from $\mathbf{b}(t)$ and contain only the numbers 0 and 1.[42] These matrices also serve to make the formal connection between the fate matrix $\mathbf{C}$ and the reduced fate matrix $\mathbf{C}'$:

$$\mathbf{C}' = \Xi' \cdot \mathbf{C} \cdot (\Xi')^{\mathrm{T}} \tag{9.43}$$

and between the damage matrix $\mathbf{D}$ and the modified damage matrix $\mathbf{D}'$:

$$\mathbf{D}' = \begin{bmatrix} \mathbf{D} \cdot (\Xi')^{\mathrm{T}} \\ \Xi'' \cdot \mathbf{C} \cdot (\Xi')^{\mathrm{T}} \end{bmatrix} . \tag{9.44}$$

The following section summarizes the findings under the title of the second fundamental equation.

A final remark at this stage is that the vector of stressors $\mathbf{q}$ is built of a large number of elements that fall into two main categories: transient stressors $\mathbf{c}$ and permanent stressors $\mathbf{d}$. A natural question is how these two categories should be seen in a comparative view. And in particular, do we judge permanent stressors to be more serious than transient ones? And with what type of inter-stressor weighing would we be able to put the two categories on the same level?[43] The discussion in this section does not go into that question, as it concentrates on the analytical step of describing the stressors in a quantitative representation, and not on their relative interpretation. The discussion on impacts (Chapter 10) and in particular that on problems (Chapter 11) present this issue in somewhat more detail.

42 Although the term orthogonal matrix is by definition restricted to square matrices and therefore does not apply here, the matrices Ξ' and Ξ'' could be considered to be orthogonal, in the sense that the product of each of them with its inverse yields the unit matrix $\mathbf{I}$.

43 Notice that such a weighing factor would allow us to establish an effective time horizon in social preference.

9.2.6 The Second Fundamental Equation

In the previous sections, two measures of exposure to environmental commodities were developed: the time-integrated presence or absence of degradable chemicals and renewable resources for transient stressors, and the permanent presence or absence of persistent chemicals, non-renewable resources, and economic commodities for permanent stressors.

In Part Two, a fundamental equation was derived that indicated the environmental interventions associated with any choice of consumers' external demand. The first fundamental equation was developed from the notion that different economic processes have to be active for a specific time period in order to produce a net amount of commodities that exactly satisfies the external demand. Denoting the final demand by **a**, the operating times of the processes by **t**, and the input and output rate of the processes by a technology matrix $\bar{\mathbf{A}}$, it was found that $\mathbf{t} = \bar{\mathbf{A}}^{-1}\cdot\mathbf{a}$. The environmental commodities were seen to flow during the same operating times. As they were characterized by technical coefficients in the intervention matrix $\bar{\mathbf{B}}$, the environmental interventions followed from $\mathbf{b} = \bar{\mathbf{B}}\cdot\mathbf{t}$. The first fundamental equation was constructed from these two equations:

$$\mathbf{b} = \bar{\mathbf{B}}\cdot\bar{\mathbf{A}}^{-1}\cdot\mathbf{a}. \tag{9.45}$$

The discussion on environmental processes has been cast into an equation that links the vector of environmental interventions **b** via the reduced vector $\mathbf{b}'$ to the time-integrated presence or absence **c** by means of $\mathbf{c} = -\mathbf{C}'^{-1}\cdot\mathbf{b}'$, where $\mathbf{C}'$ is the reduced fate matrix, and to the permanent amount that is present or absent **d** by means of $\mathbf{d} = \mathbf{D}'\cdot-\mathbf{C}'^{-1}\cdot\mathbf{b}' + \begin{pmatrix}\mathbf{0}\\ \mathbf{b}''\end{pmatrix}$, where $\mathbf{D}'$ is the modified damage matrix. We are now in a position to summarize another fundamental equation, which will be called the second fundamental equation:

$$\mathbf{q} = \begin{pmatrix}\mathbf{d}\\ \mathbf{c}\end{pmatrix} = \begin{pmatrix}\begin{pmatrix}\mathbf{D}\cdot(\boldsymbol{\Xi}')^{\mathrm{T}}\\ \boldsymbol{\Xi}''\cdot\mathbf{C}\cdot(\boldsymbol{\Xi}')^{\mathrm{T}}\end{pmatrix}\cdot-(\boldsymbol{\Xi}'\cdot\mathbf{C}\cdot(\boldsymbol{\Xi}')^{\mathrm{T}})^{-1}\cdot\boldsymbol{\Xi}' + \begin{pmatrix}\mathbf{0}\\ \boldsymbol{\Xi}''\end{pmatrix}\\ -(\boldsymbol{\Xi}'\cdot\mathbf{C}\cdot(\boldsymbol{\Xi}')^{\mathrm{T}})^{-1}\cdot\boldsymbol{\Xi}'\end{pmatrix}\cdot\mathbf{b}. \tag{9.46}$$

This complicated-looking equation is not so complicated to work with in practice. On the contrary, a computer package that is able to deal with matrix multiplication and inversion can handle this expression. For future reference, some of the matrix products will be abbreviated. We define the matrices

$$\check{\mathbf{D}} = \left[\begin{bmatrix} \mathbf{D}\cdot(\boldsymbol{\Xi}')^{\mathrm{T}} \\ \boldsymbol{\Xi}''\cdot\mathbf{C}\cdot(\boldsymbol{\Xi}')^{\mathrm{T}} \end{bmatrix} \cdot -(\boldsymbol{\Xi}'\cdot\mathbf{C}\cdot(\boldsymbol{\Xi}')^{\mathrm{T}})^{-1}\cdot\boldsymbol{\Xi}' + \begin{bmatrix} \mathbf{0} \\ \boldsymbol{\Xi}'' \end{bmatrix} \right] \tag{9.47}$$

and

$$\check{\mathbf{C}} = -(\boldsymbol{\Xi}'\cdot\mathbf{C}\cdot(\boldsymbol{\Xi}')^{\mathrm{T}})^{-1}\cdot\boldsymbol{\Xi}', \tag{9.48}$$

and jointly in

$$\mathbf{Q} = \begin{bmatrix} \check{\mathbf{D}} \\ \check{\mathbf{C}} \end{bmatrix}. \tag{9.49}$$

These definitions allow one to write concisely the time-integrated presence and absence and the permanent presence and absence as

$$\mathbf{q} = \begin{bmatrix} \mathbf{d} \\ \mathbf{c} \end{bmatrix} = \mathbf{Q}\cdot\mathbf{b} = \begin{bmatrix} \check{\mathbf{D}} \\ \check{\mathbf{C}} \end{bmatrix}\cdot\mathbf{b}. \tag{9.50}$$

We may now concisely combine the first and the second fundamental equation:

$$\mathbf{q} = \mathbf{Q}\cdot\bar{\mathbf{B}}\cdot\bar{\mathbf{A}}^{-1}\cdot\mathbf{a}. \tag{9.51}$$

The results of the discussion on environmental processes may now be summarized as follows.

> The second fundamental equation summarizes the influence of environmental processes on the environmental interventions that are attributed to an economic activity according to the first fundamental equation (Section 5.4.1). The result is a vector of environmental stressors of two types: the transient stressors that correspond to the time-integrated presence of degradable chemicals and the time-integrated absence of renewable resources, and the permanent stressors: the permanent present or absent amount of persistent chemicals and non-renewable resources and of economic commodities that are affected by environmental processes.

Denoting the environmental interventions by **b**, we first construct two matrices that separate the environmental commodities into transient ones ($\mathbf{b}'$) and permanent ones ($\mathbf{b}''$) by

$$\begin{pmatrix} \mathbf{b}'' \\ \mathbf{b}' \end{pmatrix} = \begin{pmatrix} \Xi'' \\ \Xi' \end{pmatrix} \cdot \mathbf{b}.$$

The time-integrated presence or absence of transient commodities is given the symbol **c** and the permanent present or absent amount of permanent commodities is given the symbol **d**. Together they are put into a vector $\mathbf{q} = \begin{pmatrix} \mathbf{d} \\ \mathbf{c} \end{pmatrix}$ that is calculated by means of

$$\mathbf{q} = \mathbf{Q} \cdot \mathbf{b},$$

where $\mathbf{Q} = \begin{pmatrix} \check{\mathbf{D}} \\ \check{\mathbf{C}} \end{pmatrix}$ and the matrices $\check{\mathbf{D}}$ and $\check{\mathbf{C}}$ are given by

$$\check{\mathbf{D}} = \left(\begin{pmatrix} \mathbf{D} \cdot (\Xi')^{\mathrm{T}} \\ \Xi'' \cdot \mathbf{C} \cdot (\Xi')^{\mathrm{T}} \end{pmatrix} \cdot -(\Xi' \cdot \mathbf{C} \cdot (\Xi')^{\mathrm{T}})^{-1} \cdot \Xi' + \begin{pmatrix} \mathbf{0} \\ \Xi'' \end{pmatrix} \right)$$

and

$$\check{\mathbf{C}} = -(\Xi' \cdot \mathbf{C} \cdot (\Xi')^{\mathrm{T}})^{-1} \cdot \Xi'.$$

The matrices **C** and **D** denote the fate matrix and the damage matrix, the first of which represents the inputs and outputs of environmental commodities related to environmental processes, and the latter representing inputs and outputs of economic commodities.

9.2.7 The Assumption of Linearity of Environmental Processes and the Connection with the Epistemological Basis

In the previous part the linearity of economic processes was discussed (Section 5.2.4), as was the validity of the constancy of the technical coefficients in the technology matrix $\bar{\mathbf{A}}$ and the intervention matrix $\bar{\mathbf{B}}$. It was concluded that, although economic processes in reality may certainly behave in a non-linear way, the particular question addressed at present – the attribution of environmental problems to economic activities – calls for a linear interpolation.

A next question is of course the nature of the environmental processes that build the fate matrix **C** and the damage matrix **D**. As noted above, there is no simple linear time dependency of inputs and outputs of environmental processes. That was one of the reasons to develop an alternative to Isard's framework. The question is now to what extent the alternative formulation satisfies some form of linearity. Obviously, the second fundamental equation is an equation which displays a linear dependency of **q** on **b**. In that sense it is in accordance with the linear attribution rule. A more fundamental question is why we went into the modelling of environmental processes at all, and did not apply the same procedure as we used for economic processes (see Section 5.2.3): observe the flows during a certain time period and derive technical coefficients, disregarding the physical and chemical details of what is happening inside the process.

An answer to that question can be found by studying the relationship between steady-state amounts or concentrations and continuous environmental intervention flows: $\mathbf{b}_{\text{bg}} = -\mathbf{C}^{-1}\cdot\boldsymbol{\phi}$ (see also the beginning of Section 9.2.2). The continuous flow $\boldsymbol{\phi}$ may be conceived as a train of pulse interventions of magnitude $\Delta\mathbf{b}$, each of them separated in time by an (infinitesimally small) interval Δt, such that $\Delta\mathbf{b} = \boldsymbol{\phi}\Delta t$. If we now attribute a vector of environmental interventions with magnitude **b** to a certain economic activity, we may say that we attribute a time period $t = b_i/\phi_i$ of the prevailing steady-state amount or concentration $(\mathbf{b}_{\text{bg}})_k$. In other words, we attribute a quantity

$$(b_{\text{bg}})_k t = \sum_i -(c)^{-1}{}_{ki}\phi_i t = \sum_i -(c)^{-1}{}_{ki} b_i \tag{9.52}$$

to the interventions b_i that make the vector of environmental interventions **b**. This may be rewritten as $-\mathbf{C}^{-1}\cdot\mathbf{b}$, and we can easily make the identification with the vector **c** in Equation (9.26). So, in principle the proposal of Section 9.2.1 to consider the time-integrated presence or absence of environmental commodities as a measure of environmental exposure is compatible with the epistemological principles outlined in Section 2.1.2, and in particular with the proportional attribution to every activity that contributes to environmental interventions, exposures, impacts, or problems.

This compatibility with the epistemological principles is essential for the scientific basis of the present work. The "historical" question that remains to be answered is why we did not argue according to the above arguments throughout this chapter. The answer lies in the recognition that the fate matrix

C could often not be inverted, and that there was a desire to include deterioration of economic commodities by environmental processes as well. The procedure which follows from direct argumentation of the epistemological principles gives no clue to these problems; the argumentation from time-integrated exposure did. Therefore the more elaborate and apparently indirect path was followed. Nevertheless, the connection with the epistemological basis was a missing link in the argument.

> Although environmental processes, like economic processes, are essentially non-linear in their behaviour, the epistemological basis chosen to answer the attribution problem requires a fully linear treatment. Matrix algebra facilitates this linear calculus to a large extent.

9.2.8 Is the Fate Matrix Square?

The second fundamental equation contains the inverse of the reduced fate matrix $\mathbf{C}'$. After the complicated discussion in Section 6.1 on the topic of the rectangularity of the technology matrix $\bar{\mathbf{A}}$, it must be asked if the fate matrix is square, if so if it is always non-singular, and if not how to proceed. Perhaps an allocation procedure would be required here as well.

The first thing to observe is that in going from Figure 9.1 to Figure 9.2, the meaning of the columns changes. A certain column does not denote an individual environmental process, such as degradation, transport, or formation. Rather, it represents the aggregated fate aspects of a particular environmental commodity. For instance, c'_{ik} indicates the time rate of change of the amount of commodity i that is present per unit amount of commodity k, according to

$$\frac{\mathrm{d}b_i(t)}{\mathrm{d}t} = \sum_k c'_{ik} b_k(t) \text{ or rather } c'_{ik} = \frac{1}{b_k(t)} \frac{\mathrm{d}b_i(t)}{\mathrm{d}t}. \qquad (9.53)$$

Because the fate matrix is defined in this way, the environmental commodity that is indicated by a particular row, say row i, is the same as the environmental commodity that is represented by the column with the same index i. Hence the fate matrix is square by definition.

A next question then concerns the invertibility of the fate matrix. In general the unreduced fate matrix **C** will be singular, as was already discussed above. That is exactly the reason to define the reduced fate matrix and to transfer persistent chemicals and non-renewable resources to the vector $\mathbf{a}'(t)$ that contains the economic commodities. So here we have a procedure to ensure that the fate matrix is reduced to an invertible matrix.

> The fate matrix is square by definition, and rows and columns will be transferred to the damage matrix, so that it becomes invertible.

Chapter 10

Environmental Impacts

10.1 REPRESENTATION OF AN ENVIRONMENTAL IMPACT

10.1.1 What is an Environmental Impact?

Up to now, we have found a way of describing the time-integrated result of environmental processes like transport, degradation, and formation. From the vector of environmental commodity flows **b** we were able to find the time-integrated presence and absence of amounts of transient stressors, the vector **c**. If one particular element of this vector turns out to be, say, 5 kg·hr, this means that 5 kg of the corresponding environmental commodity is present for 1 hr, or 1 kg for 5 hr, or in whatever combination. In a similar way, the vector of permanently present or absent stressors **d** could be found. Here the interpretation is in terms of permanent presence: a value of 5 kg means that (asymptotically) 5 kg of a certain commodity is present. All this needs further interpretation. In this interpretation we will for the time being concentrate on transient stressors.

Until now, the meaning of the term environmental impact has been kept quite implicit. Some examples were given: the number of killed species, a reduction in offspring, etc. It is remarkable that most books that discuss environmental impacts in relation to economic activity are also implicit about the meaning of environmental impact. I can do no better than quote from Victor's *Economics of pollution* the somewhat related problems in defining pollution:[1]

> Many people who write about pollution begin by noting the inadequacy of existing definitions of the phenomenon, which they then seek to remedy by offering what invariably turns out to be yet another inadequate definition. Perhaps a lesson may be learned from Lord Morley, who said he was unable to define an elephant but he would be sure to recognise one when he saw it. Something similar might be said about pollution though very often it is our other senses, and not sight alone, that signal its presence. A complicating factor, however, is that there are some forms of pollution whose effects are not immediately perceived by our senses and yet damage living and non-living matter just the same. Then there is the problem that, in so far as pollution necessarily causes damage, and most people seem to think that this is an essential characteristic of pollution, then agreement must be reached as to what constitutes damage.[2]

I will save myself and the reader the trouble of attempting to define environmental impact.[3] Rather, I will reproduce (Figure 10.1) a chain of environmental impacts from Fava et al. (1993). It clearly demonstrates that environmental impacts have to do with mostly undesired changes in environmental quality, and that impacts can be defined at many levels, from abstract properties (the acidity of the rain) to concrete phenomena (dead fish). The impact chain hides another aspect which is very important to reveal: there is:

(a) a set of causes (stressors in the above);
(b) a set of consequences (impacts);
(c) a set of relationships between the set of causes and the set of consequences.

We seek to define more exactly these two sets in order to establish relation-

1 In fact, the concepts of environmental impact and pollution are very much related: it has quite often been suggested to categorize environmental impacts in three main groups, i.e. depletion, pollution, and disturbance; see also note 8 of this chapter.

2 Victor (1972*b*, p. 7).

3 The interested reader is referred to Fava et al. (1993, p. 12) for a discussion on the meaning of environmental impact within life-cycle assessment, to Schaltegger & Kubat (1995) for an extensive German–English glossary, and to the ISO documents on environmental management.

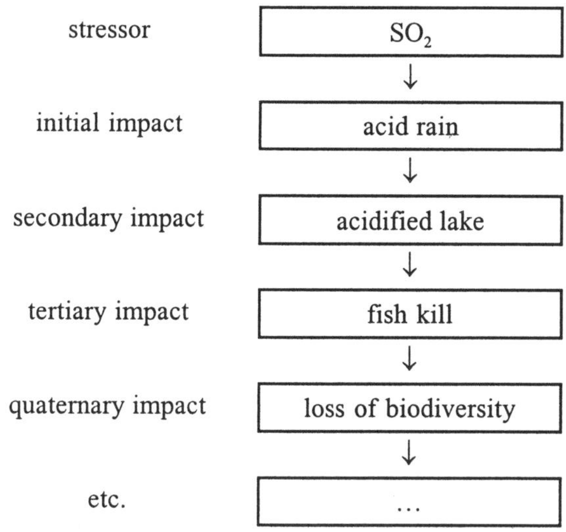

FIGURE 10.1. A simple example of a chain of environmental impacts (adapted from Fava et al. (1993, p. 13)).

ships between elements of them.[4]

(a) First the cause side, what Fava et al. call the stressors. They consider these stressors to be the environmental interventions which have been specified in the inventory analysis, but qualitatively grouped according to their potency to contribute to certain categories of impacts. Acknowledgement of the fact that environmental processes may convert an environmental commodity that exerts one type of environmental impact into another environmental commodity that exerts another type of environmental impact makes us realize that this definition is not particularly useful. For instance, emissions of nitrogen oxides may be considered to have a eutrophying impact, but – via environmental conversion into N_2O – to have a global warming impact as well (Rotmans (1990)). That would mean that an enormous amount of environmental commodities would be coupled to nearly all types of impacts. It also would mean that fate of NO_x would be modelled for

4 In the discussion that follows, the historic emphasis is on the considerations of impact analysis (or assessment) within life-cycle assessment. The reason for this is that impact analysis in LCA is much more developed than in SFA, and that it is much more general in set-up than in EIA or RA.

eutrophication as well as for global warming, whereas it would be much more efficient to do this only once for the substance itself, without paying consideration to the types of impact it contributes to (Wegener Sleeswijk & Heijungs (1996)).

A solution that is much more useful is achieved by relating the result of the environmental processes – the time-integrated presences and absences and the permanent amounts, what are called stressors in the present text – to a number of impact categories. The relation between intervention and presence/absence is then left to the modelling of fate, and is clearly separated from the discussion of impacts. An argument in favour of this separation is to be found in the procedure for risk assessment of chemicals, where the aspect of fate belongs to the exposure assessment, and the aspect of impact to the hazard identification (Van Leeuwen (1995); see also Section 1.3.2). The combination of release assessment, exposure assessment, and hazard identification then results through risk characterization in a quantitative judgement of the associated risk; see also Sections 1.3.2 and 7.5. In the present framework for life-cycle assessment the procedure is less transparent, as was already concluded from Figure 10.1. There is a classification with the intention to assign impacts to interventions[5] in a qualitative way, and a characterization which quantifies the degree to which the interventions contribute to these impacts. The influence of environmental processes is not separated from the harmfulness of the substances, so that nitrogen oxides indeed have to be classified as having a climate impact.[6]

(b) The second point of discussion is the consequence side, the impacts. As illustrated by Figure 10.1, many levels may be distinguished here. If we draw these impact chains for several chemicals, and if we know that different types of impact may influence each other in synergistic or antagonistic ways, we get a very complex web of impacts (Guinée (1994)). It is therefore very important to select impact categories in such a way that overlap and double-

5 Or the other way around, of course, assigning impacts to interventions.

6 In what is known as parallel impacts (e.g., part of the SO_2 leading to human toxic impacts and part leading to acidification; see Udo de Haes (1996, p. 20)), it is sometimes suggested that the emission is to be 'allocated to the relevant categories in proportion to its contributions' (Lindfors et al. (1995*e*, p. 12)). It is rightly recognized that this partitioning can only be made on the basis of a fate analysis. However, since fate analysis is invariably proposed to take place in the characterization which succeeds the classification, this proportional classification is logically impossible. The same possibility is being advocated by ISO.

counting is avoided (Assies (1994)).[7] For instance, one should somehow exclude dead fish from the assessment of the consequences of acidifying substances when dead fish are chosen as an endpoint for the assessment of releases of toxic chemicals. Or, alternatively, one could choose the impact level of dead fish for both acidifying and toxic substances. Lindfors et al. (1995*e*) list four requirements in this respect: completeness, practicality, independence, and relation to further steps in the procedure. Heijungs (1994*c*) offers from a less pragmatic and a more formal point of view completeness, independence, and measured in terms of a ratio scale. It could be argued that two classes of criteria should be formed: one for each category separately (like practicality and compliance with the ratio scale), and one for the set as a whole (like completess and independence).

Anyhow, within the circle of LCA scientists, a certain amount of agreement appears to have grown up on a default list of impact categories (Udo de Haes (1996)) on the basis of the first lists by Finnveden et al. (1992) and Heijungs et al. (1992*b*):[8]

- depletion and competition of abiotic resources;
- depletion and competition of biotic resources;
- depletion and competition of land;
- global warming;
- depletion of stratospheric ozone;
- human toxicological impacts;
- ecotoxicological impacts;
- photo-oxidant formation;
- acidification;
- eutrophication;
- odour;
- noise;
- radiation;

7 This is all the more true when seen in the context of the independency requirement of the attributes in a multicriteria analysis; see Section 11.1.4.

8 It may be observed that the classical typology of impacts into depletion, pollution, and disturbance, in which depletion corresponds to impacts due to extractions, pollution to impacts due to emissions, and disturbance to impacts due to physical presence and activities (Udo de Haes (1991)), is not compatible with the input–output structure of the environmental interventions. Therefore, only depletion- and pollution-related impact categories are included in this list.

- casualties.

A very important criterion for selection has been the desire to split the assessment of environmental consequences into a part that is primarily based on natural-scientific knowledge, like dose response curves and radiative forcing, and a part that is dominated by social preferences. Thus the list of impacts has been defined not only in terms of formal criteria like completeness, independency, and measured on a ratio scale, but also paying respect to the degree of scientific status on the one hand[9] and the possibility of submitting them to societal opinion on the other hand.

Although it is definitely possible to choose other impact categories,[10] we will regard impacts on this list as examples in subsequent discussions on the attribution of environmental impacts to economic activities and of environmental problems to environmental impacts.

(c) The third point to be discussed in the attribution of impacts to stressors is the strength which stressors are coupled to impacts. This is discussed in the next section.

9 In the ISO discussions on life-cycle impact assessment, a distinction between indicators and endpoints is made. Indicators are assumed to represent points in the environmental impact chain, for which a scientifically established modelling procedure is available. The endpoints are the points in this chain that are of ultimate concern, like human health and ecosystem health, but which are currently not accessible via scientific quantitative links. Therefore, the indicators represent an in-between solution: their choice is inspired by the endpoints, such that their quantification proceeds through more or less scientifically accepted methods. The origin of this reasoning probably lies in Fava et al. (1993) and Consoli et al. (1993).

10 For instance, Steen & Ryding (1993) effectively choose the impact categories biodiversity, production, human health, resources, and aesthetic values. They manage to establish quantitative relationships between, say an emission of NO_x and the five impact categories which they define in some quantitative way. It is especially the last steps in the impact chain that they model which have the largest uncertainties, and of which the scientific status is therefore doubtful. Another possibility is to choose a smaller number of indicators, e.g., energy use and waste. These choices do not meet the criteria of completeness and independence, and must indeed be seen as attempts to find an easy indicative measure. However useful this may be, the present theoretical treatment of the attribution problem will concentrate on correctness, rather than on simplicity and feasibility.

The second stage in the analysis of consequences of environmental interventions is the attribution of the time-integrated presence or absence and the permanent presence or absence to environmental impact categories. For this aim, a number of impact categories must be selected. Criteria for this are formal criteria, like completeness and independence of the categories, and other criteria, like a limitation of their number and their natural-scientific status.

10.1.2 A Measure for Environmental Impacts

Having defined a number of environmental impact categories, we must proceed to accomplish the quantitative attribution of time-integrated and permanent amounts to those impact categories. The discussion will start with some considerations on impacts of a toxic nature and be restricted to impacts of transient stressors. An extension to other impact categories and impacts of permanent stressors will be made afterwards.

If it is desired to account for the fact that some pollutants are more hazardous than others, for example because they are more toxic, a measure of these differences in intrinsic hazard must be incorporated. For this, a discussion of the toxicological impacts of chemicals will serve as an example. A subsequent discussion will generalize this to non-toxic impacts, like global warming, and to resource-related impacts *in casu* depletion.

Standard toxicology teaches us that it is possible to establish dose response relationships (or dose effect[11] curves) per pollutant. These curves demonstrate

> the relationship between dose and the magnitude of a certain effect, either in an individual or in a population. Such curves may take a variety of forms. They may be linear within a given dose range but more often they are not.[12]

11 The terms effect and impact frequently denote the same phenomenon. In dose response curves, the dose may be a real dose (in kg), a relative dose (in kg per kg bodyweight or tissue), a dose-rate (in kg per day), a concentration (in kg per cubic metre of air), and the response may be a percentage of the organisms that displays a certain response (e.g., death), or a measure of activity (e.g., the number of offspring). Both abscissa and ordinate of the dose response curve are also quite often defined as a logarithm of one of these quantities. See, e.g., Van Straalen & Verkleij (1991).

12 Tas & Van Leeuwen (1995, p. 344).

An often observed curve is a sigmoidal curve (see also Figure 2.3), the horizontal axis (y in the figure) representing the concentration of the pollutant, the vertical axis (z in the figure) representing the environmental impact, e.g., in terms of the percentage of the population or the number of species affected to some degree or the expected increased mortality.

It is tempting to apply toxicological information contained in such dose response curves. A choice that is sometimes seen is to compute the incremental environmental impact (z_a) due to a specified increased concentration (y_a). That is, the quantity

$$z_a = z(y_c + y_a) - z(y_c) \tag{10.1}$$

is regarded as the environmental impact due to some activity that introduces a dose y_a.[13] There are a number of problems associated with this choice (see Section 2.1.2 for a more detailed treatment):

- the expression often requires a concentration as input (y_a) whereas the only quantity that is available is a time-integrated amount;
- as the curve is not a straight line, the order in which activities are added will be important for the resulting impact;
- the expression does not satisfy the rule of 100%-additivity: that the sum of the attributed impacts corresponds to the attributed impacts of the sum;
- the procedure requires one unique background concentration per pollutant, while the time-integrated incrementals are the result of an aggregation over a number of processes.

An alternative that is sometimes encountered is a marginal approach:

$$z_a = \left[\frac{\partial z(y)}{\partial y}\right]_{y=y_c} y_a. \tag{10.2}$$

The same disadvantages hold here, plus the additional disadvantage that a marginal approach poses serious restrictions on the domain of the analysis. Still another possibility is formed by the average environmental impact per unit of concentration:

13 The subscript "c" denotes, as in Section 2.1.2, the current situation, while "a" stands for analytical.

$$z_a = \frac{z_c}{y_c} y_a \tag{10.3}$$

with only the first and the last drawbacks of the above list of four. A choice which enables us to circumvent the fourth problem is to consider the tangent at the linear part of the curve or the tangent at that part where the curve is steepest as a factor with which to multiply y_a.

As stated in the discussion on the epistemological basis, in principle any choice is possible (*cf.* Heijungs (1998)). Only some choices appear to be more sensible. The choice of any of these principles cannot be made at random, *ad hoc*, or as you like it. Also, ethical considerations[14] ("A choice for the tangent at the steepest part of the dose response curve brings us sooner to a sustainable economy") should preferably be outside this analytical discussion of attribution. For a scientific establishment it is absolutely essential that the choice of any of these principles follows automatically, by logical deduction, from the epistemological principle of the entire theory. Of course, the *a priori* principles themselves from which the method is derived may be inspired by ethical convictions or ideological and political doctrines. From the considerations in Section 2.1, however, the only possible choice in the context of the attribution problem is that according to Equation (10.3).

As discussed, implementation of this choice is relatively straightforward, although there are still some difficulties. Above we already saw two of these. In the remainder of this section we discuss the problem that Equation (10.3) requires a permanent concentration (or amount) as input (y_a) whereas the only quantity that is available is a time-integrated amount (or concentration) **c**. The other drawback – the requirement of a unique background concentration per pollutant – is postponed to the end of Section 10.1.3.

If a permanent concentration y_c leads to a certain permanent response z_c, we, as in Section 9.2.5, postulate that a time-integrated amount or concentration c leads to a time-integrated response e that is given by

$$e = \frac{z_c}{y_c} c. \tag{10.4}$$

As in the earlier problem of validation, we can neither prove nor falsify this relationship, but we can try to argue that it follows from the epistemological

14 See Müller-Wenk (1996) for an example of a discussion on "the shape of damage functions" that is put into the context of the desire to achieve certain goals.

principles that were exposed in Section 2.1.2. Taking Equation (10.3) as a starting point, we first generalize this to time-dependent amounts and impacts:

$$z_{\mathrm{a}}(t) = \frac{z_{\mathrm{c}}}{y_{\mathrm{c}}} y_{\mathrm{a}}(t). \tag{10.5}$$

Next we observe that the permanent amount y_{a} is not available; instead we have the time-integrated amount $c = \int_0^\infty y_{\mathrm{a}}(t)\mathrm{d}t$. Therefore, we integrate both sides of Equation (10.5) over t:

$$\int_0^\infty z_{\mathrm{a}}(t)\mathrm{d}t = \int_0^\infty \frac{z_{\mathrm{c}}}{y_{\mathrm{c}}} y_{\mathrm{a}}(t)\mathrm{d}t = \frac{z_{\mathrm{c}}}{y_{\mathrm{c}}} c. \tag{10.6}$$

We conclude that it is convenient to regard the left-hand side as the time-integrated impact that is to be attributed to the time-integrated presence of an amount c. This time-integrated impact will be denoted by e; hence we have deduced the attribution rule for environmental impacts that is given by Equation (10.4). For the permanent stressors, of which the permanent amount is given by d, the situation is relatively straightforward. Denoting the permanent environmental impact by f, we simply identify y_{a} with d and z_{a} with f, so that the attribution rule becomes

$$f = \frac{z_{\mathrm{c}}}{y_{\mathrm{c}}} d. \tag{10.7}$$

Lastly, we must generalize the expressions for the time-integrated impact e and the permanent impact f to the situation of multiple stressors and multiple impacts (i.e. the situation of parallel and serial impacts; see Udo de Haes (1996, p. 20)). When several stressors exert the same type of environmental impact (e.g., CO_2 and CH_4 both contribute to global warming), it is important to specify the specific contribution of each of the contributing stressors (e.g., the current level of global warming is according to Shine et al. (1990) for 61% caused by CO_2 and for 17% by CH_4). That is to say, we must specify $(z_{\mathrm{c}})_i$ and $(y_{\mathrm{c}})_i$ for all contributing stressors i, $(z_{\mathrm{c}})_i$ being a function of the amount $(y_{\mathrm{c}})_i$, of the nature of the stressor i, and probably including the other stressors as well to account for synergism or antagonism. We thus use the form

$$(z_{\mathrm{a}})_i = \frac{(z_{\mathrm{c}})_i}{(y_{\mathrm{c}})_i} (y_{\mathrm{a}})_i \tag{10.8}$$

under the condition that

$$z_c = \sum_i (z_c)_i. \tag{10.9}$$

Here a new epistemological problem arises: while the current emission levels of CO_2 and CH_4 can be known by measurement, how is one to know the contribution of these gases to the total global warming problem? This problem is discussed in Section 10.1.4. Supposing for the moment that it is possible to find values for this $(z_c)_i$, we can now proceed to calculate the factor that relates the average impact to the average amount, and to consider it as the factor that translates a certain time-integrated amount into a time-integrated impact, or a permanent amount into a permanent impact.

Also accounting for the fact that one stressor may contribute to more than one impact category, we end up with the following expression:

$$(z_a)_{li} = \frac{(z_c)_{li}}{(y_c)_i}(y_a)_i, \tag{10.10}$$

where $(z_c)_{li}$ represents the current contribution that stressor i makes to impact category l. The concrete form to be used in the context of the attribution problem is then the following:

$$\begin{aligned} f_{li} &= \frac{(z_c)_{li}}{(y_c)_i} d_i \\ e_{li} &= \frac{(z_c)_{li}}{(y_c)_i} c_i \end{aligned} \tag{10.11}$$

It may be observed that the current stressor level $(y_c)_i$ enters both the equation for the permanent stressors (the top one that links f_{li} and d_i) and the equation for the transient stressors (the bottom one that links e_{li} and c_i). Because the subscript i is an index that runs over some hundreds (or more) of stressors for the two categories of stressors separately, we will have different $(y_c)_i$s in both expressions. Permanent stressors contribute to permanent impact categories, transient stressors to transient impact categories, and there is not yet any connection between the two classes.

Contributions of different stressors i to the same impact category l may of course be added to an overall contribution to the impact category l:

$$f_l = \sum_i f_{li} = \sum_i \frac{(z_c)_{li}}{(y_c)_i} d_i$$
$$e_l = \sum_i e_{li} = \sum_i \frac{(z_c)_{li}}{(y_c)_i} c_i \qquad (10.12)$$

The term $\frac{(z_c)_{li}}{(y_c)_i}$ is seen to serve an important function in these sets of equations: they symbolize the relationship between a certain stressor i and a certain environmental impact l to which that stressor contributes. The quantity therefore expresses the "strength" of a unit amount of the stressor i to contribute to impact category l. It deserves a symbol and a name: as a symbol we will use r_{li}:

$$r_{li} = \frac{(z_c)_{li}}{(y_c)_i}, \qquad (10.13)$$

and as a name the term impact factor.

One thing which needs to be clarified at this point is the relation of the impact factor with the equivalency factors[15] that are used in the context of life-cycle assessment. As has already been discussed in Section 10.1.1, the separation between fate, impact, and problem that was introduced in Chapter 8 differs somewhat from the usual approach in LCA. Most texts that deal with the assessment of impacts in relation to products have the quantitative aspects of fate and impact combined in a procedure that is most often referred to as characterization (Finnveden et al. (1992), Heijungs et al. (1992*a*, pp. 43–48), Consoli et al. (1993, pp. 24–25), Fava et al. (1993, pp. 22–26), Lindfors et al. (1995*e*, pp. 16–80)). Equivalency factors can then be considered as the result of an analysis of fate and impact, that is, the equivalency factor that links the intervention of environmental commodity k to impact category l is the product of the fate factor that links the intervention of environmental commodity k to the stressor i and the impact factor that links this stressor i to impact category l. The concept of equivalency factors will not be used in the further analysis.[16]

15 Other terms that can be found are characterization factor and (obsolete) classification factor.

16 Of course, it may be practical in daily life to merge fate factors and impact factors into equivalency factors, and perhaps even merge these with the problem factors (see Chapter 11) into factors that translate environmental interventions in one step into a one-dimensional problem measure. The analytical nature of the discussion demands of keeping them separate in the present text. Moreover, it has often been stated that one-step procedures lack

The linear attribution of environmental impacts to time-integrated or permanent amounts of environmental commodities can theoretically proceed by means of impact factors, which express the "strength" of a unit amount of each stressor to contribute to a particular impact category. A combined application of the fate factors that were developed in Section 9.2 and the impact factors that were developed above represents the link between environmental interventions (the result of the analysis of Part Two) and the contribution to environmental impact categories as defined in Section 10.1.1. These combined factors are the well-known equivalency factors of life-cycle assessment. For reasons of analytical transparency, it is proposed to keep distinguishing the aspect of fate from that of impact.

10.1.3 The Third Fundamental Equation

We may now finalize the previous discussion by summarizing and interpreting the equations for the attribution of impacts to time-integrated and permanent amounts of stressors in matrix form:

$$\begin{aligned} \mathbf{f} &= \mathbf{R}\cdot\mathbf{d} \\ \mathbf{e} &= \mathbf{R}\cdot\mathbf{c}' \end{aligned} \tag{10.14}$$

or by constructing the vector **r** from the time-integrated impact **e** and the permanent impact **f**:

$$\mathbf{r} = \begin{pmatrix} \mathbf{f} \\ \mathbf{e} \end{pmatrix} = \mathbf{R}\cdot\begin{pmatrix} \mathbf{d} \\ \mathbf{c} \end{pmatrix} = \mathbf{R}\cdot\mathbf{q}. \tag{10.15}$$

The matrix **R** is called the impact matrix; an element r_{li} represents the contribution to impact category l that is attributed to a unit amount of stressor (time-integrated presence or absence or permanently present or absent amount) i. The equation

$$\mathbf{r} = \mathbf{R}\cdot\mathbf{q} \tag{10.16}$$

is called the third fundamental equation. It links environmental stressors **q** (time-integrated or permanent amounts) with environmental impacts **r**.[17] It

transparency, and that intermediate results (here, for instance, the inventory table and the stressor table) have a stand-alone value (Wegener Sleeswijk & Heijungs (1996)).

17 The vector **r** is called the impact profile; its elements are the impact scores.

may easily be combined with the second fundamental equation (Section 9.2.4: $\mathbf{q} = \mathbf{Q}\cdot\mathbf{b}$):

$$\mathbf{r} = \mathbf{R}\cdot\mathbf{Q}\cdot\mathbf{b} \tag{10.17}$$

to provide an expression that conforms to the characterization procedure of LCA; $\mathbf{R}\cdot\mathbf{Q}$ represents the matrix of equivalency factors.

> The connection between transient and permanent stressors on the one hand ($\mathbf{q}$) and environmental impacts on the other hand ($\mathbf{r}$) is expressed by the third fundamental equation:
>
> $$\mathbf{r} = \mathbf{R}\cdot\mathbf{q}.$$
>
> An element r_{li} of the impact matrix $\mathbf{R}$ expresses the "strength" of a unit amount of stressor i to contribute to impact category l.

The present state is that we have now developed three fundamental equations: the first one ($\mathbf{b} = \bar{\mathbf{B}}\cdot\bar{\mathbf{A}}^{-1}\cdot\mathbf{a}$) serves to go from external demand ($\mathbf{a}$) to environmental intervention ($\mathbf{b}$), the second one ($\mathbf{q} = \mathbf{Q}\cdot\mathbf{b}$) to go from intervention to environmental stressor ($\mathbf{q}$), and the third one ($\mathbf{r} = \mathbf{R}\cdot\mathbf{q}$) to go from stressor to environmental impact ($\mathbf{r}$). These three equations may be substituted into each other to provide the connection between the external demand of economic commodities and the environmental impacts that are to be attributed thereto:

$$\mathbf{r} = \mathbf{R}\cdot\mathbf{Q}\cdot\bar{\mathbf{B}}\cdot\bar{\mathbf{A}}^{-1}\cdot\mathbf{a}. \tag{10.18}$$

A question that may be raised is what the impact matrix $\mathbf{R}$ achieves. Of course its prime aim is to add an interpretation to the time-integrated and permanent amounts of stressors: the presence of a unit amount of mercury in the surface water makes in general a higher contribution to the toxicity problem than the presence of a unit amount of phosphate. The impact matrix, however, achieves more. If we consider the fact that there may be tens of thousands of environmental commodities, and that the default list of impact categories of Section 10.1.1 contains 14 items, we see that we have achieved a tremendous aggregation of information. Although this implies a considerable loss of detail, one should bear in mind that the aggregation is realized by adding an interpretation, which perhaps adds so much information that the loss of information is fully compensated. Mathematically, it means that the impact matrix $\mathbf{R}$ is far from square: there are many more columns than rows. In contrast to the first and second fundamental equation where a discussion on the dimensions of the matrices was required (Sections 6.1 and 9.2.6), the fact that there is no matrix inversion involved in the third fundamental equation simplifies things to some extent.

One last point in connection with the previous point of the dimension of the matrices refers to the fourth complication that was raised in the beginning of Section 10.1.2: the procedure requires one unique background concentration per pollutant $(y_c)_i$, while the time-integrated or permanent amounts are the result of an aggregation over a number of processes. These processes take place at different places and at different times.[18] A formal trick to overcome this problem is simply to expand the number of environmental commodities. Just as we introduced a distinction between the commodities mercury in water and mercury in air to account for a difference in severity related to different environmental media, we may divide this further into mercury into mercury in Italian air, mercury in coastal water, etc. An extremely large number of environmental commodities may be defined in this way, although practical considerations with regard to data availability and computational feasibility will reduce the number of commodities.

10.1.4 The Nature of the Impact Factors

In Section 10.1.2, a new epistemological problem was introduced: how to determine the contribution that a certain stressor makes to a certain impact category? If we read carefully the cited document that states the relative contributions of CO_2 and CH_4 to the global warming impact, we observe that they speak of the changed impact and not of the impact itself:

> The major contributor to increases in radiative forcing due to increased concentrations of greenhouse gases since pre-industrial times is carbon dioxide (CO_2) (61%).[19]

This suggests a link with the incremental rule (Equation (10.1)) or perhaps with the marginal rule (Equation (10.2)). An expression of the relative contributions in terms of the average rule (Equation (10.3)) is lacking here. On the other hand, such rules appear to exist in the case of acidification:

18 Even when an analysis of the regional SFA type is undertaken, this problem exists because no region and no time period is homogeneous with respect to emission patterns and background concentrations.

19 Shine et al. (1990, p. 45).

Sulfate contributes more to precipitation acidity than nitrate throughout most of Europe.[20]

The topic of this section is to investigate to what extent it is possible to express the relative contribution of a stressor to a certain environmental impact according to the average attribution rule, as is required by the epistemological principles and their consequences that were discussed in Sections 2.1 and 10.1.2.

In general, different stressors will contribute in a complicated, non-linear, and mutually dependent way to an environmental impact category. For instance, the contribution of nitrogen oxides (NO_x) to ozone formation depends heavily on the presence of volatile organic compounds (VOCs). The marginal contribution of NO_x may be positive, zero, or even negative. If there is a measure of the environmental impact category photo-oxidant formation ($(z_c)_l$), it would be impossible to express the absolute ($(z_c)_{li}$) or relative $\left(\frac{(z_c)_{li}}{(y_c)_i}\right)$ contribution that one particular substance (i, which stands for NO_x or one of the VOCs) makes to that problem. Both categories of substances are equally required to create ozone. This should not induce one to attribute 50% of the attribution problem to NO_x and 50% to VOC. In the first place, there is not one VOC but hundreds of them. This would suggest blaming every chemical with a small share smaller than 1%, which is in disagreement with an intuitive view of the role of NO_x, and it would moreover not distinguish "minor" pollutants from important ones.

It is difficult to conceive how one is to improve the situation. In fact, there is quite some resemblance with the allocation procedure for multiple economic processes that was discussed in Section 6.2. There we had the problem of how to allocate a certain input or output (e.g., use of electricity or emission of CO_2) to the two or more economic outputs that are produced by one process (such as the process that produces chlorine and caustic soda). A small number of rules could be deduced from the epistemological principles; in particular the requirement of 100%-additivity was important (Section 6.2.2).

The present situation is quite similar: the problem is how to allocate a certain impact (e.g., photo-oxidant formation) to the two or more stressors (e.g., NO_x and VOCs) that contribute to that problem. And again, we can do

20 Hordijk et al. (1990, p. 39).

no better than formulate a small number of rules, and leave the details as still to be resolved.

One requirement that can be proposed here is the requirement of 100%-additivity. That is, we postulate that the sum of the weighted current stressor levels yields exactly the current impact level. Mathematically:

$$\sum_i \frac{(z_c)_{li}}{(y_c)_i}(y_c)_i = \sum_i e_{li}(y_c)_i = (z_c)_l \tag{10.19}$$

This is probably the only requirement that can be made *a priori*.

There are a number of other requirements that could be submitted. Among them is the rule that every stressor that has a potency to contribute to a certain impact category indeed contributes to the numerical score for that impact category. This view complies with the prevention principle, which is sometimes said to form the basis for impact analysis or assessment in LCA (*cf.* Udo de Haes (1996, pp. 11–13)). It must be emphasized that this requirement is not compatible with the requirement of 100%-additivity (see also Figure 10.2, which shows that emission of a substance of which the

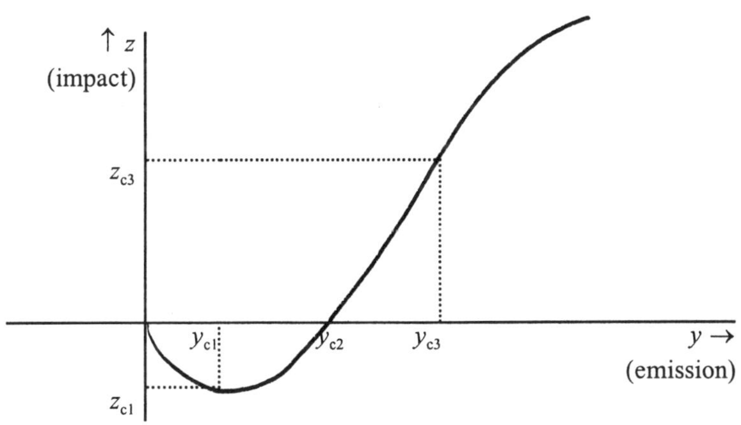

FIGURE 10.2. Negative (c1), zero (c2), and positive (c3) attribution of impacts.

current background level (c1) is suboptimal is being "rewarded", that emission of a substance of which the background (c2) exerts no impacts leads to a zero score, and that only emissions of a substance of which the background (c3) indeed contributes to environmental impacts get a positive attribution score). As such, it is not an appropriate choice in relation to the attribution problem, but rather applies to other forms of LCA, for instance, in connection with the design of long-term sustainable economic planning; see Section 14.1.1.

It must be noted that nearly all proposals that have been made to find an answer to the question of interpreting environmental stressors into environmental impact categories lack a consistent epistemological basis. It is, however, complicated to unravel the exact situation.

In the first place, the aspects of fate and impact are quite often mixed into a rather untransparent – though practical – system of equivalency factors. The global warming potentials (Shine et al. (1990)) are a combination of fate and impact characteristics. Although the impact aspect is separately reported (op. cit. (p. 53)), it is hardly if ever referred to, and the result of the fate estimation is not reported separately. This situation is not unique to global warming: the concept of equivalency factors in LCA intentionally covers the aspects of fate and impact without the need to specify them separately.

The second argument is that – again restricted to the impact analysis in LCA – the proposed measures for the different impact categories differ to quite some extent on their basis. The global warming potentials are based on the marginal increase of the impact, the toxicity measure on the basis of a certain no-effect parameter on an equivalency of "safe values" (Jolliet & Crettaz (1997)), and the measure for eutrophication (Heijungs et al. (1992*b*)) is more or less based on the average contribution of nutrients in the formation of biomass.

This study seeks to derive a number of tools for environmental analysis and decision-support from a unified epistemological principle. It will be clear that the choice for the basis of deriving the impact factor must follow from this epistemological principle. It would be very unscientific to postulate impact measures "out of the air". That the current principles outlined in Section 2.1 are not sufficient to derive impact factors (and some other items, such as allocation factors) indicates that the epistemological basis to answer the attribution problem is still too small. One or two more principles might be necessary here for a complete derivation of the tools. For instance, we could postulate that the marginal contribution of a substance to an impact category, renormalized so as to satisfy the 100%-rule, is to be used for the impact factor in the context of attribution.

The epistemological principles that were outlined in Section 2.1 do not provide sufficient material to obtain impact factors for determining the relative contribution of each stressor to each impact category. As in the allocation problem, more external principles are required to find these coefficients.

Chapter 11

The Environmental Problem

11.1 REPRESENTATION OF THE ENVIRONMENTAL PROBLEM

11.1.1 What is the Environmental Problem?

The three fundamental equations that have so far been derived allow us to attribute environmental impacts to economic activities in relation to a specified external demand. The rest of the quotation of Victor's *Economics of pollution* that was given in Section 10.1.1 offers a good starting point. Although it is geared to discussing pollution, I quote it here in the context of a discussion of the environmental problem:

> any statement of what is or is not pollution necessarily involves a value judgment. … it is at this point that reasonable men may just have to disagree.[1]

I consider the concept of environmental problem to represent the problematic value, or disutility, that we assign, according to some set of moral principles, to the state of the environment or to changes of that state.[2]

1 Victor (1972*b*, p. 8).

2 De Groot (1992, p. 5n) defines environmental problems 'as discrepancies between (actual or expected) facts and norms, at the level of impact (e.g. environment-related health), at the level of environmental parameters (e.g., toxic substances in the air) and at the level of environmentally relevant activities (e.g., a proposed highway).' The present definition differs

Consequences of this view are, first, that the environmental problem – unlike environmental impacts of which there are many types – is a one-dimensional object, and, secondly, that the environmental problem is dependent on individual or social circumstances such as cultural background and personal interests, and may consequently vary over groups or persons, or within one group of persons over time.

Given that the perception of environmental impacts amounts to a value judgement, it must be acknowledged that an environmental problem never has and never will have a natural-scientific status. Natural-scientific facts may of course influence one's opinion or one's conduct. An ethical framework will, however, only in rare cases be built upon natural science.[3] The cultural embedding, the attitudes and behaviour of other people, and many other aspects will normally play a significant role. On the other hand, social-scientific methods will help the researcher to establish sets of stated or revealed preferences, but this by no means implies that the preferences themselves have a scientific status. We must try to accept that a person's or a society's judgements may be in contradiction with certain facts, or even in contradiction with each other. A scientist, like any other person, may try to persuade people to believe in his or her personal convictions, but when they refuse to do so, there is no ground for accusing them of being unscientific.

> The environmental problem is conceived here as the one-dimensional subjective measure of the severity of all environmental impacts. Attributing a share of the total environmental problem to an arbitrarily chosen economic activity is the topic of the next sections.

from De Groot's in two respects: environmental problems only exist at the level of impacts, and they manifest themselves not only as the disutility of the state of the environment, but also of the change of that state. There is some debate with respect to the question whether a one-dimensional measure of the environmental problem can be derived directly from the inventory table; see Braunschweig & Müller-Wenk (1993) and Anonymous (1994*c*) for two quite different proposals in that direction. It has, however, been quite broadly accepted that an intermediate step in which a number of impact categories are addressed needs to be made. Evidence of this is, apart from in the cited documents like Heijungs et al. (1992*b*), Fava et al. (1993), Consoli et al. (1993), Lindfors et al. (1995*c*), the report from Braunschweig et al. (1996), in which Braunschweig and Müller-Wenk have rephrased their 1993 proposal from intervention-oriented to impact-oriented weighting.

3 Even if natural science alone were the sole building material of one's ethics, one would have to choose between competing scientific theories and to deal with "facts" with different probabilities of truth.

11.1.2 A Measure for the Environmental Problem

Section 10.1.3 discussed the aggregation of a multitude of environmental stressors into a quite limited number of environmental impacts. Our next task is to reduce the set of environmental impacts into a single figure that represents the environmental problem to which those impacts contribute. The reasoning to be followed is quite similar to the one used for the measure of environmental impacts, and can therefore be quite brief. If the total problem is denoted by g, several environmental impacts l contribute an amount $(g_c)_l$ to it, and the current amount of environmental impact l is denoted by $(z_c)_l$, we attribute the following amount of environmental problem

$$(g_a)_l = \frac{(g_c)_l}{(z_c)_l}(z_a)_l \tag{11.1}$$

to an attributed environmental impact $(z_a)_l$. In our case, we have attributed an amount r_l to a certain economic activity. The total environmental problem index to be attributed is then simply

$$g = \sum_l \frac{(g_c)_l}{(z_c)_l} r_l. \tag{11.2}$$

Again, like the quantity $\frac{(z_c)_{li}}{(y_c)_i}$ in Section 10.1.2 (the impact factor r_{li}), the quantity $\frac{(g_c)_l}{(z_c)_l}$ plays a central role in this equation: it constitutes what will be called the problem factor, and expresses the contribution that a unit amount of impact category l makes to the total environmental problem that is perceived by an individual or society. It will be abbreviated by the symbol g_l:

$$g_l = \frac{(g_c)_l}{(z_c)_l}. \tag{11.3}$$

The equation to aggregate environmental impacts into a measure of the environmental problem, the problem index g, is then simply

$$g = \sum_l g_l r_l. \tag{11.4}$$

It is clear that this measure of environmental problem is indeed one-dimensional, and that it is a multilinear function of the environmental impacts that are attributed to a certain economic activity. As such, it is in agreement with the epistemological principles that were outlined in Section 2.1. Another important feature is that the index l runs over all elements of **r**, and hence over the transient impacts **e** as well as the permanent impacts **f**. This means that the weighting allows for an aggregation of time-integrated transient impacts due to degradable and renewable environmental commodities, and of asymptotical permanent impacts due to persistent and non-renewable environmental commodities. It might appear remarkable that two such different classes are combined into one measure of the environmental problem. It is, however, precisely this character of the perceived problem which enables this miraculous reconcilation. The character of the environmental problem is an intrinsic one-dimensional measure. There is a situation of multiple impacts of many different kinds, some of them of a permanent nature and others of a transient nature. Yet individuals, groups of individuals, or society perceive or perceives this multi-impact situation as a whole and is or are able to assign one measure of undesiredness to it.

In aggregating all types of impacts into one problem measure, a new epistemological problem has been created: how to determine the problem factor g_l? This question will be discussed in Section 11.1.4.

> Using similar arguments as for environmental impacts, we may easily construct a measure for the environmental problem as the weighted aggregation of the attributed environmental impacts. The weighting factors are referred to as problem factors.

11.1.3 The Fourth Fundamental Equation

In matrix notation the weighted aggregation of environmental impacts assumes the form

$$g = \mathbf{g} \cdot \mathbf{r}. \tag{11.5}$$

Here the elements of the problem vector **g** represent the problem factors for the different environmental impacts that are weighted according to individual or societal preference. The equation is called the fourth fundamental equation, as it is the fourth and last step in the path from attributing environmental problems to economic activities.

The fourth fundamental equation expresses the relation between the set of environmental impacts that are attributed to an economic activity and the environmental problem that is attached to those impacts. The environmental problem index is calculated as

$$g = \mathbf{g} \cdot \mathbf{r},$$

where $\mathbf{g}$ is the vector of problem factors and $\mathbf{r}$ is the vector of attributed environmental impacts.

Combination of the fourth fundamental equation with Section 10.1.3 yields the "master equation" (*cf.* Section 5.4.1) that reveals this relationship:

$$g = \mathbf{g} \cdot \mathbf{R} \cdot \mathbf{Q} \cdot \bar{\mathbf{B}} \cdot \bar{\mathbf{A}}^{-1} \cdot \mathbf{a}. \qquad (11.6)$$

It is this equation which will be used – along with the other fundamental equations – in the further derivation of the concrete tools for environmental analysis and decision-support in the next section.

11.1.4 The Nature of the Problem Factors

In Section 10.1.4, the nature of the impact factors was found to be intrinsically unknowable within the epistemological principles stated in Section 2.1. The impact factors were defined as the contribution that the current level of a certain stressor makes to the current level of each impact category.

It is not surprising that the problem factors that play a central role in the fourth fundamental equation are equally unknowable. The problem factors indicate the contribution that the current level of each impact category makes to the current environmental problem. This contribution is on the one hand even more unknowable than the one related to impact factors, because in the case of the problem factors it is also the total amount (the current environmental problem) which is unknown. On the other hand, however, the fact that it is about social preference might make the situation easier to comprehend.

There is a highly developed theory on the measurement of preference and utility, and on decision theory. Of general significance are formal textbooks like Sen (1969) and Fishburn (1988). Related to decision-making in the environmental field are, for instance, Jansen (1991) and Maystre et al. (1994). It must be emphasized that these books provide excellent theoretical frameworks which can in principle be used to make decisions on concrete environmental issues, for instance, concerning the choice between two or more alternatives. Furthermore, there is a large amount of papers that describe one particular approach towards the valuation of impacts on the environment or of environmental objects; see, e.g., Bateman & Turner (1992), Sankovskii (1992), and Boxall et al. (1996).

Unfortunately quite remote from these well-founded frameworks are a number of texts which describe sets of problem factors or procedures to obtain such sets. The problem factors are intended to be generally applicable, which means that they are not specific for one specific group of alternatives, but can be used for any arbitrary problem of rank or choice. The field of life-cycle assessment in particular has produced a number of proposals; see Lindeijer (1996) for an overview. There have been only few attempts to reconcile the general decision-making literature with the attribution-related question that is posed in LCA; see Fava et al. (1993, pp. 87–100), Heijungs (1994*c*), Tukker (1994), and in particular Hofstetter (1996*b*). Unfortunately, none of these texts has been able to produce concrete numbers.

The question of finding problem factors which transform the impact scores into the problem index is far from settled.

Chapter 12

Towards Concrete Tools for Environmental Analysis and Decision-Support: Impact Analysis

12.1 GENERAL CONSIDERATIONS

While the derivation of the inventory analysis of a selection of tools for environmental analysis and decision-support in Chapter 7 was a long exercise in choosing special system boundaries and external demands, the derivation of the impact analysis is much easier. This has in the first place to do with the fact that the necessary ingredients – the environmental interventions – are already there at the end of the inventory analysis. A second reason is that there is not a crossroad of modes of analysis in the impact analysis: the tools of the CFA type and those of the ALA type can all be treated with the second, third, and fourth fundamental equation. In principle, the following sections on the derivation of the specific form of the impact analysis for the cases of life-cycle assessment, substance-flow analysis, etc. can be kept very brief.

Nevertheless, the following sections turn out to be not so short. The reason for this is the large deviation from the established framework and methods for the impact analysis of the different tools. As was already discussed, the structure of the impact analysis in LCA (where it is usually called impact assessment) is one that does not conform to the three stages of fate, impact, and problem, that has been devised as a unified framework. For SFA, there is also a problematic match: environmental processes (the fate aspect) are normally treated together with the economic processes that were dealt with in the inventory analysis in this study. For risk assessment a similar reason holds. See also Sections 1.3.2 and 10.1.1.

So much for the – with respect to numbers – immaterial differences in framework. The difference in methods originates from a difference in questions that are normally posed to the tools. The emphasis in this study is on the attribution of environmental problems (or impacts) to economic activities. Most authors in the diverse arenas of tools for decision-support have other questions: that of choice between alternatives, that of granting permits, etc. It is partly a matter of posing a clear question which determines the epistemological principles and thereby the concrete methods to be used. See Section 14.1 for a further discussion.

The derivation of the tools will be illustrated with an example impact analysis. For this we assume the fate of environmental commodities to be

TABLE 12.1. Hypothetical data for environmental processes, used to illustrate the derivation of several tools.

environmental commodity	stressor				
	"d_1": crops	"c_1": kg CO_2 in air	"c_2": kg CO in air	"c_3": kg NO_2 in air	"c_4": kg N_2O in air
"b_1"*: kg CO_2 in air	1	0	0	0	0
"b_2": kg CO in air	-0.1	1	-5	0	0
"b_3": kg NO_2 in air	0	0	0	-3	2
"b_4": kg N_2O in air	0	0	0	1	-1

* The reader is again referred to footnote 31 of Chapter 5 for an explanation of the quotation marks.

given as in Table 12.1. For example, the fourth column ("c_3") of this table expresses the differential equation

$$\frac{db_3(t)}{dt} = 0b_1(t) + 0b_2(t) + -3b_3(t) + 1b_4(t), \tag{12.1}$$

or, in words, that the rate of change of the amount of NO_2 in air correlates linearly with the amount of N_2O in air, and anti-linearly with the amount of NO_2 in air.[1] The fate matrix is thus given by[2]

1 Observe that the units that are indicated in Table 9.3 do not correspond to the quantities b and c, but are based instead on the underlying fate model.

2 Observe that the fate matrix is not the 4 × 4 matrix in the lower right corner of Table 9.3,

$$\mathbf{C} = \begin{pmatrix} 0 & 1 & 0 & 0 \\ 0 & -5 & 0 & 0 \\ 0 & 0 & -3 & 1 \\ 0 & 0 & 2 & -1 \end{pmatrix}. \qquad (12.2)$$

The inputs and outputs of economic commodities by environmental processes is simple in this example. It is assumed that there is only one economic commodity "a_1": crops, and that these are positively affected by CO_2, and negatively by CO, with coefficients 1 and −0.1 respectively. The damage matrix **D** is then simply

$$\mathbf{D} = \begin{pmatrix} 1 & -0.1 & 0 & 0 \end{pmatrix}. \qquad (12.3)$$

According to the theory that was developed in Section 9.2, the singular fate matrix must be reduced by transferring the first row and column to the damage matrix. For this aim, we introduce the two matrices $\boldsymbol{\Xi}'$ and $\boldsymbol{\Xi}''$ as

$$\boldsymbol{\Xi}' = \begin{pmatrix} 0 & 1 & 0 & 0 \\ 0 & 0 & 1 & 0 \\ 0 & 0 & 0 & 1 \end{pmatrix} \text{ and } \boldsymbol{\Xi}'' = \begin{pmatrix} 1 & 0 & 0 & 0 \end{pmatrix}. \qquad (12.4)$$

A straightforward application of the rules for finding $\check{\mathbf{C}}$ and $\check{\mathbf{D}}$, and hence **Q**, gives:

$$\mathbf{Q} = \begin{pmatrix} 0 & -0.02 & 0 & 0 \\ 1 & 0.02 & 0 & 0 \\ 0 & 0.2 & 0 & 0 \\ 0 & 0 & 1 & 1 \\ 0 & 0 & 2 & 3 \end{pmatrix}. \qquad (12.5)$$

The interpretation of this fate/damage matrix will be discussed in connection with the tools that will be derived hereafter.

For the analysis in terms of environmental impacts, the following situation is postulated. There are two environmental impacts considered here: global

but is its transpose. Related to this is the fact that the left-hand side of Equation (9.1) is $\frac{db_3(t)}{dt}$ and not c_3; see Section 9.2.2 for an argumentation.

TABLE 12.2. Hypothetical data for environmental impacts, used to illustrate the derivation of several tools.

	environmental impact		
environmental stressor	crop growth (in kg)	toxicity (number of excess deaths)	global warming (radiative forcing in W)
"d_1": kg crop	1	0	0
"c_1": $kg \cdot hr^{-1}$ CO_2 in air	0	0	300
"c_2": $kg \cdot hr^{-1}$ CO in air	0	1500	10
"c_3": $kg \cdot hr^{-1}$ NO_2 in air	0	400	30
"c_4": $kg \cdot hr^{-1}$ N_2O in air	0	0	40

warming, expressed in terms of radiative forcing; and toxicity, expressed in excess incidence of death. There is also one economic commodity involved: crops. The details of the hypothetical impact data are given in Table 12.2. For instance, the number 300 means that the current emission level of CO_2 contributes 300 $W \cdot kg \cdot hr^{-1}$ to the total global warming impact. It is left unspecified what this total impact is, and what the emission level is. Only their ratio is given. For instance, the total global warming impact might be $3 \cdot 10^{12}$ W while the total emission of CO_2 is $1 \cdot 10^{10}$ $kg \cdot hr^{-1}$. In any case, these hypothetical impact data yield an impact matrix **R** that is given by[3]

$$\mathbf{R} = \begin{pmatrix} 1 & 0 & 0 & 0 & 0 \\ 0 & 300 & 10 & 30 & 40 \\ 0 & 0 & 1500 & 400 & 0 \end{pmatrix}. \tag{12.6}$$

Finally, the interpretation of environmental impacts in terms of their contribution to what is perceived as the environmental problem. Table 12.3 gives hypothetical problem factors for the environmental impact categories global warming and toxicity, and for the impacts on the economic commodity crops. The factors may be put in the problem vector **g**:

$$\mathbf{g} = \begin{pmatrix} -1 & 8 & 5 \end{pmatrix}. \tag{12.7}$$

These numbers may be interpreted as the contribution that the current extent of the impact makes to the total environmental problem, as perceived by those who have stated the factors. It says, for instance, that the current impact of

3 Again, notice that the impact matrix is the transpose of the number in Table 12.1.

TABLE 12.3. Hypothetical data for the environmental problem, used to illustrate the derivation of several tools.

environmental impact	g: environmental problem
"f_1": crop growth (in kg)	-1
"e_1": global warming (radiative forcing in W)	8
"e_2": toxicity (number of excess death)	5

global warming is perceived more seriously than the current impact of toxicity.

12.2 DERIVATION OF LIFE-CYCLE ASSESSMENT

Section 7.2 gave an expression for the inventory table **b** as a result of the inventory analysis in LCA. This inventory table can be directly submitted to the procedure for impact analysis.

Supposing that the vector of environmental interventions is given as

$$\mathbf{b} = \begin{pmatrix} 10 \\ 0 \\ 2 \\ 0 \end{pmatrix} \tag{12.8}$$

hence an attributed emission of 10 kg CO_2 to air and of 2 kg NO_2 to air, we easily find from the fate analysis using $\mathbf{q} = \mathbf{Q} \cdot \mathbf{b}$ that

$$\mathbf{q} = \begin{pmatrix} 0 \\ 10 \\ 0 \\ 2 \\ 4 \end{pmatrix} . \tag{12.9}$$

The interpretation is as follows. There is an asymptotically permanent amount of 10 kg CO_2 in the air, there is a time-integrated amount of 2 kg·hr NO_2 in the air, and there is a time-integrated amount of 4 kg·hr N_2O in the air. There is no CO in the air, and the permanent nature of CO_2 in the air[4] has forced us to exclude the ever-increasing influence of this stressor on crops. Therefore, there is no (positive or negative) influence on crops.

This vector of stressors can be further submitted to an analysis of the resulting impacts. Although CO_2 and CO differ in their nature as stressors (the former is an permanent stressor, the latter an transient stressor), it was apparently possible to determine the contribution they make to the same impact category (global warming). Application of the impact factors to the stressor table gives by means of $\mathbf{r} = \mathbf{R} \cdot \mathbf{q}$:

$$\mathbf{r} = \begin{pmatrix} 0 \\ 3220 \\ 800 \end{pmatrix}. \tag{12.10}$$

The interpretation is that the attributed interventions make a contribution to the impact of global warming (5200 W) and to the impact of toxicity (800 excess cases of death). There is no impact on crops.

The final interpretation is in terms of the environmental problem:

$$g = 29760. \tag{12.11}$$

This number may be difficult to interpret in an absolute way: a comparative study of different alternative products, or an analysis of the contribution that different economic processes or emissions make to the attributed environmental problem will reveal the significance of this measure of societally perceived environmental problem.

> The first stage of the impact analysis in LCA is concerned with fate. The table of transient and permanent stressors is found by direct application of the second fundamental equation to the inventory table that was yielded by the inventory analysis. The interpretation in terms of environmental impacts is found by direct application of the third fundamental equation. The final interpretation in terms of the environmental problem that is to be attributed is found by application of the fourth fundamental equation.

The traditional approach to LCA differs in quite a few respects from the procedure described above. With respect to the framework, some differences

4 In reality, CO_2 has a limited residence time in the air. This has been neglected for illustrative purposes, however.

were already discussed in Sections 10.1.1 and 3.4.2. But perhaps more important are the differences with respect to the results.

In the first place, fate is not often modelled in LCA, although its importance is being realized (Udo de Haes (1996)) and some research in this area is being carried out (Jolliet (1994), Wegener Sleeswijk & Heijungs (1996)). Most guidelines for LCA suggest the use of global warming potentials for interpreting environmental commodities in terms of global warming impacts; these potentials are constructed on the basis of, *inter alia*, a fate model. For the impact depletion of stratospheric ozone and for photo-oxidant formation, the suggested use of ozone depletion potentials and photochemical oxidant creation potentials also implies the incorporation of fate. For most other impact categories, the situation is much less developed. Fate modelling for toxicity is in its infancy (Guinée et al. (1996)), while the other substance-oriented output categories acidification, eutrophication, and odour have barely been discussed in the context of fate. It may be argued that modelling of fate should preferably take place independently from the impact categories considered (Wegener Sleeswijk & Heijungs (1996)). Acknowledgement of this idea will perhaps lead to a consistent incorporation of fate in all emission-related impact categories. Fate has seldom been discussed in relation to resource-related interventions; see Guinée & Heijungs (1995) for a method to determine the depleting impacts of resource extraction including one fate aspect (regeneration). One aspect that has been introduced in this chapter and that is perhaps lacking in all of LCA literature is the reaction (decay) products that are formed in environmental processes. The proposed fate calculation sees the formation of decay products as a simple conversion of commodities into commodities, and is thus in theory perfectly able to include it in a consistent way. The practical problem of finding appropriate data to describe this phenomenon may be an important obstacle, though.

A second important difference is that the measures for the impact categories have seldom been defined in a consistent way with respect to the incremental-marginal-average question. See Section 10.1.4 for a number of examples of impact factors in LCA that comply with different epistemological principles. There is a large amount of agreement between the impact categories in traditional LCA and those of Section 10.1.1, but that is no accident, as the list proposed in Section 10.1.1 was a good deal inspired by the discussions in LCA. I do not claim that a choice for the average attribution rule is superior to the other choices, but I do think that it is superior in relation to the attribution problem. But of course, attribution is not the only conceivable question to be posed in environmental analysis and decision-making; see Section 14.1 for some further remarks. The most important recommendation for LCA is to make a consistent choice of impact factors, in line with the exact question that is asked (*cf.* Frischknecht (1997)), and consistently to include fate in an impact-category-independent way (Wegener Sleeswijk & Heijungs (1996)).

Lastly, the final interpretation in terms of the environmental problem is pertinently based on social preference in LCA (see, e.g., Heijungs et al. (1992*a*), Consoli et al. (1993), Fava et al. (1993), Finnveden (1996)), but is more and more being based on natural-scientific parameters (see, e.g., Goedkoop & Cnubben (1995), Braunschweig et al. (1996)). This, of course, can be judged as a problematic development:

> In a sense it can therefore be questioned whether [these] methods in general can be called valuation methods.[5]

Anyhow, it can be argued that problem factors that are based on dynamic considerations (such as reduction targets, costs for prevention, willingness-to-pay, marginal trade-offs) are by definition inappropriate to the attribution problem. Of course, we may decide to substitute, say, marginal problem factors for the static attribution-oriented problem factors for lack of anything better, as long as it complies with the boundary conditions, most notoriously the rule of 100%-additivity.

> There are significant differences between the proposed approach and the current practice of life-cycle assessment. These differences concern the framework of impact analysis, which is proposed to be supplied with a stand-alone analysis of fate, the inclusion of indirect aspects, due to, for instance, decay products, and the consistent choice of a static attribution principle in defining the impact factors and the problem factors.

5 Finnveden (1996, p. 30).

12.3 DERIVATION OF SUBSTANCE-FLOW ANALYSIS

The structure and procedure for the impact analysis in SFA is very similar to that of LCA, but its differences from the currently established set-up are much larger. The inventory analysis (see Section 7.3) gave a vector of environmental interventions **b** which was put with the external economic flow **a** into the vector of external flows **p**. From this vector was deduced the vector of substance flows **y** by means of the transmission vector τ. Because the fate characteristics of carbon in CO_2 are different from those of carbon in CO, a correct analysis of fate and a subsequent analysis of environmental impacts can only take place at the level of the flows in **b**, and not at that of the flows in **y**. The rules for finding the resulting stressors and impacts, and the one-dimensional problem, are exactly the same as for LCA. Presenting a numerical example does not provide any additional insight.

What is different, however, is that SFA concentrates in the presentation of the results of the impact analysis on the substance or substance group of interest. The inventory table **b** was calculated but not presented as the final result of the inventory analysis. Instead, the conversion to the vector **y** was made. The analysis of fate is quite similar in this respect. The presentation of the stressors **q** is restricted to that fraction that contains the substance that is central in the analysis. The connection with this new quantity **w** is via[6]

$$\mathbf{w} = \tau \diamond \mathbf{q}. \tag{12.12}$$

The subsequent analysis of impacts and the environmental problem of course starts from the original table of stressors **q**, not with the presented **w**. A new problem arises if one tries to attribute environmental impacts to substance flows, however. The concept of impact factors presumes that it is possible to establish a quantitative relationship between, say, a unit emission of halon-1211 (CF_2BrCl) and the depletion of stratospheric ozone. It does not, however, say anything with respect to the relation between carbon, fluorine, chlorine, or bromine and the depletion of the ozone layer. In other words, there is no scientific ground to establish partial impact factors under the current epistemological foundation. This restriction holds, *a fortiori*, for the extension to environmental problems. Only for special choices of the substances (e.g., cadmium) might it be possible to go into an attribution of

6 Care should be taken that the ordering of the commodities differs between **p** and **q**. Some reshuffling in τ may therefore be required.

environmental problems to environmental stressors.

The procedure for impact analysis of substance-flow analysis is exactly equal to that of life-cycle assessment. The presentation of the results is, however, restricted to the stressors, or, occasionally, to the impacts.

The difference with the established approach for SFA is, however, enormous. This concerns the framework as well as the exact technical procedures.

In LCA, we proposed to disentangle the usual structure for determining the influence of fate and impact into two separate steps. The modification for SFA is more drastic. On the one hand, SFA tries to model the processes in the economic and in the environmental system in an identical way ("the economy/ environment analogy"; Van der Voet (1995*a*, p. 94)). The arguments that were presented in Section 9.1.1 invoked the design of an alternative representation of environmental processes, even though the suggestions of Isard (1968) to unite the two were judged as inspiring. A crucial element in the apprehension of the deviation from the established concepts is the exact question at stake. Whereas the traditional substance-flow analysis aims to describe the flows (and probably stocks) of a substance in a certain region during a certain period of time, the starting point in the present text is the attribution problem. The question here is thus: which flows in the environment are to be attributed to the economic activity in a certain region during a certain period of time? This is markedly different from the question concerning the flows in the economy and the environment in a certain region during a certain period of time. For example, transboundary pollution of economic activities outside the region of interest into the region of interest is uninteresting with respect to the attribution problem, but is an important source of pollution from the traditional SFA point of view. Or the other way around: transboundary pollution of pollution caused by the region of interest to another region is part of the pollution-to-be-attributed, whereas it is more or less outside the system in the traditional point of view. I think that both interpretations of substance-flow analysis have their merits, and that not one or another mode is necessarily better or worse than the other(s). It is the exact question which differs, with consequences for the entire set of computational rules and numerical results.

Besides the completely different set-up for the inclusion of environmental processes, the further impact analysis is also different. Most substance-flow analyses do not consider an interpretation in terms of environmental problems. Tukker et al. (1995) provide one of those rare examples where a number of environmental impact categories is addressed. It must be stressed that it is difficult to do so in general. In the first place, it is the speciation of the substance which determines the types of impacts it may contribute to, and the strength with which it does so. A normal SFA concentrates on the specific substance, say carbon, and is hence unable to distinguish CO_2 from CO. But even if it manages to do so, the fact that fate is included in a way which is different from that described above makes the connection with impact factors cumbersome. Most substance-flow analyses therefore either stick to an "extended inventory analysis", which covers economic and environmental processes, but does not cover environmental impacts or problems, or uses specific indicators to aggregate flows and to interpret the results. Examples of these indicators are described by Van der Voet et al. (1995*d*), by Baccini & Bader (1996, p. 308 *ff.*), and by Azar et al. (1996). Despite the possible usefulness of these indicators, they fall outside the realm of the epistemological basis of this study.

> There is a large conceptual and practical difference between the proposed approach for substance-flow analysis and the established approaches. The main reason for this is the fact that the traditional approaches are not designed to give an answer to the attribution problem, but instead concentrate on the environmental situation in the region that also defined the boundary for the economic activities taken into account.

12.4 THE RELATION WITH ENVIRONMENTAL IMPACT ASSESSMENT AND RISK ASSESSMENT

The fact that the inventory analysis of all described tools for environmental analysis and decision-support ends up with an inventory table of the same type means that the impact analysis of all these tools is to a very high degree identical. The previous two sections were devoted to the impact analysis in LCA and in SFA, and already in those cases the impact analysis was identical. The longest part of those sections was devoted to a discussion concerning the differences with the established approaches with respect to the impact analysis in the context of the attribution problem. The impact analysis of environmental impact analysis (Section 7.5) and risk assessment (Section 7.6) is again fully identical; see the previous two sections for a more detailed description.

The most important point for these three tools is one of interpretation. The two tools as defined here must be understood within the question of attribution. Thus, environmental impact assessment, like substance-flow analysis, is not concerned with the impacts or the problem in a region, but with the impacts or problems that are caused by a restricted economic activity within that region. And risk assessment does not give a clue to the question of safety or lack of it, but states which part of the environmental problem is to be attributed to the production and use of a certain chemical.

> The rules for making an attribution-oriented impact assessment in the tools EIA and RA is very easy: the formalism for LCA and SFA can be applied in a direct way. Some reflection as to the interpretation of the resulting tool remains an important issue.

[illegible] T_{ij} [illegible] ... [illegible] ... [illegible] ... [illegible] ... [illegible] ...

PART FOUR

CONCLUSION

This part is structured as a mirror of the introductory Part One.

The first section gives an answer to the attribution question of Section 1.1. In fact, four answers are given, each of them corresponding to a different interpretation of the attribution problem. These interpretations give rise to the five tools for environmental analysis and decision-support developed during Parts Two and Three: life-cycle assessment, substance-flow analysis, environmental impact assessment, and risk assessment, with subsequent focal points of the interpretation: a product from the cradle to the grave, a substance in a region, a factory, and releases of a chemical.

The second section gives an answer to the position question of Section 1.2. This amounts to a comparison of the four tools discussed with respect not so much to their focal point, but more to the differences that arise in the course of the unified procedure.

Whereas Section 1.3 introduced the path towards an answer to the attribution problem and the position problem, the last sections of this part pose a number of further questions. In the first place, the limited value of attribution in the context of environmental decision-making is discussed. Reference is made to other types of questions for which the several tools are also used: planning analysis, scenario analysis, improvement analysis, and origins analysis.

Some final reflections as to the scientific meaning and the philosophical position of this type of analysis posit that the process-picture of the world is a useful one with a restricted domain, that the tools for decision-support may create a self-consistent procedure but will never tell the one and only truth because there is more than one truth, and that the academic position of the kind of environmental science that has been practised in this study deserves a rather philosophical place between theology and science.

Chapter 13

The Answers

13.1 ANSWER 1: THE ATTRIBUTION PROBLEM

13.1.1 Introduction

Section 1.1 introduced the attribution problem as the question of which environmental problems are to be attributed to which economic activity. In the previous sections, especially in Section 1.2, Chapter 7, and Chapter 12, we discussed a number of tools for environmental analysis and decision-support. From the facts that there are quite a few tools available (see the anthology of Section 1.2.1), and that at least some of these tools can be derived from unified principles (Chapters 7 and 12), we arrive at an important conclusion. The attribution problem cannot be answered without a proper context. The economic activity to which environmental problems are to be attributed must be defined in a careful way. The resulting starting point has decisive implications for the procedure to be followed and consequently for the answer to the attribution problem.

The unified framework that was introduced in Section 1.3.2 consisted of three phases of analysis: a goal definition, an inventory analysis, and an impact analysis. It is the phase of goal definition that is concerned with the exact choice and formulation of the economic activity that is subject to further analysis. In particular, the crossroad of analyses into activity-level analysis and commodity-flow accounting (Section 5.3.2) and the system boundaries as to which economic processes are included in the analysis (Section 5.3.3) follow easily from the specifications made in the goal definition.

The following main categories of economic "activities"[1] will be considered in this and the next few sections:

- a product from the cradle to the grave;
- a substance in a region;
- a factory;
- releases of a chemical.

Each of these possibilities corresponds to a certain class of economic activities, and thereby to a certain interpretation of the exact meaning of the attribution problem. Specification of the answer to the attribution problem for these cases results therefore in a number of different tools for environmental decision-support. The principles of these tools have been derived in Chapters 7 and 12. They will be repeated and summarized in the next few sections.

The tools for answering the attribution problem are derived from unified principles. This means that there are, besides the four fundamental equations, a number of common elements. These common elements on the one hand facilitate reflections as to the relative position of the tools (Section 13.2), and on the other hand allow for a concise description of the tools and a time- and effort-saving data collection procedure. The common elements are described below before the description of the specific tools. The fundamental equations will also be repeated hereafter.

Common element 1: collection and representation of data with respect to economic processes

Collect physical data (rates of inflow and outflow of economic and environmental commodities) of every process that is part of the system. The rate of flow of the ith economic commodity to and from the jth process is represented by a technical coefficient $\bar{a}_{ij}$, and the rate of flow of the ith environmental commodity by $\bar{b}_{ij}$. The inflow of commodities is represented by negative values of these coefficients; outflows are positive. Thus, if a_{ij} and b_{ij} represent the flows of the ith economic commodity and the ith environmental

1 It may be observed that not all categories appear to correspond to an activity. For instance, a product is not an activity, and neither is a region one. This is, however, a matter of semantics: what is meant here is the activities that are related to a product or the activities that take place within a region respectively.

commodity to and from the jth process during the time interval t_j that these flows are recorded, the technical coefficients are established as

$$\bar{a}_{ij} = \frac{a_{ij}}{t_j} \text{ and } \bar{b}_{ij} = \frac{b_{ij}}{t_j}. \tag{13.1}$$

The elements $\bar{a}_{ij}$ and $\bar{b}_{ij}$ are collected in two matrices: the technology matrix $\bar{\mathbf{A}}$ and the intervention matrix $\bar{\mathbf{B}}$. See Section 5.2.3.

Common element 2: determination of the allocation factors
Economic processes that provide two or more functions may need to be allocated, which means effectively that they are split into a number of independent hypothetical processes that provide one single function. The factors that are needed for this must be supplied by the user as external knowledge. An important requirement is the rule of 100%-additivity. See Section 6.2.

Common element 3: collection and representation of data with respect to environmental processes
Model the fate (intermedia transport, degradation, formation, etc.) of environmental commodities. This results in a number of coefficients c_{ik}: the rate of change of the amount of the ith environmental commodity per unit amount of the kth environmental commodity. In an analogous way, model the fate (degradation and formation) of economic commodities due to the presence or absence of environmental commodities. The resulting coefficient d_{ik} represents the rate of change of the amount of the ith economic commodity per unit amount of the kth environmental commodity. These coefficients are thus given by

$$c_{ik} = \frac{1}{b_k(t)}\frac{\mathrm{d}b_i(t)}{\mathrm{d}t} \text{ and } d_{ik} = \frac{1}{b_k(t)}\frac{\mathrm{d}a_i(t)}{\mathrm{d}t}. \tag{13.2}$$

The elements c_{ik} and d_{ik} build the fate matrix $\mathbf{C}$ and the damage matrix $\mathbf{D}$. See Section 9.1.3.

Common element 4: determination of the reduction matrices
The fate matrix is singular if its determinant is zero. In that case, select the indices of the rows that are filled with only zeroes. The reduced fate matrices are constructed by splitting a square unit matrix into two matrices by moving the rows that correspond to the singular rows of the fate matrix in the matrix $\boldsymbol{\Xi}''$

and giving the remaining matrix the symbol $\boldsymbol{\Xi}'$. See Section 9.2.5.

Common element 5: selection of impact categories and determination of impact factors
A number of environmental impact categories must be chosen. Important requirements are completeness and independence. The "strength" of a certain stressor with which it contributes to these impact categories must be established as external knowledge. An important requirement is the 100%-rule. See Sections 10.1.1 and 10.1.4.

Common element 6: determination of the problem factors
The contribution of each of the chosen impact categories to the perceived total environmental problem must be established as external knowledge. See Section 11.1.4.

First fundamental equation
The relation between the vector of externally demanded economic commodities **a** and the vector of environmental interventions of environmental commodities **b** is given by

$$\mathbf{b} = \bar{\mathbf{B}} \cdot \bar{\mathbf{A}}^{-1} \cdot \mathbf{a}. \tag{13.3}$$

See Section 5.4.1.

Second fundamental equation
The relation between the vector of environmental interventions of environmental commodities **b** and the vector of transient and permanent stressors **q** is

$$\mathbf{q} = \begin{bmatrix} \mathbf{d} \\ \mathbf{c} \end{bmatrix} = \left[\begin{bmatrix} \mathbf{D} \cdot (\boldsymbol{\Xi}')^{\mathrm{T}} \\ \boldsymbol{\Xi}'' \cdot \mathbf{C} \cdot (\boldsymbol{\Xi}')^{\mathrm{T}} \end{bmatrix} \cdot -(\boldsymbol{\Xi}' \cdot \mathbf{C} \cdot (\boldsymbol{\Xi}')^{\mathrm{T}})^{-1} \cdot \boldsymbol{\Xi}' + \begin{bmatrix} \mathbf{0} \\ \boldsymbol{\Xi}'' \end{bmatrix} \atop -(\boldsymbol{\Xi}' \cdot \mathbf{C} \cdot (\boldsymbol{\Xi}')^{\mathrm{T}})^{-1} \cdot \boldsymbol{\Xi}' \right] \cdot \mathbf{b}. \tag{13.4}$$

See Section 9.2.6.

Third fundamental equation
The relation between the vector of environmental impacts exerted on impact

categories **r** and the vector of transient and permanent stressors **q** is given by

$$\mathbf{r} = \mathbf{R} \cdot \mathbf{q}. \tag{13.5}$$

See Section 10.1.3.

Fourth fundamental equation
The relation between the one-dimensional environmental problem g and the vector of environmental impacts exerted on impact categories **r** is given by

$$g = \mathbf{g} \cdot \mathbf{r}. \tag{13.6}$$

See Section 11.1.3.

13.1.2 A Product from the Cradle to the Grave: Life-Cycle Assessment

Sections 7.2 and 12.2 were devoted to the derivation of life-cycle assessment (LCA). Life-cycle assessment was introduced as an analysis of the activity-level analysis type, under the special condition of only one economic non-material commodity output. This output is thus not a concrete product in the traditional sense, but is the function fulfilled by that concrete product.[2] The full algorithm is summarized below.

Phase 1: Goal definition
Specify the functional unit, that is, the service that is to be fulfilled by the product that can be considered as the culmination of the cluster of economic processes. Assuming that this service corresponds to the ith economic commodity, put all elements except the ith of the vector of external demand to zero, and put the ith element to a value that corresponds to the functional unit. Denote this vector by **a**. Thus put

2 As discussed in Section 7.2, we may introduce here at this point the "cradle-to-gate" analysis with a positively valued material object (a good) as its focal point, and the "gate-to-grave" analysis with a negatively valued material object (a "bad") as its focal point. The main text, however, is restricted to the "cradle-to-grave" analysis only, starting with a non-tangible positively valued object (a service).

$$\mathbf{a} = \begin{bmatrix} 0 \\ \cdots \\ 0 \\ a_i \\ 0 \\ \cdots \\ 0 \end{bmatrix}. \tag{13.7}$$

If necessary, specify the functional unit with respect to representative characteristics, especially time period and spatial scale.

Phase 2: Inventory analysis
Collect data of every economic process that might be involved according to common element 1. In the case of a rectangular or singular technology matrix $\bar{\mathbf{A}}$, postulate allocation factors to allocate multiple processes according to common element 2. Find the environmental interventions that are to be attributed to the functional unit a_i by means of the first fundamental equation.

Phase 3: Impact analysis
Collect data with respect to environmental processes that determine the fate of environmental commodities and the damage of economic commodities according to common element 3. Determine the reduction matrices according to common element 4. The transient and permanent stressors are found by application of the second fundamental equation. Select impact categories and determine impact factors according to common element 5. Apply these elements by using the third fundamental equation. Determine problem factors according to common element 6, and apply the fourth fundamental equation to find the environmental problem g that is to be attributed to the functional unit a_i.

13.1.3 A Substance in a Region: Substance-Flow Analysis

The derivation of substance-flow analysis (SFA) was presented in Sections 7.3 and 12.3. It was defined as an analysis of the commodity-flow accounting type, although it often turns into one of the activity-level type when the effectiveness of abatement measures is studied. The special aspect of SFA was that all economic activities in a certain region are included in the analysis, but that the presentation of the results is restricted to one user-defined substance or group of substances. This section describes the complete algorithmic structure.[3]

Phase 1: Goal definition

Define the region, the time period, and the representative calendar time which the substance-flow analysis is to account for. The time period is given the symbol t, and is usually one year. Also choose the substance or the group of substances.

Phase 2: Inventory analysis

Collect, according to common element 1, data of every economic process that is part of the system in agreement with the goal definition's specification of region and calendar time. The size of the flow of the jth environmental intervention is given by

$$b_k = \sum_i \bar{b}_{ki} t. \tag{13.8}$$

Construct a vector of transmission coefficient $\boldsymbol{\tau}$, such that τ_i represents the content of the substance of interest of the ith commodity. The flows of this substance to and from the environment is now expressed as elements of the vector **y**:

$$y_j = \tau_j b_j. \tag{13.9}$$

Phase 3: Impact analysis

Collect data with respect to environmental processes that determine the fate of environmental commodities and the damage of economic commodities according to common element 3. Determine the reduction matrices according to common element 4. The transient and permanent stressors are found by applying the second fundamental equation to the vector of environmental interventions **b**. The resulting stressors may be filtered to display only the presence of the substance of interest:

3 As discussed in Section 7.3, we may derive instead of a proper substance-flow analysis by concentrating on one substance, a material-flow analysis, a product-flow analysis, or an energy(-flow) analysis by concentrating on a material, a product, or energy instead. The text is restricted here to SFA.

$$w_j = \tau_j q_j. \tag{13.10}$$

Care should be taken with respect to the index j of the elements of the transmission vector $\boldsymbol{\tau}$. The extension from environmental stressors to environmental impact or even environmental problem can in general not be made.

13.1.4 A Factory: Environmental Impact Assessment

Sections 7.4 and 12.4 introduced environmental impact assessment as an analysis that is very much the same as pure commodity-flow accounting, but with a much narrower system boundary.

Phase 1: Goal definition
Define the activity, the time period, and the representative calendar time which the analysis is to account for. The time period is given the symbol t, and is usually one year.

Phase 2: Inventory analysis
Collect, according to common element 1, data of every economic process that is part of the system in agreement with the goal definition's specification of activity and calendar time. The environmental intervention of the kth environmental commodity is given by

$$b_k = \sum_i \bar{b}_{ki} t. \tag{13.11}$$

Phase 3: Impact analysis
Collect data with respect to environmental processes that determine the fate of environmental commodities and the damage of economic commodities according to common element 3. Determine the reduction matrices according to common element 4. The transient and permanent stressors are found by application of the second fundamental equation. Select impact categories and determine impact factors according to common element 5. Apply these elements by using the third fundamental equation. Determine problem factors according to common element 6, and apply the fourth fundamental equation to find the environmental problem that is to be attributed to activity during the selected time period.

13.1.5 Releases of a Chemical: Risk Assessment

Sections 7.5 and 12.4 described risk assessment as a special case of the procedure for substance-flow analysis. The difference is that one does not study the presence or the content of the chosen substance in commodities, but only as it really exists in a free form. So, not cadmium in batteries and not cadmium in a stock in a factory, but only the emission of pure cadmium to the environment. The only difference in the procedure that is described in Section 13.1.3 is a more restricted choice of the vector of transmission coefficients. Nearly of all them will be zero.

13.1.6 Discussion

The preceding sections discussed four different answers to the attribution problem. There is not one single and unambiguous answer. The relative position and meaning of the different answers is discussed in the next section, which concentrates on the second main question of this study. Some discussion needs to be devoted, however, to the question of novelty of the results. Have the tools by any means been improved?

I think that the answer is affirmative. The constant debate on what the tools for environmental analysis and decision-support ought to be can be traced back to a lack of clarity in the question and a lack of clarity in epistemological foundation. The first point will be discussed in Section 14.2.2; the second point will, it is hoped, be clear after the reader has gone through the previous chapters. Some examples from the previous discussions will demonstrate a number of proposed modifications to the existing tools.

- The impact analysis (or impact assessment) of LCA is split into three major elements: analysis of fate, analysis of impacts, and analysis of problem contribution.
- The analysis of fate in all the tools that are derived is improved by – at least theoretically – incorporating the formation of reaction (decay) products and the disappearance of natural resources that are consumed to regenerate other extracted resources.
- The focus on the attribution problem enables a clear restriction in the question that is posed, and allows us to design the tools from linear principles.
- The question that is posed in SFA is changed from an analysis of the

flows in the economy and environment in a region to an analysis of the flows in the economy of a region and the flows in the environment that are to be attributed to those economic activities.

- The current mixture of marginal and average calculus that underlies the impact analysis and parts of the inventory analysis is purified.
- The theoretically superior way to link processes in an SFA is by specifying all inputs and outputs of the processes, and not yet concentrating on one single substance or substance group.

13.2 ANSWER 2: THE POSITION PROBLEM

The previous section summarized a number of different modes of answer to the attribution problem. Depending on one's point of view, different "cross-sections" or "cut-outs" through the set of economic activities (or "the economy environment system") could be made (*cf.* Udo de Haes & Heijungs (1996)). The fact that these cross-sections were connected to tools for environmental analysis and decision-support, combined with the fact that these tools were derived within a uniform framework and from unified epistemological principles, now enables us to give an answer to the position problem that was formulated in Section 1.2.2.

For this, we will first place all tools that have been derived in an enlarged version of Figure 5.3; see Figure 13.1. The left branch corresponds to activity-level analysis, in which an external demand is specified, and the operating times of the economic processes are determined such that the external demand is satisfied. The branch on the right is the commodity-flow accounting, in which a certain operating time is chosen (most often one year) into which all economic processes in the system boundary are put. We see that substance-flow analysis, environmental impact assessment, and risk assessment are considered as special cases of this more general commodity-flow accounting. This does not mean that CFA is in any sense "better" or "more useful" than its three daughter-tools. On the contrary, the tools introduce additional information, which gives them in some respects priority over their mother. For instance, the transmission coefficients of SFA translate the result of the CFA into an analysis which is very suitable for tracing the origins of certain flows (*cf.* Van der Voet (1996); see also Section 14.1.4).

The previous sections gave a summary of the formal procedures for the different tools. The headings of the various sections already give a clue to the

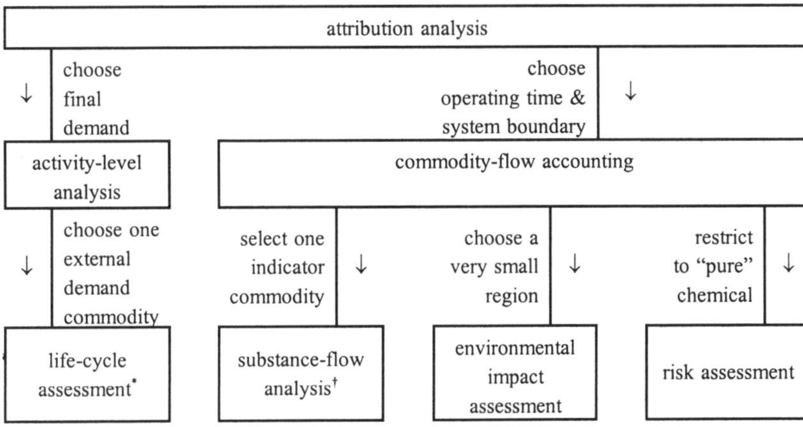

* Life-cycle assessment includes here "cradle-to-grave" analysis, "cradle-to-gate" analysis, and "gate-to-grave" analysis.

† Substance-flow analysis also includes here material-flow analysis, product-flow analysis, and energy(-flow) analysis.

FIGURE 13.1. Enlarged version of Figure 5.3, in which all analytical tools that were discussed have been placed.

position problem. More extensively, in relation to the goal definition of the various tools we arrive at the following conclusions.

Life-cycle assessment

Life-cycle assessment (LCA) is a tool for environmental analysis and decision-support that attributes environmental interventions, environmental stressors, environmental impacts, or the total environmental problem to a cluster of economic processes of which the operating time is adjusted in such a way that exactly one output service is produced.

Substance-flow analysis

Substance-flow analysis (SFA) is a tool that attributes the substance-content of a user-defined substance or substance-group of the environmental interventions or the environmental stressors to a cluster of economic activities that takes place in a certain region during a certain period of time.

Environmental impact assessment

Environmental impact assessment (EIA) is a tool that attributes the environmental interventions, environmental stressors, environmental impacts, or the total environmental problem to the cluster of economic activities that is related to a narrowly defined "region" (i.e. a set of spatially located activities), such as a factory, during a certain period of time.

Risk assessment

Risk assessment (RA) is a tool that attributes the environmental interventions, or the environmental stressors to the cluster of economic activities that takes place in a certain region during a certain period of time in so far as a certain chemical is involved in its pure form, e.g., heavy metals as such and not as contained in batteries or plastics.

We thus see that all these four tools give a different interpretation to the question of attribution. This study opened with the painted slogan against CO_2 as an example of an attempt to reduce global warming impacts. A CFA will point out that the Netherlands economy is the source of a certain amount of CO_2. An LCA will connect this to product functions, some of which will be produced but not used within the Netherlands, and some of which will be used but not produced in that country. An EIA might specify in more detail what contribution to CO_2 is made by the activity under review, but will not also point out final causes. There is no final cause: it all depends on the perspective of the decision-maker, and hence on the cross-section he or she decides to make. The tool will only help to make this cross-section. And the unified derivation of the tools will guarantee that there is no inconsistency between the different tools.

It must be emphasized once more that the compilation of emissions and extractions, the inventory table, is constructed by an aggregation over all processes that are included within the system boundary. The consequence is an omission of detail with respect to calendar time, location, and intermittent or continuous character of an intervention. This fact, added to the omission of background levels, means that the analysis of impacts necessarily assumes a rough form, which is probably good enough in the context of the attribution problem, but which is certainly not sufficient for several of the current uses of risk assessment and environmental impact assessment. In this respect, and certainly in the context of what will be discussed in Section 14.1, risk assessment and environmental impact assessment as understood in the present context are of very limited value. The intrinsic chain character of life-cycle assessment and substance-flow analysis makes the proposed description much more valuable. See, however, the next section for a number of important remarks with respect to the meaning of the results and realm of applicability.

A very important final remark is that all that has been said above applies to the particular forms of LCA, SFA, EIA, and RA that were derived:

- to answer the attribution problem;
- under the chosen epistemological principles.

There are other forms of each of the instruments, either because they were not constructed to answer the attribution problem, or because other epistemological principles were used, implicitly or explicitly. For instance, the ignorance of location in the tools that was mentioned above does not normally apply to EIA. This has to do with the fact that EIA is normally not applied to the attribution problem, but to the analysis of planning of new activities; see the next chapter.

Chapter 14

Further Reflections

14.1 THE LIMITS OF ATTRIBUTION

14.1.1 Attribution versus Planning Analysis

Section 5.2.4 discussed the assumption of fixed technical coefficients. It was concluded that technical coefficients are almost never constant, and that the indivisibility of certain commodities may be a disturbing factor as well. These limitations were accepted in the context of the attribution problem, because attribution is inherently connected to chopping indivisible commodities into pieces, and the linear attribution rule inevitably led to fixed technical coefficients.

When results from an exercise in attribution are applied in practical situations, the limitations show up, however. Many economic and environmental processes behave in a non-linear way, with discontinuities every now and then. The emissions involved in transporting a commodity by truck per unit of commodity will level off as a function of the number of commodities transported, with a sudden increase if a second truck is required. Using knowledge from this study may well result in a change of economic behaviour, so that indeed an extra truck is needed. The attribution itself did not incorporate that. More or less in line with this, Opschoor (1994) introduces the material-product (MP) chain analysis as an analysis that

> aims at linking the materials approach and the product approach ... in an

application oriented, policy relevant fashion.[1]

Here policy relevance demands that some forms of socio-economic parameters may need to be introduced, e.g., in order to achieve a proper picture of what will happen. An example application (Kandelaars & Van den Bergh (1996)) shows what could be involved here. As stated in Section 2.2.2, the modelling of socio-economic behaviour is irrelevant to the attribution problem.

We thus see a distinction between attribution and the planning or programming of economic activities. The scientific requirements for an answer to the attribution are consistency and logic. The scientific requirement for the question of planning is truth. The question of where to build which factory is one which should give an indication of what really will occur.[2] Another instance of planning is that of choosing which pesticides are to be permitted. In those cases, much additional knowledge is required: what are the background levels of pollutants and noise, which sensitive species are living where, etc. These aspects find no place in the unified methodology of this study, because the study is not concerned with planning. But it may inspire the construction of a similar theory to answer the planning problem. It may be possible to design an alternative epistemological scheme, which can then serve to derive a number of tools for environmental decision-support in relation to planning.

> The theory that has been developed in this study does not answer the planning problem that is concerned with the question of adding activities at certain locations, of installing factories, or of buying products. The unified approach may, however, inspire others to derive tools for decision-support for application to the planning problem.

1 Opschoor (1994, p. 207).

2 Environmental impact assessment is almost always exclusively used for planning purposes. The procedures that are used therefore barely resemble the procedure that was derived in this study.

14.1.2 Attribution versus Scenario Analysis

An interesting question is in what respect the inventory analysis of life-cycle assessment of Section 7.2 differs from the normal analysis of economic activities and their environmental consequences. Life-cycle assessment has a number of important characteristics:

- the external demand vector contains only non-material services (not a radio, but using a radio for a certain time);
- only one economic commodity is non-zero in the external demand vector (not a complex set of services, but one isolated service: the functional unit);
- the external demand vector is often of an arbitrary nature (not the total number of hours of radio use by an individual consumer or by the total population, but one hour or five hours).

The arbitrariness of the functional unit can be justified by the fact that the first fundamental equation is linear homogeneous: results from LCA, combined in a proper way, can build an analysis of a macro type. Mathematically we have

$$\begin{aligned}\mathbf{\Delta b} &= (\mathbf{b} + \mathbf{\Delta b}) - \mathbf{b} \\ &= (\bar{\mathbf{B}} \cdot \bar{\mathbf{A}}^{-1} \cdot (\mathbf{a} + \mathbf{\Delta a})) - \bar{\mathbf{B}} \cdot \bar{\mathbf{A}}^{-1} \cdot \mathbf{a}, \\ &= \bar{\mathbf{B}} \cdot \bar{\mathbf{A}}^{-1} \cdot \mathbf{\Delta a}\end{aligned} \tag{14.1}$$

which implies that LCA can be regarded either as an analysis of the difference in environmental flows of a world with ($\mathbf{a} + \mathbf{\Delta a}$) and without ($\mathbf{a}$) one additional service, or as an analysis of a world with only that service ($\mathbf{\Delta a}$).[3] The linearity goes back to the assumed linearity in the activity analysis (see Section 5.2.1), which in its turns goes back to the linear interpolation (defended in Section 2.1.2).[4]

3 See also the discussion on Leontief multipliers in Section 7.1.

4 Observe that under the present assumptions, LCA is not necessarily a marginal approach (see Heijungs et al. (1992*b*, p.12)), as the equation for $\mathbf{\Delta b}$ is valid for a $\mathbf{\Delta a}$ of any size. It must be noted, however, that the important restriction is the *ceteris paribus* assumption which is completely logical in the context of the attribution problem, whereas it is only to some extent acceptable in the analysis of the difference between a world with and without one additional service (*cf.* Huppes & Frischknecht (1995)). The latter type of analysis might appropriately be called the incremental problem to put it in contrast with the attribution problem.

One may think of carrying out an LCA at the macro level. If one defines the functional unit to be "having one meal", one effectively combines the functional units "drinking one glass of wine", "eating one potato", "eating one kg of fish" in suitable proportions. In a similar way, one may define a functional unit like "living of one person for one year", or "subsistence of the world's population for one year". The functional unit at the macro level is in fact a full enviro-economic activity analysis, with a certain population and its life style as its exogenously imposed driving force. The boundary between life-cycle assessment and environmentally extended activity analysis as defined in Section 5.3.2 is thus vague. Nevertheless, the definition of life-cycle assessment as an activity analysis with a restriction on external demand helps to clarify the relation with the existing forms of LCA.

Important advantages of the micro approach of LCA are the following:

- LCA allows us to determine the relative contribution of every service that is part of the life style (e.g., radio listening contributes 2% to the total environmental problem);
- LCA allows us to make comparative statements on product alternatives that produce (nearly) the same function (e.g., radios connected to the grid make a lower contribution to the environmental problem than battery-operated radios);
- LCA allows us to determine where major improvements of product systems might take place (e.g., energy consumption during use is responsible for 90% of the total environmental problem of radio listening).

These properties mean that LCA is widely used by governments, by industrial firms, and by consumer movements and environmental groups (Baumann (1995), Anonymous (1996*a*)).

However, the restriction of the subject of LCA to one economic commodity is effectively a *ceteris paribus* assumption. This assumption is obviously violated in many cases, in particular when changes at the macro level are foreseen. For instance, a complete replacement of battery-operated radios by grid-operated ones would induce a cascade of economic repercussions which would affect the battery-producing industries, their suppliers, and so on. Ultimately the external demand of a society might change in many respects, leading to quite different types of environmental impacts. The essential element here is a break-down of the hypothesis of fixed technical coefficients. In that sense, we retrieve the situation of the previous section on the planning problem. But its scope may be much wider here: it involves large-scale changes of technical characteristics and social behaviour. As in the case of the planning problem, the analysis of scenario changes calls for a "true" method that obviously involves non-linearities and other complicating factors. And again, the LCA, SFA, etc. that have been derived to answer the attribution problem do not give an answer to the scenario problem. Other forms of these tools may be developed, however, and some of the ideas that have been put forward in this study may be useful for that purpose.

> The analysis of large changes in scenarios requires other implementations of the tools than the one that is provided in the context of the attribution problem.

14.1.3 Attribution versus Improvement Analysis

In various documents on LCA, a statement like the following is included:

> The prime objectives of carrying out a LCA are: ... (3) to provide decision-makers with information which ... identifies opportunities for environmental improvements.[5]

To satisfy this objective, the established procedure for LCA contains, besides goal definition and scoping, inventory analysis, and impact assessment, an improvement assessment (or: analysis).

At the same time, it has been recognized that

> formal systematic procedures for improvement assessment are not yet established.[6]

Furthermore, it has been agreed that the

> actual redesign of a product or process is not a part of LCA – it is one of the applications.[7]

5 Consoli et al. (1993, p. 5).
6 Op. cit. (p. 6).
7 Op. cit. (p. 26).

A number of remarks must be made:

- The statement that the identification of options for product improvement on a life-cycle basis is not (yet) formalized is not true; see Heijungs et al. (1992*b*, p. 115 *ff.*) and Heijungs (1994*b*) for two methodological developments in that direction.
- There is a tendency to confuse the analytical improvement assessment with the application in the form of product improvement; this may be one reason for ISO to erase improvement assessment from the "canonical" standard for LCA.
- The attribution of the environmental problem to a product, as one "cross-section" in looking at the attribution problem, does not need an improvement assessment, and is not even compatible with it.

The remainder of this section concentrates on this latter point, but will occasionally touch upon the other points as well.

The procedure to answer the attribution problem tries to give an answer to an accounting question. There is no other goal than an analytical one. On the other hand, improvement of products is an important issue in many industrial companies (Christiansen et al. (1995)). It is felt that the attribution of environmental aspects (like interventions or impacts) to a unit of product contains important information which only needs to be revealed. The marginal analysis (Heijungs (1994*a*)) is based on that conviction. The procedure is based on the calculation of a series of parameters that indicate the sensitivity of the environmental intervention to an intentional change of the technical coefficients. The quantities $\frac{\mathrm{d}b_k}{\mathrm{d}\bar{a}_{ij}}\frac{\bar{a}_{ij}}{b_k}$ and $\frac{\mathrm{d}b_k}{\mathrm{d}\bar{b}_{ij}}\frac{\bar{b}_{ij}}{b_k}$ are considered for this purpose. A high value of these coefficients (either positive or negative) points to a technical coefficient ($\bar{a}_{ij}$ or $\bar{b}_{ij}$) that must be changed only slightly to significantly change the chosen intervention (b_k). The procedure for the marginal analysis yields a long list with sensitivity factors for all technical coefficients. The idea is that the most sensitive parameters are first considered in an analysis of options for environmental improvement. The coefficients have, however, been calculated by a non-discriminating routine. This means that quite a number of them may be irrelevant, because they correspond to physically impossible suggestions (e.g., produce more than 1 kg rolled steel from 1 kg steel), uneconomic suggestions (e.g., recycle 100% of the disposed glass), or inconvenient suggestions (e.g., do not light a candle during supper). There could be even more reasons to discard certain suggested options for improvement. The selection of these options is clearly an applied activity, which should not take place within the context of attribution or related analytical questions. The generation of the still unscreened options by means of the marginal analysis or by any other analytical means is, however, different. It does not belong to the attribution problem in the strict sense, but can in some situations be a fruitful extension. It is all the more regrettable that these analytical extensions are so rarely discussed, and that the framework of ISO has put them into the rather obscure sphere of "interpretation" that is filled with various types of miscellaneous extras. It is highly probable that this will lead to a regression of further developments with respect to analytical tools for extracting improvement options from the wealth of information that is present in LCA. For the other tools, the idea of an improvement analysis has received even less attention.[8]

> The method for answering the attribution problem contains information that may be relevant for the improvement of products or processes. The generation of improvement options itself is not part of the attribution problem, however, so that a treatment of this topic is outside the scope of this study.

14.1.4 Attribution versus Origins Analysis

The attribution problem was defined as a mapping of economic activities onto environmental problems. For some purposes, a reversed procedure, called origins analysis, may be of interest. In the context of substance-flow analysis, Van der Voet et al. (1995*b*) write:

> The origins of one specific problematical flow can be traced at several levels. … three levels are distinguished: 1. Direct causes, derived directly from the nodes balance (for example, one of the direct causes of the cadmium soil load is atmospheric deposition) 2. The economic sectors, or environmental policy target groups, directly responsible for the problem, identified by following the path back from node to node to the point of emission (for example, waste incineration is one

8 See, however, Van der Voet et al. (1995*b*) for a marginal analysis in SFA.

of the economic sectors responsible for the cadmium soil load) 3. Ultimate origins, found by following the path back to the system boundaries (for example, the import of zinc ore is one of the ultimate origins of the cadmium soil load).[9]

This section discusses possible connections between attribution analysis and origins analysis.

The search for direct causes is straightforward using the formalism derived in this study. The environmental process (node) from which a particular flow directly originates can easily be identified. The question of which economic sector is directly responsible is also not difficult to answer. The arguments of Section 1.1.1 must be kept in mind, nevertheless: although the electricity plant is most directly coupled to the emission of carbon dioxide, this direct responsiblity setting is not always obvious in a more sophisticated analysis.

The remainder of this section will be concerned with the ultimate origins analysis. This type of origins analysis may be defined as answering the question of which input flows contribute how much to a certain internal flow or output flow. In the language of Figure 7.3, the ultimate origins of x_9 are x_2 and x_6, and the origins analysis should state which fraction of x_9 is due to x_2 and which fraction is due to x_6. Van der Voet et al. (1995*b*) propose rewriting the system of equations (Equation (7.43)) in such a way that all flows except the origin flows x_2 and x_6 become dependent variables:

$$\begin{bmatrix} x_3 \\ x_4 \\ x_5 \\ x_8 \\ x_9 \end{bmatrix} = \begin{bmatrix} 0.00008 & 0 \\ 0.8 & 0 \\ 0.00008 & 0 \\ 0.2 & 0 \\ 0.00008 & 1 \end{bmatrix} \cdot \begin{bmatrix} x_7 \\ x_6 \end{bmatrix} \tag{14.2}$$

Supplying the values that were found for x_2 (18182) and x_6 (1453), we find that x_3, x_4, x_5, and x_8 originate entirely from x_2, and that x_9 originates for 99.9% from x_6 and for the remaining 0.1% from x_2.

In the case of internal loops, it may happen that internal flows are larger than the total input flow. For instance, Van der Voet et al. (1995*b*) shows a total input of 120 and an internal flow of 420. The origins analysis then states that the input flow of 20 creates an internal flow of 57, 14% of the total size

9 Op. cit. (p. 140).

of 420. A certain problematic flow may therefore be highly sensitive to the flows from which it originates, and it may hence be influenced to a large extent by a small change in the input flows. One could envisage working out a kind of Hessian matrix:

$$\begin{bmatrix} \frac{\partial x_3}{\partial x_2} & \frac{\partial x_4}{\partial x_2} & \frac{\partial x_5}{\partial x_2} & \frac{\partial x_8}{\partial x_2} & \frac{\partial x_9}{\partial x_2} \\ \frac{\partial x_3}{\partial x_6} & \frac{\partial x_4}{\partial x_6} & \frac{\partial x_5}{\partial x_6} & \frac{\partial x_8}{\partial x_6} & \frac{\partial x_9}{\partial x_6} \end{bmatrix} \tag{14.3}$$

to identify elements that are larger than one, and that therefore represent sensitive aspects. The interpretation is pretty close to that of the marginal analysis that was discussed in Section 14.1.3. The main difference is that the sensitivity coefficients are more easily established than in the case of the marginal analysis, where the presence of an inverse matrix in the first fundamental equation complicates the mathematics.

An origins analysis, in the sense of an analysis of which inputs may be held "responsible" for a certain flow, is a mode of analysis that is quite close to the attribution problem. The procedure of origins analysis can be derived from the procedures that were discussed in the context of attribution.

14.1.5 The Meaning of Attribution for Environmental Analysis and Decision-Support

We have occasionally come across questions related to attribution versus marginal, causality, unknowables, etc. This section aims to provide a somewhat broader interpretation of what attribution is and what it means in the context of environmental analysis and decision-support.

One cannot change the world. One can only make choices which affect the way the world is running in a negligible or almost negligible way. One might therefore propose that the only relevant question in decision-making is the marginal question, which starts from the *ceteris paribus* assumption and then leads to questions such as: what are the additional environmental problems if one extra product is made? This would disqualify the use of tools for the attribution problem, as these were interpreted throughout this study as achieving a static apportioning for use in environmental analysis and decision-support.

However, even if we accept that the marginal question is the relevant question in the context of decision-making, the attribution question still has a value in pointing out key issues. With an economic metaphor, for instance, we might with an attribution type of question discover that housing is "responsible" for one-third of our monthly expenses. A subsequent marginal analysis could then analyse the gain or loss of moving to another house or switching to a completely different system of shelter. So, a combination of tools might be envisaged:

- First, tools for attribution analysis are used to identify key issues (dominant aspects, hot spots).
- Next, tools for marginal analysis are used to investigate the change that is introduced by switching to an alternative.

Even without the second type of analysis (or: if switching to an alternative does not improve the situation), the attribution type of analysis is worth doing, because it confronts people with the share of particular economic activities in the total environmental problem. In that way, we become aware of the rucksack, the footprint (Wackernagel & Rees (1996)), the shadow (*cf.* Anonymous (1993)), or any other visualization of the environmental problems attributed to the economic activity under study. On the other hand, doing a marginal analysis without an attribution analysis has another type of value. It is aimed at environmental improvement without (or with only implicit) prior analysis if the problem that is being relieved was large enough to give it priority.

One probably disturbing conclusion that we may draw from this argument is that there is not one single LCA; nor is there one single SFA. There are two major types: one relating to static attribution and one to changes. The family of change-related tools may be further subdivided into tools for analysing consequences of short-term variations, mid-term variations, and long-term variations (Frischknecht (1997, p. 4)). See also Section 14.2.2.

Attribution analysis does not answer the question of effects of changes. For that, other epistemological principles have to be enunciated and elaborated as to their consequences for operational tools. However, attribution analysis may act as a source of inspiration in relation to where to analyse which changes.

14.2 FINAL REMARKS

14.2.1 Process and the State of the Environment

This study has emphasized the concept of process. Part Two and a large part of Part Three were devoted to economic and environmental processes as the central object of concern. At the same time, it was stated that there is a "something" to be changed in the course of a process. This "something" was represented by the economic or environmental commodities. One may wonder if there is a prime object of environmental concern with respect to the process commodity question. Which of the two is more "real"? Which of the two is more important?

Since ancient times, philosophers have touched on these and related questions. The most famous controversy in this respect is the one between Parmenides and Heraclitus, between the alleged permanence of substance against the tantamount alleged volatile πάντα ῥεῖ. The discourse is, however, far from settled, with Whitehead's *Process and reality* and Bergson's *L'Évolution créatrice* as the climax of the twentieth century. Without desiring to jump into an area that is remote from me and from the topic of this study, some statements could be made in the context of the attribution problem.

We may conceive the economic system and the environmental system in two different ways.

The first corresponds to the snap-shot concept of making a picture of the state of the world at time $t = 0$, and listing all that can be seen in a state vector $\mathbf{\Omega}(0)$. The elements of this state vector then represent amounts of economic and environmental commodities $\Omega_i(0)$. The nature and the location of these commodities can be specified in any desired degree (see Section 5.1.5). A typical example of this state vector is

$$\mathbf{\Omega}(0) = \begin{bmatrix} 3 \text{ radios} \\ 16 \text{ kg steel} \\ 120 \text{ kg } CO_2 \text{ in air} \\ \ldots \end{bmatrix} . \tag{14.4}$$

A snap-shot that is made at time interval T later gives a state vector $\mathbf{\Omega}(T)$. We may visualize the two pictures with their corresponding state vectors as in

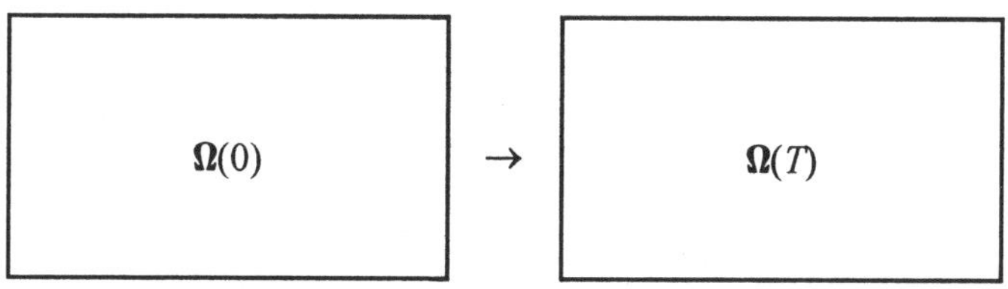

FIGURE 14.1. The commodity-picture of the world.

Figure 14.1. The two boxes represent the photographic images of the state of the economy and environment that were produced at time $t = 0$ and at time $t = T$. The arrow indicates the flow of time, and symbolizes the apparent change that has taken place in the time interval T.

The second conceptualization of the state of the world is represented in

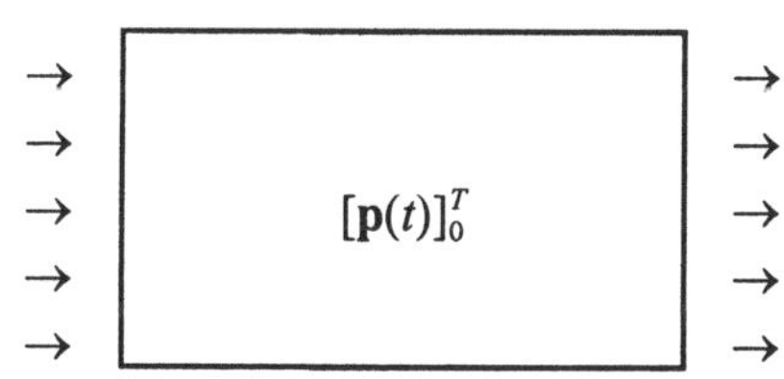

FIGURE 14.2. The process-picture of the world.

Figure 14.2. It gives a central role to process and neglects the state of the world either before or after the process. The arrows here symbolize the inflows and the outflows of sets of commodities.

The two pictures can be united by establishing a formal correspondence between the two:

$$\mathbf{\Omega}(T) - \mathbf{\Omega}(0) = [\mathbf{p}(t)]_0^T \tag{14.5}$$

or, more dynamically oriented,

$$\mathbf{\Omega}(T) = \mathbf{\Omega}(0) + \int_0^T \overline{\mathbf{p}}(t)\mathrm{d}t. \tag{14.6}$$

We must however be careful not to establish the identity of the two pictures too rapidly.

The commodity-picture is able to study the "apparent change". This means that it is unable to detect whether a change is due to a unit process or to a cluster of unit processes. It just establishes the difference between before and after, and considers this difference as the process. This view has important shortcomings in relation to the theory that was developed in this study. Part Two discussed the allocation problem in connection to the fact that more than one useful thing has happened. We established a theory of dealing with this problem that was based on the basis of splitting a unit process into two or more virtual processes. The step that was tacitly assumed to be taken before was the specification of aggregate processes as to their constituent unit processes. In the analysis of fate in Part Three, an even more complicated situation arose. It was concluded in Section 9.2.7 that it was necessary to describe the fate of environmental commodities by modelling environmental processes, and that giving a pure phenomenological description did not suffice.

The process-picture, which has therefore been chosen as a basis for this study, has however another important shortcoming. The state of the economy and the environment is outside its realm. This type of analysis is therefore unable to say anything about stocks in the economy, about background concentrations of chemicals, etc. This shortcoming must be recognized for a proper understanding of the meaning of the tools that were derived. Environmental decisions very often need to take into account this information. This should remind one once more of the incomplete character of these tools.

The above remarks should induce one to conclude that the commodity-picture and the process-picture are both useful though incomplete. They supplement each other in giving a complete picture of the world. In a more restricted context – like the attribution problem – one of the two pictures may suffice. It should be clear that, although I adhere to the process-picture in this study, I by no means position it prior to the commodity-picture. I am not a "processist", but probably half a "substantialist" (see Rescher (1996, p. 5)). I therefore reject the creed of process ontology, which is summarized below.

Process can conceivably make do without things. ... But no workable substance

> ontology can get on without a heavy reliance on processes, seeing that process-detached thing as a fifth wheel. Substances can come upon the stage of consideration only through the mediation of processes. A process ontology thus greatly simplifies matters. Instead of a two-tier reality that combines things together with their inevitable coordinated processes, it settles for a one-tier ontology of processes alone – at any rate, at the level of basics. For it sees things not just as the products of processes ... but also as the manifestations of processes – as complex bundles of coordinated processes. It replaces the troublesome ontological dualism of thing and activity with a monism of activities of different and differently organized sorts. If Ockham was right and simplicity is a crucial advantage in ontology, then process metaphysics clearly has much to offer.[10]

I consider this and similar points of view inspiring in certain contexts.

14.2.2 Is There No Truth in Environmental Science?

Although this study started with an apparently normal question in relation to an incident at the electricity producer where Greenpeace had chosen to climb the chimney, we have gradually moved into an almost metaphysical discourse on truth in environmental science. This section will give a summary and sketch some prospects.

Section 2.1 raised the epistemological problem of how to acquire knowledge in the context of the attribution. It was said that the attribution problem could not be answered by experimental methods, and that the attribution itself could be considered as an interpolation, so that any attempt to verify it is doomed to fail. The science was consequently built up from a number of epistemological principles: order-independence, amount-independence, and 100%-additivity. These three principles were more or less sufficient to derive life-cycle assessment, substance-flow analysis, etc. They were not completely sufficient. Except for the problem that data on economic and environmental processes are needed in addition, there are some other details that are missing. These are in particular the allocation factors (Section 6.2.2), the impact factors (Section 5.3.4), and the problem factors (Section 5.4.4). These three categories of factors were even claimed to be unknowable with the present epistemology, which is to say that they are not provided by the present theory; nor does the theory give a clue to how they can be obtained. Every choice which satisfies the three principles is compatible and

10 Rescher (1996, pp. 48–49).

therefore correct. This leads to a proliferation of equally correct methods and answers. The result is a paradox: a comparative analysis of the environmental problem that is to be attributed to activity x and to activity y may put forward that according to some, x is more environmental friendly, whereas others hold that y is better. The paradox is that they are both right. In other words: there is no single unambiguous truth under the present epistemological principles. Some of the quotations in Section 2.1.4 illustrated the situation.

There is another aspect that is perhaps even more disturbing. The previous point may in principle be solved by specifying one or two more principles.[11] But even the principles themselves – the three of Section 2.1 or extended with one or two more – are by no means universal. It is really like the interpolation of the power function x^n to non-integer values of n (Section 2.1.3): almost every definition is good. However, it is widely agreed upon to choose one particular form. For the attribution problem, a similar argument might hold. In the context of energy analysis, Chapman declared long ago that

> all these estimates of the energy cost of aluminium are self-consistent, they are all "correct", but they are all based on different conventions.[12]

The epistemological basis might be chosen from a completely different direction. For instance, the principle of 100%-additivity could be argued to be abandoned, in the same way as today's differential geometrists reject Euclid's parallel postulate (*cf.* Heijungs (1998)). The result is a completely different set of operational rules for LCA, SFA, etc. And again, consistent within itself, and, as long as it not in disagreement with facts, equally as valid as the tools that were derived in Section 13.1. Once more, a paradox, but now not due to an insufficient epistemology, but due to an alternative epistemology.

Still one level higher is the interpretation of the tools for environmental analysis and decision-support. What is life-cycle assessment? Is it a tool within the context of the attribution problem, as this study has been arguing? Or should we see it in the context of incremental analysis (*cf.* Huppes & Frischknecht (1995))? Here the situation is somewhat less dramatic, because it will often be possible to determine if a certain question requires an analysis with respect to attribution, with respect to marginal changes, with respect to

11 In Heijungs (1998) this would amount to the formulation of one or two more axioms.

12 Chapman (1974, p. 102).

large-scale changes, etc. But still, the terms LCA, SFA, EIA, and RA have only a vague meaning unless the exact context of attribution versus planning versus ... is specified.

At another level, there is the question of universality. It turns out that questions with respect to environmental preference cannot be answered unambiguously, even if the rules are clear. This has to do with the particular circumstances of the target group of the analysis.

> It is conceivable that LCA tells us that a household should prefer glass bottles, whereas canteens should prefer carton packages. The environmental truth is user-dependent and thus context-sensitive.[13]

We have seen that there are many competing environmental truths. This obscures environmental debate, and might be an obstacle to the belief in tools for environmental analysis and decision-support. There is not so much reason to be pessimistic, however. There are many truths in the environmental world, but the realm of many of these truths is quite restricted. A precise formulation of the question that is to be answered by the tool is a first prerequisite. Next comes the choice of the appropriate tool. Only at the level of concrete tools does the truth begin to bifurcate. An epistemological basis must be chosen. And the chosen one might be insufficient to complete all details of the procedure.

14.2.3 A Role within Environmental Philosophy

It is clear that quite some work remains to be done. It is also clear that not all work can be done, or, at least, not in a conclusive way. I end up as I began, by giving the concept of environmental science the hybrid status of philosophy and everything else that is beyond what can be perceived, and thus as a part of metaphysics.

> Philosophy, as I shall understand the word, is something intermediate between theology and science. Like theology, it consists of speculations on matters as to which definite knowledge has, so far, been unascertainable; but like science, it appeals to human reason rather than to authority, whether that of tradition or that of revelation. All definite knowledge – so I should contend – belongs to science;

13 Heijungs & Guinée (1995, p. 666).

> all dogma as to what surpasses definite knowledge belongs to theology. But between theology and science there is a No Man's Land, exposed to attack from both sides; this No Man's Land is philosophy.[14]

Conceived in this way, the construction of tools for environmental analysis and decision-support is a No Man's Land between ethics and experience. And indeed, it will be exposed to attacks from the side of dogma and from the side of science. The results may be in contradiction with well-established dogmas like the doctrine that reuse and recycling are "good". And the procedure may be in contradiction with scientifically established facts, like the impossibility of installing half a locomotive or of producing chlorine without sodium.

This, however, must not be seen as a weakness of this branch of "environmental philosophy". It should be seen as a property to which one should try to become accustomed. The subject of interdisciplinarity that was discussed in Section 2.2, together with the previous remarks concerning the position of this type of science, should stimulate the unique academic role that is potentially present: relying heavily on dogma, natural science, and social science, but not belonging to any of the corresponding disciplines.

14.2.4 Post Scriptum

Except for a few alterations and corrections, the text so far follows my Ph.D. thesis (Heijungs, 1997*b*). This section summarizes and comments on a number of developments that have taken place since that time.

Much is still valid, I think, and also still reflects the state of affairs. Within the domain of LCA, many ISO texts have been finalized and canonized: they have become an International Standard. As such, one could consider changing some terms, or being more precise. However, many of the developments in the ISO standard for LCA have taken place without a proper reference to related or similar terms in other fields, so that the ISO terms for LCA are not particularly useful for comparing or unifying LCA, SFA, EIA, RA and other tools. A lot of further practical work has been done, but the conceptual and fundamental progress has been not too great. Comprehensive texts like those by Hauschild & Wenzel (1998) and Guineé et al. (2001) and more focused articles and reports like those by Udo de Haes et al. (1999) and Anonymous (1999) should be mentioned here.

14 Russell (1945, p. xiii).

With respect to SFA, the fundamental development is perhaps even smaller. Recent key publications in this field focus on particular cases, such as countries (e.g., Adriaanse et al. (1997) and Matthews et al. (2000)) or substances (e.g., Ayres (1997), Kleijn et al. (1997), and Van der Voet et al. (2000)). More theoretical publications focus on the practice (e.g., Anonymous (2000)) or on dynamic modelling (e.g., Kleijn et al. (2000) and Bauer et al. (1997)).

With respect to the relationship between economic systems and the environment or environmental economics in general, we should mention the reference book by Van den Bergh (1999). Other publications of interest are Kandelaars (1998), Kleineidam (2000), Freire et al. (2000), Hendrickson et al. (1998), Eder & Narodoslawsky (1999) and Koenig & Cantlon (2000).

The relationship between different tools, here referred to as the position problem, has been addressed from a user's perspective more than from a foundational perspective. However, Bouman et al. (2000) provide a nice addition.

The somewhat humble tone in Section 14.2.2, about the absence of truth in environmental science, has been confirmed by a wealth of post-modern work. We mention Tukker (1998), Hofstetter (1998), Bras-Klapwijk (1999), and to a lesser extent Lundie (1999) as four pieces of evidence in one single year. Central in those books is the emphasis on participation of stakeholders in environmental analysis, not only to supply facts, but also to construct the theory, model and computational rules of the game. To a certain extent, my book identifies places for those who wish to exert their influence. For instance, the choice of axioms was shown to comprise arbitrary elements, and the fact that the chosen axioms are insufficient to guide the allocation step pointed to another arbitrary element. But I did not go so far to say that "anything goes", a quotation from Feyerabend's *Against method.* Scientific facts, so it seems, are only perceived as facts by a mind which is willing to recognize them as facts. A mind that is educated in a different culture will recognize different facts. Therefore, the post-modernists argue, facts exist only inside a certain cultural context. I agree that there is some truth in this, but it is truth with restrictions. And, perhaps more importantly, I strongly disagree with the idea that the cultural bias of evidence makes it necessary to include a diversity of cultures and opinions in an analysis of decision-support. See Heijungs (1999) for an argumentation.

Chapter 15

Summary of Findings

This study has raised a large number of topics, from the "ultimate means" (physics/technics) to the "ultimate ends" (theology/ethics) (Daly, 1973*a*). A natural question is: What's new? This concluding section summarizes a number of points which I consider to be new findings.

- Answers to the attribution problem can only be given by theoretical reasoning, not by experimental methods; this also means that there is not one unambiguous answer to the question of the attribution of environmental problems to economic activities.
- The epistemological foundation for tools for environmental decision-support is of the utmost importance; the fact that it has been neglected so far[1] is a serious barrier to scientific and therefore also to societal acceptance of these tools.
- It is possible to derive a number of tools for environmental decision-support from a quite limited set of epistemological principles.
- The harmonized framework and derived method for these tools allows for the compilation of databases that can be used for each of these

1 I cannot resist the temptation to quote Jammer's *The conceptual development of quantum mechanics*: 'In spite of its high-sounding name and its successful solutions of numerous problems ..., quantum theory ... prior to 1925, was, from the methodological point of view, a lamentable hodgepodge of hypotheses, principles, theorems, and computational recipes rather than a logical consistent theory. ... In fact, quantum theory became the subject of a special craftsmanship or even artistique technique .... In short, quantum theory still lacked two essential characteristics of a full-fledged scientific theory, conceptual autonomy and logical consistency' (Jammer (1966, p. 196)). I am inclined to think that the term quantum mechanics may easily be replaced by the terms LCA, SFA, and the like, with the substitution of 1925 by an appropriate date.

different tools.

- It is possible to derive these tools, and in particular life-cycle assessment and substance-flow analysis, from exactly the same epistemological principles. For the other two tools that have been considered, environmental impact assessment and risk assessment, it is probably less important to use the quite situation-unspecific form that has been derived.
- All these tools represent a particular "cross-section" of the attribution problem, relating to products from the cradle to the grave, to substances in a region, etc.
- There are many forms of each of these tools, each of them corresponding to a different question: that of attribution, that of planning analysis, that of scenario analysis, that of improvement analysis, and that of origins analysis. The present study has emphasized only one of these forms: that of attribution.
- The ideas that have been developed in economic input–output analysis and activity analysis are very relevant and useful for the development of methodologies for life-cycle assessment and substance-flow analysis.
- The set-up of these tools developed in this study differs in a number of respects from the conventional set-up; it is argued that the new set-up is better in the context of the attribution problem.
- The fate models that have been developed in risk assessment using steady-state multimedia models are suitable in the context of the attribution problem. A major improvement which turns out to be theoretically simple is the incorporation of reaction (decay) products.
- The epistemological basis that has been chosen in this study does not of course provide any empirical input data needed for obtaining actual results. Worse, perhaps, is that it is an insufficient basis for providing the principles for obtaining all the parameters encountered in the tools that have been derived; this applies in particular to the allocation factors, the impact factors, and the problem factors.
- The quantitative nature of the tools for the attribution problem means that a basic knowledge of mathematics is indispensable; moreover, matrix algebra[2] provides an elegant and powerful technique for the

2 A remarkable coincidence is that the above quotation occurs in Jammer's chapter 'The rise of matrix mechanics'.

derivation and formulation of the different tools.

References

Adriaanse, A., S. Bringezu, A. Hammond, Y. Moriguchi, E. Rodenburg, D. Rogich & H. Schütz, 1997. *Resource flows. The material basis of industrial sconomies.* World Resources Institute, Washington, 1997.

Aitchison, I.J.R. & A.J.G. Hey, 1982. *Gauge theories in particle physics. A practical introduction.* Adam Hilger Ltd, Bristol, 1984.

Alcamo, J., R. Shaw & L. Hordijk (Eds.), 1990. *The RAINS model of acidification. Science and strategies in Europe.* Kluwer Academic Publishers, Dordrecht, 1990.

Amir, S., 1994. 'The role of thermodynamics in the study of economic and ecological systems'. *Ecological Economics* **10** (1994), 125–142.

Anderberg, S., G. Bauer, Y. Ermolie & W. Stigliani, 1993. *Mathematical tools for studies of industrial metabolism.* IIASA, Laxenburg, 1993.

Anonymous, 1968. *A system of national accounts.* United Nations, New York, 1968.

Anonymous, 1974. *Energy analysis workshop on methodology and conventions.* IFIAS, Stockholm, 1974.

Anonymous, 1981. *Milieu-effectrapportage. II: Methodologies, scoping and guidelines. Conclusions and Recommendations.* SDU, 's-Gravenhage, 1981.

Anonymous, 1992. *Product life cycle assessment. Principles and methodology.* Nord, Copenhagen, 1992.

Anonymous, 1993. *The LCA sourcebook. A European business guide to life-cycle assessment.* Sustainability, London, 1993.

Anonymous (Ed.), 1994*a*. *First working document on life-cycle impact assessment methodology.* ETH, Zürich, 1994.

Anonymous (Ed.), 1994*b*. *Proceedings of international conference on ecobalance. Life cycle assessment for development of materials and technologies.* The Society of Non-traditional Technology, Tokyo, 1994.

Anonymous, 1994*c*. *The phosphate report. A life cycle study to evaluate the environmental impact of phosphates and zeolites A-PCA as alternative builders in UK laundry detergent formulation.* Landbank Environmental Research & Consulting, London, 1994.

Anonymous, 1995. *The life cycle approach. An overview of the product/process analysis.* OECD, Paris, 1995.

Anonymous, 1996*a*. *Life cycle assessment. What it is and how to do it.* UNEP, Paris, 1996.

Anonymous (Eds.), 1996*b*. *Tagungsband "Ökobilanzen im Städtebau. Konzepte für umweltorientierte Bewertungsverfahren".* IBÖ Verlag, Wien, 1996.

Anonymous, 1999. 'SETAC working groups 1993-1998'. *SETAC-Europe News* **10**:3 (1999), 14–20.

Anonymous, 2000. *Paradigm for substance flow analysis. Revision. Draft.* Danish Environmental Protection Agency, Copenhagen, 2000.

Assies, J.A., 1994. 'Attribution of environmental interventions to impact categories'. In: Anonymous (1994*a*, pp. 113–117).

Ayres, R.U., 1978. *Resources, environment, and economics. Applications of the materials/energy balance principle.* John Wiley & Sons, New York, 1978.

Ayres, R.U. & A.V. Kneese, 1969. 'Production, consumption, and externalities'. *The American Economic Review* **LIX** (1969), 282–297.

Ayres, R.U., 1993. *Life cycle analysis and materials/energy forecasting models.* INSEAD, Fontainebleau, 1993.

Ayres, R.U., 1994*a*. 'Life cycle analysis. A critique'. *Resources, Conservation and Recycling* **14** (1994), 199–223.

Ayres, R.U., 1994*b*. *Economics, thermodynamics and process analysis.* INSEAD, Fontainebleau, 1994.

Ayres, R.U. & U.E. Simonis (Eds.), 1994. *Industrial metabolism. Restructuring for sustainable development.* United Nations University Press, Tokyo, 1994.

Ayres, R.U., 1997. 'The life-cycle of chlorine, part I. Chlorine production and the chlorine-mercury connection'. *Journal of Industrial Ecology* **1**:1 (1997), 81–94.

Azapagic, A. & R. Clift, 1994. 'Allocation of environmental burdens by whole-system modelling. The use of linear programming'. In: Huppes & Schneider (1994, pp. 54–60.)

Azar, C. J. Holmberg & K. Lindgren, 1996. 'Socio-ecological indicators for sustainability'. *Ecological Economics* **18** (1996), 89–112.

Baccini, P. & H.-P. Bader, 1996. *Regionaler Stoffhaushalt. Erfassung, Bewertung und Steuerung.* Spektrum Akademischer Verlag, Heidelberg, 1996.

Barbier, E.B., 1989. *Economics, natural-resource scarcity and development. Conventional and alternative views.* Earthscan Publications Limited, London, 1989.

Bateman, I.J. & R.K. Turner, 1992. *Evaluation of the environment. The contingent valuation method.* CSERGE, Norwich, 1992.

Bauer, G., M. Deistler, A. Gleiß, E. Glenck & T. Matyus, 1997. 'Identification of material flow systems'. *Environmental Science & Pollution Research* **4**:2 (1997), 105–112.

Baumann, H., 1995. *Decision making and life cycle assessment.* Licentiate Thesis Chalmers, University of Technology, Göteborg, 1995.

Baumol, W.J., 1972. *Economic theory and operations analysis.* Third edition. Prentice/Hall International, London, 1972.

Beck, A. & S. Bosshart, 1995. *Umweltanalyseinstrumente im Vergleich.* Diplomarbeit. ETH, Zürich, 1995.

Berg, M. van den, D. van de Meent, W.J.G.M. Peijnenburg, D.T.H.M. Sijm, J. Struijs & J.W. Tas, 1995. 'Transport, accumulation and transformation processes'. In: Van Leeuwen & Hermens (1995, pp. 37–102).

Bergh, J.C.J.M. van den & P. Nijkamp, 1992. *Dynamic macro modelling for sustainable development: economic-environmental integration and the materials balance model.* Tinbergen Institute, Amsterdam, 1992.

Bergh, J.C.J.M. van den & P. Nijkamp, 1994. 'Dynamic macro modelling and materials balance. Economic-environmental integration for sustainable development'. *Economic Modelling* **11**:3 (1994), 283–307.

Bergh, J.C.J.M. van den (Ed.), 1999. *Handbook of environmental and resource economics.* Edward Elgar, Cheltenham, 1999.

Bergman, L., 1990. 'The development of computable general equilibrium modeling'. In: Bergman et al. (1990, pp. 3–30).

Bergman, L., D.W. Jorgenson & E. Zalai, 1990. *General equilibrium modeling and economic policy analysis.* Basil Blackwell, Oxford, 1990.

Bever, M.B. (Ed.), 1986. *Encyclopedia of materials, science and engineering.* Pergamon, Oxford, 1986.

Bloemhof-Ruwaard, J.M., 1996. *Integration of operational research and environmental management.* Ph.D. thesis, Landbouwuniversiteit Wageningen, Wageningen, 1996.

Boersema, J.J., J.W. Copius Peereboom & W.T. de Groot (Eds.), 1991. *Basisboek milieukunde. Vierde, geheel herziene druk.* Boom, Meppel, 1991.

Bouman, M., R. Heijungs, E. van der Voet, J.C.J.M. van den Bergh & G. Huppes, 2000. 'Material flows and economic models. An analytical comparison of SFA, LCA and partial equilibrium models'. *Ecological Economics* **32** (2000), 195–216.

Boustead, I., 1992. *Eco-balance. Methodology for commodity thermoplastics.* APME, Brussels, 1992.

Boustead, I., 1994. *Eco-profiles of the European polymer industry. V: co-product allocation in chlorine plants.* APME, Brusssel, 1994.

Boustead, I. & G.F. Hancock, 1979. *Handbook of industrial energy analysis.* Ellis Horwood Limited, Chichester, 1979.

Boxall, P.C., W.L. Adamowicz, J. Swait, M. Williams & J. Louviere, 1996. 'A comparison of stated preference methods for environmental valuation'. *Ecological Economics* **18** (1996), 243–253.

Braat, L.C. & Lierop, W.F.J. van, 1987*a*. *Economic-ecological modeling.* North-Holland Publishing Company, Amsterdam, 1987.

Braat, L.C. & Lierop, W.F.J. van, 1987*b*. 'Integrated economic-ecological modeling'. In: Braat & Van Lierop (1987*a*, pp. 49–68).

Bras-Klapwijk, R.M., 1999. *Adjusting life cycle assessment methodology for use in public policy discourse.* Ph.D. thesis, Technische Universiteit Delft, Delft, 1999.

Braunschweig, A. & R. Müller-Wenk, 1993. *Ökobilanzen für Unternehmungen. Eine Wegleiting für die Praxis.* Verlag Paul Haupt, Bern, 1993.

Braunschweig, A., R. Förster, P. Hofstetter & R. Müller-Wenk, 1996. *Developments in LCA valuation.* IWÖ, St. Gallen, 1996.

Bringezu, S., 1993. 'Towards increasing resource productivity: how to measure the total material consumption of regional or national economies?' *Fresenius Environmental Bulletin* **2**:8 (1993), 437–442.

Bringezu, S., M. Fischer-Kowalski, R. Kleijn & V. Palm (Eds.), 1997. *Regional and national material flow accounting. From paradigm to practice of sustainability.* Birkhäuser-Verlag, Basel, in press.

Brunner, P.H. & P. Baccini, 1992. 'Regional material management and environmental protection'. *Waste Management & Research* **10** (1992), 203–212.

Carnap, R., 1966. *An introduction to the philosophy of science.* Basic Books, New York, 1966.

Carter, A.P. & A. Bródy (Eds.), 1970. *Contributions to input–output analysis.* North-Holland Publishing Company, Amsterdam, 1970.

Chandrasekhar, S., 1987. *Truth and beauty. Aesthetics and motivations in science.* The University of Chicago Press, Chicago, 1990.

Chandrasekhar, S., 1979. 'Beauty and the quest for truth in science'. Reprinted in Chandrasekhar (1987, pp. 59–73).

Chapman, P.F., 1974. 'Energy costs: a review of methods'. *Energy Policy,* June 1974, 91–103.

Chenery, H.B. & P.G. Clark, 1959. *Interindustry economics.* John Wiley & Sons, London, 1959.

Christiansen, K., R. Heijungs, T. Rydberg, S.-O. Ryding, L. Sund, H. Wijnen, M. Vold & O.J. Hansen, 1995. *Application of life cycle assessments (LCA). Report from expert workshop in Hankø, Norway on LCA in: strategic management, product development and improvement, marketing and ecolabelling, government policies.* Stiftelsen Østfoldforskning, Frederikstad, 1995.

Clift, R., 1993. *'Life cycle assessment and ecolabelling'. Journal of Cleaner Production* **1**:3-4 (1993), 155–159.

Consoli, F., D. Allen, I. Boustead, J. Fava, W. Franklin, A.A. Jensen, N. de Oude, R. Parrish, R. Perriman, D. Postlethwaite, B. Quay, J. Seguin & B. Vigon, 1993. *Guidelines for life-cycle assessment: a 'Code of Practice'. Edition 1.* SETAC, Brussels/Pensacola, 1993.

Costanza, R. (Ed.), 1991. *Ecological economics. The science and management of sustainability.* Columbia University Press, New York, 1991.

Costanza, R., H.E. Daly & J.A. Bartholomew, 1991. 'Goals, agenda, and policy recommendations for ecological economics'. In: Costanza (1991, pp. 1–20.)

Covello, V.T. & M.W. Merkhofer, 1993. *Risk assessment methods. Approaches for assessing health and environmental risks.* Plenum Press, New York, 1993.

Cowan, C.E., D. Mackay, T.C.J. Feytel, D. van de Meent, A. di Guardo, J. Davies & N. Mackay, 1995. *The multi-media fate model. A vital tool for predicting the fate of chemicals.* SETAC Press, Pensacola, 1995.

Cumberland, J.H., 1966. 'A regional interindustry model for analysis of development objectives'. *Regional Science Association Papers* **17** (1966), 65–94.

Curran, M.A., 1996. *Environmental life-cycle assessment.* McGraw-Hill, New York, 1996.

Daly, H.E., 1968. 'On economics as a life science'. *Journal of Political Economy* **76** (1968), 392–406.

Daly, H.E. (Ed.), 1973*a*. *Economics, ecology, ethics. Essays towards a steady-state economy.* W.H. Freeman and Company, San Fransisco, 1980.

Daly, H.E., 1973*b*. 'Introduction to the steady-state economy'. In: Daly (1973*a*, pp. 1–31).

Daly, H.E., 1995. 'On Nicholas Georgescu-Roegen's contributions to economics. An obituary essay'. *Ecological Economics* **13** (1995), 149–154.

Debreu, G., 1959. *Theory of value. An axiomatic analysis of economic equilibrium.* John Wiley & Sons, Inc., New York, 1959.

Dohnomae, H., M. Tani, K. Shibita, N. Okumura, 1994. 'Input–output approach for life-cycle assessment'. In: Anonymous (1994*b*, pp. 137–142).

Dragàn, J.C., E.K. Seifert & M.C. Demetrescu (Eds.), 1993. *Entropy and bioeconomics. Proceedings of the first international conference of the European Association for Bioeconomic Studies.* EABS, Milan, 1993.

Duchin, F., 1992. 'Industrial input–output analysis. Implications for industrial ecology'. *Proceedings of the National Academy of Sciences of the United States of America* **89** (1992), 851–855.

Eder, P. & M. Narodoslawsky, 1999. 'What environmental pressures are a region's industries responsible for? A method of analysis with descriptive indices and input–output models'. *Ecological Economics* **29** (1999), 359–374.

Edmonston, J.H., 1952. 'A treatment of multiple-process industries'. *Quarterly Journal of Economics* (1952), 557–571.

Engelenburg, B.C.W. van, T.F.M. van Rossum, K. Blok & K. Vringer, 1994. 'Calculating the energy requirements of household purchases. A practical step by step method'. *Energy Policy* **22**:8 (1994), 648–656.

Enquete Commission of the German Bundestag on the "Protection of humanity and the environment" (Ed.), 1994. *Responsibility for the future. Options for sustainable management of substance chains and material flows. Interim report.* Economica Verlag, Bonn, 1994.

Erickson, P.A., 1994. *A practical guide to environmental impact assessment.* Academic Press, San Diego, 1994.

Faber, M., H. Niemes & G. Stephan, 1987. *Entropy, environment and resources. An essay in physico-economics.* Springer-Verlag, Berlin, 1987.

Fava, J.A., R. Denison, B. Jones, M.A. Curran, B. Vigon, S. Selke & J. Barnum, 1991. *A technical framework for life-cycle assessments.* SETAC, Washington, 1991.

Fava, J., F. Consoli, R. Denison, K. Dickson, T. Mohin & B. Vigon, 1993. *A conceptual framework for life-cycle impact assessment.* SETAC, Pensacola, 1993.

Fava, J., A.A. Jensen, L. Lindfors, S. Pomper, B. de Smet, J. Warren & B. Vigon, 1994. *Life-cycle assessment data quality. A conceptual framework.* SETAC, Pensacola, 1994.

Fazzolare, R.A. & C.B. Smith (Eds.), 1977. *Proceedings of the international conference on energy use management.* Pergamon Press, Arizona, 1977.

Fecker, I., 1992. *How to calculate an ecological balance?* EMPA, St. Gallen, 1992.

Finnveden, G., 1996*a*. '"Resources" and related impact categories'. In: Udo de Haes (1996, pp. 39–48).

Finnveden, G., 1996*b*. *Valuation methods within the framework of life cycle assessment.* IVL, Stockholm, 1996.

Finnveden, G., Y. Andersson-Sköld, M.-O. Samuelsson, L. Zetterberg & L.-G. Lindfors, 1992. 'Classification (impact analysis) in connection with life cycle assessments. A preliminary study'. In: Anonymous (1992, pp. 172–231).

Finnveden, G. & G. Huppes, 1995. *Life cycle assessment and treatment of soild waste.* Avfallforskningsrådet, Stockholm, 1995.

Fischer-Kowalski, M., H. Haberl & H. Payer, 1994. 'A plethora of paradigms: oulining an information system on physical exchanges between the economy and nature'. In: Ayres & Simonis (1994, pp. 337–360).

Fishburn, P.C., 1988. *Nonlinear preference and utility theory.* Wheatsheaf Books Ltd, Brighton, 1988.

Fraassen, B.C. van, 1989. *Laws and symmetry.* Clarendon Press, Oxford, 1989.

Freire, F., P. Ferrão, C. Reis & S. Thore, 2000. *Life cycle activity analysis applied to the Portuguese used tyre market.* Society of Automotive Engineers, Warrendale, 2000.

Frischknecht, R., 1997: *Goal and scope definition and inventory analysis. LCANET theme report.* LCANET, Zürich, 1997.

Frischknecht, R., P. Hofstetter, I. Knoepfel, E. Walder, R. Dones & E. Zollinger, 1993. *Ökoinventare für Energiesysteme. Grundlagen für den ökologischen Vergleich von Energiesystemen und den Einbezug von Energiesystemen in Ökobilanzen für die Schweiz. 0. Auflage.* Bundesamt für Energiewirtschaft, Bern, 1993.

Frischknecht, R. & P. Kolm, 1995. 'Modellansatz und Algorithmus zur Berechnung von Ökobilanzen im Rahmen der Datenbank ECOINVENT'. In: Schmidt & Schorb (1995, pp. 79–95).

Gale, D., 1960. *The theory of linear economic models.* McGraw-Hill Book Company, New York, 1960.

Georgescu-Roegen, N., 1951. 'The aggregate linear production function and its applications to Von Neumann's economic model'. In: Koopmans (1951*b*, pp. 98–115).

Georgescu-Roegen, N., 1971. *The entropy law and the economic process.* Harvard University Press, Cambridge, 1971.

Ghosh, A., 1958. 'Input–output approach in an allocation system'. *Economica* **25** (1958), 58–64.

Gigantes, T., 1970. 'The representation of technology in input–output systems'. In: Carter & Bródy (1970, pp. 270–290).

Ginsburgh, V.A. & J.L. Waelbroeck, 1981. *Activity analysis and general equilibrium modelling.* North-Holland Publishing Company, Amsterdam, 1981.

Goedkoop, M. & P. Cnubben, 1995. *De eco-indicator 95. Methode voor het wegen van milieu-effecten die ecosystemen en de menselijke gezondheid aantasten op Europese schaal. Bevat 100 indicatoren voor belangrijke materialen en processen. Bijlagerapport.* NOH, Utrecht, 1995.

Golub, G.H. & C.F. van Loan, 1989. *Matrix Computations.* Second Edition. The Johns Hopkins University Press, Baltimore, 1993.

Graedel, T.E. & B.R. Allenby, 1995. *Industrial ecology.* Prentice-Hall, Englewood Cliffs, 1995.

Groot, W.T. de, 1992. *Enviromental science theory. Concepts and methods in a one-world, problem-oriented paradigm.* Ph.D. thesis, Rijksuniversiteit Leiden, Leiden, 1992.

Gross, L.S. & E.C.H. Veendorp, 1990. 'Growth with exhaustible resources and a materials-balance production function'. *Natural Resource Modeling* **4**:1 (1990), 77–94.

Guinée, J.B. & R. Heijungs, 1993. 'A proposal for the classification of toxic substances within the framework of life cycle assessment of products'. *Chemosphere* **26**:10 (1993), 1295–1944.

Guinée, J.B., 1994. 'Relations between the definition of impact categories, impact chains and parallel/serial impacts in LCA. 1st draft'. In: Anonymous (1994*a*, pp. 107--112).

Guinée, J.B. & R. Heijungs, 1995. 'A proposal for the definition of resource equivalency factors for use in product life-cycle assessment'. *Environmental Toxicology and Chemistry* **14**:5 (1995), 917–925.

Guinée, J.B., 1995. *Development of a methodology for the environmental life-cycle assessment of products. With a case study on margarines.* Ph.D. thesis, Rijksuniversiteit Leiden, Leiden, 1995.

Guinée, J.B., R. Heijungs, L. van Oers, D. van de Meent, T. Vermeire & M. Rikken, 1996. *LCA impact assessment of toxic releases. Generic modelling of fate, exposure and effect for ecosystems and human beings with data for about 100 chemicals.* DGM, 's-Gravenhage, 1996.

Guinée, J.B. et al., 2001. *LCA. An operational guide to the ISO-standard.* In press.

Hansen, O.J., 1994. *Sustainable product development.* STØ, Frederikstad, 1994.

Hardy, G.H., 1940. 'A mathematician's apology.' In: Newman (1956, pp. 2003–2014).

Hauschild, M. & H. Wenzel, 1998. *Environmental assessment of products. Volume 2: Scientific backgrounds.* Chapman & Hall, London, 1998.

Hawking, S.W. & W. Israel (Eds.), 1987. *Three hundred years of gravitation.* Cambridge University Press, Cambridge, 1989.

Hawkins D. & H.A. Simon, 1949. 'Note: Some conditions of macroeconomic stability'. *Econometrica* **17**:3/4 (1949), 245–248.

Heijman, W.J.M., 1991. *Depletable resources and the economy.* Ph.D. thesis, Landbouwuniversiteit Wageningen, Wageningen, 1991.

Heijungs, R., J.B. Guinée, G. Huppes, R.M. Lankreijer, H.A. Udo de Haes, A. Wegener Sleeswijk, A.M.M. Ansems, P.G. Eggels, R. van Duin & H.P. de Goede, 1992*a*. *Environmental life cycle assessment of products. Guide – October 1992.* CML, Leiden, 1992.

Heijungs, R., J.B. Guinée, G. Huppes, R.M. Lankreijer, H.A. Udo de Haes, A. Wegener Sleeswijk, A.M.M. Ansems, P.G. Eggels, R. van Duin & H.P. de Goede, 1992*b*. *Environmental life cycle assessment of products. Backgrounds – October 1992.* CML, Leiden, 1992.

Heijungs, R. & J.B. Guinée, 1993. 'CML on actual versus potential risks'. *LCA News* **3**:4 (1993), 4.

Heijungs, R., 1994*a*. 'The problem of allocation. Some more complications'. In: Huppes & Schneider (1994, pp. 8–12).

Heijungs, R., 1994*b*. 'A generic method for the identification of options for cleaner products'. *Ecological Economics* **10**:1 (1994), 69–81.

Heijungs, R., 1994*c*. 'Valuation. A societal approach'. In: Udo de Haes et al. (1994, pp. 107–113).

Heijungs, R., 1995*a*. 'Harmonization of methods for impact assessment'. *Environmental Science & Pollution Research* **2**:4 (1995), 217–224.

Heijungs, R., 1995*b*. 'Enige gedachten over normalisatie en evaluatie in LCA'. In: Goedkoop & Cnubben (1995).

Heijungs, R. & J.B. Guinée, 1995. 'On the usefulness of life cycle assessment of packaging'. *Environmental Management* **19**:5 (1995), 665–668.

Heijungs, R., 1996. 'Identification of key issues for further investigation in improving the reliability of life-cycle assessments'. *Journal of Cleaner Production* **4**:3/4 (1996), 159–166.

Heijungs, R., 1997*a*. 'On the necessity to model all material flows'. In: Bringezu et al. (1997, pp. 87–92).

Heijungs, R., 1997*b*. *Economic drama and the environmental stage. Formal derivation of algorithimic tools for environmental analysis and decision-support from a unified epistemological principle.* Ph.D. thesis, Rijksuniversiteit Leiden, Leiden, 1997.

Heijungs, R., 1998. 'Towards eco-efficiency with LCA's prevention principle. An epistemological foundation of LCA using axioms'. In: Klostermann & Tukker (1998, pp. 175–185).

Heijungs, R., 1999. 'Does a participatory approach to life cycle assessment solve its problems?' *SETAC-Europe News* **10**:5 (1999), 9–10.

Heijungs, R. & R. Frischknecht, 1998. 'A special view on the nature of the allocation problem'. *International Journal of LCA* **3**:5 (1998), 321–332.

Hemming, C., 1995. *Directory of life cycle inventory data sources.* SPOLD, Brussels, 1995.

Hemond, H.F. & E.J. Fechner, 1994. *Chemical fate and transport in the environment.* Academic Press, San Diego, 1994.

Hendrickson, C., A. Horvath, S. Joshi & L. Lave, 1998. 'Economic input–output models for environmental life-cycle assessment'. *Environmental Science & Technology* **13**:4 (1998), 184A–191A.

Hettelingh, J.-P., 1989. *Uncertainty in modeling regional environmental systems. The generalization of a watershed acidification model for predicting broad scale effects.* Ph.D. thesis, Vrije Universiteit, Amsterdam, 1989.

Hofstetter, P., 1996*a*. 'Der Spagat zwischen standortspezifischen Fragen und Lebenszyklus-ansätzen'. In: Anonymous (1996*b*, pp. 23–33).

Hofstetter, P., 1996*b*. 'Towards a structured aggregation procedure. A multi-step approach for aggregation that includes methodologies and information supplied by environmental and social sciences'. In: Braunschweig et al. (1996, pp. 123–211).

Hofstetter, P., 1998. *Perspectives in life cycle impact assessment. A structured approach to combine models of the technosphere, ecosphere and valuesphere.* Kluwer Academic Publishers, Boston, 1998.

Hordijk, L., R. Shaw & J. Alcamo, 1990. 'Background to acidification in Europe'. In: Alcamo et al. (1990, pp. 31–60).

Houghton, J.T., G.J. Jenkins & J.J. Ephraums (Eds.), 1990. *Climate change. The IPCC scientific assessment.* Cambridge University Press, Cambridge, 1990.

Huppes, G., 1993. *Macro-environmental policy: principles and design. With cases on milk packaging, cadmium, phosphorus and nitrogen, and energy and global warming.* Ph.D. thesis, Rijksuniversiteit Leiden, Leiden, 1993.

Huppes, G., 1994. 'A general method for allocation in LCA'. In: Huppes & Schneider (1994, pp. 74–90).

Huppes, G. & F. Schneider, 1994. *Proceedings of the European workshop on allocation in LCA.* CML, Leiden, 1994.

Huppes, G. & R. Frischknecht, 1995. 'Allocation in waste management. A position paper'. In: Finnveden & Huppes (1995, pp. 64–77).

Idenburg, A.M., 1993. *Gearing production models to ecological economic analysis. A case study, within the input–output framework of fuels for road transport.* Faculteit Bestuurskunde, Universiteit Twente, Enschede, 1993.

Isard, W., 1968. 'Some notes on the linkage of the ecologic and economic systems'. *Regional Science Association* **22** (1968), 85–96.

Jammer, M., 1966. *The conceptual development of quantum mechanics.* McGraw-Hill Book Company, New York, 1966.

Jansen, R., 1991. *Multiobjective decision support for environmental problems.* Ph.D. thesis, Vrije Universiteit, Amsterdam, 1991.

Jeffers, J.N.R., 1978. *An introduction to systems analysis. With ecological implications.* Edward Arnold, London, 1978.

Jolliet, O., 1994. 'Critical surface-time. An evaluation method for LCA'. In: Udo de Haes et al. (1996, pp. 133–142).

Jolliet, O. & P. Crettaz, 1997. 'Fate coefficients for the toxicity assessment of air pollutants'. *International Journal of LCA* **2**:2 (1997), 104–110.

Kandelaars, P. & J. van der Bergh, 1996. 'Materials-product chains: theory and an application to zinc and PVC gutters'. *Environmental and Resource Economics* **8** (1996), 97–118.

Kandelaars, P.P.A.A.H., 1998. *Material-product chains. Economic models and applications.* Ph.D. thesis, Vrije Universiteit Amsterdam, Amsterdam, 1998.

Kleijn, R., E. van der Voet, H.A. Udo de Haes, 1994. 'Controlling substance flows. The case of chlorine'. *Environmental management* **18**:4 (1994), 523–542.

Kleijn, R., A. Tukker & E. van der Voet, 1997. 'Chlorine in the Netherlands, part I. An overview'. *Journal of Industrial Ecology* **1**:1 (1997), 95–116.

Kleijn, R., R. Huele & R. van der Voet, 2000. 'Dynamic substance flow analysis. The delaying mechanism of stocks, with the case of PVC in Sweden'. *Ecological Economics* **32** (2000), 241–254.

Kleineidam, U., 2000. *Modelling and control of product life-cycles.* Ph.D. thesis, Technische Universiteit Eindhoven, Eindhoven, 2000.

Klostermann, J.E.M. & A. Tukker, 1998. *Product innovation & eco-efficiency.* Kluwer Academic Publishers, Dordrecht, 1998.

Kneese, A.V., R.U. Ayres & R.C. d'Arge, 1970. *Economics and the environment. A materials balance approach.* Johns Hopkins University Press, Baltimore, 1970.

Koenig, H.E. & J.E. Cantlon, 2000. 'Quantitative industrial ecology and ecological economics'. *Journal of Industrial Ecology* **3**:2/3 (2000), 63–83.

Konijn, P.J.A., 1994. *The make and use of commodities by industries. On the compilation of input–output data from the national accounts.* Faculteit Bestuurskunde, Universiteit Twente, Enschede, 1994.

Koopmans, T.C., 1951*a*. 'Analysis of production as an efficient combination of activities'. In: Koopmans (1951*b*, pp. 33–97).

Koopmans, T.C. (Ed.), 1951*b*. *Activity analysis of production and allocation.* John Wiley & Sons, New York, 1951.

Koopmans, T.C., 1957. *Three essays on the state of economic science.* McGraw-Hill Book Company, Inc., New York, 1957.

Kornai, J., 1971. *Anti-equilibrium. On economic systems theory and the tasks of research.* North-Holland Publishing Company, Amsterdam, 1971.

Körner, S., 1960. *The philosophy of mathematics. An introductory essay.* Dover Publications Inc., New York, 1986.

Kümmel, R., 1989. 'Energy as a factor of production and entropy as a pollution indicator in macroeconomic modelling'. *Ecological Economics* **1**: (1989), 161–180.

Lave, L.B., E. Cobas-Flores, C.T. Hendrickson & F.C. McMichael, 1995. 'Using input–output analysis to estimate economy-wide discharges'. *Environmental Science & Technology* **29**:9 (1995), 420–426.

Lee, J.J., P.O'Callaghan & D. Allen, 1995. 'Critical review of life cycle analysis and assessment techniques and their application to commercial activities'. *Resources, Conservation and Recycling* **13**:1 (1995), 37–56.

Leeuwen, C.J. van, 1995. 'General introduction'. In: Van Leeuwen & Hermens (1995, pp. 1–17).

Leeuwen, C.J. van & J.L.M. Hermens (Eds.), 1995. *Risk assessment of chemicals. An introduction.* Kluwer Academic Publishers, Dordrecht, 1995.

Leontief, W.W., 1936. 'Quantitative input and output relations in the economic systems of the United States'. *The Review of Economic Statistics* **18**:3 (1936), 105–125.

Leontief, W.W., 1941. *The structure of American Economy, 1919–1939. An empirical application of equilibrium analysis.* Oxford University Press, New York, 1953.

Leontief, W.W., 1970. 'Environmental repercussions and the economic structure. An input–output approach'. *Review of Economics and Statistics* **52** (1970), 262–271.

Leontief, W.W., 1986. 'Input–output analysis'. In: Bever (1986, pp. 2339–2349).

Leroy, P., 1995. 'De Nederlandse academische milieukunde: gevangen tussen milieuwetenschap en milieu(beleids)praktijk?' *Milieu* **10**:5 (1995), 238–245.

Lindeijer, E., 1996. 'Normalisation and valuation'. In: Udo de Haes (1996, pp. 75–93).

Lindfors, L.-G., K. Christiansen, L. Hoffman, Y. Virtanen, V. Juntilla, O.-J. Hanssen, A. Rønning, T. Ekvall, G. Finnveden, 1995*a*. *Nordic guidelines on life-cycle assessment.* Nordic Council of Ministers, Copenhagen, 1995.

Lindfors, L.-G., K. Christiansen, L. Hoffman, Y. Virtanen, V. Juntilla, A. Leskinen, O.-J. Hanssen, A. Rønning, T. Ekvall & G. Finnveden, 1995*b*. *LCA-Nordic. Technical reports No 1–9.* Nordic Council of Ministers, Copenhagen, 1995.

Lindfors, L.-G., K. Christiansen, L. Hoffman, Y. Virtanen, V. Juntilla, A. Leskinen, O.-J. Hanssen, A. Rønning, T. Ekvall, G. Finnveden, 1995*c*. *LCA-Nordic. Technical reports No 10 and special reports No 1-2*. Nordic Council of Ministers, Copenhagen, 1995.

Lindfors, L.-G., K. Christiansen, L. Hoffman, Y. Virtanen, V. Juntilla, O.-J. Hanssen, A. Rønning, T. Ekvall, G. Finnveden, 1995*d*. 'Technical report No 8. Data gaps'. In: Lindfors et al. (1995*a*).

Lindfors, L.-G., K. Christiansen, L. Hoffman, Y. Virtanen, V. Juntilla, O.-J. Hanssen, A. Rønning, T. Ekvall, G. Finnveden, 1995*e*. 'Technical report No 10. Impact assessment'. In: Lindfors et al. (1995*b*).

Lipsey, R.G. & P.O. Steiner, 1978. *Economics*. Fifth edition. Harper & Row, New York, 1978.

Lotka, A.J., 1924. *Elements of mathematical biology*. Dover Publications, Inc., New York, 1956.

Lundie, S., 1999. *Ökobilanzierung und Entscheidungstheorie. Praxisorientierte Produktbewertung auf der Basis gesellschaftlicher Werthaltungen*. Springer, Berlin, 1999.

Mackay, D., 1991. *Multimedia environmental models. The fugacity approach*. Lewis Publishers, Chelsea, 1991.

Manara, C.R., 1980. 'Sraffa's model for the joint production of commodities by means of commodities'. In: Pasinetti (1980*b*, pp. 1–15).

March, R.H., 1996. *Physics for poets*. Fourth edition. Mc-Graw-Hill, Inc., New York, 1996.

Matthews, E., C. Amann, S. Bringezu, M. Fischer-Kowalski, W. Hüttler, R. Kleijn, Y. Moriguchi, C. Ottke, E. Rodenburg, D. Rogich, H. Schandl, H. Schütz, E. van der Voet & H. Weisz, 2000. *The weight of nations. Material outflows from industrial economies*. World Resources Institute, Washington, 2000.

Maystre, L.Y., J. Pictet & J. Simos, 1994. *Méthodes multicritères ELECTRE. Description, conseils pratiques et cas d'application à la gestion environnementale*. Presses Polytechniques et Universitaires Romandes, Lausanne, 1994.

McKenna, C.J. & R. Rees, 1992. *Economics. A mathematical introduction*. Oxford University Press, New York, 1993.

Meent, D. van de, 1993. *Simplebox. A generic multimedia fate evaluation model*. RIVM, Bilthoven, 1993.

Miller, R.E. & P.D. Blair, 1985. *Input–output analysis. Foundations and extensions*. Prentice-Hall, Englewood Cliffs, 1985.

Misra, K.B., 1996. *Clean production. Environmental and economic perspectives.* Springer, Berlin, 1996.

Moll, H.C., 1993. *Energy counts and materials matter in models for sustainable development. Dynamic lifecycle modelling as a tool for design and evaluation of long-term environmental strategies.* Ph.D. thesis, Rijksuniversiteit Groningen, Styx, Groningen, 1993.

Möller, A. & A. Rolf, 1995. 'Methodische Ansätze zur Erstellung von Stoffstromanalysen unter besonderer Berücksichtigung von Petri-Netzen'. In: Schmidt & Schorb (1995, pp. 33–58).

Müller-Wenk, R., 1996. 'The shape of the damage function and the choice of valuation factors'. In: Braunschweig et al. (1996, pp. 50–65).

Neumann, J. von, 1945/1946. 'A model of general economic equilibrium'. *Review of Economic Studies* **13** (1945/1946), 1–9.

Newman, J.R. (Ed.), 1956. *The world of mathematics. A small library of the literature of mathematics from A'h-mosé the Scribe to Albert Einstein.* Tempus, Redmond, 1988.

Newman, P., 1962. *'Production of commodities by means of commodities'. Schweizerische Zeitschrift für Volkswirtschaft und Statistik* (1962), 58–75.

Nieuwlaar, E., 1988. *Developments in energy analysis.* Ph.D. thesis, Rijksuniversiteit Utrecht, Utrecht, 1988.

Noorman, K.J., 1995. *Exploring futures from an energy perspective. A natural capital accounting model into the long-term economic development potential of the Netherlands.* Ph.D. thesis, Rijksuniversiteit Groningen, Groningen, 1995.

Odum, H.T., 1983. *Systems ecology. An introduction.* John Wiley & Sons, New York, 1983.

Oosterhaven, J., 1988. 'On the plausibility of the supply-driven input–output model'. *Journal of Regional Science* **28**:2 (1988), 203–217.

Opschoor, J.B., 1994. 'Chain management in environmental policy: analytical and evaluative concepts'. In: Opschoor & Turner (1994, pp. 197–228).

Opschoor, J.B. & R.K. Turner, 1994. *Economic incentives and environmental policies. Principles and practice.* Kluwer Academic Publishers, Dordrecht, 1994.

Oreskes, N., K. Shrader-Frechette & K. Bellitz, 1994. 'Verification, validation, and confirmation of numerical models in the earth sciences'. *Science* **263** (1994), 641–646.

Oude, N.T. de, 1993. 'Experts need ... experts'. *LCA News* **3**:2 (1993), 1–2.

Paelinck, J.H. & P. Nijkamp, *n.d. Operational theory and method in regional economics.* Saxon House, Westmead, *n.d.*

Parmenter, B.R., 1982. 'Inter-industry analysis: the ORANI model of Australia's industrial structure'. In: Webb & Allan (1982, pp. 69–108).

Pasinetti, L.L., 1980*a*. 'Introductory note: joint production'. In: Pasinetti (1980*b*, pp. xii–xvii).

Pasinetti, L.L. (Ed.), 1980*b*. *Essays on the theory of joint production.* Columbia University Press, New York, 1980.

Pearce, D.W. & R.K. Turner, 1990. *Economics of natural resources and the environment.* Harvester Wheatsheaf, New York, 1990.

Perrings, C., 1987. *Economy and environment. A theoretical essay on the interdependence of economic and environmental systems.* Cambridge University Press, Cambridge, 1987.

Pigou, A.C., 1920. *The economics of welfare.* Macmillan and Co., London, 1920.

Pillet, G. & H.T. Odum, 1987. *É³. Énergie, écologie, économie.* Georg Éditeur, Genève, 1987.

Plourde, C.G., 1970. 'A simple model of replenishable natural resource exploitation'. *The American Economic Review* **60** (1970), 518–522.

Popper, K.R., 1959. *The logic of scientific discovery.* Routledge, London, 1995.

Press, W.H., B.P. Flannery, S.A. Teukolsky & W.T. Vetterling, 1989. *Numerical recipes in Pascal. The art of scientific computing.* Cambridge University Press, Cambridge, 1992.

Quakernaat, J. & A. Weenk, 1993. 'Integrated life cycle management at company level. The concept of environmental merit'. *Journal of Cleaner Production* **1**:2 (1993), 99–106.

Raa, T. ten, D. Chakraborty & J.A. Small, 1984. 'An alternative treatment of secondary products in input–output analysis'. *The Review of Economics and Statistics* **66**:1 (1984), 88–97.

Raa, T. ten, 1988. 'An alternative treatment of secondary products in input–output analysis. Frustration'. *The Review of Economics and Statistics* **70**:3 (1988), 535–538.

Raa, T. ten, 1995. *Linear analysis of competitive economies.* Harvester Wheatsheaf, New York, 1995.

Ravina, M., 1993. 'Wasan and the physics that wasn't'. *Monumenta Nipponica* **48**:2 (1993), 205–224.

Rescher, N., 1996. *Process metaphysics. An introduction to process philosophy.* State University of New York Press, Albany, 1996.

Rijckeghem, W. van, 1967. 'An exact method for determining the technology matrix in a situation with secondary products'. *Review of Economics and Statistics* **49** (1967), 607–608.

Rosenbluth, G., 1968. 'Input–output analysis. A critique'. *Statistische Hefte* **9**:4 (1968), 255–268.

Rotmans, J., 1990. *IMAGE. An integrated model to assess the greenhouse effect.* Ph.D. thesis, Rijksuniversiteit Limburg, Maastricht, 1990.

Russell, B., 1945. *A history of Western Philosophy.* Simon & Schuster, Inc., New York, 1972.

Ruth, M., 1993. *Integrating economics, ecology and thermodynamics.* Kluwer Academic Publishers, Dordrecht, 1993.

Samuelson, P.A., 1951. 'Abstract of a theorem concerning substitutability in open Leontief systems'. In: Koopmans (1951*b*, pp. 142–146).

Sankovskii, A., 1992. 'Toward evaluation of natural objects'. *Environmental Management* **16**:3 (1992), 283–287.

Sauer, B.J., C.C. Hildebrandt, W.E. Franklin & R.G. Hunt, 1994. 'Resource and environmental profile analysis of children's diaper systems'. *Environmental Toxicology and Chemistry* **13**:6 (1994), 1003–1009.

Saxton, J.C. & R.U. Ayres, 1975. 'The materials-process product model. Theory and applications'. In: Vogely (1975, pp. 178–244).

Schaltegger, S. & R. Kubat, 1995. *Das Handwörterbuch der Ökobilanzierung. Begriffe und Definitionen. The glossary of LCA. Terms and expressions.* WWZ, Basel, 1995.

Schmidt, A., 1994. 'Are we describing real life LCA inventories?' In: Huppes & Schneider (1994, pp. 140–142).

Schmidt, M., 1995. 'Die Modellierung von Stoffrekursionen in Ökobilanzen'. In: Schmidt & Schorb (1995, pp. 97–117).

Schmidt, M. & A. Schorb, 1995. *Stoffstromanalysen in Ökobilanzen und Öko-audits.* Springer, Berlin, 1995.

Schrap, S.M., G.L.G. Sleijpen, W. Seinen & A. Opperhuizen, 1994. 'Sorption kinetics of chlorinated hydrophobic organic chemicals. Part I: The use of first-order kinetic multi-compartment models'. *Environmental Science & Pollution Research* **1**:1 (1994), 21–28.

Schrøder, H., 1995*a*. *Environmental input–output analysis and the software system Steady.* Danedi, Helsinge, 1995.

Schrøder, H., 1995*b*. 'Input management of nitrogen in agriculture'. *Ecological Economics* **13** (1995), 125–140.

Schuler, H. (Ed.), 1995. *Prozeßsimulation.* VCH, Weinheim, 1995.

Sen, A.K., 1969. *Collective choice and collective welfare.* Holden Day, San Francisco, 1969.

Shine, K.P., R.G. Derwent, D.J. Wuebbles & J.-J. Morcrette, 1990. 'Radiative forcing of climate'. In: Houghton et al. (1990, pp. 41–68).

Smet, B. de, P.R. White, M. Franke, R. Lentz & J.W. Owens, 1994. 'Principle for the development of environmental life cycle impact assessment'. In: Anonymous (1994*a*, pp. 68–72).

Smet, B. de, C. Hemming, K. Baumann, S. Cowell, C. Pesso, L. Sund, V. Markovic, T. Moilanen & D. Postlethwaite, 1997. *Life cycle assessment and conceptually related programmes.* SETAC-Europe, Brussels, 1997.

Smith, J.B. & S. Weber, 1989. 'Contemporaneous externalities, rational expectations, and equilibrium production functions in natural resource models'. *Journal of Environmental Economics and Management* **17** (1989), 155–170.

Sraffa, P., 1960. *Production of commodities by means of commodities. Prelude to a critique of economic theory.* Cambridge University Press, Cambridge, 1960.

Steen, B. & S.-O. Ryding, 1993. *EPS. A system for LCA impact assessment.* Avfallforskningsrådet, Stockholm, 1993.

Stewart, G.W. & J. Sun, 1990. *Matrix perturbation theory.* Academic Press, Inc., San Diego, 1990.

Straalen, N.M. & J.A.C. Verkleij (Eds.), 1991. *Leerboek oecotoxicologie.* VU Uitgeverij, Amsterdam, 1991.

Strassert, G., 1993. 'Towards an ecological-economic accounting of the provision-transformation-restitution cycle'. In: Dragàn et al. (1993, pp. 507–515).

Tas, J.W. & C.J. van Leeuwen, 1995. 'Glossary'. In: Van Leeuwen & Hermens (1995, pp. 339–361).

Thompson, D'A.W., 1917. *On growth and form.* Canto, Cambridge, 1992.

Tillman, A.-M., T. Ekvall, H. Baumann & T. Rydberg, 1994. 'Choice of system boundaries in life cycle assessment'. *Journal of Cleaner Production* **2**:1 (1994), 21–29.

Tukker, A., 1994. 'Review of quantitative valuation methods'. In: Udo de Haes et al. (1994, pp. 127–132).

Tukker, A., R. Kleijn & E. van der Voet, 1995. *A chlorine balance for the Netherlands. Part III: Background documents, appendices and peer-review*. TNO, Apeldoorn, 1995.

Tukker A. & R. Heijungs, 1995. 'Levenscyclusanalyse: bruikbaar voor m.e.r.?' *Kenmerken* **2**:6 (1995), 20-24.

Tukker, A., 1998. *Frames in the toxicity controversy. Based on the Dutch Chlorine and the Swedish PVC debate.* Ph.D. thesis, Katholieke Universiteit Brabant, Tiburg, 1998.

Udo de Haes, H.A., 1991. 'Milieukunde, begripsbepaling en afbakening'. In Boersema et al. (1991), pp. 21–34.

Udo de Haes, H.A., A.A. Jensen, W. Klöpffer & L.-G. Lindfors (Eds.), 1994. *Integrating impact assessment into LCA.* SETAC, Brussels, 1994.

Udo de Haes, H.A. & G. Huppes, 1994. 'Positioning of LCA in relation to other environmental decision support tools'. In: Udo de Haes et al. (1994, pp. 17–22).

Udo de Haes, H.A. (Ed.), 1996. *Towards a methodology for life cycle impact assessment.* SETAC, Brussels, 1996.

Udo de Haes, H.A. & R. Heijungs, 1996. 'Milieukunde: onderzoek in dwarsdoorsneden van het maatschappij-milieu systeem'. *Milieu* **11**:1 (1996), 36–41.

Udo de Haes, H.A., E. van der Voet & R. Kleijn, 1997. 'Substance flow analysis (SFA). An analytical tool for integrated chain management'. In: Bringezu et al. (1997, pp. 32–42).

Udo de Haes, H.A., O. Jolliet, G. Finnveden, M. Hauschild, W. Krewitt & R. Müller-Wenk, R., 1999. 'Best available practice regarding impact categories and category indicators in life cycle impact assessment'. *International Journal of LCA* **4**:2 (1999), 66–74 and **4**:3 (1999), 167–174.

Victor, P.A., 1972*a*. *Pollution. Economy and environment.* George Allen & Unwin Ltd, London, 1972.

Victor, P.A., 1972*b*. *Economics of pollution.* Macmillan, London, 1972.

Voet, E. van der & R. Heijungs, 1994. 'Life-cycle assessment and materials balances. Different approaches?' *SETAC Europe News* **4**:6 (1994), 3–4.

Voet, E. van der, R. Kleijn, L. van Oers, R. Heijungs, R. Huele & P. Mulder, 1995*a*. 'Substance flows through the economy and environment of a region. Part I: systems definition.' *Environmental Science & Pollution Research* **2**:2 (1995), 90–96.

Voet, E. van der, R. Heijungs, P. Mulder, R. Huele, R. Kleijn & L. van Oers, 1995*b*. 'Substance flows through the economy and environment of a region. Part II: modelling.' *Environmental Science & Pollution Research* **2**:3 (1995), 137–144.

Voet, E. van der, R. Huele, R. Kleijn, P. Mulder & L. van Oers, 1995*c*. 'SFINX: gereedschap voor de analyse van stofstromen door economie en milieu van een gebied.' *Milieu* **10**:3 (1995), 134–140.

Voet, E. van der, R. Kleijn & G. Huppes, 1995*d*. 'Economic characteristics of chemicals as a basis for pollutants policy.' *Ecological Economics* **13** (1995), 11–26.

Voet, E. van der, 1996. *Substances from cradle to grave. Development of a methodology for the analysis of substance flows through the economy and the environment of a region. With case studies on cadmium and nitrogen compounds.* Ph.D. thesis, Rijksuniversiteit Leiden, Leiden, 1996.

Voet, E. van der, J.B. Guinée & H.A. Udo de Haes, 2000. *Heavy metals: a problem solved? Methods and models to evaluate policy strategies for heavy metals.* Kluwer Academic Publishers, Dordrecht, 2000.

Vogely, W.A. (Ed.), 1975. *Mineral materials modeling. A state-of-the-art review.* Johns Hopkins University Press, Baltimore, 1975.

Wackernagel, M. & W. Rees, 1996. *Our ecological footprint. Reducing human impact on the earth.* New Society Publishers, Gabriola Island, 1996.

Webb, L.R. & R.H. Allan (Eds.), 1982. *Industrial economics. Australian studies.* George Allen & Unwin, Sidney, 1982.

Weenen, J.C. van, 1990. *Waste prevention. Theory and practice.* Ph.D. thesis, Technische Universiteit Delft, Delft, 1990.

Wegener Sleeswijk, A. & R. Heijungs, 1996. 'Modelling fate for LCA'. *International Journal of LCA* **1**:4 (1996), 237–240.

Weidema, B.P., 1994. 'Qualitative and quantitative parameters in product impact assessment'. In: Udo de Haes et al. (1994, pp. 29–35).

Weinberg, S., 1987. 'Newtonianism and today's physics'. In: Hawking & Israel (1987, pp. 3–16).

White, P.R., B. De Smet, J.W. Owens & P. Hindle, 1995*a*. 'Environmental management in an international consumer goods company'. *Resources, Conservation and Recycling* **14** (1995), 171–184.

White, P.R., M. Franke & P. Hindle, 1995*b*. *Integrated solid waste management. A lifecycle inventory.* Blackie Academic & Professional, London, 1995.

Wigner, E.P., 1960. 'The unreasonable effectiveness of mathematics in the natural sciences'. *Communications on Pure and Applied Mathematics* **13** (1960), 1–14.

Will, H., 1996. *Produkt-Ökobilanzen am Fallbeispiel der Automobil-Lackierung unter besonderer Berücksichtigung der Wirkungsabschätzung*. Ph.D. thesis, Technischen Universität München, München, 1996.

Wilting, H.C., 1996. *An energy perspective on economic activities*. Ph.D. thesis, Rijksuniversiteit Groningen, Groningen, 1996.

Woo, M.T., T. Noguchi, T. Veach Long II & R.S. Berry, 1977. 'Methodology for energy analysis'. In: Fazzolare & Smith (1977, pp. 649–664).

Wood, M.K. & G.B. Dantzig, 1951. 'The programming of interdependent activities: general discussion'. In: Koopmans (1951*b*, pp. 15–18).

Subject Index

Accumulation 73, 158, 159
Acidification 180, 186, 222, 233, 250
Activity analysis 45, 84, 114, 274, 291
Activity-level 77
  analysis (ALA) 82, 87, 89, 137, 138, 171, 244, 259
Affinity 44
Allocation 120, 125, 127, 166, 234
  factor 134, 135, 146, 285
  procedure 6, 27, 31, 43, 120, 130, 131, 132, 133, 135, 145, 217
Antagonism 222, 228
Anti-pollution 67
Attribution problem 3, 4, 5, 18, 28, 45, 85, 167, 250, 253, 259, 267, 271, 272, 286
Average 27, 28, 226, 233, 236, 250, 268
Avoided impacts 121, 126
Axiom 26, 33, 314
Background 188, 192, 200, 226, 235, 284
"Bad" 40, 57, 64, 128, 150, 151, 263
Balance 43, 67, 68, 72, 73, 81, 89, 111, 148, 155, 164
  equation 161
  volume 153
Balancing item 165, 167
Behaviour 43
Capital 55, 63
  good 62, 147
Ceteris paribus 275, 280
Chain analysis 171
Chain management 171
Characterization 222, 230, 232
  factor 230
Chemistry 190
Classification 100, 222
  factor 230
Cluster 17, 85, 133, 192
Cobb–Douglas 83
Combined waste handling 129, 132
Commodity 16, 39, 40, 70, 183
  account 98, 102, 110
  balance, see Balance
  economic, see Economic commodity
  environmental, see Environmental commodity
Commodity-based technology assumption 109, 110, 111, 113, 126

Commodity-by-process account 103, 104
Commodity-flow accounting (CFA) 82, 87, 88, 137, 138, 152, 175, 244, 259
Common element 260
Completeness 223
Concentration 196, 200
Conservation 206
Consumption 40, 41, 57, 64, 196
Coproduction 97, 100, 129, 132, 145
Corrosion 194, 205
"Cradle-to-gate" analysis 151, 263
"Cradle-to-grave" analysis 151, 263
"Cross-section" 268, 277, 291
Damage matrix 195, 196, 210, 212, 213, 216, 246
Data quality 73
Decision theory 180, 242
Degradation 75, 180, 186, 189, 190, 192, 200
  constant 190
  rate 189
Degradable substance 201, 213
Depletion of stratospheric ozone 250, 252
Depreciation 62, 147
Diffusion 191
Diffusivity 191
Discounting 197, 206
Discreteness 44
"Disservice" 40, 57, 128, 150
Dose response curve 24, 25, 225
Duration 61, 70, 77
Dynamic model 167
Ecologic commodity 70
Ecological footprint 150, 281
Ecological rucksack 150, 281
Ecology 34, 35, 46, 49
Economic
  activity 4, 5, 55, 57, 58
  commodity 67, 80, 149, 152, 183, 187, 213
  process 16, 40, 58, 61, 183, 187, 193
  value 128
Economics 34, 39, 49
Ecosphere 198
Ecotax 93
Effective time 78
Emission 66, 67, 92, 101, 155
  reduction 93
Endpoint 224
Energy 67, 72, 153, 170, 265
  analysis 6, 101, 120, 135, 139, 153, 170, 265, 286
  balance, see Balance
  saving 93
Entropy 184
Environment 36, 56, 198
  natural *vs.* thermodynamic 35
  "the" *vs.* "its" 35, 150
Environmental
  commodity 68, 80, 149, 152, 183, 188, 202
  compartment 75
  impact 180, 219, 222, 230, 236, 240, 241, 267
  impact assessment (EIA) 18, 59, 82, 140, 171, 175, 255, 266, 270, 273, 291
  intervention 80, 85, 143, 144, 155, 176, 202, 213, 230

policy 49
problem 4, 5, 46, 179, 180, 230, 238, 240, 251, 267
process 180, 187, 188, 193, 200, 222
science 34, 50
stressor 202, 208
Epistemology 19, 22, 25, 28, 44, 168, 216, 227, 229, 233, 236, 241, 267, 271, 273, 285, 287, 288, 292
Equilibrium analysis 98, 113, 114
Equivalency factor 230, 232, 236
Erosion 186
Eutrophication 221, 236, 250
Evaporation 75
Experiment 285, 290
Export 155
Exposure assessment 176
External demand 86, 91, 92, 93, 117, 138, 142, 162, 187, 204, 213, 274
Externality 42, 56
Factor of production 46, 55, 56, 82
Fate 46, 189, 202, 222, 230, 236, 250, 252, 267, 284
matrix 193, 194, 196, 201, 203, 204, 210, 212, 213, 216, 217, 245
model 196, 209, 291
Flow 62, 64, 67, 70, 87, 174, 200
chart 140, 144
Formal science 21, 44
Formation 180, 191, 196, 200
Framework 13, 15, 249, 253, 259
Fugacity 196
Functional table 102
Functional unit 143, 147, 151, 274
Fund 62, 64, 67, 70, 87, 174
Fundamental equation
1st 59, 93, 97, 106, 111, 144, 156, 167, 204, 213, 274
2nd 212, 213, 216, 217, 232
3rd 231
4th 241
"Gate-to-grave" analysis 151, 263
Global warming 180, 221, 228, 233, 236, 250
Goal definition 15, 259, 269
Good 40, 57, 64, 66, 67, 128, 150, 151, 263
Harmonization 12
Hessian matrix 280
Holism 22, 27
Impact analysis 15, 142, 244, 248, 267
Impact, see Environmental impact
analysis 15, 142, 244, 248, 267
assessment 142
category 222, 225, 239, 254
chain 220
factor 230, 236, 240, 285
matrix 231, 247
profile 231
score 231
Import 155
Improvement analysis 276, 291
Incremental 226, 233, 250, 286
Independence 223
Indicator commodity 139, 170
Indicator 224, 254
Industry account, see Process account

Initial supply 162
Input–output analysis 82, 98, 101, 102, 103, 104, 110, 114, 122, 167, 291
Institutional table 102
Interdisciplinarity 34, 50
Intermedia transport, see Transport
Interpolation 22, 28, 29, 216, 274, 285, 286
Intervention matrix 92, 93, 94, 194, 204
Inventory analysis 15, 142, 274
Inversion of matrix 92, 96, 97, 113, 117, 127, 145, 146, 162, 203, 204, 217, 233
ISO 6, 12, 16, 220, 222, 224, 277, 278
Labelling 74, 90
Land 63
Labour 55, 63, 67, 99
Least squares approximation 124
Leontief inverse 106
Leontief multiplier 138, 274
Life-cycle assessment (LCA) 6, 13, 18, 27, 31, 45, 59, 82, 87, 120, 121, 123, 133, 135, 138, 140, 141, 142, 151, 168, 171, 224, 232, 237, 245, 250, 265, 269, 271, 276, 278, 288, 293
Linear programming 78
Linearity 28, 77, 151, 168, 183, 188, 191, 215, 267, 272, 274
Lithosphere 198
Macro *vs.* micro 275
Make/use analysis 98, 108, 110, 114
Make matrix/table 108, 109
Marginal 27, 226, 233, 236, 250, 268, 280
  analysis 277, 278, 280, 281
"Master equation" 93, 242
Material 63, 64, 67, 153, 170, 265
Material-flow analysis 139, 170, 172, 265
Material-product chain analysis 272
Materials balance, see Balance
Mathematics 34, 47, 49
Matrix inversion, see Inversion of matrix
Metaphysics 30
Methodology 16, 18
Mobility 189, 191
Modified matrix 208, 212, 213
Multicriteria analysis 180
Multimedia model 197, 291
Natural science 44, 46, 239
Node 153
Non-linearity 21, 44
Non-renewable resource 201, 205, 213
Odour 250
Operating time 78, 86, 88, 109, 113, 117, 153, 173, 183, 186, 187
Optimization 44
Origins analysis 278, 291
Parallel impacts 222, 228
Partition coefficient 191, 196
Performance variable 162
Permanent
  absence 206, 208, 211, 213
  impact 228, 241
  presence 206, 208, 211, 213
  stressor 202, 208, 212, 213

Persistent substance 199, 201, 205, 206, 213
Physical 42, 43, 58, 67, 99, 100, 105, 111
Photo-oxidant formation 234, 250
Planning analysis 44, 84, 271, 272, 276, 291
Position problem 7, 9, 10, 18, 268
Power function 28, 286
Preference 239, 241, 242, 251
Prevention principle 235
Problem, see Environmental problem
  factor 240, 241, 242, 285
  index 240
  vector 241, 247
Process 70, 153, 282
  account 98, 102, 104, 107
  cluster, see Cluster
  disconnected 165
  economic 16, 40, 58, 61, 183, 187, 193
  environmental 180, 187, 188, 193, 200, 222
  technology 22, 44
  tree 140, 144
  Process-based technology assumption 109
Product 63, 67, 153, 170, 265
Product-flow analysis 171, 265
Production 40, 41, 57, 129
  function 55, 56, 63, 65, 68, 77, 82
Program 78
Pseudo-inverse 123, 124, 132
Quasi steady state 160
Ratio scale 223
Reaction product 190, 197, 250, 267, 291
Reallocation 120
Rectangular matrix, see Square matrix
Recycling 121, 129, 288
  closed-loop 132
  open-loop 132
Redefinition 120, 121, 126
Reduced matrix 207, 212, 213, 217
Reductionism 22, 27
Release assessment 176
Renewable resource 201, 213
Resource 39, 55, 63, 67, 92, 155, 191
  depletion 180
  non-renewable 201, 205, 213
  renewable 201, 213
Returns to scale 82
Risk assessment (RA) 13, 18, 59, 82, 140, 175, 222, 255, 267, 270, 291
Scenario analysis 274, 291
Serial impacts 228
Service 40, 42, 57, 62, 67, 128, 150, 151, 263
Singular value decomposition 124
Social science 43, 44, 46, 239
Solubility 196
Square matrix 127, 131, 145, 146, 217
Steady state 168
Stock 62, 73, 158, 159, 284
Stressor 211, 212, 221; see also Environmental stressor
  permanent 202, 208, 212, 213

transient 202, 204, 208, 212, 213
Subjective 180
Subsidiary product 56
Substance 151, 170, 265
degradable, see degradable substance
group 151, 152
persistent, see persistent substance
Substance-flow analysis (SFA) 13, 14, 18, 59, 73, 82, 86, 99, 139, 140, 150, 151, 153, 155, 156, 160, 167, 177, 254, 266, 269, 270, 271, 273, 280, 293
Substance-flow diagram 185
Substitution method 121, 126
Substrate 198
Synergism 21, 222, 228
System 36, 153
boundary 86, 90, 259
expansion 123
Systems analysis 37
Technical coefficient 77, 80, 82, 105, 106, 112, 162, 167, 170, 183, 192, 215, 272, 276, 277
Technology matrix 92, 93, 94, 106, 109, 114, 116, 131, 193, 194, 204
rectangular 96, 97, 98, 111, 113, 114
singular 96, 97
Technosphere 198
Theorem 26, 33, 113, 319
Thermodynamics 36, 37, 72
Time 61, 77, 87
Time-integrated
absence 201, 211, 213, 222
exposure 203
impact 197, 228
preference 197
presence 198, 199, 201, 211, 213, 222
Tool 7, 8, 9, 10, 11, 18, 259, 268, 287, 288, 290
Toxicity 222, 236, 250
Toxicology 225
Transboundary pollution 253
Transfer coefficient 162
Transient
impact 241
stressor 202, 204, 208, 212, 213
Transmission
coefficient 152, 154
vector 152, 157, 159, 170
Transport 180, 186, 189, 191, 192
Transportation 76
Truncated flows 147, 149, 150, 208
Truth 31, 285
Unification 11, 13, 18, 167, 236, 259
Use 64
matrix/table 108, 109, 110
Utility 42, 43, 44, 129, 242
Validation 28, 33, 227
Vapour pressure 196
Verification 285
Wasan 49
Waste 56, 63, 66, 101
treatment 42, 57, 151, 186

Substitution method
Systems analysis 32
Technical coefficients 77, 80, 83
Transportation
Truncated flow
Unit